The Bounds of Defense

The Bounds of Defense

Killing, Moral Responsibility, and War

BRADLEY JAY STRAWSER

OXFORD
UNIVERSITY PRESS

Oxford University Press is a department of the University of Oxford. It furthers
the University's objective of excellence in research, scholarship, and education
by publishing worldwide. Oxford is a registered trade mark of Oxford University
Press in the UK and certain other countries.

Published in the United States of America by Oxford University Press
198 Madison Avenue, New York, NY 10016, United States of America.

© Oxford University Press 2023

All rights reserved. No part of this publication may be reproduced, stored in
a retrieval system, or transmitted, in any form or by any means, without the
prior permission in writing of Oxford University Press, or as expressly permitted
by law, by license, or under terms agreed with the appropriate reproduction
rights organization. Inquiries concerning reproduction outside the scope of the
above should be sent to the Rights Department, Oxford University Press, at the
address above.

You must not circulate this work in any other form
and you must impose this same condition on any acquirer.

CIP data is on file at the Library of Congress

ISBN 978–0–19–069251–3

DOI: 10.1093/oso/9780190692513.001.0001

Printed by Integrated Books International, United States of America

*Dedicated to all of my co-conspirators in figuring this stuff out.
You know who you are.
Our disagreements make the collective inquiry stronger.
Thank you for endeavoring in the task together.*

Contents

Acknowledgments	ix
Introduction	1
Outline	9
1. Permissible Defensive Harm and Liability	17
2. The Evidence-Relative View of Liability Attribution	71
3. The Evidence-Relative View and Intricate Symmetries	110
4. A Defense of Revisionist Just War Theory	137
5. A New Proposal for Liability in War	184
6. The Puzzle of Benevolent Aggression	203
7. Towards a New Liberal Theory of Just War	224
8. Conclusion: Answering Calvin	266
Appendix: List of Cases in Order of Appearance	275
Bibliography	283
Index	295

Acknowledgments

I have worked on this book for so long now and had so many kind souls help me with it along the way for those many years that attempting to give proper acknowledgments seems like a fool's errand. But I'll be a fool and give it a go; though I'm certain to leave out many deserving thanks and gratitude. My apologies in advance for those I mistakenly omit.

There are some usual suspects—like Jeff McMahan, who inspired and mentored me to work on these issues more than any other. Jeff, no amount of scotch will ever repay my debts. Cherished mentors and friends like Michael Lynch and Steve Wall; wise and encouraging scholars who seem to serve in the role of senior statesmen for our field, like Cheney Ryan and Henry Shue; brilliant minds who inspire me both as scholars and human beings, such as Cecile Fabre and Susanne Burri—I owe you all a debt of gratitude. The late Derick Parfit must be mentioned here. The legends of his generosity with his time and feedback are true, and I was lucky enough to be one of the beneficiaries of it. My thanks to so many great friends and scholars, including the likes of David Whetham, Janina Dill, Massimo Renzo, Marco Meyer, Victor Tadros, Adil Haque, Jovana Davidivoc, Kalia Draper, Mona Simon, Lars Christie, Kimberly Ferzan, Saba Bazargan-Forward, David Rodin, Seth Lazar, Helen Frowe, Michael Robillard, Stephen Woodside, Ian Fishback, Jennifer Welsh, Linda Eggert, Kate Vredenburgh, Johannes Himmelreich, Danny Statman, Yitzhak Benbaji, Uwe Steinhoff, David Luban, Michael Gross, Nancy Sherman, Shannon French, Jim Cook, Marcus Hedahl, Judith Lichtenberg, Carl Ficarrotta, Ryan Jenkins, Shawn Kaplan, Scott Sagan, Ed Barrett, Jeremy Davis . . . And so many others: I thank you and have learned from each of you. Having too many colleagues that I am lucky enough to name as friends who have helped me in this endeavor is a good problem to have. In our little subfield, we have an amazing group of scholars and I count myself lucky to be a part of it.

To so many of my old friends who were willing to let me think out loud and discuss these topics with probing questions, often over a cocktail: Dave Alderson, Liam Doust, Rob Hayward, Patrick LeMaster, Bill Douros, Kris Lehman, Glenn Sadowsky, Tom Moylan, Todd Weaver,

Jonathan Llovio, Ken Walton, Matt Hohman, Dan Finkley, Steve Horvath, Richard J. Cerame, Terrell Maddox, DJ Joy, Justin Pederson, John Sherman, and Jon Rose. And, of course, some of my friends who are likely tired of hearing me debate these things, often with myself, for the past many years: Mark Hille, you have my thanks. Jason Redula, remember math. There's a band of brothers without whom this book would not have been written and without whom I could not have done much of anything. Glenn Paauw, Matt Burnett, Patton Dodd, Jeff Culver, Wilson Brissett, Jim Knutsen: long live the cult.

Colleagues and dear friends at the Naval Postgraduate School for whom I count myself lucky to be a member and whose impact and influence on my thinking is more than you can imagine: John Arquilla, Leo Blanken, Gunner Sepp, Tristan Volpe, Doug Borer, Anna Simons, Glenn Robinson, Ryan Maness, Camber Warren, Sean Everton, Brian Greenshields, Amina Kator-Mubarez, Frank Giordano, Gordon McCormick, Rebecca Lorentz, Michael Freeman, Siamak Naficy, Shannon Houck, Daniel Cunningham, Tommy Jamison, Jennifer Duncan, Karen Flaherty, Matt Zefferman, Carly Capson, John Tullius, Carter Malkasian, Steve Lerman, Ann Rondeau, and so many others: thank you. John Arquilla deserves special thanks: John, you have always believed in me as a scholar and backed me in ways I can never repay. Thank you.

There is my family, Abbi, Toby, and Norah, who are the light of my life and the reason I get up every morning. To say thank you is inadequate. I love each of you more than I can comprehend or express. Abbi has been helping me write this book, in her own way, for well over a decade. Thank you, Abbi. And thanks to my biggest fans, my parents, Larry and Debbie, and my mother-in-law, Vicki, for your unending support.

And there is also my Compass family, without whose support this book would have never been finished. My dear friend Lisa Strutz has helped in innumerable ways and with endless encouragement and support. This, and so many things, would be impossible without you. Lisa, thank you. Ted Lechterman and Ben Lange, you are both brothers and both push me to be a better scholar. David Whetham, your encouragement to me at the very outset of my academic career was critical to me in ways I cannot fully explain, and it has never stopped. You've long been my big brother in this academic life together and will forever have my gratitude. (You're also the only person in these acknowledgements mentioned twice.) Lorenzo Nericcio, your help and editing work has been tremendous and I'm forever in your debt. Margaux,

Eric, Teresa, Marius, Katherine, Duncan, Drew, Andrew, Anicée, Becky, Ravi, and Monika: Thank you all.

This book was lucky enough to receive not just one, but two separate workshops with some of the very best scholars I know who honored me by kindly tearing the book apart and debating me at every turn. Sincerely, I don't know how I was so fortunate to have both book symposiums. First, I owe my friend Lars Christie, and the stalwart band of scholars he assembled to discuss and debate my book in Oslo, Norway a debt of thanks: Susanne Burri, Mike Robillard, Andreas Carlsson, and Mona Simon, with excellent help from Camilla Serck-Hanssen. Second, my friend Michael Skerker organized a workshop in Monterey, California, where we examined both his recent excellent book—*The Moral Status of Combatants: A New Theory*—and this manuscript together. Alec Walen, Pauline Shanks Kaurin, Richard Schoonhoven, Jeremy Davis, and Graham Parsons—you each have my deep gratitude. Alec Walen deserves special credit and call-out for going above and beyond in his written comments on the entirety of the near final draft of this book, which he happily handed to me with the full book printed out in a binder at the workshop. What a gift. Alec, your professional generosity is matched only by your affable and warm affect. You are a credit to our field and discipline.

I was fortunate in that the initial round of peer-review for the book was honored to have the brilliant and insightful Kalia Draper, and another anonymous reviewer, give substantial and excellent feedback and guidance. Thank you Kalia and the anonymous reviewer for OUP.

My students deserve a special shout-out. There are so many I could name, and especially those whose theses I was honored to advise. Much of my earliest, embryonic thinking on these ideas actually started when I was teaching philosophy to cadets at the Air Force Academy, while I myself was serving in the Air Force. Then, later, while I was teaching at UConn. But, without question, the past decade I've now had teaching the incredible men and women who have come through the Defense Analysis Department at the Naval Postgraduate School have impacted my thinking on these issues more than any other group of people. The topics explored in this book have been hashed and rehashed out again and again with cohort after cohort of amazing NPS students I've been honored to teach. Thank you for pushing me. As real-world practitioners—warfighters—who have to live out the harrowing ethical decisions I write about in this book in such often academic and removed ways, you all have my never-ending gratitude and debt of thanks. This really is for all of my students, especially for every single student who took the advanced Ethics of War class, DA 4711. Those seminar sessions over the years are some of the greatest I've ever known. A few students must be named—though it's simply true that there are too many to properly give account. Tom McNeil, you know why. Benny Romero, you are missed. Forrest Crowell, thank you. Ted Morton. Nils French. Tom-Erik Kihl. Jon Huntsman. Scott Orr. Andy Anderson. Rob Birch. Fray Bart Doyle. JJ Hayes. Ben Silvertooth. Jon Ferrin. Andrew Charlie "Bonesaw" Rockwood. Ryan Donofrio. There are so many others I'd wish to name. To all of my students: thank you for giving me the honor of teaching you something about ethics and philosophy.

Finally, if there were an award for the most patient and supportive editor on the planet—perhaps there should be—it would not only go to Peter Ohlin, but the competition wouldn't stand a chance. Peter has supported and encouraged this book project from the start and displayed the longsuffering of a saint while it came to conclusion. To Peter and the entire incredible team at OUP, you have my eternal thanks.

Introduction

> Wars are poor chisels for carving out peaceful tomorrows.
> —Martin Luther King Jr.

Liberal conceptions of the moral justification for war have become dominant since the publication of Michael Walzer's *Just & Unjust Wars* in 1977.[1] This dominance is seen across all contemporary manifestations of just war theory: from international relations and diplomatic discourse, from the minds and proclamations of military commanders and governmental leaders, to the everyday political assertions and philosophical rationalization of most individuals. Similarly, rights-based accounts of the moral justification of individual defensive killing have been dominant since, at least, Judith Jarvis Thomson's work on the issue in the early Seventies.[2] Over the past two decades, however, these already rich fields of research—just war theory and the ethics of defensive harm—have each experienced significant and sustained resurgence. On the just war side, many scholars, notably led by Jeff McMahan among countless others, have challenged the Walzerian Orthodoxy, leading to a new and seemingly ever-expanding explosion of work on the ethics of killing in war. On the ethics of defensive harm side, many of these same scholars uncovered a multitude of ways the theoretical details of rights-based permissible killings are far more complex than most of us initially thought.

This book addresses both debates. It does so by treating both subjects as equal parts in a larger meditation on the ethics of killing generally, whether in war, collectively, or in self-defense, individually—and whatever it is that lies between. That is, I focus on the moral justification of individual defensive

---

[1] Michael Walzer, *Just & Unjust Wars: A Moral Argument with Historical Examples* (New York: Basic Books, 1977).

[2] See, for example, Judith Jarvis Thomson, "Self-Defense and Rights," in *The Lindley Lecture* (Lawrence, KS: Lawrence University of Kansas Publications, 1976).

killing in general and its application to war as a natural outgrowth of the former. The book thereby engages some of the present debate over perceived weaknesses in the standard model of just war theory and hopes to defend some aspects of a properly liberal conception of just war. More broadly, I view this entire book as an earnest attempt to take individual rights seriously in our thinking over killing and war.

Some have similarly engaged in thinking about the morality of killing and war recently and have come to rather different conclusions than I present here. Many hold that if we are to take rights seriously, war could never be just—in principle—and the notion of a "just war" is an illusory abstraction. Others think that the classic justification for war built upon the individual right to self-defense is a mistaken move in the first place. There are some scholars who agree that if we are to take individual rights seriously, we must make some quite radical changes to the traditional just war convention. However, there is debate over what these changes should be and if any plausible just war theory can survive such changes. In my view it can be done: a plausible, workable, and legitimately liberal just war theory can be found that adequately respects the rights of individuals. That is what I intend to craft (at least partially) in this book.

Allow me to put my project another way. One of the debates, examined below in some detail, focuses on whether any just war account that rejects the doctrine of the moral equality of combatants can maintain that war can still be fought justly. I defend that it can, but this debate is really only one subset of the wider question at the fore of just war thinking: as we dismantle Walzer's "legalist paradigm" and cast off central vestments of a defunct classic just war theory, can the notion of a just war survive in the contemporary world of modern warfare? I argue in the affirmative that it can be done—that the needed rejection of Walzerian relics does not destroy the project of crafting a plausible just war theory. It does, however, require ever sharpening exactly what just war demands of us. My aim in this book is to discover just what those demands are. It turns out they are exceedingly high. But as I will argue below, that is exactly what we should *expect* for any plausible notion of what morality demands of us when we try to wage war justly, or are so confident as to claim that we can do so, even in principle. The moral weight of war is tremendous and terrible. We should shudder in the face of its awful reality. I try to never wander far from the notion that it's rather audacious to presume that something as horrendous as war could ever possibly be "just" in the first place. If such a thing can be just—and I think it can—it will certainly carry with it exceedingly high moral demands on those who kill, maim, and destroy. Again, we should expect this to be the case if we take the moral significance of the horror of war with the seriousness it deserves.

Before I outline the sequence that I will work through to deliver such ends, let me first say a word about the value of contemporary moral philosophy and the importance of its applicability. Once my work here gets into the weeds, common to this kind of analytic rigor, it may appear to many that this is nothing more than trivial hair-splitting and a certain kind of logical application of concepts derived from frivolous puzzles found only in the isolated ivory tower of modern academia. This is a relatively common complaint regarding analytic philosophy in general. In other words, many will take this to be a kind of "work" (if it can even be called that), wholly divorced from the real-world difficulties, pains, complexities, and horrors of actual human experience over these same matters.[3] I think such a judgment is too quick and unfair. The realities of lived experience often do, in fact, bring with them the kind of moral complexities that take great care to unravel and understand, if only we grapple with them seriously. Moreover, I find it true that the moral realities that surround us, and especially those that arise around such intense things as killing and war, often hold hidden and almost mysterious intricacies and facets in want of careful explanation. These intricacies deserve our attention. But still, I appreciate the apprehension and skepticism many will have toward this method. I get it. What I would ask is that the reader join me in this attempt at careful, dispassionate critical reasoning and exploration, for the subject matter deserves such attention. And, it turns out, there are few methodologies available for such work if we wish to give it the logical rigor it demands. Allow me to make the case for the method by way of example.

Consider the following short and painful reflection on killing in war from a US soldier, Timothy Kudo, who was deployed to the wars in Iraq and Afghanistan. His unit had just shot and killed two innocent noncombatants on a motorcycle whom they mistakenly took to be armed combatants due to some tragically misleading evidence and difficult epistemic circumstances:

> I know that our decision was right and, given the outcome, that it was also wrong. We trained to kill for years and given the opportunity, part of us

---

[3] Fellow scholars make similar critiques of the approach. See Mark Rigstad, "Putting the War Back in Just War Theory: A Critique of Examples," *Ethical Perspectives* 24, no. 1 (2017): 123–44.

jumped at the chance to finally be Marines. Despite the school construction and shuras, that's what it meant to make a difference in uniform; it meant killing our enemies. But these men weren't enemies. They were just trying to get to a home so close that their family was able to watch them die. After the shooting, the families encircled us in hysterics as they collected the bodies. It was the first and only time I saw an Afghan adult woman's face. The wailing continued in the distance as we continued on our mission.... I remember the widows and orphans and wailing families and the faces of two men on a motorcycle. They understood they were being killed as it happened, yet they couldn't accept their fate. They died painfully. Their teeth clenched and grimacing. Their eyes open. Those eyes gave them a final pleading expression. *Why did you kill us?. . .* The Marine Hymn states that we are "first to fight for right and freedom and to keep our honor clean." Since the shooting, I've thought about what that means and decided that it was beyond good and evil. It was an accident. War doesn't distinguish between innocence or guilt, skill or incompetence, intelligence or idiocy. But we do. We see injustice in the deaths and can't accept their inevitability. But it was fated when we decided to go to war. In that sense, we're all responsible.[4]

As it turns out, such a story directly touches on many of the conceptual matters this book examines. The issues surrounding evidence-relative permissibility, the matters of liability attribution in cases of uncertainty, and even the issues of whether a given group of people can properly defend themselves and such things as "freedom" and whether it is possible to keep one's "honor clean" in war—all major issues addressed in this book—are surfaced in this small, real-world vignette from this soldier. My work ultimately contends that war is, above all else, a horrific tragedy, even in those rare instances when it can be the right thing to do, even when it is necessary. That assertion is perhaps nothing new; but the conceptual framework I offer helps make this case, it gives us a better explanatory model for understanding it, and, I hope, does some justice to the realities of war reflected in the story above.

Thus, when I at times spend pages attempting to get the moral reasoning right on some far-flung, intricate thought experiment for a seemingly small distinction between cases, it is actually because I hope to find some better

---

[4] Timothy Kudo, "On War and Redemption," *New York Times* (November 8, 2011), accessed December 20, 2011, http://opinionator.blogs.nytimes.com/2011/11/08/on-war-and-redemption/.

moral understanding of cases like the above. If our aim is clarity, it demands the kind of analytic rigor and style we have seen from moral philosophy over the past few decades. But the goal here is not clarity for clarity's *sake*. What we are after is *truth* in our moral beliefs. If that is our goal, what else are we to do? If we take this effort seriously, it will take time, work, and careful, diligent thinking—even when it seems a tad esoteric at times.

Allow me to give another story; this one far more recent, and equally tragic. This is a story of a soldier who was told by his country that he was fighting for a just cause, only to learn in painful fashion that he had been lied to and that, in fact, he was contributing to an evil war effort. Amazingly, we have an incredible account of him honestly and gut-wrenchingly wrestling with this reality, in real time, as he is discovering it right in the very midst of warfare. This—the epistemic realities and corresponding moral duties of those who fight in war, and specifically how our epistemic duties and moral duties are inextricably tied together in crucial ways, perhaps especially in the moral horror of war—is a central theme if not *the* central theme of this book. Moreover, the particular case this man was involved in is an extraordinary example of overt, unjust aggression, and a seeming indisputably clear case of an unjust cause fighting against a just cause—namely, national self-defense. This issue forms the central theme of the later chapters of the book: how can we rightly understand justifiable national defense?

I speak of Lt. Col. Astakhov Dmitry Mikhailovich. He was part of the invading Russian force in 2022 attacking Ukraine. Mikhailovich was captured by the Ukrainian defensive force and was then interviewed. His testimony and those of some of his comrades was broadcast in real time across the internet to much of the world.[5] In the video of the account, Mikhailovich appears genuinely heartbroken and simultaneously outraged at his epistemic confusion in waging the war he was just fighting.

---

[5] Note that this interview was originally published by 24Kanal, a smaller Ukrainian TV news station. In light of that, it must be taken with some degree of healthy skepticism; Ukrainian media has clear incentives to present Russian POWs in a remorseful position. Additionally, the story was not reported widely by Western news stations, most likely due to concern that Russian POWs in Ukraine may have been mistreated, or that simply using and interviewing POWs in this way for propaganda is considered wrong or at least questionable, even when the POWs themselves appear to consent and wish to give their account. Many journalist outlets wish to not be complicit in what could turn out to be misuse in this way. The *Washington Post* published an article describing this concern in depth: Isabelle Khurshudyan and Sammy Westfall, "Ukraine puts captured Russians on stage. It's a powerful propaganda tool, but is it a violation of POW rights?," *Washington Post* (March 9, 2022). That article does not include reference to the interview with Lt. Col. Astakhov Dmitry Mikhailovich, but the same concerns outlined in that piece naturally apply here. There are countless similar accounts of confusion as to the actual Russian aims by Russian soldiers in the 2022 invasion of Ukraine.

> We were told that Ukraine allegedly—we were told this while in Russia, via the media—that Ukraine was dominated—I am literally 100% wrong now, don't judge too harshly—we were told that Ukraine's territory was dominated by a fascist regime. Nationalists and Nazis had taken power, and ordinary people needed some help to get rid of this yoke. [...] I feel shame that we came to this country, to Ukraine's territory [...] I don't know why we're doing this. We knew very little. We brought sorrow to this land [...] I feel sorry for the people back in Russia. They're not guilty; their guilt is that they are misinformed.[6]

This is an incredible and painful confession of a warfighter: he has concluded that the justification for the war he was just waging, that he was compelled to wage by his state, was false; it was a complete fabrication. And Mikhailovich is wrestling with the moral responsibility and guilt that he and his fellow soldiers—and even his fellow citizens back home—carry, or should be excused from carrying, given their cloudy epistemic circumstances over the injustice of their cause.

Do the Russian soldiers who invaded Ukraine, in what appears to be a blatant and overt example of unjust aggression, bear any responsibility for their participation in that war? I speak not of those Russian soldiers who committed the many atrocities, or even stood by or failed to act to stop their fellow soldiers from committing atrocities. We all agree, one would think, that those soldiers have moral responsibility for such heinous acts, for such war crimes. I mean simply for even participating in the invasion in the first place, as part of the Russian military, are they morally responsible? Clearly, the *decision* to invade rests not with those soldiers but with the authoritarian dictator Vladimir Putin and those in his orbit. And, no doubt, maximal moral responsibility and blame is on his head. But do those who willingly carry out his criminal war bear any responsibility themselves? I argue in this book that they do. But this is

---

[6] Chris Pleasance, "Show us mercy.. we thought we were liberating Ukraine from the Nazis," *The Daily Mail* (March 7, 2022), https://www.dailymail.co.uk/news/article-10585541/Ukraine-war-Russian-POW-begs-mercy-invading-forces.html. And Yaron Steinbuch, "Captured Russian Officer https://nypost.com/2022/03/07/captured-russian-officer-apologizes-to-ukraine-for-genocide/. The interview was shared widely across Twitter by many users and accounts, some reputable, some not. Again, please note well the discussion in note 4, above, regarding the questionable tactics of interviewing POWs in this way, as well as the likely reason more mainstream and reputable press did not cover the story out of (perhaps justifiable) fear of being complicit in the wrongful treatment of POWs. I include it here because, first, this interview did indeed happen and appears veracious, and, second, it is a striking present-day example of a soldier coming to grips with not merely *jus in bello* failings but of actually being misled on the *jus ad bellum* justifications given to him by his country. In many ways, this is precisely what this book is about.

complicated. In no small part because clearly large swaths of the Russian military did not have clear epistemic insight into what they were really doing—neither the aims of the war itself, nor even the very fact that it was an invasion.[7] How do their epistemic limitations impact their resulting moral responsibility, if at all? These are some of the core questions I am after in this book.

So, I beseech the reader again to have patience when, in this book, I may at times work through some detailed aspect or another of rather academic and technical points, or split hairs over a certain conceptual distinction. Or, please, perhaps the most patience is needed when I work through some admittedly bizarre and far-flung thought experiment. In all these things, the aim is trying to divine the moral truth on exceedingly difficult, yet all too important and relevant moral questions that confront the reality of our lives today.

I offer you a "Calvin & Hobbes" comic strip written by the legendary Bill Watterson to better capture my point here.[8] In the strip (figure I.1 below), young Calvin approaches his father who is reading the newspaper in his easy chair. Calvin asks, with apparent sincerity, "Dad, how do soldiers killing each other solve the world's problems?" The next two panels show the father's shocked silence—he's dumbfounded—as he searches for a way to respond to a question so pregnant with pain and youthful innocence. Eventually, Calvin walks away without an answer, muttering to himself, "I think grown-ups just *act* like they know what they're doing."

Figure I.1. Calvin and Hobbes comic strip.[9]

---

[7] Nell Clark, "Here's how propaganda is clouding Russians' understanding of the war in Ukraine," *NPR* (March 15, 2022), accessed June 4, 2022, https://www.npr.org/2022/03/15/1086705796/russian-propaganda-war-in-ukraine

[8] I admit to being a complete fanboy of Watterson. His work is perhaps the greatest ever accomplished in his given medium; with the notable contender of Gary Larson competing for such a claim. If you, dear reader, have not spent long hours with Calvin and his beloved Hobbes, you are missing out.

[9] This comic strip is used under Section 107 of the Copyright Act of 1976 wherein allowance is made for "fair use" for purposes such as "criticism, comment, news reporting, teaching, scholarship,

My aim in this book is to answer Calvin. And to give him a real answer. The initial silence of Calvin's father is, I think, appropriate. We tend to try to answer this question too quickly, perhaps instinctively. But Calvin's question deserves a serious and thoughtful answer or, rather, a series of answers. And, more painfully, the likes of Timothy Kudo and Astakhov Dmitry Mikhailovich and their testimonies deserve proper responses, to give us better understanding and explanation, even if not solace and succor, to the lived moral realities their stories embody. Such an answer, if it is to properly respect the sincerity and import of the question, will by necessity be long and, at times, rather complicated. But we fail to answer it via analogy or simple story or narrative or picture, as helpful as those can be in human understanding. This question rightly demands careful work and damn good answers. This, then, is why I take such pains to systematically and carefully think through the questions I do below. And, note well, I am here only even attempting to do that to a small subset of the moral complexities immediately apparent. Yet, I believe that dispassionate, objective moral reasoning can bear us significant fruit. Put another way: if there were ever a vexing moral question worth our serious and sustained attention would it not be this dreadful and seemingly endless reality of human life about which Calvin inquires?

and research." Fair use is a use permitted by copyright statute that might otherwise be infringing. Non-profit, educational, or personal use tips the balance in favor of use.

Outline

The approach I take to answering Calvin's question—"How do soldiers killing each other solve the world's problems?"—can be described in broad terms very briefly. I will sketch it here in simple form. First, starting from the most basic building block, I examine if it is ever morally permissible for one human to intentionally kill another. I believe that it can be on some, usually rare (thankfully), occasions. Next, I examine just what those occasions are and how the general principles guiding moral action apply for this particular activity of killing: when someone can be killed and yet not be wronged in so doing. Following that, I try to see if this act which can sometimes be permissible can generate instances where whole groups of people can try to kill other whole groups of people, and if this too can ever be justified. Again, I find that this can indeed be the case, but, again, it is only so in rather rare and particular contexts. Understanding what those rare contexts are begins to give us an answer to Calvin's question.

That's the very short, hyper-simplified version of what I am trying to do in this book. Here's the longer outline. I begin, in the first chapter, by examining the notion of a right to self-defense. Perhaps surprisingly, self-defense has been notoriously difficult to justify on a rights-based account. I briefly review the recent history of that debate and propose a rights-based "liability account" of self-defense that follows in the tradition of Jeff McMahan, Judith Jarvis Thomson, David Rodin, and Suzanne Uniacke, among countless others. There is a long and complicated debate, however, over whether liability attribution requires responsibility or mere causation, or some other relationship to the unjust harm to be averted, on the part of the liable person. In chapter 1, I offer my basis for rejecting those views which do not require responsibility for liability. Short story, I just don't think they work. They so far exceed our moral intuitions that were we to accept them, we'd have to question all of our moral intuitions. Instead, I embrace what I call the Responsible Account for liability. Yet, within this account there are still two major, competing views for how we should understand the responsibility criterion. Each have their own compelling strengths. But, at the end of chapter 1, I show the weaknesses in both of these views and the need for a new view of the responsibility necessary for liability.

Before continuing down the road to this new view liability attribution, we stop to see something already implied by the rights-based accounts. Right out of the gate, we see that if we consistently apply a rights-based "liability account" for permissible killing to *wartime* killing, then several significant revisions must be made to the conventional understanding of just war theory. This is so obvious to anyone who stops and thinks about how we *otherwise* consider killing in any other context that it's borderline absurd that we so blithely accept killing in war at face value. I remember myself, rather briefly, having these thoughts of incredulity early in my life. But I, like I think most of us—and perhaps most of humanity across the past few centuries in the least, but likely much longer—were told a story about how killing in war is simply "different" in some important, even critical, sense. But, I worry, this is an illusion we have been sold.

Indeed, if we apply a rights-based "liability account," as it seems the best arguments available seem we should, then one of the central pieces of traditional just war theory must be rejected almost right out of the gate. Specifically, what is known as the moral equality of combatants thesis. I aim to defend this rejection and show how a plausible just war theory can remain standing without this classic tenet. But, to do so, I must first formulate my particular view of liability and the responsibility criterion. Thus, in chapter 2, I offer what I call the Evidence-Relative View of liability to defensive harm. On this view, one should become liable to defensive harm only if one violates some evidence-relative norms in a properly relevant way. I argue that an Evidence-Relative Account of liability provides a better understanding of our considered moral judgments than the competing accounts reviewed in chapter 1 can deliver. Understanding liability as something that turns only on evidence-relative norms holds greater justificatory force than competing fact-relative or belief-relative accounts of responsibility do. Moreover, the implications of this are particularly important when applied to classic debates over self-defense and war, as I will show.

This is a significant departure. Full stop. For most scholars within the Responsible tend to hold that liability should turn on matters of fact-relative permissibility.[1] While there are reasons to hold such a view, I ultimately

---

[1] I am not alone in my view—recently a handful of scholars have either come around to the right "fit" that the Evidence-Relative Account seems to give to liability cases, or have otherwise recently defended other hybrid versions of the account. It is hard to know when such theoretic moves emerge,

disagree and show that an Evidence-Relative Account should be preferred for several reasons. One reason is that an Evidence-Relative Account provides a better explanation for the important moral concept of excuse and crucial distinctions therein. Generally, the concept of excuse is a notion which ends up simply being lost on most other ways of understanding liability; or at least not able to be adequately explained. Another reason is that the Evidence-Relative View can more plausibly accommodate many of the classic challenges raised in the self-defense literature reviewed in chapter 1. Indeed, it provides precisely the kind of new view that we found was needed at the conclusion of chapter 1.

In chapter 3, I turn back to war more directly and examine the recently ascendant revisionist approach to just war theory. After briefly tracing its scholarly lineage, I show why attempts to separate the morality of war from the morality of everyday life are mistaken. I then defend the rejection of the moral equality of combatants thesis necessitated by my view against a powerful objection: is just war even possible following such revisions? I believe it is and defend my view against the many challenges it creates. One such notable challenge is what has become known as the "responsibility dilemma" pressed most effectively by Seth Lazar, and resurrected or recast in various forms by others.[2] Defending against this objection turns out to be a proper defense of the revisionist strain of just war theory more generally. Finally, I show how some other efforts made to reestablish the moral equality of

---

especially among such a vibrant community of scholars who are lucky enough to work together—collaboratively, in my mind—towards advancing the field in the ethics of war over the past decade or two. I have been convinced of the Evidence-Relative View since (at least) 2010 and have published brief mentions of the view over the years, but have yet to give my full account of the position until this book. However, thankfully, others have either taken up the view itself in the interim or else have recognized the same weaknesses in competing views that drive one to the evidence-relative views in the first place. For example, when the earliest account of evidence-relative approaches were emerging—I think first mentioned in my *Analysis* article in 2011, "Walking the Tightrope of Just War"—Jonathan Quong references that piece and mentions the view as a possible route of resolution to some problems with most approaches to liability in his 2012 article, "Liability to Defensive Harm," *Philosophy & Public Affairs*, 40, 45–77. Of particularly important note is the excellent work of Susanne Burri. Burri's scholarship deserves special discussion later in the book. Burri and I both seemed to see the overall soundness of some type of Evidence-Relative View early on within in our field. We commiserated on the regular misinterpretations of the general distinctions of evidence-relative as opposed to fact-relative moral permissions across countless conferences and papers and gatherings. In recent years, Burri herself has written on an Evidence-Relative View of liability, which is excellent: "A Subjective Impermissibility Account of Liability to Defensive Harm." Much of my work on this conceptual theory is in debt to Burri's outstanding thinking and scholarship on the topic.

[2] Seth Lazar, "The Responsibility Dilemma for Killing in War: A Review Essay," *Philosophy & Public Affairs* 38, no. 2 (2010): 180–213.

combatants similarly fail, such as the arguments that war is a kind of morally unregulated "affray" offered by Patrick Emerton and Toby Handfield.[3]

This defense of the revisionist approach to just war theory leads to outlining how the superior Evidence-Relative Account of liability attribution could be directly applied in war. Thus, in chapter 4, I offer a new proposal for how target discrimination could actually work in war in the real world if we take the revisionist account seriously. I call this proposal the "Reasonable Perceived Liability" (RPL) model and build here on previous work attempting to reconcile the revisionist approach with the realities of how war is actually fought.[4] I show how such a model could potentially function in the real world and I offer some arguments in its defense against a variety of objections.

I noted above that some question whether or not a justification for state-level defensive violence can be properly based on an individual right to self-defense. Most notably, David Rodin has raised this challenge, but the question has grown and received considerable attention from several other scholars of late. Put differently, many will come along and conclude that some kind of liability attribution can make defensive killing in individual cases justified, but they will balk at the idea that this logic could possibly hold for large groups—entire nations—setting out to kill one another. It's a tough question, and in many ways, gets to the core of Calvin's question. Hence, in chapters 5 and 6, I outline how a properly liberal just war theory *could* be constructed that is based solely on a respect for individual rights and the distinctive value liberalism places on individual autonomy. This approach and its grounding will be counter-intuitive to many and controversial—how could the value of *individual* autonomy legitimately ground group killing on a rights-based model, where each individual has different epistemic standing and, consequently, different permissions and wrongs? While the result is admittedly unexpected, I find that this approach, in fact, is precisely the best chance any rights-based approach for justifying nation-state level warfare. While the conditions for its instantiation will be quite rare, it is the just war theory that most plausibly fits with an individual rights respecting liberalism. As such, it gives us the best attempt at answering why "soldiers killing each other" can

---

[3] Patrick Emerton and Toby Handfield, "Order and Affray: Defensive Privileges in Warfare," *Philosophy & Public Affairs* 37, no. 4 (2009): 382–414.

[4] Strawser, "Revisionist Just War Theory and the Real World: A Cautiously Optimistic Proposal," in *Routledge Handbook of Ethics and War: Just War in the 21st Century*, ed. Fritz Allhoff, Adam Henschke, and Nick Evans (Routledge Press, 2013).

(sometimes, rarely) be morally justified. In other words, returning to my answer to Calvin, it is in these chapters where I move from showing that it can be morally permissible for an individual to kill another, to showing how that permission can aggregate to whole groups of people, and do so in a way that is consistent with the principles initially ascertained for self-defense.

To accomplish this, I first set up the general problem here for liberalism in chapter 5 with the puzzle of weak, conditional, benevolent aggression. This puzzle is designed to actually strengthen the core point of Rodin's challenge to see if liberalism has any way out of this justificatory conundrum, even in the most vexing of possible cases imaginable. Then, in chapter 6, I resolve the puzzle by arguing that a proper valuing of individual autonomy can, in some instances, give rise to legitimate defense of certain group projects, including the group project of self-governance. Note that I only intend in these chapters to show what the moral structure of such a project could be; I do not set out to build a complete theory. Instead, my aim is to offer some blueprints. That is, I show how a distinctively liberal theory of just war *could* be constructed that meets the above challenges consistently and does so *coherently* with the positions to which rights-based approaches are already committed. This is important work if we hope the previous chapters to have any purchase in the real world. If a basic coherent framework of a right to state defense cannot be found within the confines of liberalism in the first place, then the detailed work of taking individual rights seriously in warfare is moot.

Detailed Chapter Section Outline

Chapter 1: Permissible Defensive Harm and Liability
- 1.1. Introduction
- 1.2. The Rights-Based Account of Defensive Harm
  - 1.2.1 Positive Permissibility to Harm
  - 1.2.2 Liability
  - 1.2.3 Necessity and Proportionality
  - 1.2.4 Liable and Nonliable Cases
- 1.3. A Vicious Circle for Rights-Based Accounts?
  - 1.3.1 The Need for Asymmetry
  - 1.3.2 Grounding Asymmetry
  - 1.3.3 More on Liability Constraints
- 1.4. Is Responsibility Necessary for Liability?

- 1.5. Rejecting the Nonresponsible View
  - 1.5.1 Killing Bystanders
  - 1.5.2 The Otsukian Objection
  - 1.5.3 Defending Against Otsuka
  - 1.5.4 Opportunistic Use of Bystander
  - 1.5.5 Direct and Indirect Threats
- 1.6. Two Views of the Responsibility Criterion
  - 1.6.1 Embracing the Responsible View
  - 1.6.2 Two Views
  - 1.6.3 Exploring the Views
- 1.7. Problems with Both Views of Responsibility
  - 1.7.1 Trouble with Foreseeability
  - 1.7.2 Asymmetry or Symmetry?
  - 1.7.3 Nonreciprocal Risk
  - 1.7.4 Liability with excused culpability
  - 1.7.5 The Incomplete Responsible View

Chapter 2: The Evidence-Relative View of Liability Attribution
- 2.1. Introduction
- 2.2. Three Senses of Wrong
  - 2.2.1 A Better Framework
  - 2.2.2 Is Wrong Univocal?
  - 2.2.3 Understanding the Three Senses
- 2.3. The Evidence-Relative View
  - 2.3.1 A Tertium Quid
  - 2.3.2 Two Kinds of Excuse
- 2.4. Moral Epistemic Contextualism
  - 2.4.1 Moral Duties to Believe Rightly
  - 2.4.2 Responsible for Ignorance
  - 2.4.3 Failure of Due Diligence
- 2.5. Moral Ignorance
  - 2.5.1 Another Kind of Ignorance
  - 2.5.2 Defensive Harm and the Moral Ignorance Thesis
  - 2.5.3 Bracketing Moral Ignorance

Chapter 3: The Evidence-Relative View and Intricate Symmetries
- 3.1. Introduction
- 3.2. Tragedies as Explanatory Tool
  - 3.2.1 An Intricate Symmetry
  - 3.2.2 Resolving Tragedies: Distributing Harm

3.3. Further Complexities: Imposing Risk with Ignorance
    3.3.1 Risk Imposition
    3.3.2 Invincible Ignorance and Moral Epistemic Contextualism
3.4. Oversimplifying Epistemic Issues
    3.4.1 Evidentiary Considerations for Classic Cases
    3.4.2 Third-Party Intervention
3.5. Real-World Cases

Chapter 4: A Defense of Revisionist Just War Theory
4.1. Introduction
4.2. The Just War Tradition
4.3. A Separate Morality of War?
4.4. Revisionist Just War Theory and Its Discontents
    4.4.1 The Responsibility Dilemma for Revisionist Just War Theory
    4.4.2 The Contingent Pacifism Horn
    4.4.3 The Evidence-Relative View and the Dilemma
    4.4.4 The Total War Horn
    4.4.5 A supposed paradox
4.5. Other Possible Grounds for the MEC
    4.5.1 Affray as Grounds for the MEC
    4.5.2 Relevant Harm
    4.5.3 We're All Unintentional Ninjas

Chapter 5: A New Proposal for Liability in War
5.1. Introduction
5.2. Degreed Status
5.3. Deriving RPL
5.4. Objections and Real-World Cases

Chapter 6: The Puzzle of Benevolent Aggression
6.1. Introduction
6.2. A Justificatory Burden
6.3. The Puzzle of Alpha's Benevolent Aggression
6.4. The Puzzle's Challenge to Liberalism
6.5. Rodin's Challenge
6.6. Liberal Resolution?
6.7. The Case of Unjust Charlie

Chapter 7: Towards a New Liberal Theory of Just War
7.1. Introduction

- 7.2. The Special Value of Autonomy for Liberalism
- 7.3. The Value of Group Projects to Individual Autonomy
- 7.4. Autonomy Is to Be Respected, Not Maximized
- 7.5. The Value of Group Agency
- 7.6. The Assimilation Objection and Group Decision Thresholds
- 7.7. Summary Comments on Liberal Just War

Chapter 8: Conclusion: Answering Calvin

1
Permissible Defensive Harm and Liability

Let necessity, therefore, and not your will,
slay the enemy who fights against you.
—from Saint Augustine's letter 189 to Saint Boniface (418)

1.1. Introduction

This chapter has two aims: first, to explain a basic Rights-Based Account of permissible defensive harm understood as a right to self- or others-defense. The right is derivative from a right to life which is itself limited in scope as a right to, amongst other things, not be unjustly or wrongly killed.[1] Second, the chapter will explore a question central to any Rights-Based Account of self-defense: what conditions must obtain for someone to be liable to defensive harm? I reject that liability can be rightfully attributed to one merely for being the (nonresponsible) cause of a rights violation to another. Instead, I'll defend the view that a necessary criterion for liability must require some kind of moral responsibility for a wrongful harm to be averted. From here, however, it is still a further debate getting clear on just what responsibility for liability itself entails—what does it mean to say someone is responsible for a wrong? Some hold that liability simply tracks culpability. Others hold that the level of responsibility resulting in liability need not be simple culpability but can be some lesser form of responsibility that hinges on voluntary agency, regardless of the blameworthiness of the supposedly liable party. Both views fail to give us an adequate account of liability attribution. This sets up the next chapter where I offer a new proposal for liability attribution that better accords with our considered moral judgment and intuitions on self-defense. If all of this sounds rather technical and far removed from the moral realities

---

[1] I'll use "unjustly" killed most often throughout; but am happy to substitute wrongly, or other terms as well.

The Bounds of Defense. Bradley Jay Strawser, Oxford University Press. © Oxford University Press 2023.
DOI: 10.1093/oso/9780190692513.003.0003

of war, I'd encourage one to revisit the introduction to this book. To get this right, we have to start at the beginning.

1.2. The Rights-Based Account of Defensive Harm

Most people hold that there is such a thing as morally permissible self-defense. There are, of course, notable exceptions, but for most it is a first-order and rather simple moral truth that one can permissibly block wrongful harm to oneself (or others) with violence in at least some circumstances.[2] As Judith Jarvis Thomson first remarked, "Before we take a close look at it, we may think of self-defense as morally transparent."[3] But as her work and the explosion of scholarly work on the topic over the past few decades has shown, it is surprisingly contentious just what conditions must be met in order for defensive harm to be morally permissible. There has been so much work on the ethics of self-defense of late that that it may now be safe to say, *pace* Susan Uniacke writing in 1994, that the topic is no longer "under-analyzed," although many important puzzles remain unsolved and disagreement over key points persists.[4]

I embrace what's been labeled a Rights-Based Account for defensive harm that has emerged from this collective writing.[5] The philosophers who employ

---

[2] Those exceptions are the rare absolutist pacifist voices who contend that not only is there an absolute moral prohibition on coordinated group violence (i.e., war), but that there is a prohibition on even individual violence against other human beings in all cases. (In fact, they usually hold that the former prohibition stems from the later and would, of course, be logically entailed were the latter true.) The position is often rooted in a particular religious tradition, such as pacifist forms of Christianity or Hinduism. Examples of this in the Christian tradition include the Mennonite scholar John Howard Yoder (see Yoder, *The Original Revolution* (Scottdale, PA: Herald Press, 1971); *The Politics of Jesus* (Grand Rapids, MI: William B. Eerdmans Publishing Co., 1972); and *When War is Unjust* (Minneapolis: Augsburg Publishing, 1984).) Also, the theologian Stanley Hauerwas (see Hauerwas, "Pacifism: Some Philosophical Considerations," in *The Morality of War: Classical and Contemporary Readings*, edited by Larry May, Eric Rovie, and Steve Viner (Upper Saddle River, NJ: Prentice Hall, 2005).) There is also the view known as "contingent pacifism," but this and most discussions of pacifism, in fact, are nearly always used in reference to a moral prohibition on war and not individual self-defense. For a philosophical analysis of pacifism's role in political philosophy see: Jan Narveson, "Pacifism: A Philosophical Analysis," *Ethics* 75, no. 4 (1965): 259–71; and Narveson, "Is Pacifism Consistent?," *Ethics* 78, no. 2 (1968): 148–50. Also see Jenny Tiechman, *Pacifism and the Just War* (Oxford: Basil Blackwell, 1984).

[3] Judith Jarvis Thomson, "Self-Defense," *Philosophy & Public Affairs* 20, no. 4 (1991): 283–310.

[4] Susan Uniacke, *Permissible Killing: The Self-Defence Justification of Homicide* (Cambridge: Cambridge University Press, 1994), 2.

[5] Many scholars have labeled this approach with this or similar monikers. Jeff McMahan explicitly did so, but I do not believe he was the first to use this label. See Jeff McMahan, "The Basis of Moral Liability to Defensive Killing," *Philosophical Issues* 15 (2005): 386–404. It is also sometimes (in earlier work, in particular) referred to as the "Justice Account" or, occasionally, the "liability account."

this approach differ in several important ways in explaining how the rights framework plays out, and a great deal of disagreement remains over just what incurs liability, as already mentioned. But there is a growing consensus amongst a fairly sizable set of moral philosophers on the account's basic structure. Those scholars who take some form or other of a Rights-Based Account to permissible defensive harm include (at least) influential scholars such as Judith Jarvis Thomson, Jeff McMahan, David Rodin, Frances Kamm, Susan Uniacke, Michael Otsuka, Tony Coady, Cécile Fabre, Kaila Draper, Helen Frowe, Victor Tadros, Adil Haque, Alec Walen, and many others.[6] I will describe and analyze the account here taking some liberties to smooth over the smaller conceptual differences and henceforth my use of Rights-Based Account refers to all such accounts under this basic conceptual umbrella. Working through even a cursory overview of the account can be laborious, but it is a crucial foundation upon which the rest of this book is built.

1.2.1 Positive Permissibility to Harm

We have a basic moral presumption that harming people—much less killing them—is generally wrong. But exploring exceptions to this presumption reveals two primary ways we tend to think killing could potentially be justified. First, perhaps there are cases where the stakes are high enough such

---

[6] Thomson, "Self-Defense"; *The Realm of Rights* (Cambridge, MA: Harvard University Press, 1990); Jeff McMahan, *Killing in War* (Oxford: Clarendon Press, 2009); *The Ethics of Killing: Problems at the Margins of Life* (New York: Oxford University Press, 2002); "Innocence, Self-Defense and Killing in War," *Journal of Political Philosophy* 2 (1994): 193–221; "The Ethics of Killing in War," *Ethics* 114 (2004): 693–732; "The Basis of Moral Liability"; "Just Cause for War," *Ethics and International Affairs* 19 (2005): 1–21; "On the Moral Equality of Combatants," *Journal of Political Philosophy* 14 (2006): 377–93; "The Morality of War and the Law of War," in *Just and Unjust Warriors*, edited by David Rodin and Henry Shue (New York: Oxford University Press, 2008), 19–43. Michael Otsuka, "Killing the Innocent in Self-Defense," *Philosophy & Public Affairs* 23 (1994): 74–94. David Rodin, *War and Self-Defense* (Oxford: Clarendon Press, 2002). Uniacke, *Permissible Killing*. Frances Kamm, *Intricate Ethics: Rights, Responsibilities, and Permissible Harm* (New York: Oxford University Press, 2006). Tony Coady, *Morality and Political Violence* (Cambridge: Cambridge University Press, 2008); "Terrorism and Innocence," *Journal of Ethics* 8 (2004): 37–58; "The Status of Combatants," in Rodin and Shue, *Just and Unjust Warriors*, 153–75; Cécile Fabre, "Harming, Rescuing and the Necessity Constraint on Defensive Force," *Criminal Law and Philosophy* 16, no. 3 (2022): 525–38; Kerah Gordon-Solomon, "What Makes a Person Liable to Defensive Harm?," *Philosophy and Phenomenological Research* 40, no. 1 (2018): 543–67; Lars Christie, "Causation and Liability to Defensive Harm," *Journal of Applied Philosophy* 37, no. 3 (2020): 378–92; Jonathan Quong, "Liability to Defensive Harm," *Philosophy & Public Affairs* 40 (2012): 45–77. Helen Frowe, *Defensive Killing* (Oxford: Oxford University Press, 2014). Kalia Draper, *War and Individual Rights: The Foundations of Just War Theory* (New York: Oxford University Press, 2015). Adil Haque, *Law and Morality* (New York: Oxford University Press, 2017). Alec Walen, *The Mechanics of Claims and Permissible Killing in War* (Oxford University Press, 2019). And so many more.

that killing a morally innocent person can be justified simply due to the catastrophic consequences that would be avoided by doing so. Such instances of permissible killing, when there are such cases, would clearly wrong the victim and thereby violate her right to not be wrongfully killed, but this would supposedly be justified on purely consequentialist grounds as the lesser evil, given the dire circumstances.[7]

Call this justification of killing, simply, the Lesser-Evil Account. It is a brute calculus of the aggregate, usually substantially large harm to be avoided against the wrong of the person or persons to be harmed in order to block the large harm. Most people tend to think such a calculus could be a plausible way to morally justify killing, especially given a high enough threshold of harm to be averted, if there really are no other options before us that would cause less harm.[8] Again, if the harms are catastrophic enough, most will eventually (at some threshold), cave and agree that a lesser evil is the better of two roads to take in a forced-choice. Some people think that this approach is the right way to think about justifiable harm, period, for all cases, whether the harms be great or small.[9] Such strictly Utilitarian-only type thinking on the moral permissibility of defensive harm is rare, however, and for very good reason. Most, for example, rightly conclude that it is wrong to impose serious harm upon an innocent person merely to gain a slight advantage in overall aggregate harms avoided. And most hold this view even though we admit that there may indeed be cases where the consequential burden is so extreme that we must over-ride this general principle. The thought is that such lesser-evil cases—especially for killing—will be rare, and should be rare. And, even when they do obtain, they are a kind of tragic forced-choice—for they involve the violation or wronging of one or some, for the greater good. We all want the greater good, of course; but most hold that there are times when the moral permissibility of harm does not necessarily include the tragic trade-off. As such, we do right to look beyond the overly simple aggregate math of a consequentialist-only understanding of permissible harm.[10]

---

[7] See McMahan, "The Basis of Moral Liability," 387, for discussion on this point.

[8] Perhaps surprisingly—it surprised me—there are some who reject the Lesser-Evil Account even on catastrophic stakes; and I do not mean pacifists, referenced earlier, but those who think this way of "lesser-evil" justifying harm is wrong conceptually. Notably, Alec Walen. This is not quite what it appears at first. See, Walen, *The Mechanics of Claims and Permissible Killing in War* (Oxford University Press, 2019).

[9] See, for example, the work of Fritz Allhoff, as a recent example of this classically utilitarian approach as it applies to harm to others. See, but for one example, Fritz Allhoff, *Terrorism, Ticking Time-Bombs, and Torture* (Chicago: University of Chicago Press, 2012).

[10] There is a great deal more to say rejecting a consequentialist-only approach to the morality of harming, of course. However, the broad Rights-Based Account has become the dominant

The Rights-Based Account of permissible defensive harm, by contrast and thankfully, offers an approach to permissible killing that is not based *solely* on consequences. Rather, on this account there are cases of permissible killing that do not violate the rights of the person killed. That is, this view argues that there can be cases where killing is not a lesser evil to be outweighed, but rather that in some circumstances killing is not wrong at all—that one is not wronging a person who is killed, say, in legitimate and necessary self-defense against a wrongful attacker. There is no right that is violated in such defensive harm, and the moral justification of the act is not built on consequentialist concerns but rather the rights of those defended against unjust harm and the moral wrongdoing of the attacker. Such rights-based approaches demand that permissible defensive harm will often act as a "trump" or veto against pure consequentialist demands.[11] As David Rodin points out, this aspect of rights in general, including any right one may have to permissible defensive harm, is characteristic of what we mean by moral rights in the first place.[12] For these, and other reasons, most scholars working on this topic pursue a Rights-Based Account of self-defense rather than the pure consequentialist "lesser-evil" type approaches. Indeed, as Kaila Draper has explained, working through the ethics of defensive harm is often itself a good reason to reject not only utility-based accounts for permissible killing, but thereby all of act-utilitarianism in general. Draper writes, "It defies not just common moral intuition, but moral common sense, to suppose that the innocent victim of

---

account in the field and is the focus of my work in this book. As such, a thorough rejection of the consequentialist-only type approaches exceeds the scope of this work.

[11] To use Ronald Dworkin's terminology. Ronald Dworkin, *Taking Rights Seriously* (Bristol: Duckworth, 1977), p. xi. And Dworkin, "Rights as Trumps" in *Theories of Rights*, edited by J. Waldron (Oxford: Oxford University Press, 1984), 154–55. Dworkin originally used this phrasing, and it can still be helpful. However, since it was first used in the lexicon in this way, tragically and incredulously, the United States elected a disgraceful man named Donald J. Trump to the nation's highest office; a one-term, twice-impeached President. It is sad and regrettable, but his name's prominence has effectively ruined using the term in this way in modern English any longer as it is inextricably linked in most people's minds to the single worst failure of a President in the history of the United States. For more on this, see: Tim Natfali, "The Worst President in History," *The Atlantic* (January 19, 2021), https://www.theatlantic.com/ideas/archive/2021/01/trump-worst-president-history/617730/. For more on how this man ruined the word, see: Robinson Meyer, "Another Victim on this Election: The Verb 'To Trump,'" *The Atlantic* (October 25, 2016), https://www.theatlantic.com/technology/archive/2016/10/ave-atque-trumpe/505259/. And, Robert Weintraub, "How Donald ruined the Word Trump," *Slate* (February 14, 2017), https://slate.com/culture/2017/02/how-donald-ruined-the-word-trump.html.
[12] Rodin, *War & Self-Defense*, 55.

malicious and unjust aggression can justifiably defend herself only if she can thereby maximize utility."[13]

The Rights-Based Account begins simply enough: people have rights. That is, we all have legitimate moral claims against one another that all should respect. Although I will not outline the full account in this chapter, I adopt here what is known as a standard Hohfeldian multi-variable relational understanding for rights.[14] An example is given by Alan Gewirth in his helpful formula: "A has a right to X against B by virtue of Y, where A is the subject (or right-claimant), the right is the nature of the relationship, X is the object of the right, B is the respondent (or duty-holder), and Y is the right's justifying basis or reason."[15] Similarly, then, we can understand liability as meant to apply on a Hohfeldian three-part relational reading of rights such that if X is liable to be attacked by Y for purpose Z, then that means X has forfeited their right to not be attacked and X would not be wronged in being attacked by Y for end Z. (This will make more sense after I have explained liability below.) McMahan and others embrace this approach.[16]

So, again, we start with the simple premise: people have rights. One such right all have is, simply enough, to not be harmed unjustly. The corollary of this claim is that not all harm toward another person is necessarily unjust and there is no right against being harmed justly. That is, the right to life or non-harm is importantly restricted in scope in this way and it comes with certain conditions—it is not boundless. Hence, the title of this book: *The Bounds of Defense*.[17] As Rodin writes, "The right to life is subject to conditions specified in terms of facts about the mutual relationship between an aggressor and defender (or more generally between any two interacting parties)."[18] Just harm is harm that does not wrong the person to whom it is delivered and

---

[13] Draper, "Defense," 70. My thanks to Kalia Draper for reminding me of this broader point. As well as helpful comments and review of an earlier version of this manuscript throughout.

[14] See Wesley Newcomb Hohfeld, *Fundamental Legal Conceptions as Applied in Judicial Reasoning* (New Haven: Yale University Press, 1946).

[15] Alan Gewirth, *Human Rights: Essays on Justification and Applications* (Chicago: University of Chicago Press, 1982), 2. For a good discussion of Gewirth's formula, see Abigail Gosselin, "Global Poverty and Responsibility: Identifying the Duty-Bearers of Human Rights," *Human Rights Review* 8 (2006): 35–52.

[16] I am giving the details of this approach short shrift here; but volumes could be and have been written on the "structure" of human rights and conceptual debates therein. Nothing in my work here falls on this, so I set further exposition of it aside.

[17] And, yes, as some have noted, the title of this book also pays homage to a philosopher with a similar name to mine: Peter F. Strawson's, *The Bounds of Sense*. It is a bit of an inside philosophy-baseball joke to see who catches the references.

[18] Rodin, *War & Self-Defense*, 74.

is delivered for the purpose of blocking unjust harm to another.[19] Unjust harm is not simply the inverse—harm delivered for a non-harm blocking purpose—for some unjust harm may indeed be aimed at blocking harm, but still be wrongful. The basis for unjust harm then is not merely structural but is based critically on a moral asymmetry between two parties in a conflict. Failing to make this important distinction leads to a vicious circle for the logic of any Rights-Based Account self-defense, as I'll explain below in section 1.3. Hence, on the Rights-Based Account, if X delivers a wrongful harm against Y (or is about to deliver a wrongful harm), then that intended wrongful harm itself is what makes the defensive harm delivered against X permissible. The harm against X is permissible *for the purpose* of averting the original wrongful harm.[20]

Understood this way, defensive harm is simply an extrapolation from one of the most basic of liberal principles perhaps best articulated by Mill's harm principle, but expressed countless times before and since. As Mill writes, "the only purpose for which power can be rightfully exercised over any member of a civilized community, against his will, is to prevent harm to others."[21] But my invocation of Mill here should not confuse the matter over what is doing the justificatory work for the account. The account is not arguing for harm to one for the prevention of harm to others as purely a calculation of aggregate harm to be avoided—like the Lesser-Evil Account. Indeed, on the Rights-Based Account, there will be cases where the permissible harm delivered may well be *greater* than the impermissible harm averted. To put the notion another way and introduce a further term, there are things one can do to make oneself *liable* such that it is positively permissible to deliver harm to him or her for the purpose of blocking an impermissible violation to another that the liable person will otherwise carry out. Harming a liable person for this

---

[19] Depending on one's view of desert, another instance of just harm can be harm delivered for the purpose of punishing an actor's wrongful actions. I'll discuss desert more below in section 1.3.3.

[20] Throughout this chapter, I do not discuss any morally important distinction between permissible self-defense and third-party intervention defense of others. This is because I do not endorse agent-centric views of defense (as discussed below), but instead take a rights-based approach to defensive harm. Since I think all people hold rights universally, if one person can permissibly engage in self-defense in a given instance, then others may also permissibly intervene and defend that person. Not all versions of the Rights-Based Account agree. Thomson, for example, disagrees and thinks there is a moral difference between self-defense and others' defense based on an agent-centric self-preference. See Thomson, *Realm of Rights*. Thomson there references Nancy Davis, "Abortion and Self-Defense," *Philosophy & Public Affairs* 13 (1984) and George Fletcher, "Proportionality and the Psychotic Aggressor," *Israel Law Review*, 8, no. 3 (1973): 367–90, and Fletcher's *Rethinking Criminal Law* (Boston: Little, Brown, 1978), as all providing examples of such a view. I find these views generally preposterous, but I am not setting out to defeat them in this book.

[21] John Stuart Mill, *On Liberty* (New York: Simon & Brown, 2012), 19.

purpose has a positive moral reason for doing so rather than being merely some kind of an *excused* wrong that is outweighed by greater goods to be attained.

1.2.2 Liability

Liability is a complex technical term of art referring to a particular moral status that individuals incur in certain temporally bound contexts. Importantly, liability as it is used here does not mean *legal* liability.[22] Firstly, if one is liable to harm, in a given context, and that person is then so harmed (to the extent she is liable to be harmed), then the harmed person would have no legitimate complaint of unjust treatment; she would not have been wronged or had her rights violated. (This "no legitimate complaint" way of framing liability will often be helpful in our thinking ahead.) To become liable to defensive harm, one must be currently wronging or attempting to wrong or about to wrong another (to violate a right) by delivering unjust harm of some kind. That is, one must be in some way causing a rights violation of another person. Further, for one to be liable to harm, harming the liable person must effectively thwart the wrong for which the person is responsible.[23] Liability is importantly instrumental in this way that desert is not.[24] That is, if harming a person responsible for an impending rights violation does nothing whatsoever to effectively block that rights violation, then the person is *not* liable to defensive harm, regardless of whatever else the person may or may not *deserve*. (What one deserves, morally, is a different, separate question here.) So, liability attribution requires not only behaving in such a way that will wrong another, but the further condition that harming the liable person is part of an effort to actually block that wrong. What exactly constitutes responsibility for the violation of a right to incur liability is highly controversial and a new proposal for how to understand that responsibility will be the central focus of the next chapter. But first we must get clear on this Rights-Based Account of

---

[22] Moreover, throughout this chapter and the remainder of the book, I am not addressing legal concerns over killing and defensive harm but, rather, solely moral questions.

[23] Or the defender must reasonably believe (and have proper evidence for so believing) that doing so will effectively thwart the unjust threat. This is a point of disagreement amongst liability accounts that I will explore at length below. It is the entire focus of chapter 2.

[24] I'll discuss this important aspect of liability more in section 1.3.3. And this point is itself also contentious. For important matters around causation and related issues, see Lars Christie, "Causation and Liability to Defensive Harm," *Journal of Applied Philosophy* 37, no. 3 (2020): 378–92.

defensive harm in its basic structure and the constraints the liability concept puts on permissible defensive action.

Before we go further explaining liability, note that thus far I've been speaking broadly of liability to *harm*. Understanding the boundaries of what constitutes harm is itself controversial and I will not address this debate adequately here.[25] This is because the work I aim to do in this book revolves around acts that are on the far end of the spectrum of potential candidates for harm such that nearly all would agree the acts in question are clear cases of harm and meet whatever the correct conditions for harm turn out to be. In other words, if there is such a thing as harm at all—and there is—the cases I am dealing with in this book are perhaps the clearest cases of harm and would definitely fit within the concept of harm, regardless of whatever one makes of hard boundary cases of harm. (I apologize for being so overt and deliberate here, but there are actually debates over what harm even means.[26] I do not think these are useless, they are important in their own way. But I am setting out what I'm up to in the broader academic landscape over the past 20 years or so.) Examples would be physically harming someone by kicking them in the face, or stabbing them in the chest, or shooting them with a gun, or (as is explored in chapters 5 and 6) significantly restricting one's liberty and infringing upon one's autonomy. Some of these instances of harm will result in killing. *Killing* is, whatever else it is, a kind of harm.[27] To be liable to defensive *killing*, then, falls under the model for liability to defensive harm. Since killing is such a particularly extreme harm the thresholds to be met for the constraints on liability (discussed below) are simply that much greater. For ease of discussion, for much of the work below I will often discuss liability to be killed, but this can be read simply as liability to a particularly high degree of harm and the given claim can be modified *mutatis mutandis* for cases of lesser harms.

---

[25] For a good primer on the topic, see Seth Lazar, "The Nature & Disvalue of Injury," *Res Publica* 15, no. 3 (2009): 289–304.

[26] See Molly Gardner, "What is Harming?," in *Principles and Persons: The Legacy of Derek Parfit*, ed. Jeff McMahan, Tim Campbell, James Goodrich, and Ketan Ramakrishnan (New York: Oxford University Press, 2021): 381–96. See also Duncan Purves, "Harming as making worse off," *Philosophical Studies* 176 (2019): 2629–56.

[27] Though I recognize that this too is itself interestingly controversial. See Duncan Purves, "Accounting for the harm of death," *Pacific Philosophical Quarterly* 97, no. 1 (2016): 89–112. I actually do find these debates fascinating, though I imagine some interlocutors might here give us philosophers some chaff over debating whether or not killing someone counts as harming them.

1.2.3 Necessity and Proportionality

Being liable to defensive harm carries with it two key constraints that are usually seen as internal to the notion of liability itself: necessity and proportionality.[28] That is, as McMahan argues, these constraints on permissible defensive harm are part of what it *means to say* someone is liable to harm.[29] The proportionality constraint holds that the harm done to a liable person must be reasonably proportional to the extent of harm that is to be averted. Almost everyone holds that killing someone who is merely trying to steal $5 from you, for example, would not be a proportionate response, even if the thief is liable to some other, lesser level of defensive harm—perhaps capture or even mild injury. That is, the harm for which one is liable must correlate in some reasonable way with the rights violation one would otherwise impose on others and only the minimum amount of harm that is necessary to block the wrong may be used against the liable person. But proportionality is not simply a direct relation between the extent of expected just harm inflicted and that of the expected unjust harm averted. Many hold that to be proportionate, the expected extent of harm a just defensive act delivers must also correlate on the degree of culpability the liable person has for the wrong to be thwarted.[30] It is important to note, then, that liability itself comes in *degrees*. The degree to which people can be liable to defensive harm, and the degree of severity of the harm for which they are liable, tracks the severity of the rights violation to be blocked as well as their relative responsibility for the wrong.[31]

---

[28] I call them key constraints, and they are. But I might be better served to call them "primary" constraints, as there are other constraints, and some maybe seem obvious—though they are themselves worthy of analysis. There are other restrictions on permissible defensive harm that I do not review here, for example, such as imminence: that the harm to be averted must be reasonably imminent so as to require defensive harm to block it. For a discussion of the imminence restriction on defensive harm, see Rodin, *War & Self-Defense*, 40–43. I do not mean to suggest this is a small condition. It's significant and easily determinative in some cases. One may think—perhaps rightly—that the condition is quite critical in our modern age of warfare. Imagine, for example, the differing views of imminence of the unjust Russian invasion of Ukraine in 2022. One might conclude that a nuanced and careful understanding of the imminence condition is not only relevant, but possibly determinative here, given Russia's claims. I explore some ways in individual killing that the imminence condition can occasionally shift in important ways, given rare contexts, in Bradley J. Strawser, *Killing bin Laden: A Moral Analysis* (Palgrave Macmillan, 2014).

[29] For a good discussion on how these constraints are internal to the notion of liability, see McMahan, *Killing in War*, particularly 156 and 196.

[30] See McMahan, "The Basis of Moral Liability."

[31] McMahan calls this "narrow proportionality." This relationship between one's responsibility for an unjust harm and their liability will be explored at length below. For an in-depth discussion of proportionality, see Thomas Hurka, "Proportionality in the Morality of War," *Philosophy & Public Affairs* 33, no. 1 (2005): 34–66.

The necessity constraint holds that one may be killed only if killing that person is necessary for averting the rights violation that person poses. Put more precisely, the necessity constraint holds that only the amount of force necessary to block a wrong is permissible to use against a liable person. If a rights violation can be averted through something other than harm—such as by escape, say—then that method to avert the harm is morally preferred and defensive harm would be morally impermissible, precisely because it is not necessary. In such a case (where escape is an option over defensive harm), the responsible party would simply not be liable to defensive harm, for liability to harm is only attributed if such harm is necessary for the thwarting of the wrong to be averted.[32] It is sometimes said that necessity is "internal" to the concept of liability in this way.

But this condition is more difficult than may first appear because it can be read in at least two ways. This is an important and often neglected point about the necessity constraint. On one reading, the necessity constraint allows that a liable party be killed if killing is the *only* way of preventing the wrong to be averted. But another view of the necessity constraint holds that killing need not be the only way to prevent the rights violation, but that it is permissible to kill so long as there are no *other* means that are as *equally good* at blocking the wrong to be averted. In other words, killing must be the best way to block unjust harm.[33] This latter view is the one I endorse, but such a position is admittedly controversial. It does, however, make the necessity condition itself easier to meet.[34] Some have described the necessity restriction by claiming that defensive harm must be "indispensable" and "unavoidable" in the effort to block the rights violation.[35] But this language remains unclear on the "best means" versus the "only means" distinction. Is defensive harm "indispensable" to blocking an unjust harm when it is, say, by far the most *likely* means to do so? It is indispensable to being the *best* option, in such a case, but it is unclear if that is what is meant when necessity is described in such ways.

---

[32] See the discussion below in chapter 3 regarding the duty to retreat in connection to the Emerton and Handfield notion of "affray." This is also significantly nuanced and related to discussions of benign aggression and the defense intuition explored in chapters 6 and 7.

[33] Or, again, here and throughout, a given level of harm must be the necessary level of harm needed to thwart the unjust harm.

[34] I offer my defense of this reading of necessity in section 1.3. Jeff McMahan also endorses this latter view. Seth Lazar offers an excellent discussion of this issue and raises a variety of important objections for the view in "Necessity, and Noncombatant Immunity," *Review of International Studies* 40, no. 1 (2014): 53–76.

[35] Uniacke (in *Permissible Killing*, 32) and Rodin (in *Self-Defense*, 40), for example, each use the language of "indispensable" and "unavoidable." These ways of describing this component of self-defense are often used in legal conceptions of defensive privilege.

Both readings of necessity, however, have the same structure for cases where alternative options are each equally likely to thwart an impending rights violation. Imagine that there are two methods available in a given instance for blocking a wrongful harm, A and B. Each method is equally likely to block the threat of unjust harm, but A would kill the liable person posing the threat (by shooting him, say) and B would only temporarily restrict his liberty (with a net, say). The necessity constraint holds that a person blocking the unjust threat must use B, if indeed it was true that A and B were *equally* likely to avert the wrongful harm. This is simply because A (killing him) is not necessary to block the wrongful harm, on either reading of necessity. In fact, it is correct to say that the person posing the unjust threat is *only* liable to B and is not liable to A. A liable person is only liable to that harm necessary to block the wrongful harm to be averted. It is in this way that necessity is itself internal to liability. This results in the perhaps counter-intuitive notion that the permissible harm one is liable to receive is contingent upon the means available to block the unjust harm the liable person is posing. Of course, here we've stipulated that each means would be equally likely to avert the threat; there will be many cases in the real world where this is not the case, of course, and in those cases using a means that causes greater harm could be justifiable, depending on the relative likelihood of success.

1.2.4 Liable and Nonliable Cases

Two simple cases help illuminate the liability view sketched thus far. Consider the case:

Bystander on Bridge
Victim is being chased by Hitman who is trying to kill her unjustly. Victim comes to a narrow bridge, which is the only means of escape from Hitman. The bridge is blocked by Bystander who is sitting on the bridge. The only way for Victim to escape Hitman would be to knock Bystander off the bridge, thereby killing him.[36]

---

[36] Cases like this are famous in self-defense literature. This version is most similar to a case introduced originally by Thomson ("Self-Defense," 290), and followed by a similar case in Jonathan Quong's "birdwatcher on bridge" case in "Killing in Self-Defense," *Ethics* 119 (2009): 531.

Since Bystander is not imposing or in any way related to the wrongful harm to Victim, Bystander is nonliable and cannot be permissibly harmed in the effort to block the rights violation being imposed on Victim. If Victim kills Bystander in order to save herself, she would be wronging Victim. (Recall that is part of what the concept of liability—and its converse nonliability—entails.) That is, Victim would be wronging Bystander's right to not be killed unjustly. This is because Bystander is in no way morally responsible for the unjust harm about to befall Victim. Hitman is, of course, liable to defensive harm and if there were a means available for Victim to defend herself against Hitman (say by shooting him), then such an act would be a permissible act of defensive killing on the Rights-Based Account.

Compare *Bystander on Bridge* to another case,

Mafia Boss on Bridge
Victim is in the same unfortunate scenario as in *Bystander on Bridge*, except that instead of Bystander blocking the way she comes across Mafia Boss sitting on the bridge. Victim knows that Mafia Boss hired Hitman to kill her unjustly.[37]

In this case, Mafia Boss, unlike Bystander, is morally responsible for the unjust threat to Victim. In fact, Mafia Boss is outright culpable for the violation of Victim's right to life. As such, Mafia Boss is liable to defensive harm and Victim could permissibly knock Mafia Boss off the bridge as a necessary means to defend herself (via escape) against the threat posed by Hitman. Killing Mafia Boss in this way would be both proportional to his extent of liability (since the wrongful harm for which he is responsible is lethal) and necessary (since Victim has no other means of averting the unjust harm other than knocking Mafia Boss off the bridge to escape). Since Mafia Boss is liable to such harm, Victim would not be *wronging* Mafia Boss when she kills him; she would not be violating his rights—in this case, his right to not be killed unjustly. She would not be violating that right, because she would not be killing him unjustly, but rather justly.

Further, of course, if a third party, Hero, were operating from afar (via a sniper rifle, say), and saw the events of *Mafia Boss on Bridge* unfold, Hero

---

[37] This case is similar to a "Mafia Boss" case used by Helen Frowe in "Threats, Bystanders and Obstructers," *Proceedings of the Aristotelian Society* 108, no. 3 (2008): 365–72. There Frowe counts a person as a direct threat if he "is attached to an object that will kill" the victim. See Helen Frowe, *Defensive Killing* (Oxford: Oxford University Press, 2014).

could also permissibly kill Mafia Boss as a necessary and proportionate means to defend Victim if doing so gave her a means of escape (assuming that Hero could not directly stop Hitman for some reason).[38] So, on this Rights-Based Account of permissible defensive harm, one may permissibly harm a liable person as a necessary and proportionate act to thwart an unjust harm that would otherwise befall nonliable people (including oneself) for which the liable person is properly related.[39]

From this set up, it can quickly be inferred that in addition to a right to life (or a right to non-unjust-harm), one has a "right to defense" of those rights. Rodin makes the point that defensive rights are thus merely derivative rights, in the Razian sense that any right to self-defense or others-defense gains its normative force from some logically prior normative value, and are not core rights which "stand on their own."[40] The core right from which all defensive privileges derive, of course, is something like a right to life that should not be infringed upon unjustly (or, again, a right to not be harmed unjustly). But even that right is, in my view, derivative on some deeper normative value that we properly assign to life; rights are not somehow valuable for their own sake—they are normatively valuable for the good to which they point.[41] Because permissible defensive harm is derivative in this way partially explains *why* it has the restrictions that we think it does, such as necessity and proportionality. Defensive violence is not an intrinsic good to be promoted—of course—but, rather, a good only insofar as it serves the good from which it is derived. For example, the necessity requirement (including

---

[38] It is an interesting question whether Hero could permissibly kill Mafia Boss were he able to kill *either* Hitman or Mafia Boss. It seems both Hitman and Mafia Boss are each responsible for the unjust harm. Who is more responsible is debatable and, at any rate, it is unclear if there is an obligation to prefer delivering just harm to a more responsible agent over another. Intuitively it seems this would be the case, and the arguments I make in section 1.3 would support this view as follows: if one of the two unjust actors, Mafia Boss or Hitman must bear the burden of the costs imposed by the forced-choice they have created, it should be the one that is more responsible for the forced-choice. On that reading, the first impulse is to say that is Mafia Boss and that, hence, he should bear the burden of dying. However, one can just as easily argue that were Hitman not willing to be hired to kill, the forced-choice scenario would not have been created. So, again, even if we should morally prefer the harming of the agent more responsible for the unjust harm to be averted, it is unclear which of these two actors that would be. Some, such as Helen Frowe, make a distinction between the direct and indirect imposition of unjust harm claiming that the distinction matters morally for liability attribution. (See section 1.5.5. below.) If Frowe is correct, then that would have major implications here.

[39] Just what it takes for the liable person to be "properly related" to the wrongful harm to be averted is controversial and will be discussed next in section 1.3.2.

[40] See Joseph Raz, "On the Nature of Rights," *Mind* 93 (1984): 194–214, at 197. Also discussed by Rodin, *War & Self-Defense*, 37. Note that here and throughout my work in this book and in other places, I rely on this general Razian notion of rights.

[41] Again, see Raz, "On the Nature of Rights." Also see James Griffin, *On Human Rights* (Oxford: Oxford University Press, 2008).

its corollary requirement to retreat from an unjust threat of harm whenever possible rather than use harm to avert the wrong), is based on the idea that defensive harm is only permissible to use as a protection of a larger normative good. And, as Rodin writes, "general considerations of value will require us to choose the least costly course to that defense; in other words, the one which is least destructive of the good. This in turn requires us to inflict a harm only if it is necessary."[42]

I'll note briefly here that my move to understand the right to life as restricted in scope is not logically required for the Rights-Based Account. Another popular (and, admittedly more common) approach is to claim that the right to life is unrestricted in scope, but that it can be forfeited under certain contexts. Taking the forfeiture approach rather than the limited scope approach only slightly changes the structure thus far explained.[43] But the differences are, in my view, superficial. Whether one says that rights are limited or that they can be forfeited, we still must explain the *conditions* under which either case obtains such that delivering defensive harm *does not wrong* the liable party. That is, we must explain either what the boundaries of the right's limit are (the "bounds of defense") or what the conditions for forfeiture are. In either case, the basic model of the Rights-Based Account remains the same. Both approaches force the account to explain an asymmetry between parties that allows for defensive harm that does not violate a right of one of the parties to a conflict—as will be explained next in section 1.3.[44] So regardless of whether one favors a restricted scope view of rights or a forfeiture view of rights, the Rights-Based Account delineates a "right to defense" that will be *functionally* identical on either approach.

1.3. A Vicious Circle for Rights-Based Accounts?

Although perhaps initially plausible upon short reflection, many find that the account just described falls into a kind of vicious circle due to its use of rights talk regarding who is and who is not liable to harm. Put differently,

---

[42] Rodin, *War & Self-Defense*, 41.
[43] This and related questions are explored in Stephen Kershnar, "An Axiomatic Theory of Just War: Forfeiture Theory," in *Who Should Die? The Ethics of Killing in War*, edited by Bradley Strawser, Michael Robillard, and Ryan Jenkins (New York: Oxford University Press, 2018).
[44] Otherwise, recall, we are simply choosing between two rights violations and picking the lesser-of-two-evils. The point of the Rights-Based Account is to show that defensive harm can have *positive* justification as a permissible act, not *merely* a "lesser-evil" justified infringement of one's rights.

the division of "just" harm and "unjust" harm must be explained in some terms beyond *merely* the structural and putative ways they were used above to designate who is liable to harm, or else we may have a regress problem in any given case between a supposedly liable person and nonliable person. This gets complicated once we try to designate one actor as imposing the just harm as opposed to the other, in anything other than a non-putative way. There is a straightforward way out of the puzzle, thankfully, but first let us set it out in detail.

1.3.1 The Need for Asymmetry

The most basic case of self-defense helps describe this problem and show how the Rights-Based Account can fall into it. Consider:

Defender and Attacker
Defender is sitting on a park bench reading Tolstoy. She is in no way threatening harm, nor contributing to a threat of harm, nor responsible for a threat of harm, toward anyone. Attacker hates people who read Tolstoy. He charges Defender with the intent to kill her with a large sword he is swinging toward her head. Defender happens to find a small hand-gun sitting nearby, however, and she quickly shoots Attacker before his sword swings down upon her.

The vicious circle problem for the Rights-Based Account then is this: What if at the moment Attacker sees Defender reach for the gun to shoot him, he then changes his intentions and now aims to kill Defender purely as a necessary and proportionate means to defend *himself* from her threat of violating his right to life? That is, in that instant, he no longer was aiming to kill her for his original reasons of Tolstoy-reader-hatred. Now, he is simply trying to defend himself from her incoming lethal threat. After all, Attacker certainly has a right to life like Defender does. And the account so far argues that Attacker is not being wronged (not having his right to life violated; not being harmed unjustly) by Defender when she shoots him because his harm against her is a violation of her right to life (his harm to her is unjust). So, we define an unjust harm—simply—as one which violates one's rights. But for all we've said thus far a harm only violates one's rights if it is unjust. The circularity is as embarrassingly obvious as it is vexing for a Rights-Based Account. As Thomson famously said of the problem, "one does not mind all circles, but this circle is too small."[45]

Any adequate account of self-defense must be able to avoid this obvious absurdity, but—in some cases and on some accounts—this can be surprisingly difficult to do. Thankfully, the Rights-Based Account is able to escape this circle on a proper understanding of liability. Indeed, as I'll explain, that's precisely what the notion of liability is intended to do. The real problem here is that we need a means to ground the asymmetry between two parties in a permissible defense case such that their rights claims are not circular against one another.[46] That is, we need a block against the mutual or symmetrical claim of defensive privilege between Defender and Attacker. And that is what the notion of liability provides. It gives us a mechanism for explaining the moral asymmetry between Attacker and Defender which avoids the circularity of equal rights violation claims against the other.[47] Liability, then, can be thought of as a kind of label or sign pointing to the asymmetry between parties in a case of permissible defensive harm. Let me explain.

If you and I each have a right to not be killed by the other, but then you try to kill me, wouldn't I be violating your right to *not* be killed if I killed you in order to stop you from violating my right? Aren't I just trading one rights violation for another? There are several choices here on how to respond. One could say that, yes, self-defense is mere *preference* for one's own rights over another's. But that seems clearly wrong. Surely morality provides for more guidance than that, and most have a strong intuition that the idea of "defense" tracks something morally real beyond preference. That is, it is not *merely* a self-preference I have in defending myself over letting you kill me in such a case. Recall that the point of rights-based approaches in general is to give a moral explanation for permissible killing that does not violate the rights of the person killed and is not, simply, a choice of the lesser evil between competing disvalues. A quick story helps to make this point.

---

[45] Thomson outlines the vicious circle in "Self-Defense and Rights," The Lindley Lecture (Lawrence, KS: Lawrence University of Kansas Publications, 1976), 7. Rodin also effectively captures the circularity problem in chapter 2 of *War & Self-Defense*.

[46] As Rodin explains of the vicious circle, "We may call this the problem of explaining the "moral asymmetry" between defender and aggressor." *War & Self-Defense*, 50.

[47] And, again, as explained at the end of section 1.2 above, this same circularity problem presents itself for a forfeiture view of rights. On those views, rather than explaining why one harm is just and the other is unjust in ways that are not merely putative (which is the challenge for my view), they must explain why one actor forfeits her right to life while the other does not. At its core, it is the same problem. Thomson, for example, operates on a forfeiture model throughout *Realm of Rights*, yet she (like all rights-based approaches) deals with the same problem, as just noted.

Prisoner Decision
You and I have been captured by evil terrorists who tell us that they will kill only one of us and let the other go, but they tell me that I have to decide which one of us they kill.

In *Prisoner Decision*, if I choose that the terrorists kill you over me, then, surely, that would be an instance of mere self-preference. Presuming we are both innocent in this case, justice does not give non-agent centric guidance here on who should be killed. But would that self-preference decision be an act of morally justified self-defense? I think not, whatever else it may be.[48] This is because we think that in true self-defense cases like *Defender and Attacker*, Defender's act to defend herself is not *merely* that she chooses her life over Attacker's, but that she is *in the right* to do so in some way beyond merely her (understandable) preference for her own life over this stranger's life who is attacking her.[49] That is, we think that proper self-defense is not merely excused, but has positive moral justification. Indeed, this is what we mean when we claim one has a *right* to self-defense.

In *Prisoner Decision*, if I chose to have the terrorists kill you then your rights would be violated when the terrorists killed you *even if* it thereby saved my life. The same would be true, of course, if you told the terrorists to kill me in your place. We are *symmetrical* in our moral standing to the impending wrongful harm hanging over us. There is no asymmetry between us to ground a "right to defense" that one has over another. That is, neither of us is liable; there is no asymmetry for the liability indicator to point toward. In fact, it appears we stand in relation to one another in a relevantly analogous way to the relationship between Victim and Bystander in *Bystander on Bridge*. Victim could kill Bystander to save her own life, and I could kill you to save my own life, but neither of these acts is a permissible instance of a right to self-defense. In *Defender and Attacker*, however, Attacker's rights are not violated when Defender kills him to save her life and, hence, Defender's killing of Attacker is permissible. So how is it that Attacker's right to life is not violated by Defender's attack, while Defender's is?

---

[48] Whether that decision is morally permissible for some *other* reason or could be justified on a lesser evil account or is, in the least, partially or fully *excused* due to understandable self-preference, is another question entirely.

[49] As the reader can likely already predict, this kind of discussion has massive implications for soldiers killing one another in war. Indeed, the "it was either him or me" mentality is a regularly heard trope in discussions over opposing soldiers killing one another.

1.3.2 Grounding Asymmetry

The Rights-Based Account escapes this problem through the difference in the parties' asymmetric moral standing toward the threat in question and relational standing toward one another in a justified defense case. As Rodin puts it, it is "the normative relationship between the subject and the object of the defensive action" that allows for one's action to be a violation of a right and the correlated action blocking that violation to be a permissible act that is not a rights violation.[50] The best way to understand this is as two sides of one moral fact. The moral fact in question is the impending rights violation. The asymmetry is the different ways each party is related to that violation.[51]

In other words, who is committing the initiation of a rights violation upon the other and the two resulting sides of a moral relation that causation creates between the two parties delivers the needed asymmetry. Attacker is bringing about an impending violation of Defender's rights, while Defender is not the cause for an attack put upon her before she moves to defend herself from Attacker. That is to say, Attacker's action will *otherwise* cause a violation of Defender's right to life. Mafia Boss is similarly committing an act (or recently committed a causally relevant act in the near past) that will otherwise violate Victim's right to life. And Bystander is not causally (or in any way whatsoever) responsible for committing any action that will otherwise violate Victim's right to life. The feature which provides the required explanation for why a given victim has the right to kill her aggressor (but not a bystander) is the causal relationship the aggressor stands toward the aggressive attack which *will otherwise* violate the victim's life.[52] It is the combined causal act of the aggressor that will otherwise violate a right and the non-causation of

---

[50] Rodin, *War & Self-Defense*, 81.

[51] Another approach to escaping the vicious circle is to deny the Rights-Based Account, simply accept that one of the two parties in self-defense cases will have his or her right violated, but argue that there can be a justifiable basis for who should have his or her right violated over the other. Cheyney Ryan makes this kind of case in "Self-Defense, Pacifism, and the Possibility of Killing," *Ethics* 93 (1983): 508–24. There he argues that we can understand these cases as "forced-choice" situations whereby one of the two parties is forced to bear the cost of the impending harm and there is, usually, a fair way to determine who should bear the cost. See below in section 1.6.1 for a lengthy discussion of these issues.

[52] See Rodin, *War & Self-Defense*, 77. There Rodin is giving a responsibility as culpability approach which will be explained below in section 1.4 (what I call the "Simple Culpability View"). Here I aim to only show how any Rights-Based Account first escapes the puzzle by the asymmetrical relation each actor stands toward the impending rights violation.

the victim with respect to the impending rights violation resulting from the attack that creates their asymmetry.[53]

And this is what liability aims to capture. Attacker is *liable* to defensive harm because he will otherwise violate Defender's right by committing his attack whereas Defender is nonliable to defensive harm because she is not in any way responsible for the attack and that relational standing to the attack itself explains the asymmetry. Defender is not initiating a separate act that will otherwise violate Attacker's right; the relationship and action of each revolves around this one violation that is to be averted or not.

Explicitly, then, we can see how the vicious circle is avoided, here closely following Rodin. Defender has a right to life—to not be harmed unjustly.[54] This right is not unlimited in scope, but Defender has a presumption of it. Therefore, when Attacker attacks Defender's life, in the absence of some justifying reason for the attack on Defender's life, the attack will wrong Defender by violating her right to life. Because Defender is innocent and Attacker is committing an action which is causally responsible for the violation of her right, his claim against Defender that she should not use necessary and proportionate force against him fails to be entailed from his right to life (for its scope, just as Defenders', is limited to not being harmed unjustly). Therefore, Defender has a positive (derivative) right to kill Attacker that corresponds to the rights violation against herself that will otherwise occur. Hence, when Defender harms Attacker to defend against a violation of her rights, she does not violate his right to life, and thereby does not wrong him. *Because* she does not wrong him, she does not fail to continue to possess her right to not be harmed unjustly. This relational dynamic between Defender and Attacker—"the careful intimate moral relationship"—is thus capable of explaining why harming Attacker is a just harm and thereby not an infringement upon Attacker's right to not be harmed unjustly.[55] Since it is a just harm that Defender delivers, she does not become liable in delivering it. Since she is nonliable, *even if* Attacker then moves to defend himself from

---

[53] Again, I am here heavily reliant here on Rodin, *War & Self-Defense*, 77, but I am explicitly framing the asymmetry in a way which avoids his use of fault and moral culpability; preferring instead for a more neutral reading of the causal relationship to the asymmetry that need not require culpability at this point. It will become clear why I am framing it in this way below when we contrast the Simple Culpability View with other views.

[54] This following paragraph follows closely to Rodin's explication of the role of fault to escape the circularity problem outlined on *War & Self-Defense*, 79. But, again, I here alter the account to fit my *Defender and Attacker* case.

[55] Rodin, *War & Self-Defense*, 79.

her just harm to him, he cannot justly attack her because she has not made herself liable to defensive harm, although he has asymmetrically made himself liable to defensive harm.

Some argue that even if through his actions Attacker has made himself liable to defensive harm by being the cause of an impending rights-violation that his liability still does not thereby give Defender a *positive* justification to inflict harm.[56] But this misunderstands the moral facts of the case and the relation the two parties stand to one another. Again, it is not that Attacker being liable to defensive harm is an *independent* moral fact from Defender's moral permission to block a violation of her rights. Rather, as Rodin puts it best, "they are the *same* normative fact described from two different perspectives."[57] Again, I like to think of the relationship as two sides of one "moral coin." An aggressor has *opened himself up* to permissible defensive harm—he has *made himself liable*—to block the rights violation he will otherwise cause through his actions. This just harm to block unjust harm relation is one way and, once initiated, cannot be reversed.[58] To oversimplify things and put it in the rudimentary language of the schoolyard, "Who started it?" really does matter morally in these cases and being the cause of an act that will otherwise violate a right plays this central role in the liability relationship between parties. Put simply: one can *make oneself liable* to defensive harm by committing an act which would otherwise cause a rights violation and, once one has done so, one has no complaint of a rights violation for suffering defensive harm in accordance with one's liability that is aimed at thwarting that unjust harm.

---

[56] Uniacke makes this kind of objection. See *Permissible Killing*, 191.
[57] Rodin, *War & Self-Defense*, 75, my emphasis.
[58] Note: this presumes that the just harm delivered is necessary and proportional by the definition of just harm. If a defender attempts to deliver disproportionate harm, then they are not delivering just harm and the attacked person—even if initially responsible for breaking the state of non-harm—can now invoke just harm in defense of blocking unjust harm toward themselves since the disproportionate harm is by, definition, unjust. As such, the defender in this case, by using disproportionate harm to block a rights violation, has initiated a rights violation of their own which can be blocked: the defender has made herself liable to defensive harm to block her unjust harm. An example here helps. Imagine that Bob is trying to kick Tom in the shins. Tom can defend himself by tackling Bob, and thereby harming him slightly. This harm from the tackling would be proportionate harm corresponding to the unjust harm of Tom's shins being harmed.. But imagine instead of tackling Bob, Tom pulls out a handgun and aims it to shoot Bob. This would be disproportionate to the harm of his shins being kicked. At that point, Bob could now defend himself to block the violation of his right that Tom will otherwise commit (Tom's shooting Bob—a harm disproportionate to the rights violation to be blocked). Bob's defensive harm toward Tom would be permissible in correspondence to the impermissible (disproportionate) harm Tom is now imposing on Bob.

1.3.3 More on Liability Constraints

This way of talking about the normative asymmetry relationship between two parties in a defense case helps demonstrate how necessity and proportionality are both internal to the notion of liability. It helps illuminate, for example, that if there is a way for Victim to avert harm to herself without causing harm to Mafia Boss (say she can escape through some other route), then Mafia Boss is not liable to harm.[59] This is because for the harm against Mafia Boss to be just and not wrong him, it must *correspond* to the unjust harm (the wrong done) to Victim that is being averted by it. That is, it has to actually be true that Mafia Boss commits an act which would otherwise cause a rights violation. (For, if Victim can escape unharmed through an alternate route, then it's not necessarily true that his act would otherwise cause a rights violation unless he is harmed.) Note, then, that if Victim can escape through another route, then *no one* is properly liable to defensive harm in the situation regardless of Mafia Boss being the cause of a wrongful threatening act, because harming him is not necessary to avert the rights violation of wrongful harm. Remember: liability is not simply fault; it is a status that *can* result from being responsible for the imposition of a rights violation upon another, but will not necessarily be attributed unless other conditions are met.

Notice, however, that we may still think Mafia Boss is *deserving* of punishment even if he is not liable to harm due to Victim being able to escape. It is in this way, again, that liability is importantly distinct from desert. Liability is instrumental in this critical way in which desert is not (or need not be). Again, for someone to be liable to defensive harm, it must be the case that harming them would block some harm that a nonliable person *would otherwise* bear. That is, Mafia Boss is likely deserving of some kind of punishment for hiring Hitman, regardless of whether Victim has a means to escape that does not require her killing him and, thus, regardless of his liability to defensive harm.[60]

---

[59] Though he would, of course, still be blameworthy and deserving of proper legal remedies. See both the above and below discussions of the distinction between liability and desert. Desert is its own important area of moral philosophy inquiry, a full examination of which actually exceeds the bounds of this work. See, for an easy starting place, Fred Feldman and Brad Skow, "Desert," in *Stanford Encyclopedia of Philosophy* (Winter 2020 Edition), edited by Edward N. Zalta (Stanford University 2020), https://plato.stanford.edu/archives/win2020/entries/desert/.

[60] Although it has long been held that desert is distinct from questions of liability, and this has long been defended by McMahan (particularly in *Killing in War*), this has recently been challenged. John Gardner and Francois Tanguay-Renaud, "Desert and Avoidability in Self-Defense," *Ethics* 122, no. 1 (2011): 111–34. The philosophy web log "PEA Soup" held a discussion on this debate and it was led

Attacker *would* have a legitimate complaint against Defender, however, if we change the scenario slightly. Imagine that in addition to a gun, Defender discovered a very highly effective "Taser" stun weapon next to her that she could use equally as effectively as the gun to block Attacker's unjust harm. (And, as will be important later, particularly in chapter 2, imagine that Defender knew, with certainty, that the Taser would be equally as effective at blocking Attacker's unjust threat as the gun would be.) In such a case, if Defender uses the gun instead of the Taser and thereby kills Attacker, then she would have violated his rights and he would have legitimate cause for complaint. In such a case, it was not necessary for Defender to kill Attacker in order to block his unjust threat of harm to her that would otherwise obtain. That is, since the Taser is available to her, Attacker has not made himself liable to be killed. He has only made himself liable to that harm necessary to avert the violation of Defender's right, which in this case is liability to be stunned. This is how the degree of harm to which one is liable can change depending on the means that are available to block the unjust harm. This is admittedly counter-intuitive—that the means available to block a wrong-doing changes what that wrong-doer is liable for—but it is a key tenent of the Rights-Based Account, and it is born out of the necessity constraint.

This discussion also helps clarify the distinction between the two readings of necessity, given above in section 1.2. Recall that on one reading, the necessity constraint allows that a liable party be killed if killing is the *only* way of preventing the unjust threat. But another, alternative view of the necessity constraint holds that killing need not be the only way to prevent the unjust threat, but that it is permissible to kill so long as there are no other means that are as *equally good* at blocking the unjust threat. In other words, killing must be the *best* way to avert the unjust harm.

Imagine again that there are two methods available in a given instance for blocking an unjust threat of harm, A and B. But, to better see the difference between the two readings of necessity, imagine that this time A and B are *not* equally likely to block the unjust threat. Instead, A is *certain* to block the threat whereas there is only a 60% chance that B will block the threat. On the second reading of necessity, which I endorse, the responsible person for the unjust threat is liable to A in this instance, since A is the *best* way to block the

by an insightful précis by Victor Tadros and a response by Jeff McMahan. All of the actors just named, and many others in the broader liability discussion, participated in the discussion. See: https://peasoup.typepad.com/peasoup/2012/01/ethics-discussions-at-pea-soup-john-gardner-and-françois-tanguay-renauds-desert-and-avoidability-in-.html

unjust threat. On the alternative reading of necessity, it is unclear whether A or B should be used. This is because in this instance A is not the *only* way to block the unjust threat, but whether or not 60% is a reasonable threshold such that the defender should be required to use B over A is unclear.[61]

The necessity constraint is intended to capture the moral intuition that we should err on the side of using as minimal amount of harm as is necessary to avert an unjust harm and that the defensive harm itself is only justified in the first place as an instrumental means to block an unjust harm that will otherwise obtain. Again, liability is an instrumental notion: defensive harm is only permissible as part of a thwarting of an unjust harm or threat of harm. Hence, any harm going beyond that which is necessary to block the unjust harm is impermissible on the Rights-Based Account. The question at the heart of the two readings of necessity, then, is this: whether the liable party or the nonliable party should be required to suffer the *risk of harm* that the less certain, although less harmful, method will succeed in blocking the unjust harm. I contend that it is the party committing the unjust act that will otherwise result in wrongful harm (the liable party) who should suffer the risk of potential harm from this greater possibility of failure that comes with the less certain means of blocking the wrongful harm, not the nonliable party who is being defended from it. To do otherwise makes the nonliable party at least partially suffer unjust harm committed by the liable party, which invalidates the entire purpose of defensive harm to begin with.[62] This then is the justification for the more liberal reading of necessity that I endorsed above: one is required by necessity to use that option available which *best* blocks an unjust harm.[63]

1.4. Is Responsibility Necessary for Liability?

So much for the basic structure of the Rights-Based Account of defensive harm. Most philosophers who employ a rights-based approach of

---

[61] This difference between the two readings will become very important in my discussion of revisionist just war theory in chapter 3 and the application of my liability account to war in chapter 4. There is also a great deal to be investigated in this debate. Much work on issues of calculating risk in these kinds of cases has been done by Seth Lazar. See, for example, Seth Lazar, "Risky Killing and the Ethics of War," *Ethics* 126, no. 1 (2015): 91–117.

[62] This assumes that bearing the risk of harm can be itself a kind of harm. On this, see Thomas Rowe, "Can a risk of harm itself be a harm?," *Analysis* 81, no. 4 (2022): 694–701.

[63] Again, I am here only scratching the surface of the debate over how risk should be justly distributed in such cases. See, again, Seth Lazar, "Risky Killing and the Ethics of War."

self-defense would agree with the broad outlines of the account sketched thus far in the book. The central point of disagreement amongst those who employ this account, however, is just what one must do in order to be become liable to harm. That is, above, in explaining how a Rights-Based Account escapes the problem of the vicious circle, I said that the moral asymmetry between parties in a defensive harm case is based on which party imposed (or caused or is properly related to) the rights violation that would otherwise obtain. But just what the imposition of a wrongful harm actually entails can be radically different across cases. In some instances, one is directly morally culpable for the imposition of a wrongful harm to be averted. But in other more difficult cases, one can be the *cause* of an impending rights violation while not being *morally responsible* for that harm's imposition. Within all liability-type accounts there is a consensus that being directly morally culpable for causing an unjust threat to others easily suffices to incur liability. The debate surrounds these cases on the other extreme when someone is not directly culpable but may still be responsible in some way for an unjust harm and thereby potentially liable to defensive harm. In the most difficult cases, someone is not responsible for an unjust harm whatsoever, but the person is themselves simply the direct cause of the unjust harm. These are the cases of the "Innocent Aggressor" and "Innocent Threat" so widely used in the literature.[64] To simplify matters, I call all such actors Nonresponsible Threats.[65] Is a Nonresponsible Threat of an unjust harm liable to defensive harm? This question is cause for the major divide within the Rights-Based Account of permissible defensive harm.

Here's perhaps the most famous version of a Nonresponsible Threat case, drawn originally from Robert Nozick, and regurgitated countless times in different variants ever since, most notably by Thomson.[66]

---

[64] Thomson, "Self-Defense," 91.

[65] I use the nomenclature of nonresponsible rather than innocent because below we will deal with important cases where some writers (notably McMahan) argue that *some* kind of responsibility is still up for grabs, even if the person is not culpable. And note that I am here *really* simplifying matters, perhaps overly so. There is an entire cottage industry written on fine-grained distinctions between different kinds of nonresponsible threats. I will get into some of that literature below, but for now I am still hoping to trace the broad outlines of the Rights-Based Account.

[66] Thomson, "Self-Defense." Robert Nozick, *Anarchy, State, and Utopia* (New York: Basic Books, 1974): 34–35. Another contemporary example is, Susanne Burri, "The Toss-up Between a Profiting, Innocent Threat and His Victim," *The Journal of Political Philosophy* 23, no. 2 (2015): 146–65.

Falling Man
Through no moral fault of hers, Trapped finds herself at the bottom of a deep hole. Through no moral fault of his, Falling Man is thrown down the hole. Falling Man will crush and thereby kill Trapped, but she will break his fall and he will live. Trapped however, has a trusty ray-gun and could disintegrate Falling Man's body before he crushes her.

In these and countless other similar cases, you have a person who is morally innocent of any wrong-doing, and another innocent person who will be wrongfully harmed by that person. Thus, this person—the Nonresponsible Threat—is the cause of an impending unjust harm toward another, even though the person is not culpable for the impending wrongful harm. The debate centers on whether Nonresponsible Threats like Falling Man are thereby liable to defensive harm from the likes of Trapped (or third parties). Thomson argues that Falling Man is indeed liable to defensive harm from Trapped. This is because Falling Man is the *cause* of the impending violation of Trapped's right to life that will otherwise occur—he is literally the thing imposing the wrongful harm—and, Thomson concludes, he therefore stands in the asymmetrical relation necessary for liability attribution discussed in section 1.3 above. On Thomson's view the bare fact that Falling Man will otherwise violate Trapped's right to not be so killed is why he is therefore liable to defensive harm. And, importantly, on this account and on Thomson's view, this would mean Falling Man is not wronged by Trapped's killing him. Thus, on Thomson's view, moral responsibility is not a necessary requirement for liability attribution; one must merely be the brute cause of a rights violation that will otherwise occur, even if being such a cause is not one's fault in any way.

Let us call that subset of views in the Rights-Based Account that hold that Nonresponsible Threats can be liable to defensive harm the "Nonresponsible View."[67] This includes both Thomson and Uniacke and many others.[68] The

---

[67] Just like Victor Tadros' "Barbaric Thesis" or Derek Parfit's "Repugnant Conclusion," I attest that my labels of this views here is purely for ease of use. Any hidden implication of my opinion of such views is purely incidental. We've already seen that Thomson, Frowe, and Quong each defend various versions of the Nonresponsible Account. Otsuka, McMahan, and Rodin each defend versions of the Responsible Account, as I will explain below. Kaila Draper, "Defense," *Philosophical Studies* 145, no. 1 (2009): 69–88—also argues for a Responsible View.

[68] Also see, for example, George Fletcher, *Rethinking Criminal Law* (originally published Boston: Little, Brown, 1978; reprinted New York: Oxford University Press, 2000). Fletcher argues that one may be fully excused for the culpability of an action, but excuses do not render the action justified and, thus, an act done by an excuses actor can still be unjust and thereby permissible to defend against. Frowe and Quong (as cited above) hold more complex versions of the Nonresponsible

Nonresponsible View's criterion for liability to defensive harm is simply the matter of one person being the cause which will otherwise violate the rights of another. And, on this view, violating someone's right does *not* require culpability, responsibility, or even *agency* on the part of the violator.[69] Thus Nonresponsible Threats may violate rights and, thereby, may be liable to defensive harm to block that rights violation that would otherwise occur. Although on this view, Nonresponsible Threats can become liable to defensive harm in this way, they may still be fully excused of any wrong-doing and not blameworthy.

In contrast to this view, call that cluster of views within the Rights-Based Account which hold that only responsible threats can properly be liable to defensive harm the "Responsible View." This camp includes my own view presented here and in previous work, as well as giants like McMahan, Rodin, Otsuka, Draper, and many others—although there are major differences between all of these views on just what responsibility entails. Still, the Responsible View's criterion for liability attribution is a person being *morally responsible* for the impending rights violation of another to be averted, however moral responsibility is defined within a given account. Our first task then is to determine which view is best, the Nonresponsible View or the Responsible View.

1.5. Rejecting the Nonresponsible View

A great deal of work has been spent on answering this question of whether liability requires responsibility. The issue has become such a significant topic within this literature that discussing the full breadth of that debate would actually exceed the scope of this entire book. My aim in chapter 2 will be to offer a new proposal for liability attribution from *within* those rights-based approaches that answer the question in the affirmative; that is, those holding to the Responsible View for liability attribution. However, the debate over the possibility of nonresponsible liability has in important ways shaped how the Responsible View understands liability attribution itself. Hence, it is

---

Account as will be touched on below. Frances Kamm (in *Intricate Ethics*) holds a modified version of the Nonresponsible View but adds some complexities.

[69] See McMahan, "The Basis of Moral Liability," 389, for a discussion of this view. Thomson makes this explicit in "Self-Defense," 300–302.

necessary to outline the broad contours of that debate and provide the primary reasons that most who embrace some form of the Responsible View give for rejecting the Nonresponsible View.

1.5.1 Killing Bystanders

Michael Otsuka, famously, and several others have objected to the line of reasoning employed by Thomson for the permissible killing of Falling Man outlined above.[70] Otsuka argues that we are not justified in killing Nonresponsible Threats (that they are not liable to defensive harm) because we are similarly not justified to kill bystanders. This, he contends, is because we cannot make a relevant moral distinction between Nonresponsible Threats, such as Falling Man, and bystanders, such as Bystander in the *Bystander on Bridge* case. This argument is compelling.

Almost everyone thinks it is morally impermissible to kill Bystander—even Thomson herself was very clear that bystanders are not liable to defensive harm.[71] As Thomson famously said, to kill bystanders in such cases would be to "ride roughshod" over them and their rights.[72] And the reason for Thomson is simple enough: Bystander is not imposing a wrongful threat on Victim's life and, thus, Bystander will not otherwise violate Victim's right

---

[70] Michael Otsuka, "Killing the Innocent in Self-Defense," *Philosophy & Public Affairs* 23 (1994): 74–94, reprinted in his *Libertarianism without Inequality* (Oxford: Oxford University Press, 2003), chap. 4. Jeff McMahan, *Killing in War*; "The Problem of the Innocent Attacker"; *The Ethics of Killing: Problems at the Margins of Life*; "The Basis of Moral Liability". For similar views, also see Kimberly Kessler Ferzan, "Justifying Self-Defense," *Law and Philosophy* 24 (2005): 711–49, 733–9; David Rodin, *War and Self-Defense* (Oxford: Clarendon, 2002): 79–89; and Noam Zohar, "Collective War and Individualistic Ethics: Against the Conscription of 'Self-Defense,'" *Political Theory* 21 (1993): 606–22. This line of objection against the Nonresponsible Account is most famously associated with Otsuka, probably because his objection came about as a direct response to Thomson's "Self-Defense" paper in the same journal it was originally published (*Philosophy & Public Affairs*). But, interestingly, McMahan independently made essentially the same objection (that the status of bystanders and Nonresponsible Threats is equivalent and, therefore, if it is impermissible to kill bystander, it is also impermissible to kill Nonresponsible Threats). Even more interesting was that McMahan's articulation of the objection was published (in *Ethics*) the very same month (January of 1994) as Otsuka's article in Philosophy & Public Affairs. In McMahan's article, he notes that the objection was part of some chapters of his forthcoming *Ethics of Killing* book. Perhaps most intriguing of all, is that it is Otsuka and McMahan who are generally credited with originated the objection against the Nonresponsible Account, but Noam Zohar actually raised essentially the same objection a full year previous in his article cited above.

[71] See Thomson, "Self-Defense," 289–91.

[72] Ibid.

to life if she does not kill him. Because there is no asymmetry, there is no liability.[73] Indeed, killing Bystander would violate his rights.

This is the one point of agreement across *all* versions of the Rights-Based Account. Everyone from Thomson (on the extreme end of the Nonresponsible View) to, say, Rodin (on the opposite extreme of the Responsible View at the time of writing *War & Self-Defense*), think that it is impermissible to kill Bystander. The Bystander-type cases show us, writes Rodin, that

> *pace* Hobbes, we do not believe that "anything goes" when it is a case of "either him or me." Even under the shadow of death we recognize a duty to discriminate and not to harm certain classes of person. The requirement of excluding these cases from legitimate self-defense thus marks a significant boundary for *any* viable account of the right.[74]

And Thomson says something very similar:

> I suspect that some would take a Hobbesian line here: on their view, all bets are off when a person will otherwise kill you. Thus, they would say that the premise "Y will otherwise kill X" really is sufficient for the conclusion that X may kill Y, so that even the villainous driver may fight back. But why stop there? Why not go on to say more generally that all bets are off when you will otherwise die, and thus that the premise "X will otherwise die" is sufficient for the conclusion that X may kill Y?[75]

And the point is well taken: if we accept that it is morally permissible to kill Bystander, then we may as well give-up on attempting *any* kind of rights-based approach to defensive harm. This is because, if it is acceptable to kill Bystander, we, as Thomson says, will have lowered the threshold for permissible killing all the way back to mere self-preference. And if one thinks that mere self-preference can by itself justify killing another, then we are no longer in the game of respecting the rights of others.

---

[73] Note Thomson does not use the language of liability. Its use has been a later development in the literature; primarily due to McMahan. But I think it is fair to describe here view in this way as I have done here.
[74] Rodin, *War & Self-Defense*, 81. My emphasis.
[75] Thomson, *Realm of Rights*, 305.

1.5.2 The Otsukian Objection

So, the Rights-Based Account, for both the Responsible and Nonresponsible variants, finds it impermissible to kill Bystander; that he is not liable to harm. Michael Otsuka thereby issued a challenge to the Nonresponsible View, as follows.[76] Since Falling Man, and other such Nonresponsible Threats, are *morally* identical to Bystander, then they too should not be liable to harm on the Rights-Based Account. After all, although Falling Man's *body* is an unjust threat to Trapped, he himself has done nothing to impose that threat through his actual agency, and he has no control whatsoever over the threat his body poses. This is relevantly similar in all moral facets, the Otsukian argument holds, to the way in which Bystander's body just happens to innocently block Victim's escape, yet that is not something (rightly) for which we hold Bystander liable.[77] Therefore, if it is impermissible to kill Bystander, then it is also impermissible to kill Falling Man.

I find the Otsukian rebuttal of the Nonresponsible View successful and follow him in the line of reasoning it is based on. A person must have some degree of moral responsibility for a rights violation that is to be averted by defensive harm in order for that person to be liable to that defensive harm. That is, for a person to be liable, they must be responsible for having *done something* which incurs fault that is in some relevant way related to the unjust wrong that is to be averted.

One reason to think that liability attribution requires responsibility in this way has to do with the nature of rights themselves. To possess a right, recall, is just for others to be morally bound to respect a legitimate normative claim on them. Hence, only a responsible agent is capable of respecting or violating a right to begin with. If Falling Man is not in any way responsible for the unjust threat his body happens to pose to Trapped, it is unclear how *he* can be said to be violating Trapped's right to life.[78]

---

[76] See Otsuka, "Killing the Innocent."

[77] Otsuka even goes so far as to say that Falling Man is a kind of bystander to his own body since he has no control over it. Otsuka, "Killing the Innocent," 84–5. And that sounds right to my mind. Thanks to Jason Hanna for pointing this out. See Jason Hanna, "The Moral Status of Nonresponsible Threats," *Journal of Applied Philosophy* 29, no. 1 (2011): 1–14.

[78] Thomson makes an important distinction between one infringing on a right (just in case one did not accord another something that he had a right to) compared to wrongly infringing a right. On this view, it is only when one wrongly infringes on a right that one violates a right. See Thomson, *The Realm of Rights*, 122. On Thomson's view, then, Falling Man will violate Trapped's right because he will wrongfully infringe on her right, even though his so doing is outside of his control.

Consider: if a boulder were falling on Trapped instead of Falling Man, would the boulder violate Trapped's rights? Most think an inanimate object is not capable of violating a right. If that's correct, then the Otsukian objection argues that the Nonresponsible View for liability attribution cannot make a relevant distinction between Falling Man and a boulder. If boulders do not violate rights, then neither does Falling Man violate Trapped's rights. And if Falling Man does not violate Trapped's right, then on the Rights-Based Account, Falling Man is not liable to defensive harm to avert that supposed violation. Although it is an obvious point, it's helpful here to remember who *is* violating Trapped's right: it is the villain who pushed Falling Man down upon Trapped. Villain is violating Trapped's right by pushing Falling Man just as he would be if he had pushed a boulder down upon her. Villain is most certainly liable to defensive harm, if there were a way to harm him that would prevent him from violating Trapped's rights (and Falling Man's).

Of course, we all think that surely Trapped could permissibly vaporize the falling boulder. But what if vaporizing the falling boulder would end up killing an innocent man nearby, Max, who is innocently standing close to the path of the falling boulder? Otsuka argues that we cannot, in that case, vaporize the boulder, because in such a case, killing Max would be just the same as killing Bystander in *Bystander on Bridge*.[79] And, hence, if vaporizing the boulder would kill Max as a nearby innocent bystander, then Trapped cannot choose herself over Max; there is no relevant asymmetry. Justice gives us no basis for choosing between innocents here. But if that's true, then consider an intermediate case. What if rather than standing nearby the path of the falling boulder, Max was (through no fault of his own) somehow on top of the falling boulder? It seems that a mere difference in accidental spatial location should not matter morally. And if that's true, then Trapped cannot permissibly vaporize the boulder if Max is stuck on top of it either. As Otsuka writes, "Changing the location of the person should not make any moral difference."[80]

But then, all we must do is simply remove the boulder from the equation and have Max himself falling and have his weight be what would kill Trapped instead of the boulder. At this point, of course, we are back to *Falling Man*.

---

[79] Otsuka, "Killing the Innocent," 76. He uses the example of blowing up a javelin.
[80] Ibid., 85. I am indebted in this section to an excellent paper by Susanne Burri. She explicates a similar case with a piano. See Susanne Burri, "The Fair Distribution of Bad Luck," unpublished manuscript. Of course, we are each drawing on Otsuka's original use of the argument, in which he uses a Trolley car (!).

Otsuka again here argues that there is no moral difference between Max being innocently stuck on top of the falling boulder and now there being no boulder at all but him simply being "stuck" in space and falling toward Trapped.

In my view, this argument succeeds as an effective rebuttal against Thomson, and the Nonresponsible View broadly. But allow me here to add further weight to the general Otsukian objection against the Nonresponsible View. Recall the case of *Prisoner Decision* above. In that case, it was argued, either party choosing to have the terrorists kill the other would not be a permissible exercise of the right to self-defense, whatever else it may be.[81] But if either of us could choose to tell the terrorists to kill the other over ourselves, then either of us could be taken as the "cause" of an impending rights violation on the other that will otherwise happen unless (say) one of us harmed the other to prevent him or her from so choosing. And if that is true, then the Nonresponsible View appears to be forced to claim that you and I are both liable to defensive harm from the other in *Prisoner Decision* because we are identically aligned as imminent causes of a rights violation to the other and either could gain the requisite asymmetry by initiating the choice. But this seems highly implausible to think that either of us could be *liable* in such a case. It's much better to claim that *neither* of us is liable to harm in *Prisoner Decision*, but rather it is the terrorists in the case who are liable, as the Responsible View does.

1.5.3 Defending Against Otsuka

An advocate of the Nonresponsible View may here defend the account by claiming that *Prisoner Decision* is not relevantly analogous to *Falling Man*. The advocate would argue that the killing of one another in *Prisoner Decision* is more objectionable than the killing of Falling Man due to this dis-analogy

---

[81] As mentioned, some might think that such a decision would be excusable on an agent-centered view. Perhaps some other kind of non-rights-based justification could be invoked, such as utility (although it will be difficult to see how one could be situated so as to adequately judge the utility of their own life as more valuable than that of a fellow human caught in the case—but it's not necessarily impossible. Imagine, for example, that rather than you and I caught by the terrorists, it was I and my elderly grandfather. And imagine that my grandfather was terminally ill (unbeknownst to the terrorists). Further, I have a family that relies on me to provide for them, whereas he no longer bears such duties to others. In such a case, perhaps one could make a justification for me to choose that the terrorists kill my grandfather over myself. I have doubts that even here all the justification could amount to would be anything *more than* a mitigating excuse for the choice or simply the choice of the lesser-of-two evils. Notice, whatever it is, it is *not* a rights-based justification for the choice—and that is the point of *Prisoner Decision*.

and that, therefore, they can avoid the implication that their view entails the permissible choosing of one another in *Prisoner Decision*. They could argue, for example, that the cases are relevantly dis-analogous because it is the terrorists who will impose the rights violation in *Prisoner Decision* whereas, in *Falling Man*, the other party himself poses the threat.[82]

This defense becomes unconvincing, however, when we see that we could easily adapt *Prisoner Decision* so that the terrorist would literally use one of our bodies to kill the other. Say, after I chose the terrorist to kill you, the terrorists pick me up and throw me at you in such a way so that the impact will kill you, but I will live.[83] Should the fact that my body is used by the terrorists rather than their gun to kill you matter in determination of my liability? It does not appear that the case would be different in any way that should be morally meaningful. Thus, if we reject the notion that we are both liable to defensive harm from the other in *Prisoner Decision*, so too should we reject the attribution of liability in *Falling Man*. The Otsukian objection remains.

This dialectic offers a nice example of the various attempts that have been made to save the Nonresponsible View from the general Otsukian objection. Notice that the objection does not even necessarily entail that the Nonresponsible View is incorrect. Rather, it forces a dilemma on the account: If you maintain that Victim cannot permissibly kill Bystander, then you must deny that Trapped can permissibly kill Falling Man. (As the Responsible View does.) Or, alternatively, the Nonresponsible View can "bite the bullet" and claim that Victim *can* permissibly kill Bystander and then so too can Trapped kill Falling Man. But, again, almost no one who embraces the Rights-Based Account wants to grant that we can permissibly kill bystanders. (Because, at that point, it hardly even seems worth defending a Rights-Based Account—defense is mere preference.) Yet the Nonresponsible View *also* does not want to deny that Trapped can permissibly kill Falling Man. Thus, to maintain this position, it must show how the killing of Falling Man is morally distinct from the killing of Bystander. The attempts to do so follow the same pattern, above, in the possible defense—I have speculated— an advocate for the Nonresponsible View would give to the implications of *Prisoner Decision*.[84] This usually involves crafting thought experiment cases

---

[82] Or, more accurately, the other party's *body* poses the threat.

[83] The terrorists happen to be experts at human survival conditions, bio-mechanics, and applied physics.

[84] One will note that you and I function essentially as bystanders *toward one another* in *Prisoner Decision* as I've set it up. Hence, it is not surprising that it can press the same normative dilemma on the Nonresponsible Account as Otsuka's Bystander cases do.

of Nonresponsible Threats whereby a supposedly important moral distinction can be isolated between such Nonresponsible Threats and Bystander. And that, on the basis of this moral difference, the killing of Bystander is more objectionable than the killing of Nonresponsible Threats.

1.5.4 Opportunistic Use of Bystander

I find that all such attempts to rescue the Nonresponsible View fail in similar ways that the attempt to block the implication of *Prisoner Decision* fails. One particularly notable approach is worth reviewing here. It claims that there is a way in which a defending person *uses* Bystanders in a particularly egregious way that they do not so use Nonresponsible Threats. This difference, supposedly, constitutes permissible defense against Nonresponsible Threats while blocking it against Bystanders.[85] If this defense is successful, the Nonresponsible View is saved from the Otsukian objection.

To set up the defense, consider another bystander-type case.

Bystander Sheila
A villain throws a javelin at Tom. Tom can save his life only by grabbing nearby woman, Sheila, and using her as a human shield, placing her body between himself and the incoming javelin.[86]

Compare *Bystander Sheila* to *Falling Man*. In both cases the person under attack (Trapped and Tom, respectively) kill someone as a necessary means to avert his or her own death. But the Nonresponsible View argues that it's impermissible for Tom to kill Sheila, but permissible to kill Falling Man. How can this be? Because in killing Sheila, Tom takes advantage of her in an "opportunistic" way—he exploits her innocent presence to his benefit.[87] Victim, however, does not exploit Falling Man's presence—rather just the opposite. For Victim it would be better if Falling Man did not exist. Victim's treatment

---

[85] Quong and Frowe both independently offer different versions of this defense.

[86] This case is a slightly modified version used by Frowe in "Threats, Bystanders, & Obstructers," 279, and later by Hanna, "Nonresponsible Threats," 2.

[87] The use of opportunistic here is borrowed from Warren Quinn's use of the term (and "eliminivistic" below). See Warren Quinn, "Actions, Intentions, and Consequences: The Doctrine of Doing and Allowing," *The Philosophical Review* 98, no. 3 (1989): 287–312. This description of this particular defense of the Nonresponsible View relies heavily on Hanna's discussion in "Nonresponsible Threats," 2–6.

of Falling Man, rather, is "eliminative" rather than the "opportunistic" treatment of Sheila by Tom. The argument, then, is that opportunistic treatment of others in defense cases uses them in some way that does not properly respect them as rights-bearing persons or, however we wish to classify it, using people in this way is more distasteful and objectionable than treating them in merely an eliminative manner.

Jason Hanna points out that even if this argument succeeds in showing a relevant distinction between *Falling Man*-type cases and *Bystander* cases, it does not on its own succeed in proving the Nonresponsible View correct.[88] What it would show, if successful, is that the primary analogy upon which the Otsukian objection is based is flawed—that Bystanders are, in fact, relevantly morally different from Nonresponsible Threats. If correct, this alone would be a significant gain for the defense of the view.

But, alas, the argument cannot even succeed in doing this. Recall the case of *Bystander on Bridge* with which this chapter began. In that case Victim's treatment of Bystander is entirely eliminative, not opportunistic. Bystander is already on the bridge and is innocently blocking Victim's escape. Victim is not taking advantage of Bystander or using him in the opportunistic way described in *Bystander Sheila*. Indeed, just as with Trapped and Falling Man, it would be better for Victim if Bystander did not exist. Hence, the defense does not even successfully establish the distinction it relies upon for all cases of simple bystanders. Therefore, the defense cannot rely on this supposed difference to claim that the analogy between Bystanders and Nonresponsible Threats is flawed.

1.5.5 Direct and Indirect Threats

Some advocates of the Nonresponsible View don't give up here, however. Many have argued that there is still a further difference between most Bystanders and Nonresponsible Threats (even those whose killing is eliminative like in *Bystander on Bridge*). To wit: some claim there is a distinction between being the *direct* cause as opposed to the *indirect* cause of an unjust harm to be averted by defensive harm and that this distinction matters morally for liability attribution. This defense for the Nonresponsible

---

[88] Jason Hanna, "The Moral Status of Nonresponsible Threats," *Journal of Applied Philosophy* 29, no. 1 (2011): 1–14.

View has been around since, at least, Thomson's first explication of the view. Uniacke also makes a similar distinction and, most recently, Helen Frowe has delivered a thorough defense of this distinction and how it allegedly rescues the Nonresponsible View from the Otsukian objection.[89] I imagine the view will continue to arise in this debate, for it has some initial appeal. But it is ultimately illusory; and it is worth explaining why this is so before concluding our rejection of the Nonresponsible View.

Here's how the move runs. Frowe first defines a threat as anyone who makes (or would make, if not stopped) the defending person worse off through his or her actions or presence. From there, Frowe separates direct threats from indirect threats, as follows. Direct threats are those threats that will kill the defending person unless defensive harm blocks the killing. Indirect threats make the defending person worse off, but will not themselves kill him or her. *Mafia Boss on Bridge* gives us nice examples of both kinds of threats. Mafia Boss is a clear case of an indirect threat and Hitman a clear case of a direct threat. Frowe's contention is that once we recognize this distinction, we find a correlating moral difference for who can be permissibly killed in defensive cases and who cannot. She argues that it is morally permissible for a defending person to kill a direct threat to him or her *whether or not* the attacking person is responsible for so being a threat. Whereas a defender may *only* permissibly kill an indirect threat if the threat is responsible for the unjust harm he or she poses. Hence, since Bystander in *Bystander on Bridge* is not responsible for being an indirect threat to Victim, it is impermissible for Victim to kill him in self-defense and Frowe thinks that is *why* we find it impermissible to kill him. Mafia Boss in *Mafia Boss on Bridge*, on the other hand, *is* responsible for being an indirect threat, and, thus, Victim is right to kill him in self-defense. And since, on Frowe's account, direct threats are liable to be killed whether or not they are responsible for being a threat, Falling Man is liable to be killed since he is a direct threat. Hence, if this distinction is right, she's able to make a distinction between Falling Man and Bystander that delivers different moral conclusions over whether a defender can permissibly kill them.

In one sense, we can view this move by Frowe as trying to split the middle between the Responsible and Nonresponsible Accounts, with the ultimate aim of saving the claim that Trapped can permissibly kill Falling Man. This

---

[89] Thomson, "Self-Defense." Helen Frowe gives this kind of defense of the Nonresponsible View in "A Practical Account of Self-Defence," *Law and Philosophy* 29, no. 3 (2010): 245–72. Suzanne Uniacke (in *Permissible Killing*) argues that the right of self-defense (and other-defense) is a "corollary of the victim's right not to be *killed*." Also see Frowe, "Threats, Bystanders and Obstructers."

is because for indirect threats, she thinks responsibility for the threat *does* matter, but for direct threats she thinks responsibility for the threat doesn't matter. Does this defense work? I think not. Jason Hanna points out that, "For Frowe's view to be successful, we need *some reason* for thinking that the distinction between direct and indirect threats is morally relevant. Yet it is far from clear that such a reason can be offered."[90] We see that this reason is lacking when we find, in fact, that the distinction the defense relies on only obtains in some of the cases Frowe intends, but not all. In other cases, the distinction and the corresponding difference it supposedly makes vanishes, and it actually delivers the *opposite* results the move is supposed to gain for the Nonresponsible Account. This, in the least, significantly weakens the plausibility of relying on the direct/indirect distinction to defend the view. At worst, it suggests the distinction itself may be arbitrary, rather than grounded in an important moral fact about the actors in defense cases.[91] And, indeed, that is the conclusion I reach—that this supposedly critical moral distinction is, in fact, *ad hoc* reasoning simply designed to get the outputs of the *Falling Man* case where Frowe thinks it should land.

To see this, recall, once again, the case of *Prisoner Decision*, but this time, rather than one of us knowingly making the choice for whoever the terrorists should kill, one of us will do so unintentionally. I have to make the case rather elaborate to show this, but stay with me. Imagine the following scenario:

Prisoner Unintentional Decision
You and I have been captured by evil terrorists who have decided that they will kill only one of us and let the other go. They will decide which one of us to kill by carefully watching me. If I scratch my head with my right hand, they will kill you. If I scratch my head with my left hand, they will kill me. They have not informed me of any of this information—I am in the dark. But they inform you of all of this. But you are gagged and have no way of informing me.[92]

---

[90] Hanna, "Nonresponsible Threats," 6. Emphasis mine.
[91] My reasoning here is similar to the way in which Hanna rejects Frowe's move. I, however, rely on a much simpler refutation involving my *Prisoner Decision* case. Hanna uses his far more complicated "Look-Alike" case, and then further complicates the matter with what I find to be an unneeded confusion over the way in which the killing occurs. While Hanna's conclusion in rejecting Frowe's move here is correct, his route to get there is unnecessarily befuddled. A simpler rejection is all that is needed, as I demonstrate below.
[92] This modified version of my *Prisoner Decision* case is, in some ways, relevantly similar to Hanna's "Look-Alike" case ("Nonresponsible Threats," 7). I was unaware of the similarity when I first came up with this response against Frowe, but discovered the similarity after reading Hanna.

In this scenario, I am an indirect threat to you in the sense that Frowe intends. This is because if I scratch my head with my right hand, you will be made worse off, although not by me but by the terrorists. So, what if you see me begin to raise my right hand to scratch my head which you know would (unknowingly to me) move the terrorists into action to kill you (by shooting you, say)? Could you permissibly kill me to block this indirect threat to your life? Frowe's account would say that you cannot because I am not responsible for being an indirect threat.

So far so good for Frowe's distinction. But remember the slight modification that we put on *Prisoner Decision* originally to block the initial complaint by the Nonresponsible Account. I suggested that rather than using a gun, what if the terrorists picked up my body and threw me at you as their method to kill you rather than use a gun. Imagine that the terrorists originally plan on shooting you with a gun but then change their minds at the last second after I scratch my head and decide to kill you by throwing me at you. Well, if the terrorists do that, then on Frowe's account I will have suddenly shifted from being an indirect threat to a direct threat. (Falling Man, after all, is a direct threat on Frowe's account.) But if that's true, then Frowe's account says that now you may permissibly kill me, simply because the terrorists changed their mind about what method to use to kill you. And this seems quite strange, for all that has changed is the method by which the terrorists chose to kill you. *My* responsibility in the matter did not change whatsoever. And *my* moral standing in the scenario did not change whatsoever. And it seems implausible that something completely independent of me and as arbitrary as the means that the terrorists use to try to kill you can be the proper basis for a complete switch on *my* liability status to defensive harm from you.

Hanna makes a similar argument and agrees that such a small difference for a Nonresponsible Threat—going from being an indirect threat to being a direct threat—"does not appear to make a moral difference."[93] Making these kinds of apparently irrelevant changes not only relevant to, but *determinative* of, someone's liability seems mistaken. Hanna, again, makes the same conclusion I do here (substituting my case for his):

> I find it difficult to believe that you are morally permitted to kill [me, if the terrorists use my body to kill you] and, yet you are morally forbidden from killing [me, if the terrorists use a gun to kill you]. Unless we are prepared to

---

[93] Hanna, "Nonresponsible Threats," 7.

accept this result, we must apparently reject the view that there is a morally relevant distinction between direct threats and indirect threats.[94]

And, of course, we should not be prepared to accept such a result. To do so makes liability attribution appear entirely capricious and arbitrary. This gives us good reason to doubt that the direct/indirect threat distinction can save the Nonresponsible Account. The other similar moves like it, designed to show a relevant difference between Falling Man and Bystander, similarly fail and, hence, the Nonresponsible Account still stands in need of a defense against the Otsukian objection. If none is forthcoming, we are right to reject it as an adequate account of liability attribution to defensive harm and we should instead embrace some version of the Responsible Account.

1.6. Two Views of the Responsibility Criterion

So, although I have only briefly here dipped into the large body of work on the Nonresponsible View, for the purposes of this book, I will move forward with the conclusion that we should reject the Nonresponsible View and accept the Responsible View. This holds that *some kind* of responsibility for the wrong to be averted by defensive harm is a necessary criterion for liability attribution.

1.6.1 Embracing the Responsible View

To give further intuitive force to the Responsible View, let me cast permissible decisions to kill in self-defense in another light. I mentioned, in note 51, the notion of a forced-choice model, advocated by Cheyney Ryan, as a means to escape the vicious circle. As I explained in that note, if understood as a means to arbitrate between two lesser evils, this model is not a good application of the Rights-Based Account and, in fact, is an explicit departure from it. However, if we look at defense cases through the lens of a forced-choice model as a way of understanding the relevant moral asymmetry between actors to determine who would be in the *right* to defend themselves, it can be quite helpful.[95]

---

[94] Ibid.
[95] McMahan (in *Killing in War*) uses the language of the forced-choice at length to discuss the moral asymmetry between parties.

A forced-choice scenario is one in which two parties are in a situation such that at least one of them will die no matter what either party does. Yet, one of them (or both of them) can do something (or refrain from doing something) such that they determine *which* of the two of them will die. Looking at forced-choice scenarios from the standpoint of the Rights-Based Account makes us search for the relevant moral asymmetry between the parties trapped in a forced-choice to determine who must "bear the burden" of the cost the forced-choice imposes.[96] One of them must die—one of them must bear the burden—so the Responsible Account argues that the one who is morally responsible for the scenario obtaining and its resulting cost should be the one morally required to bear the burden of that cost. In pure bystander versus bystander cases (*Falling Man, Prisoner Decision*) neither party is more responsible for the forced-choice over the other—there *is no moral asymmetry* between them—and so, neither *should* bear the burden over the other, even though one of them ultimately will. This, then, is the normative force behind the Responsible Account. Since the two parties in such forced-choices are morally identical in relation to the forced-choice, neither should be liable over the other in its resolution.

1.6.2 Two Views

Thus, for the reasons just given and for the articulation of the Otsukian objection given above in section 1.5, I embrace the Responsible Account. For the remainder of this book, the Responsible Account will be the working assumption. But there is a sharp divide within the Responsible Account over just what responsibility for liability entails. This division is, by comparison, relatively under-explored in the literature as the debate between the Responsible Account and the Nonresponsible Account initially dominated most scholarly discussion of this issue.[97] There are two primary views on

---

[96] Again, this is different than how Cheyney Ryan uses the forced-choice model ("Possibility of Killing"). He intends it as an alternative to the Rights-Based Account, not as a potential corollary to it as I have tried to co-opt it here. An example of use of the language of "forced-choice" for a Rights-Based Account is, again, McMahan.

[97] McMahan first set up the divide when he presented his "responsibility account" as a separate approach to liability attribution from what I label below the Simple Culpability View (which, at the time, was the only real view available for the Responsible Account); but the division has been relatively unengaged thus far. Seth Lazar analyzed how McMahan's view of responsibility has evolved over time and challenged it in his important paper "Responsibility, Risk, and Killing in Self-Defense," *Ethics* 119 (2009): 699–728. I rely heavily on Lazar's work in the following discussion and next section. Lazar, however, did not extend his purview in that piece to those accounts rejected by

offer for the Responsible Account for liability attribution. The first I call the Simple Culpability View, and the second I call the Agency View. After I review these two different ways of understanding the responsibility criterion, I will discuss some problems they each encounter that give us reason to think that both are inadequate to serve the Responsible Account. In the next chapter I will propose a new, third view for how we should understand the moral responsibility necessary for liability attribution that better meets this challenge.[98]

The Simple Culpability View holds, as you would expect, that the moral responsibility necessary for liability attribution to defensive harm is, simply, culpability. Thus, if someone can be said to be morally blameworthy or culpable for the given wrong to be averted, they can be liable to defensive harm. This means, among other things, that if someone is posing an unjust threat, but they have a full excuse such that they would not be culpable for that unjust threat, then they are not liable.

The second view, I call (for lack of a better term) the "Agency View." The view was developed most prominently by Jeff McMahan in an effort to defend the Responsible Account while allowing it to apply liability in some cases where an individual is not fully culpable for an unjust threat, yet is still responsible in a morally relevant way.[99] This view holds that someone can be morally responsible for liability attribution even if they are not fully culpable or blameworthy for a wrongful threat. It is an attempt to create a middle-road position between someone being nonresponsible and culpable—resulting in three categories: nonresponsible; responsible but not culpable; and responsible and culpable. On this view, to be responsible, the liable person must voluntarily commit an act which will result in unjust harm to another and

---

McMahan, such as the Simple Culpability View I articulate here. Beyond McMahan, more recently some scholars who formerly held a Simple Culpability View have gradually moved ever closer to the Agency View. The clearest example of this is David Rodin. Rodin was formerly the view's biggest defender and most important proponent. Recently, however, Rodin has himself seemed to embrace a view closer to McMahan's Agency View, described below. Rodin does this in "The Moral Inequality of Soldiers: Why *Jus in Bello* Asymmetry Is Half Right," in *Just and Unjust Warriors: The Moral and Legal Status of Soldiers*, edited by Henry Shue and David Rodin (New York: Oxford University Press, 2008): 44–68.

[98] Thankfully, this view has attracted some attention. See note 9 above in the Introduction Chapter.
[99] McMahan originally called this alternative approach to liability attribution the "responsibility account" which is confusing, given my division within the Rights-Based Account, between the Nonresponsible Account and the Responsible Account, the resulting discussion over just what responsibility means. Hence, I call it the "Agency View." The reason for this shift in nomenclature, of course, is because I think this view gets the notion of responsibility wrong, as I will show.

it could have been foreseen that the act had the *risk* of potentially imposing such harm. This is a very "thin" conception of the responsibility necessary for liability attribution. It is so minimal that it is perhaps better called "bare-agent responsibility"—referring to McMahan's emphasis on mere agency for a wrong as fulfilling the requirement in some cases.

So, for example (in the most extreme cases), McMahan claims that a person can act morally permissibly according to all the evidence available to him or her—they do nothing wrong as far as they could possibly know—yet, if it turns out his or her evidence is mistaken and the voluntary act impermissibly harms someone relative to the actual facts, then the actor can thereby be "responsible" and, hence, liable. Since one can be acting permissibly according to the evidence available to them, the primary issue here is one of risk imposition. That is, the person, when acting permissibly, according to the evidence available, was aware that there was a foreseeable risk (however small) that her act may, in fact, impose a wrongful harm on others. And, in a forced-choice case between two actors wherein one of the parties must die, this imposition of nonreciprocal risk can (supposedly) make the difference needed to provide the relevant moral asymmetry between them for who has a right to self-defense and who does not. That is, in forced-choice cases, this view argues that the smallest difference in responsibility makes *all* the difference.[100] And even if the moral difference between two actors in a forced-choice scenario is not something that we would think equates to culpability, it can still be enough "responsibility" to result in liability simply by one taking a nonreciprocal risk that they *may be* actually acting wrongly against the other. As Lazar describes the view, between two actors A and B in a forced-choice scenario such that one of the two must die, "where A's voluntary conduct—however blameless—imposes risks on B, A should lose his right not to bear the costs when those risks eventuate in B being forced to choose between their lives."[101]

1.6.3 Exploring the Views

So, on this Agency View, one can be liable to harm even if they are not culpable. Note, they are still claimed to be morally *responsible*, but their

---

[100] To use a phrase used often by McMahan in *Killing in War*.
[101] Lazar, "Risk, Responsibility," 702.

blameworthiness is excused such that they are not at all *culpable*.[102] Both views—the Simple Culpability View and the Agency View—will make more sense by way of example. The famous *Dignitary & Guest* Case (originally devised by Otsuka) works nicely here.

> *Dignitary & Guest*
> Guest extends his hand to shake the hand of a foreign Dignitary at a reception. Unbeknown to Guest, a third-party projects a stunningly realistic holographic image of a pistol onto Guest's hand. Dignitary, who is accustomed to threats on her life, sees the hologram, thereby forms the justified belief that Guest is about to assassinate her, and coolly draws a pistol in order to shoot Guest down in self-defense.[103]

Now, imagine that Guest himself was also armed such that he was able to prevent Dignitary from killing him by pulling out his own gun and shooting Dignitary first, once he sees her pull the gun on him.

In such a case, is Dignitary liable to defensive harm to avert the wrongful threat she poses on Guest's life? The Simple Culpability view says no, she is not liable. This is because, although she is, in fact, about to wrongfully harm Guest (since he has done no actual wrong and is not posing an unjust threat to her), she is not culpable for this wrongful action since there is no way she could have known that she was wrongfully harming Guest (given the evidence available to her). Indeed, she acted *justly* in regard to the evidence she had available to her. These epistemic constraints excuse her culpability. Since she is not culpable for the wrongful harm to Guest, then, she is not liable to defensive harm to avert that wrongful harm. So says the Simple Culpability view.[104]

The Agency View would argue, however, that Dignitary is responsible in such a way that she should be liable to defensive harm to avert the wrongful harm done to Guest. This is because she is, according to the actual facts, acting impermissibly and committing a wrongful act (albeit unknowingly). Since she is voluntarily doing an act which *turns out* to cause wrongful harm,

---

[102] Elinor Mason offers another interesting interpretation of the distinction between cases of blameworthiness and those of liability in "Between Strict Liability and Blameworthy Quality of Will: Taking Responsibility," *Oxford Studies of Agency and Responsibility* 6 (2019): 241–64.
[103] I have modified Otsuka's original version found in "Killing the Innocent in Self-Defense," 91.
[104] An interesting reply to this view may be found in Saba Bazargan-Forward, "Defensive Liability Without Culpability," in *The Ethics of Self Defense* (Oxford University Press, 2016); see also Massimo Renzo, "Manipulation and Liability to Defensive Harm," *Philosophical Studies* 178 (2021): 3483–501.

and since she is engaging in an activity (shooting someone) which has a well-known high risk of potentially imposing wrongful harm on others, she is responsible, on McMahan's Agency View. Note well: in her act, she does not think there is a high risk of imposing wrongful harm; after all, she thinks she is acting justly given the evidence before her. But, on McMahan's view, there is a significant risk that one could be acting wrongly, *anytime* one engages in an act such as shooting. That is, there is always a risk you could be in the wrong. And, as such, Dignitary is imposing that risk on Guest, and she should thereby be liable.

This latter element of committing a "risk-imposing activity" is key for the Agency View. This is because the view does *not* hold that liability attribution is simply a matter of a morally responsible agent causing harm through his or her own voluntary action. That is a necessary first step, but it is not enough to attribute responsibility. The agent must voluntarily be committing an activity (to quote McMahan):

> of a type that is known or can be seen to impose a risk of significant harm on others, even if the probability is comparatively low.... I will assume that it is a condition of responsibility for an unjust threat that the action that gave rise to the threat either was of a risk-imposing type or was such that in the circumstances the agent ought to have foreseen that it carried a non-negligible risk of causing a significant unjust harm.[105]

McMahan uses several cases to show why he holds this view. I will focus on two of his cases. The first is supposed to be an example where McMahan thinks enough responsibility for an unjust threat obtains such that liability can be attributed. The case is:

Conscientious Driver
A person, Driver, keeps his car well maintained and always drives cautiously and alertly. On one occasion, however, freak circumstances cause the car to go out of control. It has veered in the direction of Pedestrian whom it will kill unless she blows it up by using one of the explosive devices with which pedestrians in philosophical examples are typically equipped.[106]

---
[105] McMahan, "The Moral Basis for Liability," 397.
[106] Ibid., 393. I have slightly modified the case for ease of discussion.

On the Agency View, Driver is liable to defensive harm from Pedestrian because he is voluntarily committing an act which will impose wrongful harm on Pedestrian and, further, that he was engaging in an activity that carries with it a "non-negligible risk of causing a significant unjust harm."[107] That is, driving a car carries with it known risks that one could inadvertently harm another person. Note that the view is not arguing that Driver is liable because only *he* could avoid the forced-choice coming about; Pedestrian didn't have to go out for a walk and that would have avoided the forced-choice as well. And going out for a walk brings with it some risks, however small. Rather, as McMahan explains, "the claim is that the [Driver] is liable because he voluntarily engaged in a risk-*imposing* activity and is responsible for the consequences when the risks he imposed eventuate in harms."[108]

Most defenders of the Agency View admit that the moral difference here between Pedestrian and Driver is rather slim. Engaging in the "risk-imposing" activity of driving, after all, is not something morally monstrous. The vast majority of American adults do this every day. But the Agency View holds that it is, indeed, a moral difference between them and that, although Driver is not *culpable* for the impending harm on Pedestrian, he is responsible for it in this non-trivial way such that there is a moral difference between the two actors with regard to the forced-choice. And recall that, according to McMahan, even the smallest difference can make all the difference in a forced-choice when we are trying to determine who should bear the full burden of its cost. *One* of them must bear the entire cost, after all. So, the Agency View argues, since Driver is in this small way "'responsible" for the harm, he should be the one to bear the cost and, hence, he is liable.

Another example is used to show why the Agency View does not hold one liable solely for voluntarily committing an act which eventuates in the wrongful harm of another. That is, for why the non-reciprocal risk-imposition is an additional necessary component of the responsibility required for liability. Consider:

Unwitting Cell Bomber
A villain has secretly tampered with Todd's cell phone in such a way that if Todd presses the "send" button, he will detonate a bomb to which Meredith has been tied by this same villain. The villain has trussed Meredith up so

---

[107] Ibid., 397.
[108] Ibid. My emphasis.

that she cannot escape or alert Todd to her plight. But the villain has given Meredith a weapon with which she can kill Todd.[109]

In this case, Todd is a morally responsible agent whose voluntary action will impose a wrongful harm on Meredith. But McMahan holds that Todd has not made himself liable to defensive harm from Meredith because using a cell phone is not the "right kind" of risk-imposing activity. This is because, "pressing a button on a cell phone is not the kind of act that typically carries any risk to others, however slight."[110] And, thus, McMahan thinks that Todd could not have plausibly foreseen that his action was a possible risk-imposing one, like Driver can foresee about driving. McMahan calls this the "foreseeability condition" for moral responsibility that can result in liability attribution.[111] Because he could not foresee that his action was potentially risk-imposing, he cannot be held responsible for his action actually being risk-imposing. Thus, according to the Agency View, Todd is a Nonresponsible Threat, like Falling Man, and is therefore nonliable. The Simple Culpability View, of course, would not hold Driver, Todd, nor Dignitary liable to defensive harm because none of them are culpable.

1.7. Problems with Both Views of Responsibility

I think there are sufficient problems with each of these accounts of responsibility that they merit concern for the Responsible View. These problems do not constitute strong enough reasons to reject either view outright on their own. But combined they do give us reason to search for a better view, if one can be found. To conclude this chapter, I will review some of those problems here, and then offer an improved version of the Responsible View that avoids these problems in the next chapter.

1.7.1 Trouble with Foreseeability

First, of course, whether one finds the Simple Culpability View or the Agency View more plausible will hinge on certain key moral intuitions for cases like

---

[109] Again, I have slightly modified McMahan's original case for ease of discussion.
[110] McMahan, "The Moral Basis for Liability," 398.
[111] Ibid.

Dignitary & Guest and *Conscientious Driver*. I find that neither Dignitary nor Driver should be liable to defensive harm, even if there *is* this small difference in their responsibility that the Agency View aims to highlight. Remember what we are asking in these cases when we ask if either party should be liable. We are thereby asking if one of them would not be wronged, were he or she killed as an act of defensive harm. Put differently, we are saying it is right to kill them with defensive harm. And, to my mind, claiming either Dignitary or Driver as someone who *should* be held liable to be killed is wildly counterintuitive. Remember: it may be in these cases that someone has to die, and perhaps there are even lesser-evil based reasons to choose one over the other, or some other reasons. But to claim one party is liable is to say that morality provides a reason such that one would not be wronged if they received defensive harm. And, to my mind, that is a morally absurd thing to suggest for either party in either case. But that's just an assertion of my intuitions. Let me attempt to argue why I reach such conclusions in these cases.

Part of the problem is that the "foreseeability condition" will be difficult to maintain in such a way that it does not become simply arbitrary. It seems reasonable that Todd could not have foreseen that using his cell phone would set off a bomb, and McMahan agrees. But many will think that Driver should also not be held responsible because he could not reasonably foresee his car spinning out of control and killing Pedestrian. I've been driving for thousands of hours, across my life, and I've never had a car do that, nor seen another car do that. Sure, it's possible it could happen. After all, it's *possible* that *any* action of ours could result in a chain of events that unjustly kills someone. Whether or not it is reasonably foreseeable will always be a matter of degree. We could construct cases where the reasonable foreseeability of being a risk-imposing activity falls between the foreseeability in *Conscientious Driver* and *Unwitting Cell Bomber*. Eventually the difference between cases and whether or not an action is "foreseeably" risk-imposing will become incredibly small. Yet, the Agency View will be forced to hold that this miniscule difference is the entire basis for liability in one case and the lack of attribution in another. And this seems a hard pill to swallow. It would be preferable if the basis for a complete shift in liability attribution was more significant and could not become so trivial.[112]

---

[112] Susanne Burri offers an important qualification to this view in "Morally Permissible Risk Imposition and Liability to Defensive Harm," *Law and Philosophy* 39 (2020): 381–408; see also Helen Frowe, "Risk Imposition and Liability to Defensive Harm," *Criminal Law and Philosophy* 16, no. 3 (2022): 511–24.

Recall again, McMahan claims that the difference between the two—Driver versus Todd—is that a cell phone doesn't *typically* impose risks on others. But there is, of course, a risk, however small, that something won't behave as it typically does (as the thought experiment itself shows). And this itself seems like a kind of risk that Todd could be held liable for imposing on others—the risk that a thing which typically does not impose risks on others may behave wildly differently in this one instance and thereby actually impose risks on others. If this sounds like a ludicrously small basis for which liability should hinge upon, I agree. But that is my point. This risk seems no different in kind than other incredibly small risks people may take that McMahan thinks are enough to "make all the difference" in liability attribution. The hoped-for distinction here of activities that "typically" are not risk-imposing contra those that typically are risk-imposing breaks down, for there's always a (small) risk that any typical activity will behave non-typically. If the difference is supposed to be based on the risk of imposing harms on others, then there is no principled distinction here; merely a difference in degree of risk. But mere degree of risk is not what McMahan wants to base the liability attribution on in these cases. (Remember, even Pedestrian takes certain risks going for a walk.) Rather, he wants a difference in principle that can ground the asymmetry needed for liability. But, as shown, this is an illusory basis to find it.

1.7.2 Asymmetry or Symmetry?

This brings us back to the required asymmetry that we found to be the necessary basis for liability attribution in any self-defense case. We saw, above, that to ground a right to self-defense in a way that escapes the vicious circle problem, some asymmetry must be isolated between actors. But, as just shown with the foreseeability condition, it seems the Agency View identifies a rather miniscule difference (if there even is one at all) as the basis of this asymmetry, and that difference itself breaks down as one of mere degree at best. Should such a seemingly insignificant difference be, given the significance of determining moral asymmetry and thereby grounding liability?

Part of the problem here is the emphasis on searching for an asymmetry in all cases to begin with. I fear that many of these approaches to permissible defensive harm are so focused on grounding permissible defense (and escaping the vicious circle) on a moral asymmetry that they'll search for any difference whatsoever to do the job, even if it's one that upon reflection we think is, in fact, *not* morally relevant. Particularly, in the Nonresponsible Threat cases, we see this at play time and again in the literature. It is nicely demonstrated by this remark of Tim Scanlon's in reference to the work of Thomson and her peers:

> It is either permissible to kill a [Nonresponsible Threat] in self-defense, or it is impermissible. Either way, there has to be a moral asymmetry between the threatened person and the threat, an asymmetry that favors either the victim, in which case the killing is permissible, or the threat in which case it is impermissible. It is our task as moral philosophers to identify and explicate this asymmetry.[113]

But what if there is no *relevant* asymmetry to be found? It seems to me that we miss how incredibly morally *symmetrical* the parties are in these Nonresponsible Threat cases by searching for some miniscule asymmetry to ground liability. Recall that Thomson, Uniacke, and the like, defending the Nonresponsible Account find that the supposed moral asymmetry runs toward the Nonresponsible Threat—such as Falling Man—such that he is liable to defensive harm. But notice something not mentioned previously: those Responsible Account defenders, like McMahan, will be forced to claim not that there is no asymmetry for many of these cases, but that it actually runs the other direction—toward Trapped. This is because when she takes her gun to vaporize Falling Man, she is the responsible agent who is acting voluntarily and, according to the Responsible Account, she is shooting a nonliable person. Hence, she is the one committing the impending wrongful harm and Falling Man could permissibly engage in counter-defense on these views, if he was so able (say if he had his own ray gun).

I'll discuss this in more detail in the next chapter, but this seems an odd result for the Responsible Account. The very basis of moving to the Responsible Account away from the Nonresponsible Account was because we saw that Nonresponsible Threats are relevantly like Bystanders and cannot, therefore, be found liable. So, in these forced-choice models, we should think that moral *symmetry* rules the day and neither party is liable (just as neither Bystander nor Victim are liable in *Bystander on Bridge*). Yet to think that, in fact, one is

---

[113] T. M. Scanlon, "Thomson on Self-Defense," in *Fact and Value. Essays on Ethics and Metaphysics for Judith Jarvis Thomson*, edited by Alex Byrne, Robert Stalnaker, and Ralph Wedgwood (Cambridge, MA: The MIT Press, 2001): 206. I am indebted here to Susanne Burri for bringing Scanlon's discussion of this point to my attention.

liable over the other (as the Agency View ends up being forced to admit with permissible counter-defense) seems to violate this intuition which drove us to the Responsible View in the first place.

Seth Lazar has also argued against the Agency View along a similar vein. He argues that it is too permissive in whoever it says can be permissibly killed because the moral asymmetry it bases liability attribution on is too insignificant.[114] Lazar also raises an objection borne out of the forced-choice model and the triviality of the asymmetry involved. If the asymmetry is so small between parties, then, Lazar writes, "rather than allowing it to be so definitive, we should attempt a fair distribution of risk, proportionate to this small difference."[115] And, the thought is, that killing is not *proportionate* to the small difference. It would be better in the *Conscientious Driver* case, for example, for Pedestrian to try to throw her explosive device next to the car in such a way that it would make Driver veer off course, but not kill him. Even if this was not a certain way of defending herself (imagine that this attempt had a reasonable but not certain chance of successfully causing Driver's car to miss her), this would be a better distribution of this small difference rather than the "full" distribution of the cost onto the Driver by killing him. Or, perhaps even better, would be if there was some way for the two to bear an equal "fair" division of the unjust harm they both face. If there were a way to adjust the directional path of the car such that it resulted in a crash that, indeed, harmed Driver and harmed Pedestrian, but killed neither or them, then that would be a better distribution of wrongs in the forced-choice than Pedestrian or Driver having to bear the full unjust cost him or herself.[116]

1.7.3 Nonreciprocal Risk

There's another obvious point here that is incredibly problematic for the Agency View. In fact, it's probably the most damaging objection. And it is simply this: the supposed difference the Agency View points to between Driver and Pedestrian is, in fact, *not* one of non-reciprocal risk imposition by Driver on Pedestrian. That is because they are both imposing risk on the

---

[114] Lazar, "Risk, Responsibility."
[115] Ibid., 715.
[116] Susanne Burri suggests that a coin-flip could be another fair distribution of harm citing the work of John Broome on how the fair distribution of resources could work. I'll discuss this at some length in chapter 2.6.2.

other and engaging in a "risk-imposing" activity. How is it that Pedestrian imposes a risk on Driver? Well—this is perhaps an odd side-effect of the kinds of thought experiments we come up with to test moral principles in analytic moral philosophy—but walking around town carrying explosive devices that could potentially be lobbed at cars if they spin out of control through no fault of their drivers certainly seems risk-imposing in the relevant way McMahan wants to claim that driving is. Hence, Pedestrian is knowingly going about town engaging in a "risk-imposing" activity by having such a means to kill Driver with him, just as Driver is when he drives his car around town.[117]

This is an example of where these thought experiments become so obtuse in their effort to find the searched-for principle (the nonreciprocal risk the Agency View hopes to rely on, in this case), that they miss something rather obvious about themselves needed for the desired result to obtain. In this case, what is missed is that carrying (with the possibility of potentially using) pocket-sized explosive devices that deliver enough force to change the direction of an on-coming car is not something we can simply write off as irrelevant to the moral relationship between parties. At least, that is, we cannot write it off as irrelevant *if* we are at the same time going to hold Driver's risk of conscientiously driving as relevant to his moral standing. Liability is about the moral relationship between parties; both risk-imposing activities would be relevant, if that's what the Agency View wants to hang its hat on.

1.7.4 Liability with Excused Culpability

So, it seems the difference the Agency View turns on may not always hold up under scrutiny. And, at any rate, it seems it is inadequately small to make a morally innocent person lose his right to life. One may think, as a result, that we should abandon the Agency View and return to the Simple Culpability View—that one must, simply enough, be morally culpable for an unjust threat to be averted in order to be liable to defensive harm. That seems like the obvious move, given these problems for the Agency View combined with a rejection of the Nonresponsible View. But there are also real problems with the Simple Culpability View as well. For it does seem, indeed, that there *are*

---

[117] See Lazar, "Risk, Responsibility," 716, for a good discussion on this point.

some cases where one can be liable to defensive harm even if they are not (fully) culpable. Here's one possible example:

Coerced Killer
A mafia ring has captured a man, Sam, and his family. They have threatened to kill his entire family if he does not do their bidding. They give him a gun and command him to go kill an innocent woman, Sarah. Sam finds Sarah and raises his gun to kill her. Sarah is unaware of the coercion Sam is under. She just sees a random stranger trying to kill her. Sam knows full well he is killing an innocent person. He whispers to himself as he pulls the trigger, "may God forgive me."

If Sarah has the means to defend herself against Sam and thereby avert the unjust harm that he will deliver, it certainly seems permissible for her to do so. Yet, because of the coercion he is under, many will think that Sam is not fully culpable for posing this unjust threat to her. That is, he is acting *wrongly* but that we think he is *excused* of this wrong-doing (either partially or fully excused, given the extent of coercion). To what extent his culpability is mitigated is up for debate. If one thinks that the threat of killing his family is not enough to mitigate his culpability, then we can imagine another thought experiment whereby the coercion is enough such that Sam's culpability is full. Yet, we still think—quite obviously to my mind—that he should be liable to defensive harm from Sarah, given her relational moral standing to his threat. That is, to perhaps put it best, Sarah would not wrong Sam if she killed him to defend herself. (And I think Sam would agree.) Yet, the Simple Culpability View cannot account for this.

Relatedly, there are also problems for the Simple Culpability View with the inverse of these cases. That is, there are times when we think we *should* hold someone liable even if they are not actually culpable of imposing an unjust harm, but are simply intending to impose harm. It is these kinds of cases that lead McMahan to press the Agency view in the first place. Here is an example of such a case, originally raised by McMahan.

Unknown Unloaded Gun
A Gunman, fully intending to kill Mark, points his gun at Mark and slowly begins to squeeze the trigger. Mark is innocent and nonliable to be killed. Gunman and Mark both reasonably believe that the gun is loaded but in

fact it is not. Mark has just enough time to defend himself and kill Gunman with his own concealed gun before Gunman pulls the trigger.[118]

Notice that in this case the Gunman is not actually culpable for imposing a real unjust threat of harm *that would otherwise obtain*. This is because, since the gun is not loaded, no harm would ever actually obtain. But liability to defensive harm on the Simple Culpability View, recall, requires that someone be culpable for imposing an actual unjust threat that would otherwise obtain if it is not averted. So, the Simple Culpability View is in the embarrassing position of claiming that Gunman in *Unknown Unloaded Gun* is actually not liable to defensive harm and that Mark wrongs Gunman when he kills him. (Notice the absurd view that would then follow from that is that Gunman could then in theory try to kill Mark to avert the wrongful harm that Mark is now imposing!) To avoid this, the view would have to be amended to liability being attributable for someone culpably *attempting* to commit wrongful harm. But this leads to serious problems regarding how far out we can remove the attempt from the act such that soon the critical necessity criteria for defensive harm is lost. This is no small matter for liability. For example, could the Gunman be liable the night before the incident above when he prepared the gun? Or the week before we formed the intention? Months? Clearly this way out of the problem only adds further difficulty to the view.[119]

1.7.5 The Incomplete Responsible View

Again, I do not find any of these problems just discussed to be completely devastating or insurmountable to either view of liability attribution for the Responsible View. This is primarily because the problems are mostly due to differing intuitions over these particularly difficult cases. Moreover, it seems some version of the Responsible View is clearly right over the Nonresponsible View. But these difficulties do give us reason to search for a better version of the Responsible View. In particular, two problems seem most pressing: the inability to deal with the tragedy of symmetrical cases in a satisfying manner (particularly for the Agency View), and the problem of cases of excused culpability wherein we still think liability obtains (for the Simple Culpability

---

[118] The case is drawn from McMahan, "The Basis of Moral Liability," 390.
[119] McMahan explains these problems for the view in Ibid., 391–94.

View). These leave the Responsible Account incomplete. To add some final punch to the need for a better account of responsibility than these two views offer, consider again the case of *Dignitary & Guest*. This is an incredibly complex case, to say the least. Dignitary is behaving in ways wholly permissible with what she can possibly know of the situation—she thinks, rightly, based on all the evidence available to her, that someone is unjustly threatening her life. Yet consider Guest. If he attempts to defend himself against Dignitary's action—her action which will, indeed, wrongfully harm him even though it is done by her wholly innocently—if he attempts to defend himself from that harm, he too will be wrongfully harming her even though he would be behaving in a wholly permissibly way, given what he could possibly know of their tragic situation. Neither view, it seems to me, gives us an adequate accounting or even explanation of this complex moral relationship between these two actors. Both views have some truth to them: the Simple Culpability View is correct that neither is culpable; yet the Agency View is correct that there is, indeed, wrongful harm being willfully delivered, however innocently. How do we resolve this?

We need a way to deliver the core intuition of the Responsible Account— that liability requires responsibility—yet do so consistently and in a way that does not fail to deliver the correct results in these difficult cases. In the next chapter, I will offer a view of liability attribution that avoids these problems. I find that it delivers more normatively appealing results in these cases and, more importantly, it gives a stronger and more coherent reason for the liability results it proffers than the weak "risk-imposing activity" basis used by the Agency View. It is also able to capture and explain the complex intricate moral relationship between actors in these tragic cases such as *Dignitary & Guest*. Finally, the new view I will offer has positive inferences that make it a better view for liability beyond simply avoiding the problems that plague the other views. In particular, it will be quite helpful in our theorizing on killing in war—which is what, ultimately, this book is about. Recall that the goal of this book is to explicate why soldiers can be justified in setting out to intentionally kill other soldiers in war. Understanding when it is ever the case when one can be killed justly, and not be wronged in being killed, is a central step in answering that question; perhaps *the* central step. The new view I offer in the next chapter will help us take that step.

2
The Evidence-Relative View of Liability Attribution

> At what point is someone precluded from availing themselves of the justification of self-defense because of their own poor judgment?
> —Dan Gelber, writing on the killing of Trayvon Martin

2.1. Introduction

What must one do in order to open themselves up to justifiable defensive harm? What do we think is a fair standard to hold someone liable to bear the cost of averting a wrong? Nearly everyone agrees that it is permissible to kill you if it is necessary to stop you from willfully killing an innocent person. But is it permissible to kill you in order to stop you from unknowingly, or nonresponsibly, or even innocently killing an innocent person? Is that a fair treatment of you and a proper respect of your rights? And if we do not kill you in such a case, is that a fair treatment and proper respect for the rights of the person you would otherwise kill? Human beings have been hurting, maiming, and killing each other for a long time. When is it not merely *better* to take such action, all things considered as perhaps a "lesser evil," but actually *right* to do that to one another?

To merely call these difficult questions that demand our attention does not quite capture their importance. It is a disservice to the deep normative values from which these questions arise to treat them as any other analytic puzzle. To be sure: they are difficult questions, and, indeed, they deserve serious, careful engagement. But they are more than that. To my lights, these questions strike at the heart of human value itself, what respect we owe to one another as required by that value we all possess, and any attempt we may make to take the notion of rights seriously. If we believe human life has distinct and deep normative value and that human life itself is supremely important, as I do, then these questions have distinct and deep normative value and are supremely important. That we do not yet have any settled answers in moral philosophy to these questions highlights rather than diminishes their importance. My attempt in this chapter to craft a better understanding of moral liability to defensive harm is to merely nibble at the analytic edges of these weighty questions.

As we saw in chapter 1, there are many different ways writers have tried to answer these questions about permissible defensive harm. Some answers are better than others; all have difficulties and problems. In this chapter, I offer my evidence-relative approach as a new proposal for how we should understand the responsibility criterion for liability attribution. The view attempts to carve out a coherent and plausible conceptual space between the Simple Culpability View and the Agency View. I call it the Evidence-Relative View. This account holds that one may become liable to defensive harm only if they have violated norms that they could be properly held responsible for ascertaining. On this view, one can be properly morally responsible for an act in a variety of different ways which can constitute being liable to defensive harm. If one is directly culpable for the act, then he or she can become liable to defensive harm to avert it. All three views agree on this. But my view goes further. It contends that one can also be morally responsible for an act resulting in liability to defensive harm when one fails to form the belief licensing that act in a way that is properly responsive to the evidence available. This can matter for liability because, in a range of cases, the failure to properly form the correct belief upon the available evidence regarding the permissibility of an act is itself a *moral* failing. It can be a moral failing because the agent did not give the act the proper epistemic consideration it deserves correlative to the moral significance of the act, and not giving proper epistemic consideration to an act of moral significance is morally wrong, not merely epistemically wrong, or so I will show. Put another way, one can become liable to defensive harm if one has done something that, given the evidence available, he or she could have reasonably concluded was impermissible and *should* have so concluded, given the moral stakes involved. Put simply: the view is an attempt to get at an understanding of the moral responsibility necessary for liability attribution that is tied in a critical way to the ethics of belief formation. This has several important implications.

First, the view is more restrictive than the Agency View. This is because it requires some failure of sensitivity to the evidence available in the determination of an act's permissibility, when one acts *unknowingly* impermissibly.

The Agency View holds that there are some cases wherein one can fulfill all of one's epistemic duties with regard to the permissibility of an act in question, and then behave permissibly according to that evidence available, and yet still be liable. That is, the Agency View holds that there are times when someone could not have reasonably known otherwise that her action was wrong, and yet that act still grounds her liability. The Evidence-Relative View counters this and claims that if one has fulfilled all of his or her epistemic duties in determining the permissibility of an act and then acts accordingly, then that person cannot be held liable for the resulting act, even if it turns out to be impermissible on the facts of the case. On the Evidence-Relative View, if the person turns out to be mistaken with regard to an act's permissibility through no failing of any kind on his or her part, then he or she cannot be held liable. Yet, at the same time, it is *less* restrictive than the Simple Culpability View in that it allows for liability attribution in some cases where a given party may be excused from culpability whilst still morally responsible for acting against the permissions delivered by the available evidence.

I will argue that this model for liability to defensive harm holds both in traditional self-defense cases *and* in the case of killing in war. Indeed, it is in its application to these latter cases that the full depth of the view is best on display. Moreover, the very fact that it can be consistently applied across both kinds of cases of permissible killing, and deliver consistently plausible results, is one of its greatest strengths. The Evidence-Relative View has many advantages over the other accounts, particularly its ability to distinguish two importantly different types of excuses as well as its far superior explanation of tragic defense cases. It also avoids the pitfalls that plague the other accounts and makes better sense of our moral intuitions for many of the classic cases in the self-defense literature. Perhaps the strongest element of the evidence-relative approach to liability, however, is the many advantages it delivers to recently ascendant revisionist understandings of just war theory. This application of my proposal will be dealt with in chapters 3 and 4. In this chapter, I aim to simply lay out the account in its basic form as it is applied to individual cases of defensive harm.[1] The above is an initial pass at describing the view, but it must be unpacked and explained in detail.

---

[1] The account does come with some costs, of course, but many of the objections that can be raised against it are best done so in the context of war. Hence, I will investigate the majority of those in chapters 3 and 4 as well. At the end of this chapter, I delve into some of the further complexities the view raises for many of the classic cases, and this will (tangentially) address several of the standard objections as well.

2.2. Three Senses of Wrong

In chapter 1 we saw that within the Rights-Based Account of defensive harm, there are two broad views: those who hold that some responsibility for an unjust harm is necessary for one to be liable to defensive harm (the Responsible Account) and those who hold that one only needs to be the cause of a rights violation to another and that culpability, responsibility, or even agency is not required for liability attribution (the Nonresponsible Account). I rejected the Nonresponsible Account. Within the Responsible Account, we found two different approaches for explaining the responsibility that is deemed necessary for liability. The first, the Simple Culpability View, holds that liability simply tracks culpability. The second, the Agency View, holds that a very thin concept of responsibility—what I called "bare agent-responsibility"—can make one liable to defensive harm, even though not necessarily culpable for the harm to be averted. We found that both of these views for liability attribution are inadequate to meet the demands of the Responsible Account. We need a new model for capturing the understanding of responsibility necessary for liability attribution.

2.2.1 A Better Framework

One reason we need a new model is revealed in the shifting of many of these writers' positions between the Simple Culpability Account and the Agency View over time and across the debate.[2] This is due, at least in part, to the basis of separation between these camps being conceptually muddled in some instances. This drives me to think we are in need of a better way to *frame* the debate. Simply proposing my view for liability attribution will help in this regard because it provides a stronger, clearer terminological framework for

---

[2] This is particularly true of McMahan and Rodin themselves. As already noted in chapter 1, Rodin's views regarding the responsibility criterion have shifted away from the Simple Culpability View and more towards the Agency View. McMahan's own views, however, have also shifted significantly over the years. Early on, he followed Otsuka and essentially held a Simple Culpability View. It was not until his 2005 article, "The Basis of Moral Liability"—well into his vast corpus on the ethics of permissible killing—that McMahan embraced the Agency View. In conversation and personal correspondence, however, McMahan can still sound less than perfectly clear on where exactly he stands between the two views. He often stresses the moral responsibility required of the Responsible Account for any liability attribution which, at times, make his arguments come across as searching for a comfortable position on responsibility somewhere south of the Agency View's thin conception, yet not all the way to the Simple Culpability View.

discussing the different ways in which an individual can be morally responsible for a wrong. But, further, once we set out this framework and apply it to self-defense cases, the core disagreement between the two views becomes stark and, simultaneously, we see that a new, third option presents itself. This third option—the Evidence-Relative View for liability attribution—is located conceptually between the Simple Culpability View and the Agency View, with clear lines of distinction from each. From this vantage, it is better able to handle many of the cases that give each of the other views trouble, it is able to make a key distinction between two different kinds of excuse, and it better accords with our moral intuitions for defensive harm more broadly.

To properly present the view, first consider a way of distinguishing three different senses in which an act can be wrong. We saw above that the Agency View holds that a person can be acting permissibly according to all the evidence available to her, yet, if it turns out that she is mistaken and actually impermissibly harms someone, she can be liable, on that view. We do better to explain this via a distinction regarding the different ways or manners in which an act can be wrong. This distinction is based on an assumption that there is no single, univocal way to understand the concept "wrong" but that there can be different *senses* to understanding moral permissibility. As Derek Parfit famously explains:

> Some acts of ours would be *wrong* in the *fact-relative* sense just when this act would be wrong in the ordinary sense if we knew all of the morally relevant facts... and [others would be] *wrong* in the *belief-relative* sense just when this act would be wrong in the ordinary sense if our beliefs about these facts were true... and [others would be] *wrong* in the *evidence-relative* sense just when this act would be wrong in the ordinary sense if we believed what the available evidence gives us decisive reasons to believe, and these beliefs were true.[3]

I follow Parfit's terminology and divide senses of wrong into these three categories of belief-relative, evidence-relative, and fact-relative wrongs.[4] Using this language we can say, for example, that the Agency View holds that one can be acting permissibly in the evidence-relative sense, yet still turn out

---

[3] Derek Parfit, *On What Matters, Vol. 1* (New York: Oxford University Press, 2011): 150–51.
[4] I am neutral as to whether this division is exclusive. Some have recently tried to expand this three-way division. See, for example, David Rodin's paper, "Authority and Determination-Relative Wrongdoing," delivered at the 2015 Annual Oxford ELAC Conference held jointly with the Stockholm Centre for the Ethics of War and Peace.

to be acting impermissibly in the fact-relative sense. We then see that the Agency View contends that liability tracks violations of these fact-relative norms, so long as the individual engaged in a given act voluntarily and (following McMahan's version) it was a foreseeably "risk-imposing" act. But even that, notice, simply means that the act was all-things-considered evidence-relative permissible, but that the agent herself could, in theory, foresee that there was still a risk that it could possibly turn out to be fact-relative impermissible. (We will get much deeper into these kinds of complexities later in the chapter.)

The corollaries of this three-way normative division of wrongs are many and include, for example, evidence-relative permissibility as opposed to fact-relative permissibility, evidence-relative obligation and fact-relative obligation, and countless other derivations I will use frequently.[5] Of course, most of the time and for the large majority of human action, an act is permissible in all three ways at the same time (or impermissible in all three ways at the same time). It is only when they "come apart" in some way or another that we have these difficult cases. But recognizing that an act's different senses of permissibility do occasionally come apart in these ways is crucial for us to get to the core of what we think proper moral responsibility for liability attribution should entail. And that's exactly what happens in, for example, *Dignitary & Guest* and other similar cases, as I'll explore below.

2.2.2 Is Wrong Univocal?

First, however, we must get clear on an important point regarding what these three distinctions themselves mean for morality. Some writers think that one of these three senses of wrong is the "correct" view of wrong-doing or the dominant view, or some such other way of preferring one sense over the other in terms of which is "actually" the right way to understand wrong. That is, some contend that one of these ways of understanding normative

---

[5] I will employ all of the following terminology: evidence-relative wrong, evidence-relative permissible, evidence-relative justified, evidence-relative impermissible; and the like, and all of the same derivations for both fact-relative and belief-relative permissibility. Note: that the proper usage is to say that "act X is evidence-relative permissible" and, so forth, as opposed to "act X is evidence-relative*ly* permissible" and the like. I find this to be the correct usage of the terminology because we'd say that an act is permissible relative to the evidence; hence, the act is evidence-relative permissible. That is, the evidence-relative part of "evidence-relative permissible" is not an adjective modifier on all of permissibility—rather, evidence-relative permissibility is one kind of permissibility as opposed to another kind, such as "fact-relative permissibility."

right and wrong *just is* the ordinary sense of moral obligation and the other senses are dependent upon it; that it has logical priority over the other two or that one is the fundamental sense of obligation. These writers think that one of these senses is the *correct* way to understand moral wrong-doing and ascribing moral right or wrong to acts in the other senses is either simply mistaken or, even if descriptively helpful, does not capture the foundational sense of moral obligation.[6]

Michael Zimmerman, for example, argues that "ought" should be understood in only one distinct sense.[7] He finds the claim that there could be multiple distinct senses of moral obligation for a particular case from different perspectives "strains credulity."[8] Zimmerman argues that there is only "one kind of overall moral obligation" and therefore, "only one corresponding ought."[9] Those who share Zimmerman's view on the univocality of moral obligation usually base it on the felt need to be able to give an unequivocal answer to someone, in any case or circumstance, when one asks, "What ought I to do?"[10] Imagine a person, Jill, is in a scenario whereby her act's permissibility conceptually comes apart in the ways outlined above by Parfit. Presume that we have the "God's eye view" of the scenario and she asks us, "Is my act morally permissible?" Zimmerman demands that it is foolish of us to say to her, "Well, it is permissible in one sense, but impermissible in another sense." He thinks that will be no help to her. He thinks that she wants to know, "Yes, but what ought I *really* do? Should I do this act or not?"[11]

I respect Zimmerman's point here, so far as it goes. However, I think it may miss the descriptively helpfully point of the distinction. Parfit objects with those who think that one of these views of moral permissibility is dominant

---

[6] An example of a writer who holds this view is Gideon Rosen. See Rosen, "Culpability and Ignorance," *Proceedings of the Aristotelian Society* 103, no. 1 (2003): 61–84. And Michael Zimmerman, *Living with Uncertainty: The Moral Significance of Ignorance* (Cambridge: Cambridge University Press, 2010). Zimmerman, "Moral Responsibility and Ignorance," *Ethics* 107, no. 3 (1997): 410–26. Also see, Zimmerman, "Is Moral Obligation Objective or Subjective?" *Utilitas* 18, no. 4 (2006): 329–61. Examples of those who think there is no priority between different senses of ought and that morality is not univocal in this way are Parfit (see *On What Matters*) and W. D. Ross, *Foundations of Ethics* (Oxford: Clarendon Press, 1939).

[7] Zimmerman, *Living with Uncertainty*, 5.

[8] Ibid., 7.

[9] Ibid.

[10] Zimmerman gives an answer to the question. He calls it the Prospective View of moral obligation which he defines as follows: "An agent ought to perform an act if and only if it is probably the best option that he has." (*Living with Uncertainty*, 6).

[11] I am here basing this case of Jill on one of Zimmerman's examples, but am modifying the case to fit Parfit's terminology. I am also over-simplifying the case, quite radically—Zimmerman and Parfit both explore far more complicated variations than I will in this chapter.

over the other and that such efforts to point to one sense of wrong as prior to the others are hopeless. Again, on Parfit's view, there simply is no univocal way to understand wrong—none is logically dominant over the other—there *just are* these different conceptions or senses or ways of being wrong that sometimes come apart for certain actions. As Parfit writes, "We ought to use 'wrong' in all these senses. If we don't draw these distinctions, or we only use some of these senses, we shall fail to recognize some important truths, and we and others may needlessly disagree."[12]

For my purposes here, this disagreement over whether moral obligation is univocal need not trouble us. The reason is that I am in search of the proper basis of responsibility needed for liability and this debate over moral obligation is, in fact, much broader than the narrower question of liability. Determining in what sense we should understand moral obligation more closely relates to the task of what the proper sense of culpability should be. Presuming we reject the Simple Culpability View, as I do, then I need not take a hard stand here on the proper way to understand culpability. Ultimately, I find Zimmerman's arguments for his Prospective View of moral obligation to be highly persuasive.[13] However, I think Parfit is correct in that, at least *conceptually*, these other senses of wrong-doing remain—that much, anyway, is hard to deny—and that morality has this room within it to make these kinds of distinctions. And that is all I need for my project here: these different ways of *conceiving* of wrong. Thus, for the purposes of presenting the Evidence-Relative View for liability, I will agree with Parfit and assume a non-univocal sense of wrong for the remainder of this book.[14] Note, however, that one could hold that one of these ways is the "correct" way to understand "ought" over the others, and my arguments throughout this chapter for liability attribution would still stand. Nothing critical to my project (in this chapter or in the book as a whole) hinges on whether wrong-doing is to be understood as univocal or not. Thus, while attracted to the Prospective View (for reasons that will become obvious below and dovetail nicely with my view of liability), I bracket the debate over wrong-doing's actual univocality at present and can remain officially agnostic on the matter.

---

[12] Parfit, *On What Matters*, 151.
[13] Gideon Rosen's work ("Culpability and Ignorance") also offers arguments for conclusions on this point very similar to Zimmerman's.
[14] A full defense of the non-univocality of our understanding of wrong takes us far beyond the scope of this work in this book. For Parfit's defense of the non-univocality of wrong, see *On What Matters*, 150–72.

To see why this bracketing is easy to do for my project, return to Jill, who is asking, "OK, but what ought I do?" Let's imagine her act is permissible in the fact-relative sense, but impermissible in the evidence-relative sense. If she then asks us "What ought I do?"—and we had the God's eye view—all we need to do is explain the evidence to her that she is missing that is creating the gap between the senses of her permissions. That is, we would not say, "Well your act is permissible in this way, but impermissible in this way." We would, rather, say, "Well, the evidence available to you makes you think that your act is permissible—that is, to you it is evidence-relative permissible. But it is, in fact, fact-relative impermissible, and if you knew this evidence X, Y, and Z—which we have now just told you—your act will suddenly become evidence-relative impermissible because we just changed your evidentiary standing to the act. So, of course, what you ought to do is R; that is, that which is fact-relative permissible." This is why Zimmerman and others' objection that we need to be able to give one "answer" to someone's question of "ought" is not going to bother us here for liability attribution. Perhaps Zimmerman is correct that one of these ways of understanding wrong is somehow proper over the other—but simply being able to conceptually distinguish them is all that is needed to ascribe liability in the manner I propose. Since I am dealing with evidentiary questions of permission that weigh on liability attribution, if one is ever in a position to *tell someone* else of the separation between his or her fact-relative and evidence-relative permissibility, then that just means one is in a position to *change* the person's evidentiary standing to the act. Doing so would thereby change the person's evidence-relative norms. In questions over our responsibility for our actions, none of us, sadly, *ever* stand in a God's-eye view; we always have only a better or worse evidence-relative perspective on our acts. This will become clearer as we analyze the three senses of wrong through particular cases. Further, as I'll explain below in section 2.2.3, we'll see why we can bypass the debate between Parfit and Zimmerman when we see that *all it means* to say someone has evidence-relative permissibility is that the person *takes himself* to have fact-relative permissibility, and to do so correctly according to the evidence available to him.[15]

---

[15] It is a further question whether to say that someone has belief-relative permissibility just means that the person believes that they have evidence-relative and fact-relative permissibility—I think this is the case in the vast majority of human experiences—but it could be, rarely, that someone actually knows they don't have proper evidence for a false belief they have, yet they believe it anyway. See section 2.2.3.

2.2.3 Understanding the Three Senses

So, all that is needed for my purposes in this book is to, at least, conceptually recognize these three ways in which an act may be *understood* as wrong.[16] Consider the following three stories which give us pictures of these three different conceptions of wrong-doing.

Bill

Bill has evidence available to him that if he backs his car out of the driveway, he will run over his neighbor's child. But, even though Bill has accessible evidence for this (say he can clearly see the child in the rear-view mirror as he begins to back out, or he can recall that the child was behind the car right before he got in), Bill somehow comes to believe that his backing up the car will cause no such harm to anyone and, thus, based on that belief he further believes that it is thereby morally permissible to back up his car. Bill thus proceeds to back up his car and kills the neighbor's child.

Ethan

Ethan does not have any good evidence that if he backs his car out of the driveway he will run over the neighbor's child. He cannot see anyone in the mirrors, which he checks diligently, and there was no one behind him when he got in the car. Imagine Ethan is particularly careful about checking all his surroundings anytime he backs his car out, this case included. The child discretely snuck up behind the car after Ethan got in, completely out of the purview of his sensory perception. Consequently, Ethan believes that backing up his car will not harm anyone and, based on that belief, he further believes that it would thereby be morally permissible to back up his car. Unfortunately, the neighbor's child was in fact behind the car and when Ethan backs up his car, he kills the child.

Morton

Morton is in an identical situation to Bill. Morton, however, correctly believes due to the evidence accessible to him that his backing up the car will run over the neighbor's child, and he believes that it would thereby be a morally impermissible act. Morton decides to back up the car anyway and

---

[16] And, of course, to even *present* the Prospective View as Zimmerman does (and other competing views do) we must be able to at least recognize the different *conceptions* of wrong identified by Parfit's terminology above.

he kills the child, just as he believed he would and had evidence that he would and as he believed would be wrong to do.

In all three stories, backing up the car is fact-relative impermissible; all three men actually commit a fact-relative impermissible act: killing an innocent child. But from that similarity onward the cases come apart for they were each wrong in importantly distinct ways. Recall Parfit's definitions of the different senses of wrong above. Bill's action was fact-relative impermissible because in actual fact his act killed the innocent child. Killing an innocent child, *ceteris paribus*, is wrong. Bill's action was *also* evidence-relative impermissible because there was evidence accessible to Bill such that his action was going to kill the child. That is, the evidence available to Bill gave him (or *could have* reasonably given him) decisive reason to believe that his act was fact-relative impermissible, and therefore it was evidence-relative impermissible. Bill's action was, surprisingly, belief-relative permissible, however, for he believed, despite the evidence in front of him, that his action would not cause any wrongful harm and was thereby permissible. If this belief *were* true and, in fact, had his action not caused any harm, then the act would not be fact-relative impermissible; hence, since Bill held this false belief about the fact-permissibility of his action, his act was belief-relative permissible.

Notice that in determining whether Bill had belief-relative permissibility for the act it does not matter *how* Bill came to have the belief that his action would not commit a wrongful harm. Whether it was by incredible powers of self-deception, utter epistemic negligence and disregard for the evidence, some terrible mental illness, or villainous mind-control, it is irrelevant for determinations of belief-relative permissibility. Regardless of how he was able to form a false belief in spite of the evidence to contrary, he did so.[17] Thus, since he *held the belief* that his act was fact-relative permissible (even though it actually was not), his act was belief-relative permissible.

Ethan's action, on the other hand, was both belief-relative permissible *and* evidence-relative permissible. He had no reasonable way of coming to believe (no reasonable access to evidence) that his action would, in fact, cause wrongful harm.[18] That is, he had no evidence that his act would be fact-relative

---

[17] How one comes to have a belief, however, will of course be critical to the determination of one's *responsibility* for holding that belief, as I'll discuss below. It will also be critical, as the astute reader is likely already imagining, when we turn to soldiers killing one another in war.

[18] There are certainly ways Ethan *could* have come to know this, but his action did not demand that he take investigative epistemic steps significantly beyond those that he took. That is, he met his moral

impermissible—as it turned out it was since his action killed the innocent child. Because Ethan had accessible evidence to reasonably conclude that his act was fact-relative permissible, his act was evidence-relative permissible. Of course, had his evidence been veracious, and had the resulting beliefs he held been true, then his act would have been fact-relative permissible. But, because his evidence and beliefs conflicted with the facts of the case, Ethan's evidence-relative permissibility (and simultaneous belief-relative permissibility) for the act "came apart" from his fact-relative permissibility.

Finally, there is Morton. Morton is a moral monster. Morton's action was both fact-relative impermissible and evidence-relative impermissible, just as Bill's, but his act was also belief-relative impermissible because he also held the belief that his act was impermissible. That is, his act was *in fact* wrong, he was *able* to know it was wrong, and he *did* know it was wrong. In *Morton*, the three senses of wrong did not come apart. Interestingly, Morton, unlike Bill, did fulfill his epistemic obligations in this case in rightly coming to conclude that backing up his car would be wrong. But then, of course, he failed in his moral obligation to not do that which he knew it was wrong to do. We will return to this important difference between these cases below.

Before moving on, allow me to make a couple obvious but important points for what follows. All three actors—Bill, Ethan, and Morton—committed fact-relative impermissible acts, yet our moral judgment of all three of them in terms of culpability or blameworthiness is quite different. The easiest case is Morton. He is clearly culpably wrong and committed by far the gravest moral wrong. The *Bill* case is more complicated and the most difficult to assess. Most of us will want to know *how* on earth he came to have his false belief that his action was fact-relative permissible since it was clearly not so through the evidence available to him. If Bill was under villainous mind-control that forced him to form his false belief, say, we would fully excuse him of any moral culpability and blameworthiness.[19] But the reason we would do so is because, at that

---

epistemic obligations in regard to the evidence available to him. What those epistemic obligations are, then, become central to a proper understanding of evidence-relative permissibility. I will discuss this at length below in section 2.2.4.

[19] Note: above, I mentioned he would have belief-relative permissibility however he came to form the belief. Technically that is true. But I'm not sure that if a belief is formed via villainous mind-control that Bill even *has* formed the belief. That is, I'm not sure if it can be properly said that Bill even "possesses" the belief that his backing up the car wouldn't harm anyone under the circumstances or whether he would be simply controlled like an unthinking automaton. Thankfully, outside of Descartes' Evil Demon and Thomson's mind-controlling murderous villains and the like, we don't have to deal with mind-control too often in the real world.

point, we would not consider the act to even be his own in any proper sense of the word. That is, it would not be his agency that was responsible for the fact-relative wrong-doing. For defensive harm and liability discussions, of course, this will align nicely with the Otsukian objection given in chapter 1 against the Nonresponsible Account. If Bill was under the mind-control of a villain who was forcing him to use his body (or his brain) a certain way to come to the false belief he did, then he does not seem relevantly different than if his arms and legs were literally forced to move via invisible string like a human marionette doll. Someone in that situation is just as much a bystander in relation to the impending harm his body is about to deliver as Falling Man is to the harm his body will impose on Trapped.

Yet, if Bill was somehow able to force himself by choice of will to have that false belief—if that's even possible—then we'd be far less forgiving and, in fact, hold him just as culpably wrong as Morton.[20] We'd also hold Bill culpable if he came to have the false belief through sheer epistemic negligence—a complete disregard of the evidence before him.[21] This latter point will turn out to be crucial in my exposition of the new view I am offering on responsibility for liability, below. Ethan, notice, although committing the identical fact-relative impermissible act as the other two, is fully excused from being morally blameworthy because of his constrained epistemic vantage. I tend to think that cases like Bill are quite rare in the real world.[22] I imagine that cases like Morton are also rare, but, in my view, they do occur.[23] Tragically, cases like Ethan happen with mournful regularity in this imperfect world

---

[20] I set aside questions of whether such a thing is possible as outside the scope of this book. For my purposes, we simply need to have the conceptual categories clear. Of course, the question itself is fascinating. This is the question of "doxastic involuntarism" and whether it is possible to ever have any kind of control over our beliefs. For a good collection of views on this debate, see Matthias Steup, ed., *Knowledge, Truth, and Duty: Essays on Epistemic Justification, Responsibility, and Virtue* (New York: Oxford University Press, 2001). See Carl Ginet, "Deciding to Believe," in *Knowledge, Truth, and Duty*, for an argument that we do have some level of control over our beliefs.

[21] I will examine this in section 2.4.3 as a "Failure of Due Diligence."

[22] Again, many think they are *impossible*, at least on the strong "epistemic voluntarism" reading wherein one just forces oneself to believe something contrary to evidence available to them through sheer force of will. However, there are far more difficult (and presumably more common) Bill-like cases where one has access to some evidence that an act is fact-relative impermissible but does not complete the required epistemic diligence we think is reasonable relative to the importance of the act in question and, thereby, comes to the wrong conclusion in their beliefs about the act (i.e., they believe that the act is fact-relative permissible, even though they did have access to evidence that could have (correctly) convinced them otherwise). I will discuss such cases at some length below in section 2.4 on Moral Epistemic Contextualism.

[23] Some disagree and think that one can never knowingly do something she believes is wrong and that Morton is impossible. They hold that a person's very act of doing act Z reveals that she doesn't *really* think that Z is wrong. This is a much larger debate that goes far beyond the scope of my intentions to propose a

and these are the kinds of cases that will be central for my account of liability, and must be dealt with for any account.

These three stories also help illuminate a common point of confusion about the three senses of wrong. This confusion plagues these discussions, so it's good to get clear on it here.[24] To say that person X has belief-relative permissibility for an act *just means* that X believes she has fact-relative permissibility. That belief itself may turn out to be true or false. And to say that X has evidence-relative permissibility for an act *just means* that X has evidence such that it is epistemically correct for her to believe that she has fact-relative permissibility for that act.[25] Again, in the vast majority of cases in real life, these three senses of permissibility do not come apart. Thus, usually when X has belief-relative permissibility and evidence-relative permissibility for a given act, her beliefs that (and her evidence for that belief that) an act is fact-relative permissible are correct and she does, in fact, have fact-relative permissibility. This awkward and perhaps unnecessary sounding clarification will be important below in dealing with a common objection which contends that one can have belief-relative permissibility but still "know" that her action will commit a fact-relative impermissible action. (We'll also see this objection as particularly important in chapters 3 and 4 as it relates to soldiers participating in just and unjust wars.) This is confused, of course, because if one *knows* that her action will commit a fact-relative impermissible action, then she does not, in fact, have belief-relative permissibility after all.

---

new account of liability. But, to be unfairly brief, I find this line of thinking to be simply nonsensical and wildly outside the bounds of actual human experience. It certainly seems *possible* for people to do an act which they take to be wrong. To believe otherwise relegates all acts of evil throughout human history to *Bill*-like cases. And it is hard to fathom how the Turkish soldiers tossing babies in the air and impaling them in Dostoevsky's *The Brothers Karamazov* could have possibly believed there was no moral prohibition on their action. Perhaps someone will claim that people who commit such heinous atrocities must be mentally ill to the extent that they truly can't "tell right from wrong." If that is true, then it's possible they do not believe their actions to be wrong when they commit them. Our first response, after all, when we hear of the most vile of acts is to claim that the given actor must be "crazy." But even if we can set aside many of history's greatest evil cases to such an explanation, it is hard to believe that *every* single case was committed by someone so out of his or her mind as to not be able to form a correct thought about the moral status of his or her actions. Has there never been one "rational Nazi" who knowingly committed a wrong? Or, if one still is not convinced, just consider banal, everyday wrong-doings—not grave evils. Certainly, there has been a case in human history where someone knows it would be wrong to lie to his mother, and yet he does it anyway. I think most of us, if we are but honest with ourselves, can admit that we have done things that we knew were wrong, yet did them anyway.

[24] I'm genuinely surprised how often the kind of confusion I describe here occurs in discussions among philosophers. I've heard this mistake at nearly every conference I've attended over the past five years or so where the evidence-relative distinction has come up. My thanks to, and camaraderie with, Susanne Burri on our shared frustration on these persistent confusions.

[25] What standards we use for "epistemically correct" will depend on the moral importance of the act, as I will explain in section 2.4.

2.3. The Evidence-Relative View

I propose that liability should hinge on evidence-relative norms; that the violation of evidence-relative norms as part of posing an unjust threat is the proper basis of the moral responsibility required for liability attribution to defensive harm. That is, the wrongful harm to be averted must be evidence-relative impermissible to the actor committing the wrongful harm in order for him or her to be liable to defensive harm. I call this the Evidence-Relative View for liability attribution. Because it requires responsibility for liability, it is a version of the Responsible Account for permissible defensive harm. Yet it is importantly distinct from both the Simple Culpability View and the Agency View. As I will show, it is thereby able to thread the needle between the two and avoid many of the problematic issues that arise for each of these alternative views.

2.3.1 A Tertium Quid

As seen, alternative versions of the Responsible Account define the minimal responsibility required for liability in one of two ways. On the Simple Culpability View, the minimal required responsibility must be robust; it equates responsibility with culpability. On the Agency View, the minimal required responsibility can be anemic; mere "bare agent responsibility" can be enough for liability. The Evidence-Relative View is markedly different from both of these alternative views of the required responsibility for liability. It differs from the Agency View in what will be rather obvious ways. The Agency View, as mentioned above, holds that one can be acting in ways that are evidence-relative permissible, yet still be liable. The Evidence-Relative View's divergence from the Simple Culpability View, however, is more subtle, yet equally important. Rather than culpability, it holds that the minimal required responsibility for liability is committing an act which is evidence-relative impermissible. As will be shown below, we usually hold that culpability tracks closely to evidence-relative norms, but not always. There are cases when one may commit an evidence-relative impermissible act yet be excused from culpability, as I'll show below. The view's distinction from both alternative views gives it conceptual normative advantages over each. It splits the middle between the views and gives us an attractive *tertium quid*.

Recall the case of *Dignitary & Guest*. All three views—the Simple Culpability View, the Agency View, and the Evidence-Relative View—hold that Dignitary is committing a fact-relative impermissible act when she pulls out her sidearm to shoot Guest. This is because, despite appearances to the contrary, Guest is not actually threatening her with unjust harm. The Simple Culpability View holds that she is not liable, because she is not culpable for this unjust harm she will deliver to Guest. She is not culpable because she has been deceived by Villain into thinking that Guest is unjustly threatening her; her epistemic conditions excuse her culpability.[26] The Agency View, however, holds that she is liable to defensive harm from Guest because she is responsible for the unjust harm by voluntarily committing an act that runs a significant risk of actually harming someone despite her relevant evidence. That is, the act is "risk-imposing," to use McMahan's terms: there is sufficient risk that shooting someone may, indeed, impose unjust harm on someone—even when one believes they would be imposing just harm. I showed in chapter 1 why we should find it implausible on any version of the Responsible Account that Dignitary should be liable *over* Guest since the two are morally symmetrical in their standing to the unjust harm in question. We also saw in chapter 1 that this symmetry is complex and is not adequately explained by either view. Further, the Agency View's reliance on the risk-imposing nature of Dignitary shooting in apparent self-defense as the basis of responsibility is both too thin a conception of responsibility for liability to turn on and, worse, it misses that Guest is symmetrically engaging in a risk-imposing activity himself by being armed and knowingly deploying potentially fact-relative impermissible harm.[27]

---

[26] Notice, when I discuss an unjust harm against someone, I will not speak in fact-relative, evidence-relative, or belief-relative terms with regard to that unjust harm. This could easily be done, of course (e.g., fact-relative unjust harm, belief-relative unjust harm). But there is no need for such terminology and distinction. The reason: when someone is wrongly harmed, all that matters for the questions pursued here is that the person was, in fact, wrongly harmed. That is, fact-relative unjust harm is all that matters for our moral reasoning with regard to defensive harm aimed at blocking an unjust harm. If a given harm appears to be, on the evidence available, unjust ("evidence-relative unjust harm") but turns out to be fact-relative just imposition of harm, then no wrongful harm is actually delivered. Now, this mistaken evidence for the justice of a given harm may, indeed, lead someone to act in evidence-relative or fact-relative permissible and impermissible ways. But that can all be captured in terms of their evidence-relative norms for behavior (e.g., if a harm appears evidence-relative unjust, when in fact it was fact-relative just, and a person then defends themselves against the evidence-relative unjust harm, we can say, simply, that they behaved evidence-relative permissibly). Thus, applying the evidence-relative and fact-relative standards to the justice of harm itself thereby becomes redundant. All the work needed can be done by focusing on the sense of permissibility for a given act.

[27] And, recall, we can switch Guest from being armed to serendipitously finding a side-arm in the nearby holster of a guard, if we must. And it is implausible that such a small, arbitrary difference

In *Dignitary & Guest*, the Evidence-Relative View agrees with the Simple Culpability View: Dignitary is not liable to harm. This is because her act which is posing the unjust harm to Guest is not evidence-relative impermissible. She is acting permissibly according to her evidence-relative norms; hence, she is not liable. Neither is Guest liable, of course, when he responds with defensive harm himself, for he too is acting permissibly according to his evidence-relative norms.[28]

Consider a contrasting case, such as *Coerced Killer*. In that case, Sam committed a fact-impermissible act by killing Sarah and, again, all three views of responsibility under debate agree on this point. But his act was *also* evidence-relative impermissible. Sam knew that Sarah was innocent, was nonliable, and should not be killed. The Simple Culpability View, perhaps surprisingly, holds that Sam is not liable because he is not culpable for the killing; his extreme coercion excuses his culpability. I showed, in chapter 1, why we should find it implausible on any version of the Responsible Account that Sam is not liable to defensive harm from Sarah. This is because even *if* the coercion he is under fully excuses his culpability, we still think he is morally asymmetrical from Sarah in an important way for consciously choosing to impose knowingly wrongful harm on her—even if excused and non-blameworthy harm. The Agency View, of course, holds him liable because he voluntarily committed a wrong which he knew was risk-imposing and not only could, but *would*, impose fact-relative impermissible harm.

In this case, the Evidence-Relative View I'm offering agrees with the Agency View that Sam is liable. This is because Sam violated his evidence-relative norms in his killing of Sarah. Even though his culpability may be excused, he still knowingly does something which he knows will wrong another. So, in these two cases, we see the key strength of the Evidence-Relative View over the competing views for liability attribution. Unlike the competing views, it gets both cases *right*. That is, its conclusions accord with our reasoned moral intuitions on the cases and avoid the problems each case poses for one of the other views.

---

should matter morally for his or Guest's moral standing and resulting liability. They both engage in "risk-imposing" activities in the way McMahan intends it.

[28] Below I call cases like this—where two people are morally symmetrically aligned in their nonliability yet each is posing an unjust harm to the other—Tragedies, as a technical term of art. I discuss this below in section 2.6. This Tragedy way of understanding cases of symmetrical defensive harm is another benefit of the Evidence-Relative View.

2.3.2 Two Kinds of Excuse

These cases demonstrate how the Evidence-Relative View makes a key distinction, and is even *able* to make such a distinction, between two kinds of culpability mitigating excuses. This is one of its primary advantages over the Simple Culpability View. The Evidence-Relative View allows us to distinguish between epistemic excuses and coercion excuses. It allows for a sharp distinction between them which, importantly, treats these excuses differently in our assessment of moral responsibility and the resulting moral asymmetry between actors. Properly speaking, in one sense the Evidence-Relative View is not even interested in epistemic excuses for, while relevant to the mitigation of culpability and blameworthiness, there is no liability attributed when one has a full epistemic excuse. This is because having a full epistemic excuse just means that one did not violate the evidence-relative norms governing his behavior. And if one does not in any way violate their evidence-relative norms, then one is not liable; just as Bystander is not.

I find this to be a highly plausible and powerful feature of the Evidence-Relative View. Traditionally these two kinds of excuse are (almost) always run together. In both cases just given, it is assumed that the perpetrator who holds such excuse has their culpability mitigated to whatever degree the excuse warrants—possibly full mitigation. So, on the Simple Culpability View, both kinds of excuse could, and in many cases do, excuse liability. (Recall that liability comes in degrees, so whatever degree the excuse mitigates culpability would be the same degree to which the excuse mitigates liability, for this view. This is important.) The Evidence-Relative View, however, allows for these two kinds of excuses to come apart in conceptually distinct ways, by which they can have different implications for moral responsibility and, thereby, for liability attribution. Notice: on my view, both coercive excuses and epistemic excuses still have the same effect on culpability and blameworthiness that most of us take them to have. Yet they have different effects on liability, which is intuitively quite appealing.

There is more work here to be done for, just as the Evidence-Relative View has these gains, it also results in some difficult cases of its own. Moreover, the view faces a variety of immediate objections; some illusory, some significant. But there is also much more to say of the advantages this view brings to discussion over defensive harm. I will address most of these points in chapter 3. In so doing I will lay the groundwork for how the Evidence-Relative View becomes a particularly good fit for a revisionist just war theory, which will be addressed in chapters 4 and 5. First, however, I must explain how and *why* we think that someone's failing to behave justly according to available evidence can have moral consequence as well as the ways in which different moral contexts affect our judgment of one's epistemic duties.

2.4. Moral Epistemic Contextualism

Before going further, then, let me show what the view is not and explain an understanding of moral epistemic duties central to the view. First, obviously but crucially, my proposal for liability attribution is *not* a Belief-Relative View. This is a simple but critical confusion. Such a view would hold that liability should only hinge on the violation of belief-relative duties in posing an unjust threat to another person. I am not interested in such a view. Rather, I think people can be said to be properly responsible (which can result in liability attribution) for acts they commit under the evidence they have available to them, *regardless* of whether they then come to the correct conclusions for their actual beliefs, given that evidence. There are many reasons to reject the Belief-Relative View for liability attribution. Some of these will become most apparent when I apply the Evidence-Relative View to war in chapters 3 and 4. But I think the best reason is simply that there is a moral duty to ensure, to some reasonable standard, that one's beliefs line up with one's evidence when one's beliefs affect how one treats (or could treat) others. Allow me to explain.

2.4.1 Moral Duties to Believe Rightly

Whether someone *believes* his act is right or wrong can be separated from whether he *should* so believe that his act is right or wrong, given the evidence available to him. The question of whether there are moral reasons to believe in accordance with proper evidence is not a new one. William Clifford famously argued, in 1877, that "it is wrong always, everywhere, and for anyone, to believe anything upon insufficient evidence."[29] But the notion that we can be morally responsible for failing to have certain true beliefs—responsible for our ignorance—is a complex claim. It presupposes that there are certain

[29] W. K. Clifford, "The Ethics of Belief," *Contemporary Review* 34 (1877): 1–10.

duties regarding our belief regulation, that we can fail to meet these duties, and that at times these duties can be moral and not merely epistemic.[30] For the Evidence-Relative View to avoid the pitfalls of the Belief-Relative View, it must be true that if one fails to meet these moral duties to meet certain epistemic investigative standards for some act in question, then that failing can be a proper basis of assigning moral responsibility resulting in liability. Call this failing to come to the correct belief when it was reasonably possible for a person to come to the correct belief, given the evidence available to him, a Failure of Due Diligence. When someone commits a Failure of Due Diligence we can, depending on the context of the case and the act in question, assign moral responsibility for that failing. Depending on what epistemic standard is in play for a given action, that moral responsibility can be great enough to result in liability attribution. A Failure of Due Diligence will not always be a moral failing, but it *can be* a moral failing if it results in false beliefs that then lead one to act in a way that treats others unjustly. Just what epistemic standard towards one's beliefs about a given action we think is fair and proper depends on the *kind* of act in question.

This discussion of changing epistemic standards and correlative investigative demands, dependent upon the particular context of belief in question, brings the view known as Epistemic Contextualism to mind.[31] Many versions of Epistemic Contextualism argue that the standards for knowledge shift depending on the epistemic context of a given belief.[32] There is a view that applies this aspect of Epistemic Contextualism to our moral beliefs in the way I'm suggesting here for the Evidence-Relative View, articulated particularly well by Alexander Guerrero.[33] Call this view Moral Epistemic Contextualism. Although it will take some space to formulate properly, the basic idea is simple and intuitive. Most of us upon reflection hold that, as Alexander Guerrero writes, "when making certain sorts of decisions, or

---

[30] See Alexander Guerrero, "Don't Know, Don't Kill," *Philosophical Studies* 136, no. 1 (2007): 59–97.

[31] Such as, most prominently, the version of Epistemic Contextualism espoused by Keith DeRose. See DeRose, *The Case for Contextualism: Knowledge, Skepticism, and Context*, Vol. 1 (Oxford: Clarendon Press, 2009). "Contextualism and Knowledge Attributions," *Philosophy and Phenomenological Research* 52 (1992): 913–29. "Assertion, Knowledge and Context," *The Philosophical Review* 111, no. 2 (2002): 167–203. For a good primer on this vast topic, see Patrick Rysiew, "Epistemic Contextualism," in *Stanford Encyclopedia of Philosophy*, edited by Edward N. Zalta (Stanford University 2020),http://plato.stanford.edu/entries/contextualism-epistemology/index.html.

[32] I am indebted to Guerrero, "Don't Know, Don't Kill," (particularly at 68) for applying this version of Epistemic Contextualism to my Evidence-Relative View for liability. I lean heavily on his work in that paper for the remainder of this discussion of Moral Epistemic Contextualism, as noted.

[33] Ibid.

preparing to take certain sorts of actions (or to refrain from taking certain actions), what is required of us from an epistemic point of view may be sensitive to what is at stake from a moral point of view."[34]

The view holds that the more morally significant a given act is that a particular belief will support, justify, or deem permissible, then the more stringent the epistemic demands are on that belief that must be met before one is justified to act on it. That is, the level at which the epistemic standard that must be met before one can be said to have met their epistemic duties and reasonably claim to be justified in believing a certain belief is directly correlative to the moral significance of the act that belief will justify.[35] As Guerrero notes, "Importantly, this 'increase' in the epistemic demands is required by *moral* considerations, not epistemic ones."[36] That is, there are certain moral epistemic demands that adhere to some of our beliefs based on the moral significance of the actions those beliefs will (or will not) justify. To demonstrate this, consider the following case:

Hunter & Photographer
Paul is a nature photographer and Mike is a deer-hunter. Both are independently in separate wildernesses but are in identical evidentiary circumstances: they each see something coming through the bushes toward them. They can't quite tell what it is yet based on the evidence available—it could be a deer, or it could be a human being. If it's a deer, Paul wants to take a picture of it, but he doesn't want to take a picture of a human hiker (he doesn't want to waste the film, say, on pictures of humans). To get the shot he wants (the deer emerging from the bushes) he'll have to decide now on whether to start snapping pictures. Similarly, in Mike's identical evidentiary circumstances, if it's a deer, he wants to shoot it, but he doesn't want to shoot a human (of course). Just like Paul, Mike's best chance to bag the deer is to shoot right before it emerges from the bushes and sees him and flees.[37]

---

[34] Guerrero, "Don't Know, Don't Kill," 68.
[35] Ibid.
[36] Ibid., 69. Guerrero notes that we may think the stakes move along another axis as well: "We might also think that what is at stake, morally, in believing p actually alters when one is justified in believing p, but I am primarily concerned just with the question of when one is justified in acting as if one is justified in believing p." Guerrero, "Don't Know, Don't Kill," 69.
[37] It must be imagined for this case to work that we still live in the long-ago, ancient era where actual film was required for photography. This case is my own, but Guerrero gives a helpful case of two different people inspecting a house—one for the purposes of demolition and the other for the purpose of census taking—that has a similar argumentative point.

In this case, Mike's epistemic investigative duties to figure out if it is a deer or a human are far greater than Paul's. Imagine that to figure out if it's a deer or human before taking their respective actions, they each yell out, "Who's there?" in a loud voice. After not hearing anything in response, Paul is convinced that it is a deer, and not a human, and thus begins shooting his camera. We may think Paul is (epistemically) justified in his belief that it is a deer at this point. But, if Mike took the same exact investigative action and reached the same conclusion and, thus, began shooting his gun into the bushes, we would *not* similarly think that he was justified in his belief that he was shooting at a deer. What is the basis for this difference? Clearly, the difference is found in the divergent *moral* significance of the action that the belief in question will license in each case.[38]

Guerrero defines Moral Epistemic Contextualism as follows:

> How much one is morally required to do from an epistemic point of view with regard to investigating some proposition p varies depending on the moral context—on what actions one's belief in p (or absence of belief in p) will license or be used to justify, morally, in some particular context.[39]

This view contends that whether one can act (morally) permissibly in taking her belief in p as (epistemically) justified, given the evidence available to them, depends on what action that belief will itself give permission to do. I find that some version of Moral Epistemic Contextualism is true, and its truth helps to significantly strengthen the Evidence-Relative View for liability attribution in many ways. If some form of Moral Epistemic Contextualism is true, then the epistemic duties that people have in various circumstances are driven, in part, by moral demands. And this means that a Failure of Due Diligence will mean different things depending on the morally imposed epistemic duties one is under in a given case. And if one fails to come to have a

---

[38] As Guerrero explains of such distinctions in these kinds of cases: "The obligations regarding epistemic investigation go up, precisely because of what is at stake, morally." "Don't Know, Don't Kill," 68.

[39] Guerrero, "Don't Know, Don't Kill," 69. Another important point is where the locus of contextualism falls. It is not on the belief itself, per se, but on when it is morally permissible for the individual holding the belief to act as if he or she is justified in the belief in order to act on it. As Guerrero explains: "Importantly, it is contextualism not about when it is true to say that some individual S knows or is justified in believing something or not, or whether that individual can justifiably assert p, but rather when it is morally appropriate for S to act as if S possesses justified true belief or certainty with regard to some issue." Ibid., 69.

proper belief—if one is ignorant about belief *p*—one can be responsible for that ignorance, and thereby liable.

2.4.2 Responsible for Ignorance

Guerrero has attempted to build a case for the possibility of culpable ignorance against the account offered by Gideon Rosen.[40] For the Evidence-Relative View, I do not need to go quite so far as claiming that one is *culpable* for his or her ignorance, just that one can be in some way morally responsible for it and that responsibility can be enough to result in liability, in at least some cases. Of course, on the Evidence-Relative View—unlike the alternative views—we need not quibble over degrees of responsibility per se. Instead, we must simply determine if a person has met whatever her epistemic duties are in relation to the moral significance of the belief in question driving the action under consideration. If she has not met her epistemic duties and thereby comes to a false belief, and that false belief is the basis for a fact-relative impermissible act, then she is, ipso facto, in violation of her evidence-relative norms. In that case, if the fact-impermissible act will harm someone, she is thereby liable to whatever harm is necessary and proportionate to block the impermissible harm resulting from that action.[41]

Guerrero provides a rich and elaborate case to give support to Moral Epistemic Contextualism that also provides a nice framework for discussing evidence-relative impermissibility as opposed to belief-relative impermissibility. It will turn out to be a very helpful case, so I will give a slightly modified and shortened version of it here.

Dogsitter
Dogsitter is taking care of a dog. Dogsitter falsely believes that dogs cannot feel pain, because he has read Descartes and believes that non-human animals are no more than automata, intricate machines, and that machines cannot feel pain. Assume that Dogsitter has evidence available to him that dogs are not automata and that they can feel pain—there are issues of

---

[40] This is opposed, in fact, to both Gideon Rosen and Zimmerman, cited above, who both hold, although in different ways, that one should not be held responsible for one's ignorance, whether factual or moral, as I'll discuss below in section 2.5 on Moral Ignorance.

[41] This is assuming, of course, that defensive harm could be deployed in a way that would block the harm.

Scientific American sitting on his coffee table that attest to this in exhaustive detail, he knows a friend who is an expert in animal psychology, he has himself witnessed many dogs exhibiting behavior that suggests they are in pain, and so on. He has even considered whether the views of a 17th century philosopher should be relied upon in this case, and has considered consulting some of the other evidence available to him with an eye to reconsidering his belief. Still, he hasn't done this, and hasn't pursued any of the evidence available to him, and he maintains his false belief. While taking care of the dogs he routinely has to roll a heavy wheelbarrow through the garage and into the yard. If he goes one route, the wheelbarrow will roll over the dog's tail while it sleeps in its bed. He could go another route, but it is slightly further, so he decides to go the route that will result in the heavy wheelbarrow rolling over the dog's tail, since it won't cause any permanent functional harm, and he believes that dogs do not feel pain. He goes this route, and the dog routinely appears to be in great pain due to the heavy wheelbarrow rolling over its tail. Still, Dogsitter tells himself, the dog is not actually feeling pain, and so Dogsitter takes himself to have no moral reason to go a different route next time. If he believed that the dog was feeling pain, he would take himself to have a moral reason to go a different route, and would do so. But he doesn't believe this, and so he doesn't go a different route.[42]

On the framework I am advancing, Dogsitter is committing an evidence-relative impermissible act by rolling the wheelbarrow over the dog's tail. (He is also, of course, committing a fact-relative impermissible act, but he is not committing a belief-relative impermissible act.) Moral Epistemic Contextualism holds that, given that his action is of some significant moral consequence if he is wrong, he is committing a moral failure in his failing to meet the investigative epistemic standard that obtains for his act. That is, he is committing a Failure of Due Diligence.

One upshot of this, for now, is that we see why belief-relative permissibility is a very poor basis for liability attribution. Imagine if liability *was* determined by (mere) adherence to belief-relative norms. Then there could be cases where someone believes an act Z is fact-relative permissible, even though given overwhelming evidence available to them and the moral significance of the act in question, they should obviously not so believe. And,

---

[42] This is a shortened and slightly modified version of the scenario presented by Guerrero in "Don't Know, Don't Kill."

in fact, as the overwhelming evidence would suggest, it turns out act Z is not fact-relative permissible. That is, we could have cases like *Bill*. And, as discussed above, presuming that Bill came to the belief through his own epistemic negligence (and not via some evil villain using mind control), we would not want to let Bill off the moral responsibility hook (and therefore off the liability hook). Yet a Belief-Relative View for liability attribution would do precisely that. Bill could not be held morally responsible on the Belief-Relative View for his act whatsoever, simply because he came to have this false belief in spite of the evidence available to him. His Failure of Due Diligence would be irrelevant to his responsibility, and thus also liability, on such a view.

This is important for several reasons for the Evidence-Relative View in comparison to the other accounts. The largest reason is simply that by not being a Belief-Relative View, it misses the vast majority of criticisms that have been leveled by writers against such a potential view. Part of this is terminological. McMahan, for example, spends time arguing against the plausibility of what he calls a "subjective" account of the responsibility criterion for liability.[43] Because he uses the term "subjective," it may be unclear whether, by use of this term, he intends an Evidence-Relative View or a Belief-Relative View. But we see the target of his attack is Francisco de Vitoria who held a "subjectivist" account of both permissibility and justification.[44] Since Vitoria held to something like a Belief-Relative View, then, for liability, we see that McMahan's discussion centers on that view and does not, usually, directly address the Evidence-Relative View.[45]

We left the actual cause of how Bill came to have his false belief open in the case above, however, and therefore it's not the best case for analysis for the Evidence-Relative View. And although Guerrero's *Dogsitter* case helps give us clarity on Moral Epistemic Contextualism and what I call a Failure of Due Diligence, it is not a case of defensive harm. So, here's a different case, then, wherein someone commits a Failure of Due Diligence and that failing is directly related to defensive harm. Consider:

---

[43] See McMahan, Killing in War, 60–65, as well as "Innocence, Self-Defense and Killing in War," *The Journal of Political Philosophy* 2, no. 3 (1994): 193–221. In later work, he occasionally used this nomenclature, and more recently has been using derivations of Parfit's delineation that I rely on.

[44] See Francisco de Vitoria, "On the Law of War," in *Political Writings*, edited by Anthony Pagden and Jeremy Lawrence (Cambridge: Cambridge University Press, 1991).

[45] Below and in chapters 3 and 4 I will explore some of the objections McMahan does offer that would be relevant to the Evidence-Relative View as they apply to war. Seth Lazar also offers several challenges to a "subjectivist" account (again meaning primarily a Belief-Relative View) in Seth Lazar, "War and Associative Duties" (D.Phil. diss., University of Oxford, 2009).

Caroline's Confusion
Caroline is sitting in her home quietly reading Steinbeck. Brian enters the house through the front door. He was told by Caroline's husband, Ralph, to stop by the house and pick-up Ralph's guitar, which he forgot and needs for their band practice that evening. Ralph thought that his wife Caroline was still out of town on a trip, but, unbeknownst to him, she has arrived home early. Ralph told Brian that no one was home, and that Brian should use the key under the front mat to unlock the door, go inside, and grab the guitar which was in the living room. Brian does so. Upon seeing a strange man enter the living room, Caroline is frightened that it may be an intruder and an attacker—and she believes as much. So, she grabs her nearby revolver and shoots Brian.[46]

Imagine that Brian could defend himself from Caroline's gunfire in this scenario with necessary and proportionate harm to block it. Is Caroline liable to defensive harm? I think so and the Evidence-Relative View coupled with Moral Epistemic Contextualism explains why.

Caroline did not meet her epistemic duties morality requires of her before shooting Brian. We have stipulated that she has the belief that Brian is an attacker unjustly threatening her life. Thus, her act was belief-relative permissible. However, it was not evidence-relative permissible. This is because there was evidence accessible to her to which she did not avail herself which would have corrected her false belief about her fact-relative permissibility to shoot Brian. This would have required her to take some simple investigative steps, such as calling out, "Who's there?" before shooting. Or, she could have realized that her husband Ralph did not know that she would arrive home early from her trip and perhaps that explained why there was an unexpected man entering her house. And so on. That she did *not* take any of these epistemic steps—that she did not live up to the epistemic standard we think would be required for such a morally significant and weighty act as shooting someone—means that she committed a Failure of Due Diligence. This is because although she had some evidence available to her that Brian may be an unjust attacker, she did not have sufficient epistemic justification for that belief, given the moral significance of the action she took based on that belief: shooting a human being. That is, we can rightfully hold her to a

---

[46] Note: this case is very loosely based on a similar story from an episode of the television series *The League*, entitled, "The Guest Bong."

higher standard of epistemic norms than she met, precisely because of the moral significance of her act. And because she had this failing (her Failure of Due Diligence) as part of posing unjust harm towards a nonliable person (Brian), we can hold her morally responsible for her mistake.[47] Hence, she would be liable to defensive harm on the Evidence-Relative View. We would say the same thing about Mike the deer-hunter in his belief that the thing coming through the bushes was a deer. But notice, of course, that we would *not* make the same claim of Paul the photographer coming to the very same conclusion based on the very same evidence. And that is because in Paul's case, he did meet the epistemic standards required of him to form the belief he did, because his epistemic standards were significantly lower. They were lower due to the act he was going to engage in because of that belief—taking a picture—being far less morally significant.

2.4.3 Failure of Due Diligence

It's important to get clear on when we think a Failure of Due Diligence obtains and when it does not. This will also help us further understand Moral Epistemic Contextualism and the key role it plays in the Evidence-Relative Account for liability attribution. Recall *Ethan* and our moral judgment of that case. Perhaps one would disagree with my excusal of Ethan's culpability for killing the neighbor's child based on his epistemic constraints. Perhaps, instead, we can imagine one would want to hold Ethan to *very* high epistemic standards for gathering evidence such that he should have got out of his car and checked it once more just to be extra sure that a random child hadn't snuck up behind. We can imagine the distraught parents of the killed child making these kinds of demands out of anger and grief. Perhaps, they would claim that Ethan should have got out of his car to check a second or even third time before backing out, or asked a friend to watch behind him while he slowly backed out, and so forth. But even if we were understanding of the parents' grief behind such demands, we also know that such demands would be clearly unreasonable. The reason is because we think an action like carefully backing one's car out of the driveway usually does not have a high likelihood of harming others and that, therefore, the efforts Ethan took to determine whether his action was permissible were proper, given

---

[47] That is, we can hold her responsible for her ignorance in this case.

the kind of activity he was undertaking. That is to say, although his act did, indeed, end up having a grave moral significance, he could not be reasonably held to know that his act would have such significance, for this kind of act only rarely does have such significance. There are many cases when we can keep searching for further evidence than what is at first available to us. And it seems in some cases we should do precisely that, such as in *Caroline's Confusion*. But in other cases, like *Ethan*, it seems he took sufficient epistemic steps in checking his mirrors and checking behind his car before he got into it. And that's all we should expect him to do.

Notice that a slight change in *Ethan* may change what epistemic duties we think we should hold him to such that perhaps we'd claim that he did, in fact, commit a Failure of Due Diligence. Let's say there was a child in the neighborhood who had a regular tendency of sneaking up behind people's cars as they were backing out of the driveway, and the neighbors had been discussing this widely amongst themselves recently and warning each other of this dangerous possibility. Indeed, there was a neighborhood meeting about this issue the day prior, and all agreed that they must be exceedingly extra careful every time they backed out of their driveway to watch for this child doing this. In such a context, we would, indeed, hold Ethan to a higher epistemic standard, given that he would then know that his backing out of the driveway had this greater potential for major moral significance that it would not normally deliver. Note that this seemingly small point—that the surrounding context will itself impact the degree to which we think a given act should be treated with higher or lower epistemic standards—will come to have tremendous importance later in the book when we examine killing in war.

This also shows us, importantly, that one need not have *invincible* ignorance in order to meet the demands of evidence-relative permissibility when an act's evidence-relative permissibility and fact-relative permissibility come apart. One need only have met the epistemic duties that act demands correlative to its moral significance in order to have met one's evidence-relative permissibility. This is a crucial point for the Evidence-Relative View, particularly in comparison with the other two views for the responsibility criterion for liability. This will be critical, for example, when we return to the Agency View's reliance on the foreseeability condition for liability in chapter 3.[48] I should stress here that in all that I have just said and will say below regarding

---

[48] McMahan, indeed, relies on invincible ignorance that one's actions *could* be threatening, in order to *fully* exempt an otherwise innocent actor from responsibility.

ignorance, belief formation, and related doxastic duties, I am not attempting to offer nor am I defending any particular big story about the truth or falsity of epistemic contextualism, or any controversial claim about epistemology more broadly. Rather, I am only making the *moral* case as it relates to these issues, not the broader epistemic case. I'm here concerned with forming beliefs in a morally responsible way; not the larger epistemology debates about belief formation *qua* belief formation.

2.5. Moral Ignorance

Thus far, I've been discussing cases of actions done from *factual* ignorance and I've argued that a person is morally responsible for an action licensed by factual ignorance only if she is also morally responsible for the ignorance. I've argued further that, in some cases, people *can* indeed be responsible for such ignorance, as in *Confused Caroline* and *Dogsitter*. Call this the Factual Ignorance Thesis:

> Whenever an agent acts from factual ignorance, he is morally responsible for the act only if he is responsible for the ignorance from which he acts.[49]

In the cases we've examined, the factual ignorance is ignorance of the given action's fact-relative permissibility. But if a person has met her epistemic duties in forming her beliefs about the act's fact-relative permissibility, then she is not morally responsible for her ignorance about the act's fact-relative impermissibility. That is, her act is evidence-relative permissible. Consequently, I argue she should not be held liable to defensive harm to block an unjust harm that the act may deliver. But in some of the cases the actors did not live up to their moral epistemic duties (they committed a Failure of Due Diligence) and, therefore, their acts were evidence-relative impermissible in addition to being fact-relative impermissible, because they failed to draw the right conclusion that they should have from the evidence available to them.

---

[49] This formulation follows similar formulations by both Rosen and Guerrero, although they explicitly formulate the Ignorance Thesis to include both factual and moral ignorance and do so in terms of culpability rather than responsibility. I am here trying to separate factual ignorance from moral ignorance, for reasons that will be apparent shortly. See Guerrero, "Don't Know, Don't Kill," 60, and Rosen, "Culpability and Ignorance," 64.

2.5.1 Another Kind of Ignorance

There is another kind of ignorance, however, that I have not yet addressed. Namely, how should we treat cases of *moral* (non-factual) ignorance? To get clear on what this even is, recall our various "drivers backing out of the driveway" cases given above. The *Bill* case is not a matter of moral ignorance. In that case, Bill somehow came to have factual ignorance, in spite of the evidence available to him. That is, Bill believed that his backing up wouldn't harm anyone, not that his backing up over a child would be morally permissible. To demonstrate moral ignorance, we'd need to add a fourth case to our previous three backing-up drivers. Such as:

Phillip
Phillip is in an identical situation to Morton. That is, Phillip correctly believes due to the evidence accessible to him that his backing up the car will run over the neighbor's child. However, unlike Morton, Phillip does not conclude that this is morally impermissible. Rather, Phillip comes to the moral conclusion that backing up one's car over neighbors' children is a morally permissible thing to do.

Should a person, such as Phillip, be held morally responsible for coming to the wrong conclusion on a moral matter after they know all the relevant facts? This is a different and, perhaps surprisingly, more difficult question than that of responsibility for factual ignorance. Since I accept the Factual Ignorance Thesis, should I also accept the same principle as applied to Moral Ignorance? Consider the Moral Ignorance Thesis:

Whenever an agent acts from moral ignorance, he is morally responsible for the act only if he is responsible for the ignorance from which he acts.[50]

It appears I should accept such a thesis, simply for the sake of consistency. But this is more complicated than may first appear. We readily find cases like *Caroline's Confusion* wherein we think an actor is responsible for her act from *factual* ignorance because we conclude that she is responsible for

---

[50] Guerrero forms this Moral Ignorance Thesis as a restriction of Rosen's broader Ignorance Thesis noted above. See Guerrero, "Don't Know, Don't Kill," 60. And Zimmerman, "Moral Responsibility and Ignorance," 411. Zimmerman, again, puts the claim in terms of culpability rather than responsibility.

that ignorance in some way. However, it is much harder in cases of *moral* ignorance to point to one's Failure of Due Diligence upon which to pin responsibility. And yet, in many cases of moral ignorance, unlike factual ignorance, we may feel compelled to assign responsibility for an act resulting from it *regardless* of the actor's responsibility for that kind of ignorance, as I'll show below.

This important issue of moral ignorance and responsibility has only fairly recently in the history of moral philosophy began receiving the scholarship it deserves.[51] Below I will try to get clear on what moral ignorance is, how it could factor into questions of responsibility (and therefore liability), and offer a reason based on permissible defense to think that someone could (and perhaps should) be held morally responsible for acts done with moral ignorance even if one is not responsible for the moral ignorance itself. But, first, let me say at the outset that whichever way of understanding the question of responsibility for moral ignorance goes, I think the Evidence-Relative View can be modified to accommodate it. That is, nothing critical to the success of the Evidence-Relative View for liability attribution ultimately hinges on the outcome of the debate over moral ignorance and responsibility. The view is compatible with either conclusion one draws from the debate below, as I will explain. Still, despite this, the issues surrounding moral ignorance and responsibility are closely related to the issues around evidence-relative norms, so it is necessary to explore. Moreover, when we do so, we uncover a fascinating implication of whichever way one wishes to go on the question of moral ignorance.

So, first, let us get clear on our target. There is the *empirical* question of whether one is even capable of coming to the correct belief about one's moral permissions for a given act when one's *moral* epistemic reasoning is severely constrained (by prevailing cultural norms, perhaps) such that it would be very difficult for them to reach the correct moral conclusion even granting that they possess adequate *factual* evidence. I think this first question, while helpful for getting clear on our target, is quite easily answered by simply looking to the historical record of moral reformers. That is, no matter how difficult it may be, it is clearly *possible* to come to the correct moral conclusion in difficult moral epistemic circumstances. If it was literally impossible

---

[51] It had gone mostly unexplored in analytic philosophy until the work done by Michael Zimmerman and Gideon Rosen, cited above. The primary exception is W. D. Ross. Ross explored questions related to this issue in W. D. Ross, *Foundations of Ethics* (Oxford: Clarendon Press, 1939).

for one to come to the correct moral conclusion against the cultural norms of one's day, then we never would have moral reformers of any kind. We would have never seen the likes of abolitionists such as William Wilberforce, to pick one example, who spoke out against the moral evil of slavery long before it was an accepted moral belief of his surrounding culture.[52]

So that question is easily resolved—it is at least possible. But that is not what we are after. The more pressing and difficult question—the question we are after—is whether morality holds such a person *responsible* for acts licensed by this moral epistemic failure in such conditions; or for *any* act one commits out of moral ignorance under any conditions. The famous and well-worn case here is that of the ancient slaveholder who believed (in line with the prevailing cultural norms surrounding him at the time) that his action of keeping slaves was morally permissible.[53] For ease of discussion, here is a fictionalized version of this historical case:

Ancient Slaveholder

Hittite Lord is an ancient man who lived long ago in a culture very different from ours today. The prevailing cultural norms of his time held that there was nothing morally impermissible in slave holding. The legitimacy of chattel slavery was simply taken for granted. Hittite Lord owns slaves, buys and sells human beings, requires forced labor from them, breaks up families to do so, and all the corollary activities that go along with slaveholding. He does all these acts while believing, falsely, that they are morally permissible.[54]

Presume that Hittite Lord did, in fact, believe that his slave owning was morally permissible (i.e., that the ancient slaveholder is acting like Bill—he believes his act is permissible—and not like Morton who believes his act is wrong but does it anyway). Should the ancient slaveholder be held morally responsible for acts resulting from this moral ignorance?[55]

---

[52] See Eric Metaxas, *Amazing Grace: William Wilberforce and the Heroic Campaign to End Slavery* (New York: HarperOne, 2007).

[53] This example was first offered by Michael Slote and used at length by Rosen ("Culpability and Ignorance"), as well as Michelle Moody-Adams, and Guerrero ("Don't Know, Don't Kill"). See Slote, "Is Virtue Possible?," *Analysis* 42 (1982): 70–76, at 71. See Moody-Adams, "Culture, Responsibility, and Affected Ignorance," *Ethics* 104, no. 2 (1994): 291–309.

[54] I, here, paraphrase many of the uses of this example cited above. The phrase "taken for granted" is Rosen's. As he writes, chattel slavery "was simply taken for granted" and that "until quite late in antiquity it never occurred to anyone to object to slavery on grounds of moral or religious principle" (Rosen, "Culpability and Ignorance," 64.). See also Guerrero, "Don't Know, Don't Kill," 62.

[55] I am assuming here, of course, that slaveholding is, indeed a morally impermissible activity.

There are two competing views on how to answer this question. The first view holds that *Ancient Slaveholder* is a case where Hittite Lord's moral ignorance (his false belief that slaveholding is morally permissible) is blameless. That is, this view claims his moral ignorance is not his fault and he is not in any way blameworthy for it. Rosen, a defender of this view, writes: "Given the intellectual and cultural resources available to a second millennium Hittite lord, it would have taken a moral genius to see through the wrongness of chattel slavery."[56] The implication, apparently, is that we should not hold people to a standard of having to be a "moral genius." Hence, on this view, Hittite Lord is not blameworthy for his moral ignorance. It is used as part of an effort to defend the Moral Ignorance Thesis and that, since Hittite Lord is not responsible for his moral ignorance that slaveholding is wrong, he is similarly not responsible for his acts resulting from that ignorance—his slaveholding and related acts.

The alternative view argues that Hittite Lord is, in fact, responsible for his moral ignorance. Alexander Guerrero has written persuasively on this view. Guerrero, as discussed above, contends for Moral Epistemic Contextualism: that what epistemic standards of diligence morality demands of any person are contextually dependent on the moral significance of the act that will result from that belief. And, just as with factual ignorance, Guerrero thinks that Moral Epistemic Contextualism can apply in the moral ignorance case. The act of owning someone as a slave is a massively morally significant act and, hence, Guerrero argues that we are right to hold Hittite Lord to a high bar of epistemic duty for the belief that licenses such action. If we do so, we can rightly hold Hittite Lord morally responsible for, at least, not taking the time to more seriously wrestle over the question of the moral permissibility of his various slaveholding acts, and not simply taking it for granted that they are permissible. The implication is that *had* Hittite Lord—moral genius or not—fulfilled the incredibly high epistemic duties, we can rightly hold him to, for an action such as slaveholding, then he would have come to the correct moral conclusion regarding its impermissibility. Or, better, in the least, the idea is that he *could* have come to the right conclusion, and that possibility is all that is required for assigning responsibility. He did not have invincible moral ignorance. Thus, Hittite Lord is at least responsible for, to use my terminology, a Failure of Due Diligence.[57] If that is true, then he is not

---

[56] Rosen, "Culpability and Ignorance," 66.
[57] This is no longer following Guerrero's argument—I am here significantly merging his line of reasoning and my own. This is important to note because Guerrero does not argue positively for this

blameless for his moral ignorance.[58] The thought is that if Hittite Lord really is morally blind to the heinous act of slaveholding, he should be held responsible for his blindness justifying that act.

Occasionally, we encounter raw moral blindness on something as clearly morally laden as war. Take this discussion of happiness, traditionally attributed to the infamous warmonger Genghis Khan: "Happiness lies in conquering one's enemies, in driving them in front of oneself, in taking their property, in savoring their despair, in outraging their wives and daughters." The fact that moral ignorance occurs over acts of waging war will, of course, be very important in the broader discussion on war, in chapters 3 and 4.

Notice that regardless of whether one holds Hittite Lord responsible for his act, licensed by this moral ignorance, it is a separate matter from whether the Moral Ignorance Thesis is true. The view contending that we can, indeed, hold Hittite Lord responsible for his act resulting from his moral ignorance does not contradict the Moral Ignorance Thesis. Rather, it simply claims that this *is* a case where one is responsible for one's moral ignorance. It is a further question whether people who are *not* responsible for their moral ignorance can ever be held morally responsible for it: the central point of the Moral Ignorance Thesis. This debate over how to understand the *Ancient Slaveholder* case is just the first salvo between these two views.[59] Rosen and Zimmerman defend the Moral Ignorance Thesis. Guerrero argues against it. To do so, Guerrero only needs to show one case where an agent, acting out of moral ignorance, is not responsible for that ignorance, and, yet, is properly responsible for the act.[60] He believes he succeeds in doing this by offering a case of a modern day human being killing a pig in order to consume it for dinner. Guerrero thinks the killing of animals for food is morally impermissible and he attempts to use this case as an example of moral ignorance for which we can hold the ignorant responsible for the act that is based on the ignorance.

---

conclusion, but merely against Rosen's restricted Moral Ignorance Thesis. That is, I am going significantly further than Guerrero does in my claims here, and I do not want to lead the reader astray into thinking that Guerrero necessarily agrees with this implication.

[58] This is an important case because so much is built on it in the larger debate over the moral ignorance thesis discussed next.

[59] But it is a critically important case for the camp holding the moral ignorance thesis—they use it as a central example in their view's defense. Rosen takes the slaveholder case to be "beyond dispute" ("Culpability and Ignorance," 64) that it is an instance of blameless moral ignorance. I have serious doubts.

[60] Guerrero, "Don't Know, Don't Kill," 60.

This full debate over whether the Moral Ignorance Thesis holds in all cases is a much larger debate that far exceeds the scope of this book. While I am sympathetic to his aims, I think Guerrero's attempt at providing a counter-example has significant problems, not the least of which is that it is particularly ineffective against those scholars who do not find the eating of meat to be morally impermissible.[61] We need not delve deeply into this debate here for, as I show in section 2.5.3, my proposal for liability attribution is compatible with either conclusion one may reach over responsibility for moral ignorance. There is, however, an interesting argument against the plausibility of the Moral Ignorance Thesis that arises from considerations of defensive harm that has not been previously offered in this literature. It is worth offering here, as I believe it may be an entirely new and potentially powerful way to argue against the Moral Ignorance Thesis, as well as an important point, in its own right, within the defensive harm debate. Thus, I will quickly sketch how such an argument would run.

2.5.2 Defensive Harm and the Moral Ignorance Thesis

The argument is a *reductio ad absurdum* against the Moral Ignorance Thesis. To begin, let us grant the view held by defenders of the Moral Ignorance Thesis, like Rosen, that the Hittite Lord is *not* responsible for his moral ignorance regarding the permissibility of his slaveholding. According to the Moral Ignorance Thesis he also cannot, therefore, be held morally responsible

---

[61] Such as myself. Jeff McMahan once remarked to me (in conversation with Todd May) that he cannot understand how a contemporary analytic philosopher working on ethics today could be anything other than a vegetarian. First, I think the case is more complicated than the recent ascendancy of vegetarian arguments has made it seem, particularly for causal impotence reasons (see my "Eating Meat and Causal Impotence," unpublished manuscript). But, second, if enjoying perfectly rare prime rib is morally impermissible, I'm not certain that I want to be right, and that's a real problem for my ability to objectively assess the strength of the relevant arguments. That is, as David Foster Wallace suggested in "Consider the Lobster," I worry that my deep, lifelong meat-eating biases here may simply be too strong for me to give the issue the rational and objective analysis it deserves. But, to be clear, my worry here is that this bias issue for something so basic as whether to eat the food upon which our human species has relied for so many thousands and thousands of years is not simply relegated to the carnivorous side of this debate; but that the bias cuts *both* ways—that the Peter Singers of the world have their own biases here too, however much they'd prefer to deny them. Indeed, I find most vegetarianism arguments to also be built upon a kind of inclination or impulse for a certain aesthetic. But I get ahead of myself; I cannot defend the permissibility of eating meat in a footnote. Suffice to say, the effectiveness of Guerrero's supposed counter-example against the Moral Ignorance Thesis depends heavily on whether one agrees with Guerrero's intuitions over eating meat. And if one does not, unfortunately, the strength of his argument is significantly weakened. That aside, I still find his position against the Moral Ignorance Thesis to be strong and highly compelling.

for the act to which that ignorance gives license: the act of his slaveholding. Now consider one of this man's slaves, Telemaque:

Ancient Slave
Telemaque is one of Hittite Lord's slaves. He has been forced to do punishing hard labor his entire life by Hittite Lord, he has been kept in enslavement by brutal physical force, he was forcibly removed from his parents and siblings at an early age, and he has been otherwise abused and had his rights violated in ways commensurate with being a slave. Telemaque decides to defend himself from this enslavement. One morning, when Hittite Lord orders Telemaque to work, Telemaque refuses and tries to escape his captivity. Hittite Lord blocks him and does not allow him to escape. It has become clear over many years that the only way for Telemaque to escape is that he will have to kill Hittite Lord while trying to escape. Telemaque does so, and escapes to freedom.[62]

Is Telemaque's killing of Hittite Lord an instance of morally permissible defensive harm? I think it is.[63] This is because it is both necessary and proportionate for Telemaque to kill Hittite Lord in order to escape the unjust harm he is under. It is necessary to kill Hittite Lord to escape, made putatively so in the case. It is proportionate to kill Hittite Lord if one accepts that the harm of a life of unjust imprisonment and forced labor is bad enough to justify killing in order to prevent it. I think most will find this to be so. It's almost incomprehensible to me how somehow could not reach this conclusion, and that Telemaque's killing of Hittite Lord was a morally permissible act.

So far so good. Now return to the Rosen assumption that Hittite Lord is not responsible for his moral ignorance and (by the Moral Ignorance Thesis) is therefore not morally responsible for the act of his slaveholding. If that is true, then it means that Hittite Lord is a Nonresponsible Threat to Telemaque (as the term was defined in chapter 1). If that is the case, and if it is true that Telemaque's defense against Hittite Lord is permissible (in every sense), then some version of the Nonresponsible Account of permissible

---

[62] The name Telemaque in this case is used in honor of the historical Telemaque (also known as Denmark Vesey), who conspired to lead a slave rebellion in South Carolina in the 1820's. See Douglas R. Egerton, *He Shall Go Out Free: The Lives of Denmark Vesey*, 2nd ed. (Lanham: Rowman and Littlefield, 2004).

[63] And I do not distinguish in which sense it is permissible because it is a case where the fact-relative, evidence-relative, and belief-relative senses of permissibility do not "come apart"—that is, it is morally permissible in all of these ways.

defensive harm must be true. But, as was shown in chapter 1, we should reject the Nonresponsible Account. If the Nonresponsible Account is false, yet we wish to hold Telemaque's defense permissible, then we must reject the Moral Ignorance Thesis and claim that, despite his lack of responsibility for his moral ignorance in this case, Hittite Lord is still morally responsible for the act of his slaveholding resulting from that ignorance.

Because I reject the Nonresponsible Account, is the most plausible conclusion to reach from my Telemaque argument. But, of course, one could run the *reductio* the other direction and use the Moral Ignorance Thesis as a *defense* of the Nonresponsible Account. I will not here quibble over the intuitions for how to take the case—there is a large body of work behind each view here in tension.[64] But what my argument does show is that if one rejects the Nonresponsible Account, as I have in this book, then one should *also* reject that the Moral Ignorance Thesis always holds. That is, one should so reject it, assuming that they think it is permissible for Telemaque to kill his master as a necessary and proportionate defensive harm means of escape. And, *vice versa*, if one holds firmly to the Nonresponsible Account, they should actually defend the Moral Ignorance Thesis. My assumption is that that realization would not be a welcome one for many holders on the Nonresponsible Account.

It seems most plausible to claim for the *Ancient Slave* case that Telemaque permissibly harms Hittite Lord because Hittite Lord is morally responsible for his act of enslaving Telemaque. If that's true, then Telemaque's defensive harm is permissible on the Responsible Account, of course, but we must reject that the Moral Ignorance Thesis holds for all cases. Again, this is granting Rosen's view that Hittite Lord is not responsible for his moral ignorance. Another way out of the problem for a holder of the Nonresponsible Account would be to simply deny this assumption: that Hittite Lord *is* blameless for his moral ignorance upon which his slaveholding is based. As was discussed above, Moral Epistemic Contextualism gives us good reason to suspect this may be true (that Hittite Lord is responsible for his ignorance). But there may be other cases where one is not responsible for his moral ignorance, and the same *reductio* used here could be derived from those cases. In either case, it shows that there is an interesting divide across views of moral ignorance that can be based on intuitions over permissible defensive harm.

---

[64] As reviewed in chapter 1 for the Nonresponsible Account. See chapter 1.4.

2.5.3 Bracketing Moral Ignorance

But notice that for the Evidence Relative View to hold for liability, one need *not* take a side in this debate. That is, I can bracket the larger debate over moral ignorance and responsibility for the remainder of this chapter and book. The reason is because the Evidence-Relative View is compatible with either view of the Moral Ignorance Thesis. All I have to show is that *if* there are cases where one's moral ignorance is, in fact, properly his or her responsibility, then we can say that person commits a Failure of Due Diligence with regard to his or her moral beliefs and on those grounds can be liable to acts licensed by such beliefs. That is the conclusion that the Evidence Relative View produces on the matter of ignorance generally. It seems plausible that just as there are cases like *Caroline's Confusion* wherein a person's factual ignorance is, indeed, her fault, and just as there are also cases like *Ethan* wherein the factual ignorance was not his fault, that so too may there be cases where one's moral ignorance is one's fault and other cases where one's moral ignorance is not one's fault. Further, I generally think Guerrero is right and there may even be cases where we can hold some people responsible for their actions done out of their own moral ignorance even *if* they are not responsible for that moral ignorance itself. But perhaps I am mistaken in this hunch. So be it. Nothing critical to the Evidence-Relative View for liability rests upon it. If people are not in any way morally responsible (not even as Failures of Due Diligence) for genuine instances of moral ignorance, then that simply means that moral ignorance would not be a proper basis for liability attribution.

Further, if they are not to be held responsible for acts emanating from moral ignorance even when they are not responsible for the ignorance (if that is possible), then their moral ignorance would not be a proper basis for liability in those cases either. On this view, cases of moral ignorance would be to liability like the case of *Ethan* is with regard to factual ignorance—moral ignorance is not something for which people are responsible. While this would be surprising for the result shown above (that Telemaque would not have fact-relative permissibility to use defensive harm to free himself from Hittite Lord), it is technically possible that this could be true. Again, my strong intuitions are contrary to this view, and I find that moral ignorance is something for which people can be responsible. But *either* view of responsibility for moral ignorance is compatible with the Evidence-Relative View of liability attribution. I therefore set aside further analysis of moral ignorance for the remainder of this book. In what follows, I will generally discuss factual ignorance. But what I say there could be substituted, *mutatis mutandis*, for moral ignorance, on either view of responsibility for moral ignorance just discussed.

In the next chapter, I will continue to explore the Evidence-Relative View for the responsibility criterion of liability attribution. Therein we will see how it is this view, and not the other standard views on offer, that is best able to explain many of the moral tragedies that arise in both self-defense cases and, ultimately, in war. I will also show the intricate ways one's evidentiary standing to a particular case can significantly alter our moral conclusions on it, and the paucity of attention this crucial fact has received in the literature. Moreover, we will see how the ignorance we can have, and often have, regarding the relative risk that our actions may or may not impose unjust harm on others, applies serious pressure upon most views within the Responsible Account. It is only the Evidence-Relative View that can give a compelling and satisfying answer to this matter—a point upon which McMahan and many others have based the very distinction between the Simple Culpability View and the Agency View. After these matters are worked through in chapter 3, I will turn more directly to questions surrounding permissible killing in war, in chapters 4 and 5.

3
The Evidence-Relative View and Intricate Symmetries

all the men held tall with their
chests in the air, with courage in
their blood and a fire in their stare
it was a grey morning and they all
wondered how they would fare
till the old general told them to go home

He said: I have seen the others
and I have discovered
that this fight is not worth fighting
I have seen their mothers
and I will no other
to follow me where I'm going

—from "The General" by Dispatch

3.1. Introduction

Thus far, I have examined the difficult moral question: when is it not simply the least bad option to kill someone—a lesser-evil—but actually morally permissible and just to kill? That is, when is someone *liable* to be killed such that we do not wrong them when we kill them. In the last chapter, I proposed that the Evidence-Relative View of liability attribution gets the answer to this question right. The next two chapters (4 and 5), following this present chapter, will rely on the Evidence-Relative View for liability attribution as it is applied in war. Its application to debates, in what is known as revisionist just war theory, is particularly important. The view's many successes and advantages therein will themselves serve as a further defense of the view. That is, I offer this new proposal for liability attribution in the last chapter and continue my explanation of that proposal in this chapter, but much of my defense for it will be demonstrated in the following chapters as I show how effectively it deals with various problems in revisionist just war theory accounts. It is successful not only in avoiding problems that plague the competing accounts as I've already shown in chapter 2, but also in the greater ease with which it is able to handle the many thorny issues raised revisionist just war theory. There are also some important objections to the view I have not yet reviewed because they are more easily discussed in the direct relation they bear on war. I will examine those objections in chapters 4 and 5. However, there is still much more to be said regarding the Evidence-Relative View in general terms. Hence, in this chapter, I will cover some further complications including risk imposition, applying evidentiary questions to classic cases, and the many issues surrounding third-party intervention.

At the conclusion of the last chapter, we bracketed the thorny issues surrounding moral ignorance. With those set aside and with the twin tools of Moral Epistemic Contextualism and the Failure of Due Diligence at our disposal, we can return to some further advantages the Evidence-Relative View holds over the competing views. First, I will introduce the key notion of Tragedy that the Evidence-Relative View can provide as an explanatory tool. Tragedy is a term of art for the account, and it captures many of the normative features of prominent cases in the literature as well as offering a better explanation for the complex symmetrical relationship between agents in those cases. Introducing Tragedies will uncover and resolve a common confusion about the Evidence-Relative View. We will also see, more generally, that recasting these cases in evidentiary terms reveals that many supposed problems for liability attribution on any account simply dissipate. I will review some of the more complex ways this occurs later in this chapter. As we will see, this notion of Tragedy that the Evidence-Relative View is able to articulate captures a wide range of real-world cases far better than the competing views. This will be poignantly true for cases of killing in war examined in the next two chapters. Sadly, as I will argue, in war there are times when soldiers on each side of a conflict behave permissibly according to the evidence available to them, and thereby are nonliable, and yet (and hence) each behaves in fact-relative impermissible ways when they tragically kill the other. Particularly see chapter 4.4.5, on Lazar's paradox, and chapter 5.4 on how many real-world wars are instances of Tragedies, in at least some aspects.

In any case, the Evidence-Relative View's explication of Tragedy provides an explanatory mechanism for this that the other views lack. Looking through the lens of Tragedy and evidentiary issues more generally, shifts many of the important moral questions in the classic cases used throughout this literature. I will show this in two ways below. First, in sections 3.2.1 and 3.2.2, I argue that the Evidence-Relative View better accounts for the normative intuitions driving the Agency View's reliance on the nonreciprocal risk-imposing nature of some acts. Second, I will show in section 3.3 how many of the classic cases are quickly resolved by looking carefully at evidentiary concerns of the actors in those cases. This is because once we step away from putative imposition of certain "God's eye view" knowledge of various facts in these cases, it turns out that many of the actors are not, after all, symmetrical in their evidence-relative behavior. In section 3.3.2, I examine third-party interventions and what evidentiary issues they would similarly face. Finally, it turns out that there are actual real-world cases of Tragedy abounding—we need not look only to the far-flung world of philosophical thought experiments to see the phenomenon instantiate. I will show this in section 3.4 with the Brandon Lee case and discuss how the 2022 Russian invasion of Ukraine likely contains multiple other cases for many of the soldiers involved.

3.2. Tragedies as Explanatory Tool

People often say that war is a tragic affair, which seems obviously true. And of course, it is always tragedy in at least some general sense when people die, intentionally killed, or unintentionally killed as is often the case in war, at the hands of other human beings. The wanton death and destruction brought about by war is an enduring shame of mankind. But I find that it is a deeply moral tragedy in another way as well. I intend my use of the term Tragedy here as a specific, technical, term of art. Namely: a Tragedy is a case where two parties are both acting permissibly towards one another according to their evidence-relative norms, but (yet) are each acting wrongly toward one another according to the fact-relative norms. But my choice of the term Tragedy here is also used to remind us that the horrors and evils of war are not merely the wrongful harm wrought upon so many. But that, rather, even those intending in good faith to do good in war and act rightly and behave so according to their best evidence, often end up being the unwitting culprits of great evil. This is its own kind of tragedy, and, it turns out, those intending and trying desperately to do good in war, but turning out to do the opposite, often tragically involve the majority of actors on both sides of a given war.

3.2.1 An Intricate Symmetry

The Evidence-Relative View of the responsibility criterion for liability attribution gains traction in our understanding of many of the classic nonresponsible threat cases which have been the cause for so much dispute. For example, it offers a way out of the assumed asymmetry between actors that many writers demand of these cases. Upon reflection, I find that this—circumventing a presumption of necessary asymmetry in these cases—better aligns with our considered moral intuitions regarding the imagined individuals. Allow me to explain how the Evidence-Relative View is able to do this.

Consider again the case of *Dignitary & Guest*. Guest is clearly not violating any evidence-relative norms when he approaches Dignitary and sticks out his hand (he has no way of knowing the villain would project the gun hologram upon his hand), and thus, on this view of liability attribution, he is not liable to defensive harm. This means that, indeed, Dignitary is committing a fact-relative impermissible action when she pulls her gun on him because, despite the evidence she has, the fact is that Guest is not liable to defensive harm. However, Dignitary is *also* not violating any evidence-relative norms herself in doing so and is thus similarly not liable to defensive harm. Thus if, say, Guest was also armed and tried to defend himself by shooting Dignitary when he sees that she pulls a gun on him, he too would be acting impermissibly, in the fact-relative sense, because Dignitary is not liable to defensive harm because, again, liability turns on evidence-relative norms.

There is a simple confusion some have on first encountering the proposed Evidence-Relative View. Some object that because Dignitary is not liable (since she is not violating evidence-relative norms) and making a nonculpable *mistake*, that it is unfair to Guest that he loses his right to life due to her mistake.[1] That is, people object: "I shouldn't lose my right to life if I am innocent because of someone else's mistake." But the Evidence-Relative View, of course, does not claim this. Guest does *not* lose his right to life

---

[1] Seth Lazar has made this objection against the view, personal correspondence, December 2010.

because of Dignitary's mistake. If he is unable to defend himself in time, he will be (fact-relatively) wrongfully killed. But Dignitary is not responsible for Guest's (fact-relative) wrongful death such that she should not be liable to defensive harm. Similarly, however, Guest is making a mistake when he correctly (given the evidence he has) concludes that Dignitary is a wrongful threat to himself. If Guest defends himself against Dignitary, then she will also be (fact-relatively) wrongfully killed. But, just as with Dignitary if she kills Guest in such a context, Guest is not responsible for Dignitary's (fact-relative) wrongful death such that he should not be liable to defensive harm. In other words, the thought that Guest should not lose his right to life (on forfeiture formulations) because of Dignitary's mistake, is only half right—because Dignitary should also not lose her right to life because of Guest's mistake. Their moral relationship is symmetrical.

So, it is not that *either* actor loses his or her right to life due to a mistake made by the other. Rather, in such cases you have two people attempting to harm each other wherein each is acting justifiably in the evidence-relative sense, yet both are acting impermissibly in the fact-relative sense. And this is where things get complicated: the *reason* both are acting impermissibly in the fact-relative sense is precisely because both are acting permissibly in the evidence-relative sense are thereby nonliable—hence, harming them is harm that is delivered to a nonliable person and thereby fact-relative impermissible. Thus, the reason neither is liable over the other is not simply because of a lack of relevant or significant *enough* moral asymmetry between parties here (as the Simple Culpability View holds). Rather, there is a nuanced, complex, and fragile symmetry between the actors—a symmetry grounded in the intricate relationship created by both of them behaving according to their evidentiary norms which itself results in each performing a fact-relative impermissible act towards the other.

I call these kinds of symmetrical cases Tragedies, as a technical term of art for the Evidence-Relative View. Indeed, *Dignitary & Guest* is an archetypal case of Tragedy. Stating it again: a Tragedy is a case where two parties are both acting permissibly towards one another, according to their evidence-relative norms, but are each acting wrongly toward one another in a fact-relative sense. In Tragedies, then, neither party is liable to defensive harm from the other, since neither has violated evidence-relative norms. However, and this is critical: since neither has proper evidence to know that fact (the nonliability) about the other, then neither party is wrong in the evidence-relative sense to defend oneself from what one (rightly!) takes to be a fact-relative and, from their available evidentiary standing, an evidence-relative wrong committed by the other towards themselves. That is, they each correctly (in the epistemic sense) *take* the other to be violating evidence-relative norms and thus be liable to harm (on the Evidence-Relative View), given the evidence available to them. Yet neither is *actually* liable since neither has actually violated evidence-relative norms.[2]

Recall one of the dissatisfactions with both competing views of the responsibility criterion for liability reviewed in chapter 1.7.2. There I argued that it should strike us as strange that some versions of the Responsible Account find an asymmetry between Nonresponsible Threats such as Falling Man. Recall that the Nonresponsible Account, of course, holds that there is an asymmetry that points the liability label toward Falling Man for his causal imposition of a wrongful harm. But the Agency View of the Responsible Account *also* finds an asymmetry—surprisingly enough—but this time pointing the liability label towards Trapped for imposing wrongful harm on Falling Man when she voluntarily shoots him since he is nonresponsible (and nonliable). In that section, I discussed why this is a less than preferred outcome for any version of the Responsible Account. Better to say that, indeed, the parties are symmetrically morally related to the impending unjust harm here, and neither is liable. But without something like the Evidence-Relative View, the Responsible Account has no way to explain this. For, as just shown, both Guest and Dignitary are imposing fact-relative wrongful harm on the other. But, because each is acting justifiably according to evidence-relative norms, neither is liable. And, hence we have a Tragedy.

The Simple Culpability View agrees here and says that there is no asymmetry between actors, but the *reason* it gives for the symmetry is dissatisfying and overly simplistic: both are non-culpable, and, hence, there is no asymmetry, and no liability. But, again as shown in chapter 1.7.2, this is a poor representation of the incredibly complex normative facts obtaining in these cases. We recognize that, indeed, each actor is committing something which is an awful thing—a fact-relative impermissible act attempting to wrongfully take a life—yet there is something true that the Simple Culpability View identifies in that neither is culpable. Both views—the Simple Culpability View and the Agency View—have some element of truth to them regarding the actors in the cases, but the answers both give fail to capture the full moral

---

[2] Recall, on my view, the *fact* of liability hinges on the *fact* of whether or not one is violating evidence-relative norms.

picture. The Evidence-Relative View, however, is able to properly portray the moral complexity of these cases. It declares a symmetry of liability non-attribution, but an intricate complex moral symmetry that is based on the tragic reality that each actor is committing a fact-relative wrong, yet each is evidence-relative justified *because of* the others fact-relative wrong and, hence, nonliable. It is this intricate symmetry that the view is able to correctly explain which I label a Tragedy.

3.2.2 Resolving Tragedies: Distributing Harm

What is the morally correct way to resolve a Tragedy? The version of the Rights-Based Account of permissible harm I'm proposing argues that, strictly speaking, *there is no* morally correct way to resolve a Tragedy—and that this should hold on any Rights-Based Account. This is because there is no moral asymmetry between the actors in a Tragedy with regard to their liability. And, as was shown above, if there is no liability asymmetry then someone will have their rights violated and be wronged in such forced-choice scenarios. There is no means of resolution whereby someone will not be wronged. Recall Scanlon's quote from the previous chapter referring to Thomson's and other scholars' work:

> It is either permissible to kill a [Nonresponsible Threat] in self-defense, or it is impermissible. Either way, there has to be a moral asymmetry between the threatened person and the threat, an asymmetry that favors either the victim, in which case the killing is permissible, or the threat in which case it is impermissible. It is our task as moral philosophers to identify and explicate this asymmetry.[3]

But in these Tragedy cases, like *Dignitary & Guest,* the killing of either party is fact-relative impermissible and *yet* each actor's act of killing is

---

[3] T. M. Scanlon, "Thomson on Self-Defense," in *Fact and Value. Essays on Ethics and Metaphysics for Judith Jarvis Thomson*, edited by Alex Byrne, Robert Stalnaker, and Ralph Wedgwood, 206 (Cambridge, MA: Bradford Books, the MIT Press, 2001). I am indebted here to Susanne Burri for bringing Scanlon's discussion of this point to my attention. I think it is precisely this Scanlonian impulse here, that our job as philosophers is to find and explain this asymmetry, that has driven so much of this scholarship to wrongly point to scant differences in moral standing in order to try to uncover some suitable asymmetry to base liability on. This drive is wrong-headed in our complex world which is actually, tragically, often filled with Tragedies.

evidence-relative permissible. There is no asymmetry to be found upon which we should properly base liability attribution. Thus, on my view, a proper Rights-Based Account simply has no answer as to who should rightfully be killed—the best we can do is to move to making a choice between a lesser of two evils. That's not quite right; I shouldn't say that a proper Rights-Based Account has *no* answer. Rather, its *answer* is that neither person should be killed; neither can be permissibly harmed in defense—so we must look to "lesser-evil" options.

How then, given the intricate symmetry of Tragedies, should they be resolved?[4] There is a view here which is helpful. We can embrace the liability symmetry between actors in Tragic cases and, since neither party should bear wrongful harm in these forced-choices, a Rights-Based Account can look for a just resolution through theories of fair distribution of scarce resources. In this case, the scarce resource is life.[5] (I discussed this view of searching for a "fair distribution of harm" tangentially in reviewing Lazar's objection to the Agency View in chapter 1.7.2. That is, since neither party deserves to bear the wrongful harm, we can ask what would be the fairest way to distribute this wrongful harm.

The first answer to fair distribution is that if there *were* any way, of course, to divide the burden and have each party share it, then that should be pursued. If, for example, rather than one of them dying, there was a way that they could each be severely injured, we should prefer that resolution over either person's death. Note, importantly, that this kind of resolution is not, as one may think, already covered by the necessity constraint. This is because the necessity constraint applies to cases of *liability* whereby only the necessary harm needed to avert an unjust threat should be delivered to a liable party. In such cases, the nonliable party is not required to receive harm to lessen what harm the liable party receives to avert the unjust harm. In *Attacker & Defender*, after all, we would not expect Defender to suffer some harm (say she had to be severely injured) in order to create an equal distribution of harm between her and Attacker, if that were a possible as an alternative to Attacker being killed. But in Tragic cases, since there is no liable party in the forced-choice, a fair distribution of harm should be aimed for, if possible, including any way to divide the harm.

---

[4] Here I am after the question of what the correct distribution of harm should be for Tragic cases. Below, in section 3.3.2, I'll look specifically at third party interventions.
[5] This move of a fair distribution of the wrongful harm is suggested by Susanne Burri in her paper "Fair Distribution of Bad Luck." It is also examined and briefly suggested by McMahan in *Killing in War*, at 180. Finally, as noted, Seth Lazar discusses the notion in "Risk, Responsibility," at 715.

If there is no way to divide the harm, however, then there should be a fair distribution as to who should bear the full burden of the wrongful harm. Put differently, when two parties each have an equal claim to a good, then we should distribute it as equally as possible between them. But if there is no way to divide the good, then we should aim for some fair solution to achieve the maximal best distributive justice possible.[6] Susanne Burri makes this case for such instances of symmetrical defensive harm. She relies on John Broome's argument that if a good in question is indivisible, a lottery may be the best way to achieve maximum distributive justice. As Broome writes:

> [If the good in question is indivisible] ... the candidates' claims cannot all be equally satisfied, because some candidates will get the good and others will not. So some unfairness is inevitable. But a sort of partial equality in satisfaction can be achieved. Each person can be given a sort of surrogate satisfaction. By holding a lottery, each can be given an equal chance of getting the good.[7]

Burri aims to apply this to these symmetrical liability cases of lethal harm such as *Falling Man*. A perfectly fair lottery between two people, of course, is just a fifty-fifty chance between them. Hence, Burri suggests that, in (what I call) Tragic cases,

> the right thing to do for the potential victim is to flip a coin. The victim [able to affect the outcome] is charged with the distribution of an indivisible good. ... Given this, the victim should aim at a distributively just solution, and should thus give an equal chance of getting the good both to the innocent threat and to himself.[8]

This sounds like a plausibly fair way—or fairest way possible—of resolving the intricate symmetry of Tragedies. To be clear, I'm not suggesting that in Tragic cases the actors could actually, literally, flip a coin. But that, rather, a fifty-fifty distribution of harm, or risk of receiving the full indivisible harm, appears to be what morality gives us as the best (least bad/lesser-evil) option in terms of just resolution. So, by "resolving," I here only mean the way in

---

[6] See John Broome, "Fairness," *Proceedings of the Aristotelian Society*, 91 (1991): 87–101. Also see George Sher, "What Makes a Lottery Fair?," *Nous* 14, no. 2 (1980): 203–16.
[7] Broome, "Fairness," 97.
[8] Burri, "Fair Distribution," 7. Again, this follows Broome, "Fairness."

which justice resolves the moral question, conceptually, if not pragmatically. And, of course, if there were any way to bring that fair distribution about, or even approximate it, in a Tragedy case, that would be a better alternative than wrongly claiming that one actor is liable over the other. I'll discuss this further below in cases of third-party intervention to Tragic cases in section 3.3.2.

3.3. Further Complexities: Imposing Risk with Ignorance

This notion of Tragedy that the Evidence-Relative View is able to articulate captures a wide range of real-world cases far better than the competing views. This will be poignantly true for cases of killing in war as I will show in the next two chapters. Sadly, as I will there argue, in war there are times when soldiers on each side of a conflict behave permissibly according to the evidence available to them, and thereby are nonliable, and yet each behaves in fact-relative impermissible ways when they tragically kill the other. Particularly see chapter 4.4.5, on Lazar's paradox, and chapter 5.4 on how many real-world wars are instances of Tragedies, in at least some aspects. In any case, the Evidence-Relative View's explication of Tragedy provides an explanatory mechanism for this that the other views lack. In this section, I will show how the Evidence-Relative View better accounts for many of the normative intuitions driving the Agency View's reliance on the nonreciprocal risk-imposing nature of some acts.

3.3.1 Risk Imposition

As reviewed in chapter 1, the Agency View claims that liability ought to turn on violations of fact-relative norms. In *Dignitary & Guest*, Dignitary acted voluntarily, as required by the view, and, according to McMahan, because she acted in a way that appeared permissible to her but was one in which she knew there was a risk that she could be acting impermissibly. And because this risk of acting impermissibly was (supposedly) nonreciprocal, the stakes were so high, and it was a forced-choice, the Agency View concludes that she is liable to defensive harm from Guest. By translating the case into the framework provided by Parfit's terminology, we see that Dignitary acted wrongly in the fact-relative sense (because she was going to otherwise harm someone who was actually not wrongly threatening her). Yet, she acted permissibly in the evidence-relative sense (because the evidence available to her made it epistemically correct to conclude that someone was trying to wrongly harm her). What we see the Agency View is actual claiming, then, is that evidence-relative permissibility is *irrelevant* to liability when it comes apart from fact-relative wrong-doing, as it does in this and similar cases. And this is to be expected because, recall, the Agency View is intended as a medication for the Responsible Account so as precisely to avoid those cases where an agent is not culpable but still seen as having some "thin" conception of responsibility in some way (the "bare-agent responsibility" described in chapter 1).

So, the Agency View could be more accurately labeled, simply, the Fact-Relative View of liability attribution. That is, that liability should hinge on voluntarily committed actions that violate fact-relative norms. Of course, McMahan's requirement of the act also being a risk-imposing activity complicates the matter. Until, that is, we understand what that even means on this terminology. For an act to be reasonably seen to be a risk-imposing activity just means that an activity is properly deemed permissible in that instance by the actor (it is evidence-relative permissible), but that it is *possible* that it could be fact-relative impermissible. This addition to the Agency View should be considered a net gain, then, as it allows for evidence-relative norms to have some relevance on liability. The problem with this, however, as shown in chapter 1.6.3, is that nearly *any* evidence-relative permissible act that we do whatsoever could be a fact-relative impermissible act if enough implausible conditions obtain. McMahan admits this and *Unwitting Cell Bomber* shows this to be so. It's possible when we press send on our cell phones that we are, in fact, detonating a bomb that kills an innocent person. Driving a car is further down the spectrum of likelihood—that is, the risk is higher—for the possibility of it impermissibly harming someone. Further still down the spectrum of likelihood—quite a bit more likely—that your act may potentially harm someone impermissibly is the act of shooting someone. That is, these acts are progressively riskier that they may turn out to wrongly harm someone, even if done from an evidentiary vantage point of permissibility.

Where are we to draw the line for this likelihood-risk threshold for responsibility? McMahan claims that the line is along some understanding of "foreseeability."[9] But, if literally any activity could possibly result in impermissible harm towards other, what likelihood is needed for it to be a sufficiently risk-imposing activity such that that risk imposition itself can be the entire basis

---

[9] See McMahan, "The Moral Basis for Liability," 397.

of responsibility (and thereby liability) attribution between two actors? The foreseeability condition as a basis for this line is, to put it mildly, unclear. For this reason, among others, many holders of the Responsible Account find that this risk-imposing requirement is too weak and muddled to serve as the basis for something as important as liability.

But there's a further and more vexing problem that emerges for the view from this weakness. Recall in chapter 1, I pointed out that, in *Conscientious Driver*, McMahan claims that Driver, by sending a giant hunk of metal down the road, is engaging in a risk-imposing activity. Yet, embarrassingly for the view, Pedestrian, by walking around town with an explosive device that she will lob at cars if they come at her, is *also* engaging in a risk-imposing activity. For it is potentially the case anytime she lobs her explosive device at what appears to her to be an unjust threat against her life that, in fact, she could be mistaken. Be it in a complicated hologram case like *Dignitary & Guest* or some other wild variant, it seems that throwing explosive devices around town is a massively risk-imposing activity that Pedestrian is engaging in. Once we see that, we see that this risk imposition suggestion as a supposed basis for a relevant asymmetry fails.

Notice as well, although I did not discuss this in chapter 1, that this same criticism of the Agency View for *Conscientious Driver* can be said of the very kind of case it was designed to explain: the *Dignitary & Guest* case. For while it's true that Dignitary is voluntarily committing a risk-imposing activity in shooting Guest in (apparent) self-defense, notice that Guest, simply by being armed with a concealed weapon with the intent to possibly use it, is engaging in a similar risk-imposing activity.[10]

Compare all of the above problems with nonreciprocal risk imposition for the Agency View to the Evidence-Relative View. The Evidence-Relative View captures the normative intuitions behind the idea of nonreciprocal risk much more elegantly, and avoids the problems just mentioned in so doing. Recall the case of *Unwitting Cell Bomber*. McMahan, arguing for the Agency View, notes that it is, indeed, an act performed voluntarily that could possibly be risk-imposing. Yet McMahan argues that because it is not *sufficiently* foreseeable that it could be so risk-imposing, that Todd should not be held responsible. This obviously seems right, but how much better, then, to simply

---

[10] Lazar argues that even if we modified the case so that Guest was not armed but instead pulled a gun out of the belt of a nearby security guard (and was able to do so in time to defend himself against Dignitary), that this would not save him from the risk-imposing activity. For simply the act of shooting someone carries the necessary risk of wrongful harm. See Lazar, "Risk, Responsibility," 725.

capture these cases in terms of Moral Epistemic Contextualism? Pressing send on your cell phone is not the kind of activity that has a high epistemic investigative demand borne out of proper concern over its moral significance. And because it does not, and because Todd therefore behaves permissibly, according to his evidence-relative norms, he should not be liable. That is, Todd does not commit a Failure of Due Diligence. That is why we do not hold Todd liable; not because he is *not* foreseeably imposing a risk-imposing activity, but because he did not commit a Failure of Due Diligence over whether his act could plausibly wrongfully harm others. But one may here quibble that this is a distinction without a difference because what matters is that we do not hold him responsible for predicting that his act would set off a bomb—on that point the views agree. And, on that interpretation, perhaps the Agency View is really just a nascent version of some kind of Moral Epistemic Contextualism. This may appear so on the surface but, in fact, McMahan argues for a much stronger claim: that *invincible* ignorance of a potential wrong is required to escape responsibility. Since that is the standard used by the Agency View, it is not, after all, a form of applied Moral Epistemic Contextualism, as I will show next in section 3.3.2.

3.3.2 Invincible Ignorance and Moral Epistemic Contextualism

The Agency View's reliance on the foreseeability condition to determine which risk-imposing activities makes one responsible may sound like a mild or early version of applying Moral Epistemic Contextualism to responsibility required for liability. But it is not. McMahan's Agency View holds such a thin concept of responsibility that he, in fact, demands *invincible ignorance* of the potential risks an activity could impose on others to escape the foreseeability condition. Once we see this, we see that, indeed, the Agency View does not endorse a Moral Epistemic Contextualism. (Recall chapter 2.4.3 where I discussed why Moral Epistemic Contextualism does not hold to a standard of invincible ignorance and, in fact, is explicitly intended to avoid this. Ethan, for example, did not have invincible ignorance, yet we think he met his epistemic duties in the context he was in.) McMahan thinks there's a significant epistemic difference between Driver and Todd in the *Conscientious Driver* case. He writes, "intuitively it seems [Todd is] less responsible for the threat he poses than [Driver]. The reason why this is so is that, unlike [Driver], he does not intentionally kill, knowingly kill, or even knowingly impose on others a risk of being killed."[11] But McMahan here is mistaken. First, this is simply not true. What these crazy thought experiments like *Unwitting Cell Bomber* show us it is possible that *any* action whatsoever could, in some remote possible world, "impose on others a risk of being killed." If that's true, then there is always a risk on others we are "knowingly" imposing in all our actions, however scant.

In discussing *Conscientious Driver*, again, claiming that Driver somehow has some responsibility for the threat his car poses, McMahan writes, "Although [Driver] did not intend to harm anyone, [he] does know that [his] action carries a small risk of causing great though unintended harm. Although [his] act is of a type that is generally objectively permissible, and although [he] has taken due care to avoid harming anyone, [he] has had bad luck."[12] But we should not allow this move. First, again, *every* act carries *some* "small risk of causing great though unintended harm." McMahan thinks Driver has bad luck because the risk that he knew his action carried came to actually pass. But can't we just as reasonably say that Pedestrian had bad luck? Recall the point made above that simply walking around with an explosive device that you may have to use on an out-of-control car carries with it a risk that you may end up causing someone great, wrongful harm. So, didn't Pedestrian simply *also* have bad luck that the small risk she was aware of came to pass? Or what of Todd, the cell phone operator? If we are really talking about *small* risks here, and if any action we do whatsoever has some infinitesimal chance of harming others, then did not Todd simply also have "bad luck"? The point is that this seems to be a very poor basis for assigning responsibility and, hence, grounding an asymmetry which results in liability to be *killed*.[13]

The invincible ignorance standard can never be met if we are dealing with and taking seriously such small risks. McMahan claims that what is "singular about [Todd's] case [over cases like Driver]... is that he is nonculpably and invincibly ignorant that he poses any kind of threat or risk of harm to anyone."[14] So this claims that it takes invincible ignorance that there is some

---

[11] McMahan, *Killing in War*, 167.
[12] Ibid. Note McMahan's confusing use of "objectively permissible" here (this is used because of the contrast he discussed early with the subjective account), as discussed in section 3.4.2.
[13] See also Dana Kay Nelkin, "Liability, Culpability, and Luck," *Philosophical Studies* 178 (2021): 3523–41.
[14] McMahan, *Killing in War*, 168.

risk that one's action could impermissibly harm others for one to avoid responsibility attribution on the Agency View. But this has the result, however, of making every single act we take, including pressing the send button on our cellphones, one which we could be held responsible for on the Agency View. To show the absurdity of this, recall the *Bystander on Bridge* case. Bystander did *not* have invincible ignorance of the *possibility* that his sitting there could cause him to be in the way of escaping Victim. Surely it is possible for him to have considered this far-flung possibility. So, should we perhaps thereby hold him responsible for taking this risk-imposing activity, however small its actual risk was? Of course, this would be absurd. And clearly the Agency View—since it is a version of the Responsible Account—does not want to embrace this.

Instead, the Agency View should give up its imperfect basis for responsibility attribution and the incredibly high requirement of invincible ignorance of the risks one's actions could impose on others. Rather, by embracing Moral Epistemic Contextualism paired with the Evidence-Relative View, we end up capturing the same normative impulse behind McMahan's rejection of Todd's responsibility and the broader notion of different degrees of responsibility for different degrees of foreseeable risk of harm. Ethan from chapter 2, for example, did not have invincible ignorance that his backing out his car would not harm others. But, as discussed in chapter 2.2.3, it would have been possible for him to overcome this ignorance by taking further investigative steps (getting out of his car for a second or third time, having a friend watch behind him as he backed out, etc.). Thus, he was not invincibly ignorant. But, given the context of his normally innocent act of backing up his car, we do not hold him to such an extreme epistemic standard. And Moral Epistemic Contextualism explains why this is. The Agency View is right that for some other types of actions—like shooting people—we should hold people more responsible for the risks they knowingly take in committing such acts. But Moral Epistemic Contextualism accounts for this by raising the epistemic duties that bear on people correlative to the moral significance of their action. We do this, for example, with Caroline when she shoots Brian, or for when Mike the deer-hunter shoots into the bushes.

Again, what these thought experiments like *Unwitting Cell Bomber* show us is that it is conceivable that any action could pose a risk of unjust harm to others. And this is not just a luxury (or curse) of philosophers. Ask anyone, "Is it *possible* that your action X could, given some wild assumptions, pose a wrongful harm to others?" If they understand what the concept "possible" means, then they will answer in the affirmative. And if this is true, then no one can have the kind of invincible ignorance that McMahan claims Todd has in *Unwitting Cell Bomber*, about *any* action.

So, too, for the *Coerced Killer* case. The normative punch behind the case for the Agency View is that Sam is knowingly, intentionally, and completely *within* his agentic control, imposing a wrongful harm—a harm which he knows is wrongful—on Sarah. The Simple Culpability View is correct here, perhaps, to demand mitigation of his moral blame. And the Evidence-Relative View actually grants the excusal of his culpability, since culpability does not always perfectly track evidence-relative norms the way liability does. But surely for Sam—by being the one to voluntarily, intentionally, and knowingly impose wrongful, lethal harm on a person he knows is wholly innocent—this constitutes a moral asymmetry between him and Sarah that matters for which of the two of them should bear the cost of the forced-choice. It is the mafia, of course, who is morally blameworthy for the forced-choice coming about. But now that Sam and Sarah are trapped within it, and one of them must bear the unjust cost, what is the fair distribution of that wrongful harm? In this case, unlike *Falling Man* where there is no apparent or particularly important moral asymmetry between the actors, it seems that it is fair for Sam to bear the burden of that cost since he is responsible for the forced-choice in a meaningful way that Sarah is not. Importantly, Sam knows that he is responsible for the resulting forced-choice between two non-culpable actors when he acts. That is, he knows she is innocent and should not be harmed; as well as knowing, of course, the coercion he himself is under. The Evidence-Relative View, which assigns liability to Sam, accounts for this intuition which is at the core of the Agency View. Yet it also accounts for the intuition behind the Simple Culpability View that Sam's moral culpability is excused, whether in whole or in part, depending on the severity of the coercion.

3.4. Oversimplifying Epistemic Issues

I find that the majority of cases used in the defensive harm literature tend to oversimplify the moral issues they raise. This is done because nearly all these cases are given on the pretense of trying to isolate a moral asymmetry between actors and then uncover the principle behind that case. Yet these cases tend to do all their work along the axis of fact-relative permissibility without paying attention to evidence-relative norms. Additionally, they usually fail to consider the moral complications that third party intervention would entail, given differing epistemic vantage points. In this section, I endeavor to show how paying better attention to the evidentiary standing of actors in these cases changes many of our moral conclusions about them. In so doing, we also discover, perhaps unsurprisingly, that the Evidence-Relative View turns out to be a far better explanatory theory for such cases.

3.4.1 Evidentiary Considerations for Classic Cases

Once we complicate the picture by working along both the fact-relative and evidence-relative senses of wrong-doing, two things happen in our thinking over permissible defensive harm. First, we begin to see that many of the cases previously taken to be informative to our moral intuitions are actually vexed by implausible or vague evidentiary assumptions, or lack thereof, for the actors. Second, in many such cases, once we start filling in these gaps, the difficult moral dilemma facing one of the actors often disappears. Before I demonstrate this, by way of aside, let me say that one of my goals in my work is to recast many of these cases along evidentiary lines. I do not have this aim because *only* evidence-relative norms matter for our moral analysis of these cases; surely not. Again, I find that all the different senses of wrong-doing have moral import, even if just conceptually or in our analysis of moral cases.[15] But, rather, I have this goal because most scholarly attention has traditionally ignored the epistemic conditions of actors in defense cases. And, if nothing else, I hope that I have shown that what morality expects of someone depends in crucial, inescapable ways on what he or she can be expected to know in a given context.

Consider a new case, this one first offered by McMahan.

The Resident
Twin is the identical twin of a notorious mass Murderer, but is ignorant he even has a twin as they were separated at birth. Twin is driving in the middle of a stormy night in a remote area when his car breaks down. Twin is nonculpably unaware that his twin brother, Murderer, has within the past few hours escaped from prison in just this area, and that the local residents

---

[15] See the discussion of whether morality is univocal above in chapter 2.2.2.

have been warned of the escape. Murderer's notoriety derives from his invariable *modus operandi*: he violently breaks into people's homes and kills them immediately. As the twin, whose car has broken down, approaches a house to request to use the telephone, the resident of the house (Resident) takes aim to shoot him, preemptively, believing him to be Murderer.[16]

The Evidence-Relative View, of course, holds that neither Resident nor Identical Twin is liable to harm. In fact, it is a rather pure case of Tragedy. But what if Twin knew of his twin brother and had some reasonable way of knowing that Resident would likely take him to be his Twin brother in this instance? In that case, of course, he should not be approaching the house in the first place and the case becomes rather boring. In that case, Twin would be taking on some kind of relevant moral failing for the forced-choice scenario arising and he would no longer be nonliable. Further, he would no longer have evidence-relative permissibility to kill Resident in self-defense because he would know that Resident's attempted action against him was evidence-relative permissible *to* Resident. We can generalize this as follows. As soon as one party in a Tragedy is aware that the other party is, in fact, acting according to their own evidence-relative permissions, then that now-knowledgeable party loses his or her own evidence-relative permission to harm the other in defense. The reason is because the party, now in the know, is now aware that the other party is, in fact, nonliable (since the other party is behaving according to evidence-relative norms). Thus, as soon as one becomes aware of the other's relevant evidentiary problem, the entire case shifts and it is no longer a case of Tragedy. This generalization has tremendous impact on a wide-swatch of permissible defensive harm cases, and especially killing in war, as I will show.

Once we start to ask evidentiary questions of the various cases, we see a kind of principle develops for them: if it is reasonably possible for a nonliable victim to know that the opposing Nonresponsible Threat is, indeed, a Nonresponsible Threat (i.e., behaving according to evidence-relative norms), then (nearly always) the (now-knowledgeable) nonliable victim should have avoided the situation in the first place. If not—if they do not make every effort to avoid the situation even though they know it will result in the opposite actor becoming a nonliable threat—then they can become liable for that

---

[16] See McMahan, *Killing in War*, 164. I have here simplified the original case he uses and slightly edited it for clarity.

failing to avoid the situation which gave rise to the forced-choice between innocent parties in the first place.

That is, in forced-choice cases of Tragedy such as *Dignitary & Guest* or *Identical Twin*, the victim (Guest or Twin) either has access to evidence that they are not taking reasonable precaution to avoid the impending forced-choice situation, or they do not have such evidence. That is, if Twin had some reasonable way of knowing that approaching the house would result in the forced-choice that results, or if Guest had some reasonable way of knowing that the third party would project the gun on his hand resulting in the forced-choice between he and Dignitary, and so forth, and yet they still both proceeded into the forced-choice, then they do not have evidence-relative permissibility to defend themselves against the opposing actors harm because they now know that the other is nonliable. Since they know the other actor is nonliable, were they to go on to defend themselves against that party, they would be knowingly killing a nonliable person. Thus, they would be acting against their evidence-relative permissions and, hence, be liable to defensive harm themselves.

This perhaps sounds trivial, but if we imagine the cases in the real world, we see that it is not. Consider *Identical Twin*. Couldn't Resident do something other than engage in pre-emptive defensive harm so quickly? What if, for example, he did not open the door but instead called the police, then got his firearm, aimed it at Twin through a flanking window that was a safe distance away, and then called out to Twin, "Don't move! I have you in my crosshairs and the police are on their way! If you move a muscle I will shoot!" If he did that, Twin would almost certainly realize that this was something other than just a random roadside house he was asking to use the telephone. Indeed, he'd probably freeze, as instructed, until the cops got there. If Twin did not freeze, and instead took actions that could be interpreted as hostile, then it seems Twin would, at that point, be relevantly responsible in an asymmetrical way for the forced-choice that arises and, once again, we'd escape a Tragedy.

So, this means, given some rather plausible options for both actors, that it seems the case is not a Tragedy after all. Resident could have done many things to respond differently and, following that, Twin could have done many things to respond differently. In each case, their evidence-relative norms would thereby be significantly different, and neither can be said to be perfectly nonresponsible. For the case to hold and be used in the literature as it's designed, we must make unrealistic putative claims about what the actors could and could not do with regard to relevant evidence and possible investigative acts. It is the possibility of these investigative acts, and the moral demand to do so given the stakes, that changes the equation.[17]

Once we get into the weeds for the evidentiary standing of actors in these cases, we soon see that in almost every case—even the most important ones in the literature—are significantly altered by these considerations. Take, for example, even the famous case *Falling Man*. This case has been by far the singularly most important, and still continues to be, for self-defense literature in analytic moral philosophy of the past several decades. One might think that this case won't have these problems because of the clear non-responsibility of Falling Man and Trapped. But how on earth could someone have the evidence necessary to be justified in believing the putative beliefs that are ascribed to Trapped? Specifically, how could she possibly have the belief that if she does not vaporize Falling Man that her body will break the fall of his body in such a way that not only will she die but *he will live*?

I do not mean here to quibble over the assumptions necessary for these thought experiments but getting clear on these issues of belief and evidence in these cases refines our moral thinking on them. It is worth genuinely exploring: how *could* someone possibly know that at that exact height, velocity, etc., that Falling Man was falling that it would be the exact correct amount of force such that his falling body would survive but that Trapped would die? I can only think of a couple of scenarios in which this could possibly obtain. Here's one rather fanciful one: Trapped is a scientist who has been running precise tests on exactly what height, weight, etc. is needed such that for a falling body another human body would be able to cushion the force of impact to the exact right amount so that the falling body would live but the "cushioning" body would die.[18] Imagine this scientist version of Trapped, in fact, has been running experiments on this exact hole that she is now trapped in. In such a case, and such incredible evidentiary circumstances, Trapped could be faced with a real choice between vaporizing and not—between her life and Falling Man's life. But in nearly *any other case*, it seems like most of us would conclude *either* that Falling Man's impact would kill *both* he and Trapped or, alternatively, that it would kill *neither* of them but only severely

---

[17] The question often naturally presents itself here, to many, that this will have implications for what investigative actions we can hold people responsible for, especially given life or death stakes, and what that will mean for soldiers' responsibility to investigate the justificatory claims given them regarding wars in which they fight. We will explore this below.
[18] Imagine something like Jamie Hyneman running such experiments as they do on the television show Mythbusters.

injure them both. In either of these radically more plausible scenarios, there is no forced-choice. And, note, it's not only that it is more plausible that either they would both die or both live, but it's radically more plausible that one of those conclusions would be what a reasonable person in Trapped's situation would conclude.

3.4.2 Third-Party Intervention

A further way we can see how complicated the moral permissions are for these far-flung cases once we add evidentiary concerns is by considering how a third-party should intervene in them if one could. Imagine a third party who is watching the *Dignitary & Guest* Tragedy unfold from afar and has a sniper rifle with which he could intervene (call him Sniper). What should Sniper do? Fact-relatively, both parties are nonliable, so neither should die. If Sniper had full access to all information—the God's eye view, including each of their evidentiary standings—he should try to distribute the unjust harm as fairly as possible, as discussed above in chapter 2.6.2. This could include, perhaps, flipping a coin if there was time—though there most likely would not be time to determine an equitable division of unjust harm, given the case. But, regardless, Sniper would most likely not have the God's eye view on the case. What would it then be evidence-relative permissible for Sniper to do? Well, of course, that will depend on what evidence Sniper has accessible to him.

Let's consider two possibilities. First, imagine that from Sniper's vantage he cannot see the hologram of a gun projected onto Guest's hand by the villain. In that case, all the evidence available to Sniper would make it appear that Dignitary is unjustly trying to pull a gun to kill Guest and that Dignitary is thereby liable to harm to avert the threat she poses to him. In such an epistemic context, it would be evidence-relative permissible for Sniper to kill Dignitary in defense of Guest. Of course, his doing so would be a fact-relative impermissible harm delivered to Dignitary because Dignitary is, in fact, nonliable since she is acting in accord with her evidence-relative permissibility. This shows the ways in which the Tragedy can be extended to further parties. That is, this becomes a three-way Tragedy in that Sniper is behaving according to his evidence-relative permissions but will thereby deliver fact-relative wrongful harm to Dignitary, even though she herself is acting according to her evidence-relative permissions in delivering fact-relative wrongful harm; and it is this fact that gives Sniper the (incorrect) evidence that she is acting contrary to evidence-relative norms.

In a second case, imagine that Sniper also sees the projected hologram gun on Guest's hand, just as Dignitary does (and Guest, recall, does not). But, further, imagine that Sniper sees the Villain who is projecting the image and knows that it is fake. In that case, he sees that Dignitary's response is perfectly evidence-relative permissible, given the hologram and her evidentiary standing. In that case, he would not have evidence-relative permissibility to take Dignitary as liable and kill her in defense of Guest, though he may ultimately have reason to kill one over the other as a result of a fair distribution mechanism (such as flipping a coin, perhaps) to avert the Tragedy, or perhaps through some lesser-evil derivation. Notice, critically, that the Agency View here would (in this epistemic context) say that Sniper should kill Dignitary. Yet this seems wholly impermissible for, in this scenario we are considering, Sniper knows that both Dignitary and Guest are acting entirely permissibly according to the evidence available to each of them. Better, then, to say that this is a Tragedy, as the Evidence-Relative View does, and that Sniper has no *liability-based* reason to intervene and choose one life over the other.

What Sniper should do in this second scenario, of course, is to desperately try to figure out a way to break the epistemic confusion each actor is under which divides the actors' evidence-relative permissions from their fact-relative permissions. That is, if Sniper could somehow signal to Dignitary that Guest's gun is not real, or signal to Guest that Dignitary thinks he is pointing a gun at her, and so forth, then that is what he should do. If there is no way or no time to do that, perhaps he can shoot something near them to distract them until the epistemic confusion is cleared up. If there is no way to do that, perhaps he can injure one of them (by shooting them nonlethally) in such a way that it would avoid either of them fatally shooting the other. Of course, in that case, we'd have the same problem of distributing this unjust injury as we would for killing one of them over the other. But, clearly, harming one of them would be better than either of them killing the other. To decide which should be harmed by Sniper to prevent either death should, again, be some fair decision mechanism such as a coin-flip, for there is no liability difference between them.[19]

---

[19] Again, the Agency View thinks there *is* a liability difference between them (however small), and that small difference should make all the difference and that Dignitary should be shot to defend Guest.

Of course, in these cases we could add even a fourth party who sees Sniper's action. What if this fourth party could see all the relevant facts, but Sniper was just as epistemically constrained as Dignitary and so he was going to shoot Guest? Should this new fourth party kill Sniper to block that harm? Such questions could continue—and the Tragedy could be extended further out—infinitely. As odd as this sounds conceptually for a case like *Dignitary & Guest* where we have only one original imposition of unjust harm between two parties—and thus further extension beyond Sniper sounds implausible—such an extension of Tragedy in these ways (layers of people each acting in ways where their evidence-relative permissibility comes apart from their fact-relative permissibility) is precisely what I think happens in many contexts of war, as I will show in chapters 4 and 5.

3.5. Real-World Cases

To reflect on some of these above points and to better demonstrate the normative appeal of the Evidence-Relative View, there are some actual real-world cases that highlight the strengths of the evidence-relative account for liability in defensive harm beautifully. I'll focus on one case in particular for individual defensive norms at play, and then look wider and see how some examples in recent modern warfare vividly demonstrate elements of the view. The key case in question, first raised in scholarly work by David Rodin, centers on the circumstances surrounding the death of the actor Brandon Lee in the filming of the movie *The Crow*. Here I simplify and slightly change some of the details of the case for ease of discussion; but the relevant features of the case actually occurred in the real world.

Crow Shooting
Brandon Lee, the son of Bruce Lee, was a professional actor and was filming a movie called *The Crow* in 1993, in North Carolina. On one day of shooting, they were filming a scene where Lee's character enters a room and discovers his fiancée being beaten and raped by a gang of criminals. One of the actors playing the role of one of these criminals, Actor, was scripted to shoot a gun at Lee as he entered the scene. The prop used for the gun was supposed to be loaded with a kind of "dummy cartridge," similar to "blanks," that would appear to be real bullets, but would not actually be harmful. In addition to this prop, there were other prop effects staged in the room such that it

would appear as if the gun was really firing at Lee (e.g., things like small explosions going off to create the appearance of bullets striking nearby, etc.). The filming was behind schedule and the actors were not well briefed on the details of the chorography of the scene. Unfortunately, through an unintentional mix-up with the prop technicians, Actor's gun was loaded with real bullets. The mistake went unnoticed by all until filming of the scene began. Actor fired the real bullets at Lee. The bullets struck Lee and, eventually, killed him. Nearly all on set did not realize they were real bullets initially given the other special effects in the scene, and it took some time to clear up the confusion that Lee had actually been shot. Actor did not realize he had shot Lee with real bullets for some time.[20]

Again, this is a true, and tragic, story. But now consider a very slight adjustment to it. Imagine that rather than the first shots taken by Actor successfully hitting Lee, that they missed him slightly, but he (Lee) was thereby able to tell that they were real bullets. Also imagine that Actor was not so able to tell that they were real bullets (as he was unable in real life), and, hence, continued with the scene, and continued shooting at Lee. Lee was a highly trained martial artist. If such a scenario had unfolded, would Lee have had moral permission to defend himself with lethal force against Actor? Imagine Lee could have thrown a weapon of some kind—like a nearby martial arts throwing star, which were real props in the scene—at Actor to stop him from firing further. Would this have been permissible?

Given that Lee could have assumed that a mistake had been made concerning the props and that Actor is not maliciously trying to kill him, Lee thereby could conclude that Actor was not violating any evidence-relative norms in his shooting at him. That is, Lee knows that to Actor, it will appear that the special effects and the like are behaving normally, and that Actor takes himself to not actually be threatening Lee. According to all the evidence available to Actor, he is committing no wrong against Lee. That is,

[20] The death was ruled an accident. See Robert W. Welkos, "Bruce Lee's Son, Brandon, Killed in Movie Accident," *The Los Angeles Times* (April 1, 1993). For a detail accounting of the historical case, see Bridget Baiss, *The Crow: The Story Behind the Film* (New York: AbeBooks, 2000). For another discussion, see Joanne Cantor, "'I'll Never Have a Clown in My House'—Why Movie Horror Lives On," *Poetics Today* 25 (2004): 283–304. More recently, an accidental and unknowing shooting occurred while filming the movie *Rust* in October 2021. In this case, the actor Alec Baldwin fired a live bullet from a prop gun and accidentally killed the cinematographer Halyna Hutchins and injured director Joel Souza. See "What We Know About the Fatal Shooting on Alec Baldwin's New Mexico Movie Set," *New York Times* (April 2022), https://www.nytimes.com/article/alec-baldwin-shooting-investigation.html.

his act is evidence-relative permissible, even though it is fact-relative impermissible. And, critically (and rather amazingly and exceedingly rarely, in these kinds of cases), Lee would *actually know this* about Actor's epistemic situation. Since Lee knows that Actor is not violating any evidence-relative norms in this case, he knows that Actor is nonliable, and Lee therefore further knows that he would be in the wrong to kill Actor in self-defense. I find this fits better with our moral intuitions than does the alternative accounts of this case. The Agency View, for example, would here argue that Actor is liable since he is voluntarily engaging in an act which could be risk-imposing and that, therefore, Lee can permissibly kill Actor to defend himself, even though Lee *knows* that Actor is not knowingly trying to wrongfully harm Lee.

Notice that we could adapt the Lee case fairly easily, and in ways that could quite plausibly happen in the real world, such that it would then become a Tragedy. Consider:

Conspiracy Crow

For a couple of weeks leading up to the incident described in *Crow Shooting*, several cast members of *The Crow* have been spreading rumors that one of the actors has it out for Lee and wants to kill him. Further, the rumors speculate that one of the actors may try to kill Lee during filming. The rumors are being spread by a malicious Prop Tech who really does have it out for Lee. The rumors have reached Lee's ears and he has good reason, say, to take them seriously and is therefore concerned about his safety and worried that an actor may try to kill him during filming. The Prop Tech is the one in charge of the guns used in filming and he intentionally gives Actor the gun loaded with real bullets with the hope that Actor will unwittingly kill Lee. From here the case proceeds as it does in *Crow Shooting*.

In this case, because of the surrounding rumors and legitimate concerns, Lee could plausibly take Actor to be intentionally harming him. In such a case, Lee would be acting permissibly according to his evidence-relative norms to defend himself against Actor. Actor, of course, could then justifiably take Lee to be wrongfully harming him (since, recall, Actor is not even aware that his prop is actually threatening Lee—to Actor it would appear as if Lee were suddenly going off-script and trying to unjustly harm him). Such a case would be an instance of Tragedy. The two actors in the story would be trapped in an intricate symmetry whereby each behaved permissibly according to evidence-relative norms yet behaved fact-relative impermissibly, and that fact-relative impermissible action would be the very basis for the other's evidence-relative permissible, but fact-relative impermissible, action against the other. Note as well that this different epistemic context Lee is under in *Conspiracy Crow* (because of the rumors) offers a nice demonstration of how our moral intuitions regarding the permissibility of his defensive harm are shaped in accordance with Moral Epistemic Contextualism.

I mentioned, above, the more recent shooting case that occurred on during filming on the set of *Rust*. And there are likely other real-world cases like this between individuals. Such cases, like the Brandon Lee case, sound almost like thought experiments designed by a philosopher to elicit or unpack a key ethical intuition. But in addition to the individual cases, we can also imagine large-scale Tragedy occurring in the real world of this kind. I believe, horrifically, that Tragedies on such a scale are, in fact, often what occurs in war. Most recently, we can look to the 2022 Russian invasion of Ukraine and find countless cases where it appears, especially in the earliest days of the war, that many Russian soldiers were acting from positions of rather extreme epistemic confusion and ignorance. I reviewed this from one soldier's perspective, Lt. Col. Astakhov Dmitry Mikhailovich, in the introduction to this book. But note that this case is not properly a Tragedy, if Ukrainians defending their home is just—both evidence-relatively and fact-relatively—which it seems is surely the case. Even in those cases where a Ukrainian force knew, imagine, that an enemy Russian force was so confused as to their own cause, their own justified defense holds. We see that the Russian invasion for such soldiers is more like the original *Crow* example, where Lee likely knew that Actor did not understand the reality of the situation. Recall in that case, there's no liability-based reason for Lee to kill, but rather a kind of "lesser-evil" justification. The same would be true here for the Ukrainians. However, what this case shows is that even in that case, the Ukrainians likely have a "lesser-evil" based justification, even if they know the enemy soldiers are confused. Of course, we can then get into the questions of whether or not the Russian soldiers fulfilled their due diligence in determining the justice of the cause of the war they were fighting.[21] If they failed in that, then they could be found liable on those grounds. It's tragic, even if not a technical Tragedy. And it shows the sorrowful nature of war more broadly. Also note, that just as in the other

---

[21] Whether this should even hold and whether it's possible and thereby revisionist approaches to just war theory become irrelevant to the real world has been recently explored in Uwe Steinhoff, "The Indispensable Mental Element of Justification and the Failure of Purely Objectivist (Mostly "Revisionist") Just War Theories," *Zeitschrift Für Ethik Und Moralphilosophie* 3, no. 1 (2020): 51–67.

epistemically constrained cases above, the best move for an actor to make is to break the epistemic confusion. That is, to try to inform the Russians they are in the wrong.

As I conclude this chapter and the book moves to the application of this theory thus far presented to broader themes, such as war, I have to make a confession. It is a problem that plagues much of contemporary moral analytic philosophy. And the confession is this: I admit that this intricate, complex moral symmetry between actors caught in Tragedies, as I've been explicating for the last three chapters of this book, may sound like just so much arguing over the number of angels that can fit on the head of a pin. But, if I am correct thus far in the book, and the Evidence-Relative View is the correct understanding of the responsibility criterion necessary for liability attribution, then this analysis represents quite a bit more than just academic rumination and philosophical curiosity. Rather, it tells us what morality demands of us, if ever we are to kill justly. Though most of us believe it can be permissible to kill in some rare instances, claiming *justice*, for such a thing as taking a human life, thankfully seems far afield from our everyday lives. But in that human endeavor known as war, large-scale intentional killing is a central act. And if we think that soldiers may ever wage war justly, at least in some wars, and if we think that soldiers may kill one another justly, in at least some cases—and if maybe even this horror can ultimately ever be for the good and the right—then we owe it to ourselves to do the hard analytic work to get this question right. My hope is that these complex moral theories over when it is ever morally permissible to kill, can now help us think clearly about how it could ever be morally justifiable for soldiers to kill one another in war. That, as you'll recall, is the question this book hopes to answer, at least in part. It is to that issue that the remainder of this book now turns.

4
A Defense of Revisionist Just War Theory

> We make war that we may have peace.
> —Aristotle, *Nicomachean Ethics*, Book X.7

4.1. Introduction

Philosophical treatment of the ethics of war has a long and labored history. A particular set of dominant views on the morality of war has formed over many centuries and across countless scholars. Today we call this body of claims the just war tradition, the just war convention, or, simply, just war theory. It is not properly a single unified theory regarding why war can be just, but rather a series of claims and arguments regarding particular criteria that must be satisfied for a group to be properly justified in going to war (known as *jus ad bellum*) and for soldiers to behave justly within war (known as *jus in bello*). The criteria imply, of course, that war *can* be just, at least in some circumstances. It is thereby conceptually distinct from pacifism in that it thinks war *can be* morally permissible.[1] It is also sharply distinct from that collection of views known, variously, as Political Realism, International Realism, or Realpolitik, or sometimes, simply Realism in political science circles, in that just war theory takes war between states to be a moral matter, not an amoral question to be answered simply by an analysis of pure state self-interest. Out of these just war theory stipulations for *jus ad bellum* and *jus in bello*, a variety of doctrines have been developed, such as the distinction between combatants and noncombatants, the notion of interstate aggression, the (supposed) moral equality of soldiers within war, and noncombatant immunity, to name a few. The just war tradition has been remarkably stable. Relatively little has changed from its early instantiations in the Western canon in the writings of Saint Augustine all the way to its detailed exposition

---

[1] See note 1 in chapter 1 for more on various forms of pacifism.

by Michael Walzer in his 1977 book *Just and Unjust Wars*.[2] In more recent years, however, a dedicated group of scholars have revolted against many of the core principles of the long-held standard view. This revisionist approach to just war theory, as it is often called, rejects that the morality of war should somehow be cordoned off from the morality of everyday interpersonal life. Instead, it begins from a simple but powerful basis: the individual rights of all people. These revisionists argue that our approach to war must respect and take seriously people's rights, including the right to not be killed unjustly, just as those rights demand respect in any context outside of war. They conclude that in order to do this, some of the central vestments of the just war tradition must be discarded.[3]

One such cornerstone of traditional just war theory is that combatants on both sides of any conflict are equally legitimate targets of attack. This is not because they are engaged in wrongdoing but simply because they each pose a threat to one another. So long as they follow the *jus in bello* rules of proportionality and discrimination, the tradition contends, those soldiers who fight for an unjust cause and those who fight for a just cause are moral equals: both may permissibly kill and both may permissibly be killed. This is the doctrine known as the "moral equality of combatants thesis" (henceforth, MEC) and it has long been the standard view.[4] Indeed, the MEC is in many ways *the* fundamental lynchpin of the entire just war tradition superstructure. This is because it is the MEC that allows for the standard division of *jus ad bellum* and *jus in bello* to begin with and, many think, is what allows for the possibility of just war at all. The revisionist challenge to the MEC, however, is simple. It argues that one is not liable to be killed if one (merely) fights for a just cause. People have a presumptive right against being killed, after all, so why should a soldier fighting for a just cause lose that right for posing a *justified*

---

[2] Michael Walzer, *Just & Unjust Wars: A Moral Argument with Historical Examples* (New York: Basic Books, 1977).

[3] Note, of course, that there remain many opposed to the revisionist account, and this work and larger debates continues seemingly indefinitely—see Uwe Steinhoff, "The Indispensable Mental Element of Justification and the Failure of Purely Objectivist (Mostly "Revisionist") Just War Theories," *Zeitschrift Für Ethik Und Moralphilosophie* 3, no. 1 (2020): 51–67—as well as fascinating hybrid views on the obligations combatants face, like Massimo Renzo, "Political Authority and Unjust Wars," *Philosophy and Phenomenological Research* 99, no. 2 (2019): 336–57. And, although he would likely demur over such a label, I consider Michael Skerker's recent excellent work to be a form of a hybrid view as well. See Skerker, *The Moral Status of Combatants: A New Theory of Just War* (London: Routledge, 2020).

[4] See Walzer, *Just and Unjust Wars*, 34–41, for the classic exposition. For a fascinating look at modern views towards the moral equality of combatants, see Scott Sagan and Benjamin Valentino, "Just War and Unjust Soldiers: American Public Opinion on the Moral Equality of Combatants," *Ethics and International Affairs* 33, no. 4 (2019): 411–44.

threat against an unjust enemy? This is the central challenge pressed by the revisionists against the MEC and traditional just war theory more broadly. If there is no good answer forthcoming, then it seems we must reject the MEC. But doing so, and embracing the resulting revisionist position, greets its own multitude of objections and problems.

In this chapter, I have three aims. First, I'll briefly review the principles of conventional just war theory and will argue that there is no good basis for separating the morality of war from the morality of everyday life. If that is the case, then the moral rules that govern our thinking over permissible harm should also govern our thinking over the ethics of war. In the previous three chapters, I've laid out my approach to permissible defensive harm—an evidence-relative version of the Rights-Based Account. Applying this view to the ethics of war forces us to reject the MEC as well as several other elements of traditional just war theory. These rejections lead me to embrace a moderate version of revisionist just war theory.

Second, I will defend the revisionist position against a powerful objection raised against it: that without the MEC it is impossible to justify our convictions about legitimate and illegitimate targets. The worry is that the revisionist account is simply incompatible with the possibility of just war. The objection centers on the difficulty of being able to actually determine individual liability in war. If liability is not based on merely posing a threat, as the MEC would have, but is instead based on responsibility for posing a *wrongful* threat, then the determination of such responsibility could be problematic, or perhaps even impossible. At one extreme, nearly all on the unjust side (including civilians) might be liable to attack, depending on one's read of "'responsibility." At the other extreme, virtually no one may be liable (including even enemy soldiers). Either possibility fails to deliver just war. I will show how revisionist just war theory is not trapped by this dilemma and that just war is still possible without the crutch of the MEC. As one may predict, since so much of this objection is rooted in epistemic questions regarding the evidence one can have for another's liability, or for one's cause for war, the Evidence-Relative View is particularly apt at responding to it.

Finally, third, I will examine one recent alternative attempt at maintaining the MEC in the face of the revisionist challenge. I show that this attempt to ground the MEC also fails. What we are left with is a new approach to the ethics of war that cannot rely on a separate realm of morality for the rules of killing in war that are cut off from all other forms of killing. This makes fighting a war justly extremely difficult—although not, I contend, impossible.

In the next chapter, then, I will propose some new and pragmatic ways that the traditional rules of warfare could be adapted to fit this new revisionist paradigm. That is, how this could actually be done in the real world.

4.2. The Just War Tradition

Sometime around 418 A.D., the fifth century philosopher and theologian Saint Augustine wrote a letter to Boniface.[5] The matter at hand was Boniface's recent conversion to Christianity and his military service. At the time, Christianity was a distinctly pacifist religion—following the injunction of Jesus to love one's enemies, rather than to (say) kill them.[6] Thus, Boniface, who happened to be one of the few remaining competent generals in the fading Roman Empire's military, suffered a crisis of conscience.[7] But Augustine reassured Boniface. He told him that it was not impossible to please God through military service. Indeed, he instructed Boniface to embrace the spirit of a peacemaker even while he waged war and that he should accord mercy to his vanquished foes. Augustine pronounced that war should only be fought as a necessity, but that when it was so necessary it can indeed be just.

> Peace should be the object of your desire; war should be waged only as a necessity, and waged only that God may by it deliver men from the necessity and preserve them in peace. For peace is not sought in order to the kindling of war, but war is waged in order that peace may be obtained. Therefore, even in waging war, cherish the spirit of a peacemaker, that, by conquering those whom you attack, you may lead them back to the advantages of peace; for our Lord says: "Blessed are the peacemakers; for they shall be called the children of God."[8]

---

[5] While we have most of the letters (they had a long correspondence), just which historical Boniface he was writing to is not perfectly certain. But it was most likely "Count" Boniface, the general and governor of Northern Africa. See E. M. Atkins and R. J. Dodaro, ed. *Augustine: Political Writings* (Cambridge: Cambridge University Press, 2001).

[6] This is drawn, most directly, from the "Sermon on the Mount." See the Gospel of Matthew, Chapters 5 through 7. Note that the Christian pacifist tradition mentioned in chapter 1 (exemplified by the likes of Yoder and Hauerwas) still follows this basic line of thinking and regards itself, *contra* Augustine, as the correct understanding of Jesus's injunction.

[7] Given the shaky security of Rome to outside forces at the time, it's fair to assume that Augustine's worries were not merely the spiritual health of the newly converted Boniface.

[8] From "Letter 189" to Boniface, 418 A.D. See Atkins, *Augustine: Political Writings*.

And so, as the Roman Empire's decline set in, we see some of the earliest sparks of just war theory's fundamental principles expressed in the Western world. Augustine's articulation that war is something which should be done only out of necessity, with the restoration of peace as the ultimate goal for all involved, is still a bedrock tenet of *jus ad bellum*.[9] So, too, his concern that Boniface be merciful to his defeated foes—a rather radical notion in the ancient world—offers some of the first glimmers of the principles of *jus in bello* being positively argued for by a philosopher.[10]

From this point forward, the just war tradition continuously developed over the course of Christian scholarly history as a necessary justification for the evils of war to the Church. We can see that as the Church gained ever greater dominant power throughout Europe, it become more and more necessary for its scholars to write on the justification of war.[11] This is seen especially in the work of Thomas Aquinas in the 13th Century, whose work closely followed Aristotelian and Augustinian thinking.[12] But after the Reformation

---

[9] I am here indebted to many conversations with Martin Cook regarding the seeds of just war theory that can be mined in the letters Augustine wrote to Boniface. See Martin Cook, *The Moral Warrior* (Albany, NY: SUNY Press, 2004).

[10] Several centuries earlier, the Roman philosopher Cicero developed a legal or contractual understanding of how war should be fought in conflicts amongst those "within" the empire. (That is, Cicero did not think any notion of the "rules of war" applied to conflicts with the "barbarians" outside of the Empire's borders.) In Cicero's writing, we see some of the earliest *jus ad bellum* notions of proper authority and public declaration, and the *jus in bello* concept of discrimination. For a good discussion of Cicero's role in the development of just war theory, see Donald Davidson, *Nuclear Weapons and the American Churches: Ethical Positions On Modern Warfare* (Boulder, CO: Westview Press, 1983). In particular, see the chapter therein title "The Development of the Just War Tradition," pp. 1–18. But, as important as Cicero's work was, just war theory scholarship really only took off in full after Augustine. See Ronald Bainton, *Christian Attitudes Toward War and Peace: A Historical Survey and Critical Re-evaluation* (Nashville: Abingdon Press, 1960). There were, of course, even earlier thinkers who wrote on war such as, most notably, Aristotle. And we can hear some basic premises of *jus ad bellum* even in his words when he wrote, "We make war that we may have peace" in *Nicomachean Ethics*, Book X. And outside of the Western tradition, unsurprisingly, we also find a variety of ancient writers discuss issues closely related to the principles of the just war convention from Eastern and Near Eastern traditions. See, for example, Valerie Morkevicius, "Hindu Perspectives on Just War" and "Shi'i Perspectives on Just War" both in Howard Hensel, ed. *The Prism of Just War: Asian and Western Perspectives on the Legitimate Use of Military Force*, 145–68; and 169–94 (London: Ashgate Press, 2010).

[11] It would be difficult for a pacifist Church to maintain power across all of Christendom, after all.

[12] Aquinas developed a natural law concept of justice and applied that to his view of just war theory. Aquinas listed three specific *jus ad bellum* criteria as: right authority, just cause, and right intention. Aquinas also, of course, developed the incredibly important ethical concept known as the "Doctrine of Double Effect" (DDE). The DDE is used widely within the just war tradition to justify the unintentional, even if foreseen, killing of noncombatants as justifiable "collateral damage." For a thorough discussion of Thomistic views on just war theory, see Davidson, "The Development of Just War." Also see Waldo Beach and H. Richard Niebuhr, *Christian Ethics: Sources of the Living Tradition*, 2nd ed. (New York: John Wiley & Sons, 1973). Also see Frederick Russell, *The Just-War in The Middle Ages* (New York: Cambridge University Press, 1975). Also see Abbott A. Brayton and Stephana Landwear, *The Politics of War and Peace: A Survey of Thought* (Washington D.C.: University Press of America, 1981). Aquinas's work on just war theory here discussed is to be found, of course, in the

of the sixteenth century and the bloody wars of religion that followed, the need for a secular formulation of just war theory was apparent. We find this in the work of Hugo Grotius, the "Father of International Law," and his development of *jus gentium*—a "law of nations" that would be *valid etsi deus non daretur* ("even if there is no God").[13] Grotius' critical development of the just war tradition and the very notion of the "law of war" relied heavily on the just war scholarship of the natural law theorists Francisco Vitoria and Francisco Suarez the century prior.[14] From this point forward the development of the moral tradition of just war continued as eventual codification into our present international legal tradition including the first Geneva Convention in 1864 and later conventions, the Hague Convention in 1907, and the voluminous body of international law developed post-World War II in various conventions and international treaties.[15]

It is not overstating the case to say that the academic scholarship of this long just war tradition reached its apex in the work of Michael Walzer's *Just and Unjust Wars*.[16] It is also not overstating the matter to point out that essentially all Western academic scholarship on the ethics of war since 1977 to the present has in some way or other been in response to, or defense of, Walzer's articulation of just war theory. His presentation of the tradition in that work brought together most of its various manifestations in Western thought over the previous centuries and attempted to synthesize it into one coherent theory of the moral parameters guiding international conflict.[17]

Summa Theologica. See Thomas Aquinas, *Thomas Aquinas: Selected Writings*, ed. Ralph McInnery (New York: Penguin Classics, 1999).

[13] See Stephen C. Neff, ed., *Hugo Grotius on the Law of War and Peace: Student Edition* (1625; repr. Cambridge: Cambridge University Press, 2012). Again, I am here indebted to Martin Cook for many helpful discussions on this point.

[14] See Anthony Pagden and Jeremy Lawrance, ed., *Vitoria: Political Writings* (Cambridge: Cambridge University Press, 1992). And Benjamin Hill and Henrik Lagerlund, ed., *The Philosophy of Francisco Suarez* (New York: Oxford University Press, 2012). Another important jurist from this era was Samuel Pufendorf. See Craig Carr and Michael Seidler, ed., *The Political Writings of Samuel Pufendorf* (New York: Oxford University Press, 1994).

[15] Another helpful example of codification of just war theory principles, from the 19th century, was the "Lieber Code" on military operations in the American Civil War. (See The Lieber Code can be found in US War Department, *The War of the Rebellion: A Compilation of the Official Records of the Union and Confederate Armies* (Washington D.C.: Government Printing Office, 1899), Series III, Volume 3, pp 148–64.)

[16] Walzer, *Just and Unjust Wars*.

[17] This attempt to theorize the various claims of just war theory, many of which are merely presented as opposed to argued for in *Just and Unjust Wars*, has often come from Walzer after the original 1977 book. We see this effort primarily in the many new editions that have come out of *Just and Unjust Wars*, as well as in works such as, *Arguing About War* (New Haven: Yale University Press, 2004) and Walzer's many responses to the various criticisms and challenges his orthodoxy has received.

Just war theory, as mentioned, divides the principles for just war into two categories, *jus ad bellum* and *jus in bello*. Traditionally, it is held that the *jus ad bellum* criteria must *all* be met for a given group to be justified in going to war.[18] Different writers specify different particular criteria of *jus ad bellum*, and disagreement persists over whether certain criteria should be lumped together conceptually with others, but there is a strong consensus amongst traditional just war theorists on the most central criteria. They can be enumerated easily. For a state to be justified to go to war they must have satisfied all of the following *jus ad bellum* criteria: just cause, just intent, last resort, proper authority, reasonable hope of success, final aim of peace, public declaration, and (global or strategic) proportionality.[19] The traditional principles of *jus in bello* are two: proportionality and discrimination. Some writers will also include military necessity as a further *jus in bello* principle, while others think that *in bello* proportionality already encapsulates the military necessity condition.

These criteria for just behavior in war and for going to war generate several central just war theses. For example, the *in bello* principle of discrimination (that soldiers must discriminate between combatants and noncombatants and only intentionally target combatants), entails the highly morally intuitive doctrine of noncombatant immunity for war. The *ad bellum* principle of just cause (and the notion that a set of criteria must be met before war can be justly declared) implies a strong presumption of peace and entails that anytime war is justly waged it is in response to another state breaking the peace and doing wrong (i.e., through committing the international crime of aggression).

Traditionally, the *ad bellum* and *in bello* distinction is not seen as merely some heuristic means to keep the various concepts straight. Rather, the division between the two is itself a central mainstay in the just war tradition and theoretically substantive. This division is perhaps well captured by the clichéd line in Alfred Tennyson's "Charge of the Light Brigade," cynically taken to mean that it is not a soldier's place "to make reply / Theirs not to reason why / Theirs but to do & die."[20] The thought is that it is on the soldiers'

---

[18] A "given group" here is traditionally conceived of as a state—particularly since the Treaty of Westphalia gave rise to the modern notion of a nation-state. But it need not as demonstrated by some of the earliest writers, such as the *jus ad bellum* claims made far earlier by the likes of Augustine.

[19] See Martin Cook, *The Moral Warrior*, for a good discussion of these various criteria. For an argument that nearly all the *jus ad bellum* criteria are properly understood as falling under the criteria of just cause, see Jeff McMahan, "Just Cause for War," *Ethics and International Affairs* 19 (2005): 1–21.

[20] Alfred Tennyson, "Charge of the Light Brigade," in *Tennyson: Selected Poems*, edited by Christopher Ricks (New York: Penguin Classics, 1995): 215–17.

shoulders to behave justly within war; but it is not their responsibility to determine the justice of the war for which they fight.[21]

This is why the MEC is so crucial to conventional just war theory. The MEC claims that so long as combatants on both sides of any war fight according to the rules of *jus in bello*, they are morally blameless for their acts within war. If that is the case, then it is wholly irrelevant whether or not a group of soldiers from a given side has met the *jus ad bellum* criteria to their ability to behave justly in war. Thus, there is a sharp divide between *jus in bello* and *jus ad bellum* and this is by design. That is, it is taken as a feature, not a bug, of the just war tradition. We also see how the very *jus in bello* notion of discrimination becomes so critical. If all soldiers who fight, regardless of the justice of their cause, are legitimate targets of attack, then all that matters (morally), on the question of who they kill in war, is simply that they only kill one another—that they only target other combatants like themselves.[22]

Walzer delivers an in-depth presentation of the MEC throughout *Just and Unjust Wars*. And his assertions are not out of thin air, of course. He contends that the experience of soldiers as purely instruments of the state, which is using war to accomplish a political end, results in them *properly* understanding themselves as victims of that instrumental use. Thus, contends Walzer, soldiers hold that the opposing soldier who is fighting against them, "though his war may be criminal, is nevertheless as blameless as oneself."[23] And Walzer thinks this is not just a phenomenological matter soldiers encounter in war, but that it is the correct moral conclusion to draw of war and soldiering generally. By recognizing how they view themselves, claims Walzer, "we draw a line between the war itself, for which soldiers are not responsible, and the conduct of the war, for which they are responsible, at least within their own sphere of activity."[24] The basis Walzer uses for who is and who is not a combatant is based on the notion of mutual threat within the confines of war. According to this traditional view, it is this mutual imposition of threat on the other that opens up a soldier for legitimate attack. For

---

[21] See, for example, the speech from William Shakespeare's *Henry V* wherein one of the king's soldiers makes a remark about his own culpability for the justice of their cause, "for we know enough if we know we are the King's subjects. If his cause be wrong, our obedience to the King wipes the crime of it out of us." (*Henry V*, Act IV, Scene 1.) Many thanks to Martin Cook for first pointing out this passage to me and its relevance to the *ad bellum* and *in bello* distinction.

[22] One can't help but here be reminded of Calvin's inquiry to his father discussed in the introduction to this book: "How do soldiers killing each other solve the world's problems?" (See figure I.1 in the Introduction.)

[23] Walzer, *Just and Unjust Wars*, 36.

[24] Ibid., 36.

example, Walzer argued that a soldier "can be personally attacked only because he already is a fighter. He has been made into a dangerous man, and though his options may have been few [e.g., he may have been conscripted], it is nevertheless accurate to say that he has allowed himself to be made into a dangerous man. For that reason, he finds himself endangered."[25]

4.3. A Separate Morality of War?

The structure of traditional just war theory, just laid out, carves out a unique moral realm for the killing done in war that is wholly separate from how we normally conceive of the morality of killing. Many think this is how it should be. War is a distinctly special moral case, they claim. And when it comes to the horrific realities of war, we cannot try to apply the rules of everyday morality. To do so, they argue, misunderstands the nature of war itself.

Michael Walzer, of course, has been by far the most influential and important proponent of this view. Henry Shue has been another.[26] Walzer has generally relied on assertions of soldiers' experiences, like that mentioned above, to make this point.[27] Shue, however, offers a far more nuanced view with substantive, and often compelling, arguments in defence of the traditional view. It is not that there are two moralities, one which applies to ordinary life and one which applies to war, argues Shue. Rather, due to the distinctive features of war, it is governed by unique moral realities quite distinct from that of

---

[25] Walzer, *Just and Unjust Wars*, 145. Thomas Nagel also argued for the MEC on the same basis of mutual threat. Thomas Nagel, "War and Massacre," *Philosophy & Public Affairs* 1, no. 2 (1972).
[26] Shue's particular defense of a unique understanding of the morality of war is found in "Do We Need a 'Morality of War'?," in *Just and Unjust Warriors*.
[27] Assertions which have occasionally been flagrantly dismissive of the revisionist challenge to traditional just war theory orthodoxy. Of particular note here is the many ways and instances in which Walzer has simply dismissed the arguments of the most influential revisionist, Jeff McMahan, rather than even address his claims with counter-arguments or reasoned defense of the traditional view. See, for but one example in print, Michael Walzer, "Response to McMahan's Paper," *Philosophia* 34 (2006): 43–45. I myself have witnessed such treatment of the revisionist challenge firsthand. At the annual McCain Conference hosted by the Stockdale Center for Ethical Leadership, in Annapolis, Maryland, in 2011, Walzer was invited to give the keynote address. After his talk, during the question and answer session, Jeff McMahan presented a careful and well-reasoned objection, complete with a highly plausible thought experiment to make the point—a thought experiment that could easily obtain in the real world. Rather than even consider the objection, Walzer simply replied, after a deep sigh, "I don't know Jeff. Who knows? That's a philosopher's question. And I'm not a philosopher." That claim, of course, is one hell of a dodge. Needless to say, in my view, the response embarrasses Walzer far more than his intended target and belies the lack of an adequate response to the challenges posed to the traditionalist by the revisionists.

life outside war.[28] The claim is that those revisionists who hope to apply our moral thinking on permissible killing in interpersonal self-defense cases to war "beg the question by assuming a false analogy or continuity between the rules appropriate to war and the rules appropriate to other aspects of ordinary life."[29] Since war is so different from ordinary life, the acts committed in war are "necessarily incompatible" with many of the strictures of ordinary morality—or so is the claim.

The recent revisionist approach to just war theory contends, *pace* Walzer and Shue and more or less the entire just war theory canon, that there can be no such separation between realms of morality. And, indeed, that the same moral basis for permissible killing we use in "ordinary life" should apply universally, be it in "ordinary life" or war. And that moral basis, recall, is that only a liable party should be killed as a means to avert an unjust wrong. Applied to war, this means that only soldiers who have made themselves liable to be killed, should be killed. But Shue complains, understandably, that if we hold to an *individual* moral liability criterion for killing in war—given the kind of activity war is—that combatants in war could never determine whether an individual soldier is properly liable. Because of this, Shue thinks we are left with a difficult choice. On the one hand, "all bets are off" and some kind of naïve realpolitik amorality to war will result. That is, there is no plausible moral restriction on behavior in war *at all* if we try to conceive of the killing in war like that of ordinary life. Alternatively, "if we are to have a morality of war at all, it must presuppose a criterion for liability that is very different to that appropriate in contexts outside of war."[30] That is, in other words, traditional just war theory holds that in war one can be liable as a legitimate target of attack in ways that we would never grant outside of war, but that we *must* grant this different model of liability for war if there is to be any attempt to fight war justly. We simply cannot expect soldiers in war, Shue contends, to be held to the same kinds of moral strictures on killing people that we do in ordinary life.[31] To do so is a fool's errand.

---

[28] Henry Shue, "Do We Need a 'Morality of War'?," *Just and Unjust Warriors*; Michael Walzer, "What is Just War Theory About?," unpublished paper, presented Israel Institute for Advanced Study, July 11, 2011.
[29] Rodin, "Superior Law," presented at Oxford's Ethics, Law, and Armed Conflict Center's Annual Workshop on War (Oxford, UK, August 2011). I am indebted in this section to Rodin's work therein.
[30] This is Rodin here explaining the argument on behalf of Shue. See Rodin, "Superior Law."
[31] As Shue writes, "The fundamental problem with [the revisionist] view, I believe, is the assumption that it would ever generally be possible during deadly combat to make judgements about the moral liability to attack of individuals (whatever the content of the criterion of liability, short of a highly nonstandard conception). At most, combatants can sometimes make judgements about threat, which is one traditional basis for considering others to be combatants; being "non-innocent" means threatening

Shue's words here are particularly instructive, and my argument in this chapter is primarily focused on a position best articulated by Shue, so I will quote him at length on this point. Shue writes,

> The fundamental problem with [the revisionist] view, I believe, is the assumption that it would ever generally be possible during deadly combat to make judgements about the moral liability to attack of individuals (whatever the content of the criterion of liability, short of a highly non-standard conception). At most, combatants can sometimes make judgements about threat, which is one traditional basis for considering others to be combatants; being 'non-innocent' means threatening harm. But to require regular judgements of individual moral liability would be to require that the combatant judge not only whether there is a threat of harm but also whether the threat is wrongful in each individual case. This would require making discriminating judgements about features of specific individuals in a situation in which many individuals, most of whom he or she cannot see, are routinely and relentlessly, hour after hour, day after day, trying to kill him or her. This is not generally possible, however morally desirable.[32]

Part of Shue's basis for thinking this is due to the epistemic constraints that soldiers tend to encounter in the fog and horrors of war.[33] The idea is that war is so unimaginably tragic and awful, as well as complicated and confusing, that humans simply cannot make the same kinds of moral judgments, while under war conditions, that we do in other realms. As Shue explains, "The impossibility within war of making many important ordinary moral discriminations is a large part of what is so alarmingly tragic about war and is, once again, one of the main reasons why wars must not be entered into as

---

harm. But to require regular judgements of individual moral liability would be to require that the combatant judge not only whether there is a threat of harm but also whether the threat is wrongful in each individual case. This would require making discriminating judgements about features of specific individuals in a situation in which many individuals, most of whom he or she cannot see, are routinely and relentlessly, hour after hour, day after day, trying to kill him or her. This is not generally possible, however morally desirable." Shue, "Do We Need a 'Morality of War'?," 100.

[32] Shue, "Do We Need a 'Morality of War'?," 100.
[33] As Shue explains, "Combatants have neither the information nor the opportunity for reflection necessary for making such a multitude of individual judgements about unknown and often unseen/unheard but deadly adversaries, and a requirement of making such impossible judgements is inappropriate to the circumstances of war." Ibid., 99.

lightly as they recently have been."[34] And, given the horrors and realities of war that we all recognize, this is not implausible.

Thus, defenders of the traditional view contend, to challenge that the morality of war (as conceived by the just war tradition) is inadequate *on the basis* of being different from our moral conceptions of ordinary life is to *beg the question*. For such a challenge presupposes that there is, in fact, continuity between the moral rules governing everyday life and the moral realities of war.[35] They hold that there is no such continuity.[36] But the revisionist argues that the resulting morality of war these traditionalists thereby defend, does not properly respect the rights of individual persons. For, again, if a soldier fighting for a just cause (a "just soldier") has done nothing to make himself liable to harm—if he has done no wrong in fighting for a just cause—then is it not unfair to that just soldier to claim that a soldier fighting for an unjust cause (an "unjust soldier") has a moral permission to kill him? Why does that soldier lose his right to life due to another's wrongful action? The just soldier has a presumptive moral right to not be killed, after all. It therefore seems absurd to claim that his doing a morally justified and even morally commendable thing—such as defending his nation from attack as part of a just war, say—should actually be the *cause* of him losing his right to not be killed. Yet Walzer and Shue wish to say that the activity of war is so very different—so discontinuous from other human activity—that we simply *cannot* satisfy the same moral demands we ordinarily would. To assume otherwise is to beg the question that there should be such continuity, or so the traditional account claims.

Although there is some intuitive support for this traditional view, I ultimately find that this demand for discontinuity between the supposedly distinct moral realms of war and "ordinary" moral life is both unfounded and wrongheaded. Notice that, although it is tragic, there are many people's whose *entire lives* are lived under the duress and chaos of war. In their case, war effectively *is* "ordinary life." One might think this simple point itself refutes the traditional view on this score by making it vacuous. But the dispute here is best captured (and thereby better shown faulty) by way of analogy to other areas of our moral understanding. Rodin, in criticizing this demand for distinct moral rules for killing in war, gives us the following elegant response

---

[34] Ibid., 100.
[35] See Rodin, "Superior Law," for a helpful discussion of this point.
[36] Michael Walzer, "Response to McMahan's Paper," *Philosophia* 34 (2006): 43–45, at p. 43. "What Jeff McMahan means to provide . . . is a careful and precise account of individual responsibility in time of war. What he actually provides, I think, is a careful and precise account of what individual responsibility in war would be like if war were a peacetime activity."

which highlights the problem for the separate moral realities claim of the traditionalist. He asks us to consider a slaveholder living in the United States antebellum South having an argument with an abolitionist. What would we make of the following reply from the slaveholder?

> You tell me that slavery is morally impermissible because it is inconsistent with the dignity of persons and the fundamental precept that no human should be the chattel property of another. But this simply begs the question by applying the moral rules appropriate to ordinary life to the quite different activity of slave-holding. Nowhere have you demonstrated that there is a meaningful continuity between the moral rules appropriate to ordinary life and the moral rules appropriate to slave-holding. Indeed slave-holding is so different from ordinary life that the practice would be utterly impossible if one had to abide by ordinary moral rules such as the prohibition on owning another person. This is indeed one of the tragic things about slavery. If we are to have moral rules regulating the practice of slavery to mitigate the suffering it causes, we must recognise that the content of those regulations must be very different to the content of ordinary morality and must allow the owning of other persons.[37]

As a devastating *reductio absurdum*, this is beautiful. Most certainly, we would all reject such reasoning offered by the slaveholder for a special moral dispensation over the practice of slavery. But why should we view the arguments offered by the just war theory traditionalists arguing for a distinct realm of moral rules for killing in war any differently than this argument offered by the slaveholder? What Rodin's analogy makes clear is that simply because a certain kind of action is exceptional, this does not entail that the activity itself should be considered morally acceptable—much less that the special moral rules that supposedly govern it distinctly from the rest of our moral lives somehow obtain because of that fact. Indeed, we should infer the *opposite*. If a particular conduct is so divergent from normally permissible action that it thereby requires its own divergent moral rules, we should be suspicious of the moral legitimacy of the activity in the first place; we should not see that divergence as somehow self-justifying.[38]

---

[37] Rodin, "Superior Law."
[38] See Rodin, "Superior Law." I am here in this section heavily reliant on Rodin's argument in that piece. As he writes, "It follows neither that the rules, or the activity itself, are morally acceptable. Any practice that requires separate moral rules, divergent from the moral rules of everyday life must itself be assessed in moral terms."

Another example helps drive home the point even more powerfully, especially for killing and war. Consider that regrettable institution in the United States known as the "mafia." In these organized crime syndicates, there are various levels of operators who perform various tasks. They often end up killing one another for various nefarious reasons in support of the crime organization or against a rival criminal organization. The television series, *The Sopranos*, captured the life of one such fictional crime family and its kingpin, Tony Soprano. In one scene, Tony is speaking to his therapist, Dr. Melfi, and she asks him about the spiritual destination (and presumptive moral status) of his nephew, Christopher, who had recently murdered someone at the mafia boss's request.

DR. MELFI: [on Christopher] Do you think he'll go to hell?
TONY: No. He's not the type that deserves hell.
DR. MELFI: Who do you think does?
TONY: The worst people. The twisted and demented psychos who kill people for pleasure, the cannibals, the degenerate bastards that molest and torture little kids. They kill babies. The Hitlers. The Pol Pots. Those are the fucks that deserve to die, not my nephew.
DR. MELFI: What about you?
TONY: What? Hell? You been listening to me? No, for the same reasons. We're soldiers. Soldiers don't go to hell. It's war. Soldiers they kill other soldiers. We're in a situation where everyone involved knows the stakes and if you're gonna accept those stakes you gotta do certain things. It's business. Soldiers. We follow codes, orders.[39]

Now far be it from me to argue who is and who is not going to hell. However, I imagine a traditionalist about just war theory and the MEC would be uncomfortable with Tony's adoption of the special status, and thereby special moral exemptions towards how they engage one another, afforded to his mafia "soldiers." Tony is here giving a classic, traditionalist just war theory argument that because all involved "knows the stakes," that makes all who enter into this kind of conflict legitimate targets. But the idea that soldiers in war have consented and agreed to be killed by soldiers from the opposing side is untenable.[40] Again: a just soldier has done nothing to surrender his right to

---

[39] *Sopranos*, Season 2, Episode 9, "From Where to Eternity." The transcript can be accessed at: http://www.tvfanatic.com/quotes/shows/the-sopranos/page-2.html#ixzz1oef8Yxwv
[40] McMahan dispels this attempt to ground the MEC at length in *Killing in War*.

not be killed when he fights on behalf of a permissible cause. Arguing for the MEC for war is based on the same fallacious logic used here by Tony Soprano. When Tony Soprano employs this logic, its moral absurdity is obvious. Why then should we treat the MEC in just war theory any differently?[41] We should not. And, notice, to do otherwise reduces the claimed noble behavior of soldiers in war to being nothing more than the effective moral equivalent of a mob gang war. Viewed in this light we see that it is the traditionalist, not the revisionist, which actually denigrates soldiers and presents soldiers' lives and their endeavors as somehow less worthy than "normal" people.[42] The MEC must be rejected as a plausible moral doctrine for war.

What these examples of the slaveholder's special pleading and Tony Sopranos' demand for special moral rules reveal is that the burden is on those who would claim a special set of divergent moral rules for any particular human activity to show why this should be granted; the traditionalists must make the positive case for their presumed discontinuity. But, further, the justification for such a claim can only be achieved, as Rodin argues, "by reference to the values and principles of ordinary morality itself."[43] That is,

---

[41] Note: there are some circumstances in war when soldiers on both sides are equally liable to harm, but this will occur when both sides are equally unjust in their aims or when soldiers from each side are trapped in a Tragedy (as defined above in chapter 3). I will discuss such cases at length in chapter 5. But just the mere fact that there may be some cases where there will be liability symmetry between soldiers in war does not rescue the MEC as a moral understanding for all war. That being said, I think Tragedies, in my technical sense, occur in war with some regularity in instances of individual killing.

[42] The reader may here look to the quote from Charlie Chaplin I present in the conclusion of the book.

[43] Rodin, "Superior Law." Rodin makes the point that there are some other areas where we *do* think it is appropriate to have a localized moral rule. But in all these cases the justification for such special rules can only be achieved by reference to the values and principles of ordinary morality itself. Consider for example, the separate and divergent rules that allow prosecuting barristers to engage in aggressive questioning of witnesses or allow psychiatrists to not disclose potentially incriminating information about their clients (within reason). In each of these cases, we ask whether permitting a localized deviation from ordinary moral rules by these special codes is justifiable in terms of the broader contribution they make to those same underlying ordinary moral values. In both cases the answer is yes, though it is equally apparent that the burden of proof is held by those who propose and maintain the separate moral code. So, to be clear, it is of course possible that Shue is correct, and war does require this special set of moral rules. But the burden of proof is on him to establish that, rather than the other way around. Moreover, I think what's really going on here is that the traditionalists like Walzer and Shue are essentially laying down a challenge to the revisionists: "War cannot be made just without these special moral rules." And we revisionists are saying, "Perhaps it can be. We should, in the least, try to see if a coherent just war theory can be developed without them." That is my aim in this and the next chapter: to meet the challenge of the traditionalists and show that just war theory can survive without the crutch of the MEC. The traditionalist reliance on a special category of morality for war is a significant cost. If we can formulate an understanding of just war without this cost, we should. The traditionalists like Shue think that is impossible to do, so they accept this cost as necessary if we are to have a workable just war theory. On this reading, then, the aim of the revisionists is to show, first, that this is indeed a cost and, second, if it can be avoided (if we can formulate a workable

whether or not Shue is right in his claim that the revisionists are begging the question in assuming a continuity between the morality of ordinary life to that of how we should behave in war, will itself be judged (can *only* be judged) by the standards of ordinary morality itself. It would be circular to determine that the morality of war—or slavery, or organized crime—is governed by special moral rules already assumed to be distinct from the rest of morality. We must *first* judge whether the activity in question should have distinct moral rules. As Rodin writes, "ordinary every-day morality is thus inescapable."[44]

Hence, while one appreciates the grounds for Shue's insistence on the truly special character of the nature of war and, thereby, the desire to limit the horrors of war by means of special rules, such as the MEC, we must reject the claim.[45] We must rely on "ordinary" morality for our analysis of war. And ordinary morality holds that, other things being equal, intentionally killing another human being is (usually) one of the most basic wrong acts anyone can perform. As we've seen, there are some instances when it is permissible to kill. But that permissibility must be justified and based on a moral claim about the person being killed and the relevant context of their action, not *merely* the particular kind of human activity of which it is a part.

4.4. Revisionist Just War Theory and Its Discontents

The revisionist approach to just war theory argues the following: let us take individual rights seriously and apply the moral demands they generate to our ethical understanding of war. Recall in chapter 1. we saw that on a Rights-Based Account for the killing of one person over the other to be permissible and not be a violation or infringement of an individual's rights, one must do something to make oneself liable to harm such that the harming does not violate his or her right. That is, we saw that there must be some relevant moral asymmetry between actors to have permissible killing. When we turn to war, however, what would this asymmetry consist in? If a soldier is ever right in harming an opposing soldier, what could be the basis for that permissibility?

---

just war theory without this cost), we should, and, finally, that the cost can be so avoided without the demise of a plausible just war theory.

[44] Rodin, "Superior Law."
[45] As Rodin writes, critiquing Shue: "The supposition of a viable, separate and divergent morality of war or law of war may feel reassuring, but it is ultimately not sustainable." "Superior Law," 24.

The MEC, of course, contends that a soldier's permissibility to kill other soldiers is grounded not in asymmetry, but on a particular *symmetry* between them: opposing soldiers are each legitimate targets of attack on the basis of mutual threat. But with the revisionist rejection of the MEC, we are back to searching for a permissible basis for harm. I embrace the revisionist rejection of the MEC. This means I have the hard work of grounding permissible killing in war and, as I'll defend below and in chapter 5, how permissible targeting in war can even work without the MEC.

Recall the central argument used by the revisionists for the rejection of the MEC: a soldier fighting for a just cause (hereafter, "just soldier") has done nothing to make himself liable to be killed.[46] All people (a set which happens to include soldiers fighting in war) have a presumptive right against being killed.[47] And if just soldiers haven't lost their right to not be killed, then enemy soldiers violate that right if they kill them. But in that case, the soldiers fighting for an unjust cause (hereafter, "unjust soldiers") cannot actually discriminate at all, for if it is wrong to kill just soldiers, unjust soldiers have *no* legitimate targets whatsoever. So, it's thereby *impossible* for unjust soldiers to follow the *jus in bello* requirement of discrimination. Hence, a soldier's side must have just cause for her to even be *capable* of acting justly in war. The presumption of moral symmetry between soldiers is thus abandoned. And if the justice of the cause for which a soldier fights is necessary to be capable of behaving justly in war, then that means there is no longer a separation between *jus ad bellum* and *jus in bello*. The two run together; whether one can behave justly *in* war is intimately tied to the justice *of* a war. Contra the cynical Tennyson line, it is, most certainly, the soldier's responsibility "to question why," precisely because they are the ones who are going to "do and die." And, even more importantly, the soldiers must question why because they are the ones who are going to *kill*.[48]

With the abandonment of the MEC, we see what the basis for the moral asymmetry between soldiers required for liability to permissible harm must be: it is the justice (or lack thereof) of the cause for which the soldier fights. Recall from chapters 1 and 2 that one becomes liable to be killed only if there

---

[46] I will use "soldier" interchangeably with combatant and "civilian" interchangeably with noncombatant.

[47] Lazar calls this the "great force of a victim's right to life" in Seth Lazar, "Responsibility, Risk, and Killing in Self-Defense," *Ethics* 119, no. 4 (2009), 728. He is certainly correct that it is very difficult to over-ride this great force. But it can be done, in some cases. See McMahan, *Killing in War*, 44.

[48] This aspect of what soldiers actually do in warfare (compared to civilians) becomes a critical defense of the revisionist view below in section 4.4.3.

is some wrong for which one is responsible. One loses the right to not be killed and becomes liable to defensive killing, for example, when one is sufficiently morally responsible for a threat of proportionate unjust harm to another person. So, the wrong an enemy soldier poses—and for which he can be held responsible—is fighting on behalf of an unjust cause. If killing that unjust soldier is a necessary and proportionate part of thwarting that unjust cause carried out in the prosecution of that war, then it seems that it could be permissible on the Rights-Based Account, without relying on the MEC.

Thus, *contra* the views of Walzer and Shue just canvassed, we should morally appraise soldiers on opposing sides of a just cause, and their attempts to kill one another, quite differently. And rightly so. As McMahan writes, "The morality of war is not a product of our devising. It is not manipulable; it is what it is. And the rights and immunities it assigns to unjust combatants are quite different from those it assigns to just combatants."[49] The reason the moral realities of unjust soldiers are different from that of just soldiers is precisely the same reason the moral realities of Attacker are quite different from that of Defender in the *Defender and Attacker* case. It is because of a relevant moral asymmetry between the two; an asymmetry that makes one of them liable and the other not.

In addition to these arguments offered above for the rejection of the separate morality of war claims of the traditionalists, there is another approach we can take to show the plausibility of the revisionist view as it applies to war. And that is to simply try it and see if it works. Let us try to apply a revisionist account of just war theory to the realities of war and see if it is possible to come up with a coherent, workable, and plausible model. If it is, then so much better for the plausibility of the revisionist view and so much the worse for the traditionalist camp which demands these old theoretic relics such as the MEC are necessary for any workable model of just war. That is precisely what I will attempt to do for much of the remainder of this book.

---

[49] Jeff McMahan, "The Morality of War and the Law of War," *Just and Unjust Warriors*, 35. He is here comparing the morality of war to the constructed laws of war which are manipulable. There is large debate currently underway within the revisionist "orthodoxy" over whether the laws of war should follow the revised view on the morality of war. McMahan argues no. Rodin has recently argued yes. I responded to Rodin's argument by pointing out that, if he is right, then his arguments take us much further than he will be comfortable. That is, I think that if he is right in his claims in that paper that we would then be required to open up liability attribution in war far into the reaches of those traditionally labeled noncombatants (i.e., he could no longer maintain a blanket noncombatant immunity to both harm and legal liability). And, thus, Rodin's "restrictive asymmetry" would have to give way to permissive asymmetry. (Strawser "Response to Rodin," Oxford's Institute for Ethics, Law, and Armed Conflict Annual Workshop, Oxford, UK, August 2011.)

Below, in this chapter, I will first defend the revisionist rejection of the MEC against a particularly powerful objection. Then, in chapter 5, I will lay out a new proposal for how targeting in war could be based on the revisionist model, rather than on the MEC. Then, in the following two chapters, I show how liberalism is able to ground justification for a state to go to war on a right to individual autonomy, rather than the traditional arguments employed for national defence.[50]

4.4.1 The Responsibility Dilemma for Revisionist Just War Theory

The revisionist rejection of the MEC, and all the modifications of standard just war theory that result from it, face a serious objection. This objection is not grounded in a defense of the MEC.[51] Rather, it is internal to the revisionist view because it agrees with the rejection of the MEC as a necessary and correct result of taking individual rights seriously in war. But it contends that the rejection comes at an extremely high cost. The cost is this: that the revisionist account is incompatible with just war. In ways very similar to how Shue argued that liability attribution in war is very difficult, this objection centers on the difficulty of determining liability in war. Shue made this point to argue that, therefore, an alternative criterion for liability is required for the morality of war and, hence, the MEC remains. This objection, however, makes the same case for the difficulty with liability determination, but not in doomed defense of the MEC. Rather it claims that the revisionist account is thereby unworkable as a theory for how war can be plausibly fought justly. If liability is not based on posing a threat but is instead based on responsibility for a *wrongful* threat, then the determination of such responsibility becomes radically problematic for war. At one extreme, nearly all on the unjust side (including civilians) might be liable to attack. At the other extreme,

---

[50] Elsewhere in other work I have applied this revisionist model to present-day, real-world issues that deserve moral analysis and show how this approach can yield helpful results on applied topics. For example, I have taken the revisionist approach to the ethics of war in my work on unmanned aerial drones, the killing of Osama bin Laden, and the ethics of cyberwar. See Strawser, "Moral Predators: The Duty to Employ Uninhabited Aerial Vehicles," *Journal of Military Ethics* 9, no. 4 (December 2010): 342–68. And, Strawser, *Killing bin Laden: A Moral Analysis* (Palgrave Macmillan, 2014). And Strawser, with Henschke and Allhoff, *Binary Bullets: The Ethics of Cyberwar* (Oxford University Press, 2016)).

[51] Many of the arguments I will make in this section are drawn from my paper, "Walking the Tightrope of Just War," *Analysis* 71 (2011): 533–44.

virtually no one might be liable (including enemy soldiers). Either possibility fails to deliver just war. That is, depending on how we understand responsibility, it seems that many soldiers fighting for an unjust cause are not properly responsible for the wrong they thereby pose; or, alternatively, many whom traditional just war theory (and our considered moral intuitions) would say should be immune from harm (such as noncombatants) may indeed be properly responsible such that they should be targeted.

To my mind, this is a tremendous problem for the revisionist view. If the criticism is right and just war is impossible to fight without the MEC, then "revisionist just war theory" is misnamed for it is actually just a simple rejection that war can ever be fought justly. A few have explored this problem for the rejection of the MEC, but Seth Lazar has developed the most powerful version of the objection in great detail.[52] Lazar directed his attack at the most influential proponent of the revisionist view: Jeff McMahan. Lazar concurs with McMahan's rejection of the MEC but argues that this rejection, coupled with McMahan's model for liability, results in an internal problem—namely, that the ability of just soldiers to discriminate between legitimate and illegitimate targets is lost. In individual self-defense cases, we assign liability to those responsible for a threat of wrongful harm. Yet assigning responsibility for an unjust cause to actors in war will be more difficult. The MEC resolves this difficulty: all soldiers on both sides are liable to be killed. But without the MEC, how can soldiers know whom it is permissible to kill? Lazar contends that McMahan has no means to block the conclusion that either too many people are legitimate targets for killing (total war) or that almost no one is a legitimate target (contingent pacifism). This is Lazar's "responsibility dilemma" (hereafter, the "Dilemma") for McMahan's account and, by extension, against all those revisionist accounts that reject the MEC, including my own. I will focus on McMahan's revisionist account for most of my interaction here with Lazar's critique, since it is focused on his work. However, the debate applies to the revisionist camp as a whole. Further, as will be noted below, my particular revisionist model, which relies on the Evidence-Relative View for liability, will be better able to defend against this objection.

---

[52] Seth Lazar, "The Responsibility Dilemma for Killing in War: A Review Essay," *Philosophy & Public Affairs* 38, no. 1 (2010). Sharon Lloyd raised a similar objection earlier in, "Democratic Responsibility and Moral Liability: A Hobbesian Account," unpublished manuscript. Lloyd writes, "[McMahan's position] seems to suggest that democratic citizenry might be legitimate targets of violence, whereas the deceived, manipulated, coerced subjects of authoritarian regimes, and even military conscripts in an authoritarian state, might not."

McMahan tries to avoid the contingent pacifism horn—that just soldiers cannot permissibly kill unjust soldiers—by arguing that the vast majority of unjust soldiers are, indeed, liable to be killed in war. He argues against various mitigating considerations that can be offered for unjust soldiers' liability and concludes that these considerations, on the whole, fail as full excuses—and that, in any case, excuse is compatible with responsibility and hence with liability. Thus, just soldiers are right to take unjust soldiers as liable to be killed. But if that's the case, Lazar argues, this far-reaching liability should also extend to many who are traditionally considered noncombatants. That is, many civilians on the side of an unjust cause will be causally related to the unjust cause to a similar degree as many of the soldiers by activities such as campaigning and voting for pro-war candidates, paying taxes, and in general creating a favorable political climate for war. And if the excuses protecting the soldiers from liability fail, then so too will such excuses fail to shield the noncombatants from liability; and we've opened the door to total war. McMahan is aware of this problem and tries to block it by arguing that noncombatants escape liability because most of them are insufficiently causally and morally responsible for the threats the war poses. I think this is generally true. However, in that case, Lazar replies, this argument should succeed for many of the unjust soldiers as well—that many soldiers are also insufficiently causally related to the threats of the war. If this is right, then just soldiers cannot rightly attack anyone and victory is impossible; and we're back to pacifism. In short: if McMahan moves to make unjust soldiers liable, then so too will many unjust noncombatants be liable; hence, total war. But if McMahan argues that unjust noncombatants are insufficiently liable to be killed, then that makes many unjust soldiers insufficiently liable as well; hence, contingent pacifism. Lazar argues the Dilemma has made the just war tightrope too slender: the rejection of the MEC causes just war theory to lose its balance and fall to one extreme or the other.

As corollary to the Dilemma, Lazar presents a paradox that he thinks falls out of these observations of the revisionist position.

(1) It is impossible to discriminate between liable and nonliable combatants, because of the lack of information endemic to warfare.
(2) Many combatants are not liable to be killed, because they are not sufficiently responsible for the threats that they pose.
(3) Anybody who chooses to kill, knowing both 1 and 2, chooses to kill indiscriminately.

(4) Anybody who chooses to kill indiscriminately is maximally morally responsible for the threats that he poses, and so liable to be killed.
(5) It is therefore easy to discriminate between liable and nonliable combatants.[53]

And, thus, Lazar tells us that the conclusion (5) contradicts (1) and that (4) contradicts (2). Hence, we have a paradox the revisionist rejection of the MEC. If the claims Lazar makes in building the Dilemma are accurate, then the paradox does seem to follow. In the next sections, I will show why the Dilemma is a false dilemma for not only McMahan's account, but any revisionist view, and why the supposed paradox is similarly a mistake.

4.4.2 The Contingent Pacifism Horn

The Dilemma is based in part on the claim that unjust combatants are not liable. It is also based on the related but distinct claim that just combatants cannot have sufficient knowledge of unjust combatants' liability to make it permissible to kill them. Much of Lazar's work focuses on this later claim. Indeed, Lazar insists this epistemic bar for just soldiers is so high that it is virtually unattainable. As he writes, for just soldiers to know their adversaries are liable to be killed "they must know at least their adversaries' personal histories, the context of their decision to fight, their connection to a particular threat, their capacity for responsible agency, their beliefs and intentions, and that their own cause is just."[54] If this is right, then just combatants cannot attain permissibility to kill unjust combatants and, thus, contingent pacifism wins the day. But such claims of epistemic uncertainty are too strong. A great deal of uncertainty is involved in determining liability to be killed in war, but it is not inscrutable; at least not in all cases. Note also that there is a great deal of uncertainty any time we attempt to determine liability, war or sans-war.

Responding to this kind of epistemic uncertainty raises difficult issues. If the epistemic bar is as high as Lazar demands, it creates a standard that

---

[53] Lazar, "The Responsibility Dilemma," 197. Lazar has several other critiques and engagements with McMahan's *Killing in War* throughout the paper in addition to the Dilemma and the supposed paradox. I am limiting myself in responding only to his central argument since it is applicable to all revisionist views which reject the MEC. I also find that the main vein of his Dilemma critique (that discrimination in war is impossible) is well captured by the paradox, hence why I lay it out here.
[54] Ibid., 187.

most would find implausible for other cases of liability attribution, such as personal self-defense. Presumably, Lazar accepts that it is possible to have sufficient evidence to permissibly kill an attacker in personal self-defense. It is worth exploring, then, what knowledge is required for legitimate liability attribution in both self-defense cases and war. Imagine walking peacefully down the street when a stranger charges you, attempting to stab you with a large knife. It is certainly possible there are liability-relevant facts inaccessible to you. You would, indeed, need to know the long-list of attributes Lazar gives above to know with certainty that the stranger is liable to defensive harm. But this mere possibility of mistake does not negate the evidence you have for the stranger's liability and thus does not negate the permissibility of attacking the stranger in self-defense. To have sufficient evidence that the attacker is liable to make it permissible to use defensive force you do not need to know the attacker's entire personal history, the context of his decision to attack you, all his beliefs and intentions, and so forth.

The following knowledge could be relevant to the permissibility of defensive force in ascertaining the attacker's liability: have you done anything to make yourself liable to his attack (e.g., are you unjustly threatening him or some other)? Does the attacker have some other justification for attacking you (e.g., does it appear that by killing you he is preventing the deaths of innocent bystanders)? Is the attacker a morally responsible agent (e.g., can you see he is under some kind of mind control)? Most think there is sufficient evidence for each of these questions in what I've already said: a stranger charges you while trying to stab you and there is no reason to believe that he is morally justified in attacking you, that he is not responsible for his action, etc. Importantly, notice your knowledge of your own innocence plays a significant role in your ascertaining the attacker's liability. Most believe that you are justified in presuming the attacker to be liable and, thus, in defending yourself. If killing the stranger were both necessary for averting the unjust threat and proportional to the potential harm, then it would be permissible to do so.

For each of the kinds of relevant knowledge just discussed, the epistemic difference between personal self-defense and war is a matter of degree, not kind. All that needs to be added to the list for the war case is knowledge that one's cause is just. Lazar rightly shows it is difficult to be justifiably confident that one's cause in war is just; there are countless reasons why one might be mistaken, including deception by one's government. But it is *possible* to overcome these uncertainties and have sufficient evidence for a just cause. If so, and if one also has evidence for the liability of one's adversaries, it can be permissible to kill in war.

These are not merely abstract possibilities. There is the familiar example of the Polish soldier fighting an invading Nazi soldier. That the Pole is fighting for a just cause is the only further thing the Polish soldier would need sufficient evidence for beyond what's needed for justification in an ordinary case of self-defense. And, certainly, unprovoked aggression could count as evidence—perhaps even sufficient evidence—for that conclusion. An example, perhaps, from the nearer past could be a Kuwaiti defending against the Iraqi army in 1990. Most recently, a Ukrainian fighting in 2022 for the defense of their nation-state against naked Russian aggression seems perhaps the clearest case. Does Lazar really think it is hard for a Ukrainian defending her homeland against Putin's invasion to conclude that her cause is just? It seems not only that she is able to so conclude, but that it is nearly self-evident. Granted: for it to be permissible to kill in war one needs to determine that the particular enemy is liable because he is making a sufficient contribution to an unjust cause, that he is a responsible agent, etc. But these same epistemic hurdles exist in personal self-defense. No doubt some of these uncertainties are greater in war. In self-defense cases, for example, it will usually be easier to determine that an attacker is making a sufficient contribution to an unjust threat, in contrast to an unjust soldier carrying a gun he may never fire. But it remains true that these uncertainties still arise in self-defense cases and the difference between the cases is one of degree, not kind. Moreover, in war it will be possible to reach those conclusions about the enemy attacker. Again, return to Ukraine and the woman who took up a rifle to fight off Russian invaders. With her own eyes she sees some Russian soldiers she is actively fighting against kill and destroy her countrymen as part of their invasion. What other evidentiary standing would she possibly need to conclude that these specific Russian soldiers are liable?

The insistence on the impossibility of ascertaining unjust soldiers' liability creates an important dilemma for the Dilemma itself—the Dilemma's dilemma. If one maintains that it is impossible for just combatants to have necessary knowledge of unjust soldiers' liability, then so too will it be similarly impossible for anyone to have the knowledge necessary for permissible killing in self-defense. For, with the exception of knowing they have a just cause, all the uncertainties just soldiers face determining their adversaries' liability in war are also faced in any individual self-defense case. So, to maintain the Dilemma against the revisionist just war theory, one must insist on a high level of certainty regarding an adversary's liability in war, which will also commit us to rejecting the permissibility of self-defense in a much wider range of cases than most of us would be willing to do. If we cannot accept this, we must grant that the epistemic threshold can be crossed in war as well. Admittedly, there will *usually* be more uncertainty in war cases than in self-defense cases; but that does not defeat the possibility of successful wartime liability determination. To avoid this problem, the Dilemma's advocates might claim that self-defense justifications are never based on liability but are instead grounded in an agent-relative permission or a lesser-evil defense. But that seems a high price to pay, given (rightly) the dominance of rights-based approaches; better to reject the Dilemma.

If one thinks I'm being unfair to Lazar's claims of impossibility for a soldier's ability to discriminate, note his rather strong claims regarding the epistemic limitations on soldiers in war. To wit: "To say that we ought to kill only those who are liable to that fate is like saying that we ought to abort only fetuses that would otherwise grow up to be bad people. It is not merely difficult for combatants to know whether their enemies are liable, *it is impossible*—at least, if they are to fight at all."[55] I respect Lazar's worries regarding epistemic uncertainty, but certainly this is overreaching, and rather incredible overreaching at that. In claiming that ascertaining an enemy soldier's liability is on par with ascertaining a fetus's future moral behavior, the substantive disagreement between the two views is made clear. For, notice, most facts relevant to liability are in the past; the debate is properly over whether we have sufficient access to those facts to make a reasonable determination of liability. But the facts exist at the point of action. Whereas, in the abortion case, there are no facts to know presently. The determination of a fetus's future moral behavior would be based entirely upon (absurd) predictive claims about future facts. And, presumably, these predictions could only be based, at best, upon some kind of probability calculation. So, the parallel here is simply mistaken and Lazar, or anyone making such a claim, is left with a preposterous comparison. The epistemic difference between the abortion case and the liability in war case is the difference between assumptions about probability compared to present knowledge of facts about the past.[56] Certainly, there

---

[55] Lazar, "The Responsibility Dilemma," 211, emphasis mine.
[56] As noted above, liability is usually treated in an instrumental sense—that is, killing someone because they are liable must achieve some end, such as the thwarting of an unjust threat. This is one important way in which liability is different from desert—liability is forward-looking in this way. So, indeed, *some* facts about liability are not in the past; there must be a prediction of some future good attained (or bad averted) by the action against the party deemed liable. Still, the point remains

could be cases—perhaps even most cases—where an enemy soldier's liability couldn't be reasonably ascertained in war. That is not the disagreement. But, rather, there will also be some cases in war where the epistemic conditions are not utterly opaque. Such discussions have taken the clichéd "fog of war" and run with it to the point of absurdity. Certainly, the chaos endemic to war, as Lazar stresses, is a reality, but it is not the block against the very possibility of discrimination that this objection claims. Again, consider the Ukrainian defending her village against invading Russian soldiers, and it seems readily that both individual liability and the broader justness of one's cause can be epistemically accessible to an individual soldier in war.

4.4.3 The Evidence-Relative View and the Dilemma

A further resolution to the Dilemma becomes available if we revise McMahan's views on liability. As discussed above in chapter 1, McMahan holds to what I call the Agency View for the responsibility criterion necessary for liability attribution. McMahan claims that a person can act permissibly according to the evidence available to them, yet, if it turns out their evidence is mistaken and the act is impermissible relative to the actual facts, then they can be responsible and, hence, liable. That is, this view thinks liability turns on acts that are fact-relative impermissible as opposed to merely evidence-relative impermissible.[57] In chapter 2, I defended the Evidence-Relative View of liability attribution. McMahan and others who hold this view explicitly reject the view that evidence-relative permissibility excludes liability. However, if we were to claim that evidence-relative permissible action cannot be a ground of liability to defensive action, as the Evidence-Relative View does, then we can better handle many of the Dilemma's worries.

This is the case for at least two reasons. First, under the Evidence-Relative View, just soldiers would themselves be liable only if they killed without evidence-relative permissibility. So, they would not incur liability for killing an unjust soldier they reasonably believed to be liable, even if it turned out the unjust soldier was, in fact, nonliable. Second, by investigating what

---

that in the abortion case, *all* of the facts about determining liability for the fetus would be future predictive-looking.

[57] As discussed in chapter 2, McMahan uses "objectively permissible" and "subjectively permissible" to describe this distinction throughout *Killing in War*.

evidence unjust soldiers have regarding the justice of their cause, the just side could determine what level of evidence-relative permissibility the unjust soldiers could be reasonably taken to have. From this, the just side could then determine which soldiers should be viewed as liable and judiciously fight under such constraints. This evades much of the Dilemma's force by making liability determination more epistemically attainable since it turns on evidence available to an actor, not on facts that they cannot possibly access. This diminishes a great deal of the force behind the claims about the difficulty of ascertaining liability, as shown above. In the next chapter, I will continue to explore this possibility for the Evidence-Relative View in determining enemy combatants' relative level of liability to harm and show how it could be applied in a workable manner in the real world.

To better demonstrate how well the Evidence-Relative View handles this aspect of the Dilemma, imagine the following story of a just soldier named Becky:

Just Soldier Becky
Becky is a soldier fighting for a just cause. While in theater, Becky sees a person wildly charging at her unit as they are sitting peacefully under the shade of a tree while conversing with some members of the local populace. The charging enemy is shooting wildly (indiscriminately, even) at Becky, her fellow soldiers, and the civilians all around her. Becky, holding her rifle, quickly assesses the charging man's liability as bullets whiz by her and into those around her and she decides to shoot the charging enemy.

Now, given certain conditions, is it technically *possible* the charging man is not fully liable for his decision to kill—or at least not liable enough to incur the surrender of his right to life? Yes, indeed, it may be possible if we grant many of the conditions that Lazar gives for why he thinks discrimination is impossible. (Just as it is possible that Attacker may not be actually liable in the *Defender and Attacker* case from chapter 1.) If that is the case here, then Becky did not have fact-relative permissibility to kill the charging soldier. However, if Becky has proper evidence to believe that the cause she fights for is just, then she certainly has enough evidence to warrant evidence-relative permissibility to kill the charging man. Or, again, simply think on the countless examples of cases like this occurring to a defending Ukrainian soldier fighting against an invading Russian soldier. The evidence seems clear, and the warrant for determining liability follows.

Or consider another case, this time a real-world example from World War II:

Lt. Beaudoin
On April 6, 1945, American soldier 1st Lt. Raymond Beaudoin was leading his platoon over flat, open terrain near Hamelin, Germany—just a few miles from the still active Nazi concentration camp of Bergen-Belsen.[58] Nazi soldiers ambushed Beaudoin's unit with machine guns and automatic weapons, laying down devastating fire which pinned his unit to the ground. Beaudoin instructed his men to dig in and take up defensive positions against the enemy fire. Despite these attempted defensive measures, the platoon was losing men quickly. Things became even more dire when the enemy brought up strong reinforcements to the rear of Beaudoin's unit and was preparing to attack from that direction. Then three of Beaudoin's troops, sent back to obtain ammunition and reinforcements, were killed by Nazi sniper fire. To defend himself and his troops from the unjust enemy combatants' attack, Beaudoin decided to attack the most damaging enemy sniper nest 90 yards to the right flank, and thereby divert attention from the runner who would attempt to pierce the enemy's line and secure help. Crawling over exposed ground, he relentlessly advanced, undeterred by eight rounds of bazooka fire directed toward him or by rifle fire which ripped his uniform. Ten yards from the enemy position, he stood up and charged. Upon reaching the enemy position, he shot and killed two occupants of the nest; a third, who tried to bayonet him, he overpowered and killed with the butt of his carbine.[59]

In both of these cases, it seems the just soldier in question (Becky and Lt. Beaudoin, respectively) had evidence-relative permissibility to kill the enemy

---

[58] This was in the late stages of World War II in Europe when there was strong evidence emerging of the Nazi's genocide. Moreover, the Nazis committed clear acts of unprovoked aggression against their neighboring states to start the war. Officers such as Beaudoin most likely had some good evidence of the Nazis' genocide at this point in the conflict as well as *clear* knowledge of their unjustified invasion of other nations. Allied forces liberated the Bergen-Belsen camp only nine days after the event described here, on April 15, 1945. When liberated, the Allies found the bodies of over 13,000 murdered occupants lying unburied in piles around the camp.

[59] After this, Beaudoin attempted get his remaining troops to safety when he was struck by enemy machine gun fire and killed. Beaudoin was posthumously awarded the Congressional Medal of Honor for his actions in this firefight. This story is taken from the commendation for that medal and the narrative description is taken from an archive found at: http://www.worldwariihistory.info/Medal-of-Honor/Germany.html, accessed August 1, 2010. My telling of the story here is paraphrased from that account and at several places is quoted verbatim.

soldier. In both cases, the just soldier had reasonable evidence to believe that the enemy combatant was fighting for an unjust cause and was liable to be killed in the given circumstances. The enemy soldiers' liability stems from the contributions they are directly making and presently engaging in on behalf of an unjust cause—and unjust cause which is thereby threating to kill nonliable people, such as the just soldiers themselves.

Thus, one defense against the contingent pacifist horn of the Dilemma is made by restricting the basis for liability to norms of evidence-relative permissibility as is done by the Evidence-Relative View. If that's right, it can be evidence-relative permissible for a just soldier to kill an adversary in war, in some cases, and thereby not make herself liable even if it turns out she lacked fact-relative permissibility. But *even if* one rejects my view of liability attribution, the broader point and defense of all versions of the revisionist view still stands: the epistemic difference between standard self-defense cases and war will always be a matter of degree, not a difference in kind; and the uncertainties regarding liability can be overcome.

4.4.4 The Total War Horn

The other horn of the Dilemma is that if unjust soldiers are liable, then many noncombatants will also be liable. But then, the worry goes, nearly everyone on the unjust side of a given conflict—soldiers, civilians, even children perhaps—could potentially become legitimate targets. Lazar writes, "if small, unnecessary contributions, some of which one makes only by being in a particular space, are sufficient for liability to be killed, then many more noncombatants than is plausible will be pulled into the liability net."[60] McMahan responds by appealing to narrow proportionality. It demands we attack people only if attacking them is necessary to thwart a wrong and we restrict such attacks to the minimal force needed to prevent the wrong. So, most noncombatants, because they do not contribute to an unjust cause in the right way or to a sufficient extent and so forth, will not be liable to be killed. But the Dilemma's trap is set: for if McMahan uses narrow proportionality to protect civilians from attack in this way, then it should also apply to many combatants—since many combatants in most wars do not actually

---

[60] Lazar, "The Responsibility Dilemma," 192.

directly contribute enough to the actual furtherance of the war, the claim goes—and we are back to contingent pacifism.

My defense against the total war horn rests on the general notion that liability comes in degrees and that liability has the internal requirement of necessity for any permissible response.[61] If that is true, then having sufficient evidence to know when this necessity clause is met will be especially difficult in the case of noncombatants. And, even if some liability did extend to those traditionally considered noncombatants, that (by itself) does not mean they are necessarily legitimate targets for lethal attack. Just forces would have to know that by attacking noncombatants they could effectively thwart the unjust cause. Further, they would have to know that only by killing them could this best be accomplished. If some alternative means could equally thwart the contribution some unjust noncombatants provide (by safely capturing them, say), then killing would be impermissible. Given such constraints, it's hard to imagine just forces would attain warrant to kill noncombatants very often, if ever. The degree of liability most civilians will incur for the contribution which they could be *known* to be responsible will usually be quite low.

This is primarily because what combatants are *actually doing* in war is starkly different from what civilians are doing. Combatants are actively engaging in killing other people, destroying property, and otherwise executing the "bleeding edge" of the war, or else serving in closely related support roles directly to other combatants with that aim. Combatants' contribution to the unjust threat posed by the war is thereby both direct and clear and different in kind from the way in which noncombatants may contribute. This puts combatants in the dock for liability in a way the vast majority of noncombatants will not be. Noncombatants' contributions are indirect and, thus, harder to discern. Moreover, the vast majority of civilians' actions contribute to unjust war efforts to such a watered-down extent as to be negligible. And, importantly, it is foreseeable that such actions are negligible. The overwhelming majority of noncombatants have little reason to believe that *anything* they do will contribute in any substantive way beyond a negligible one to an unjust cause. So, notice, on an Evidence-Relative Account for liability mentioned above, the vast majority of noncombatants will not be liable; for they have no reasonable evidentiary grounds to believe they would be contributing in a non-negligible way to an unjust war effort. But even on

---

[61] McMahan argues for the degreed nature of liability, as do most scholars who work on liability. See for example Uwe Steinhoff, "The Liability of Justified Attackers," *Ethical Theory and Moral Practice* 19, no. 4 (2016): 1016–30.

the Agency View of liability, the fact that their contribution is foreseeably negligible will make most civilians essentially nonresponsible (and, hence, nonliable) agents.

This will not always be true, however. If an unjust noncombatant does have a less-than-negligible contribution, then they could be liable to some extent and, depending on the necessity and proportionality constraints, could be legitimate targets of attack. Such cases are rare and would probably apply only to high-level decision makers, etc. Even then, it would be difficult for just forces to have the epistemic insight required to determine civilian liability with justifiable confidence. But merely opening the door for such a possibility does not deliver the specter of total war, as the Dilemma contends; so, the objection fails. The possibility will not mean that all civilians are suddenly legitimate targets, or even any sizeable portion of them. At worst, it could mean that some fraction of those previously regarded as immune from attack should, in fact, be liable to attack. And this is not entirely implausible, if we look closely at some of the (albeit rare, among the total populace) roles some civilians play in war. Imagine a non-uniformed target analyst who identifies key targets for a military force to strike. Technically, one could claim that such an individual should fall under the traditional just war theory doctrine of absolute civilian immunity. But this seems implausible, given what the actual individual is doing on behalf of an unjust cause. Or imagine someone serving in the equivalent of the US Secretary of Defense role. And so forth. Admittedly, where to draw the line precisely in some cases will be difficult. But not in the overwhelming majority of noncombatant cases. The mere existence of dawn and dusk does not mean we should doubt the clarity of night and day. And, again, this would all hinge on what a just force could actually have evidence for regarding a given civilian; evidence which will usually be opaque.[62]

So, the defense against the total war horn is primarily an epistemic one. But, because of this, it could appear the response is not consistent with the previous response to the contingent pacifism horn. Recall the dialectic thus far: the Dilemma claims that, by rejecting the MEC, there is too much uncertainty to discriminate that unjust soldiers are liable. I respond that these epistemic limitations can be overcome—that unjust soldiers can be sufficiently responsible for an unjust cause to be liable and that this can be known, in at least some cases. But the Dilemma then presses: if that's the case, then why

---

[62] Cf. Helen Frowe, "Civilian Liability," *Ethics* 129, no. 4 (2019): 625–50.

168   THE BOUNDS OF DEFENSE

are civilians not similarly liable for their contribution and why cannot this be known? The reason is because epistemic limitations on ascertaining liability will usually be far greater in the case of civilians. This is because of characteristics endemic to noncombatants that make these uncertainties different in kind, not merely degree. Namely, noncombatants' contributions are both indirect and (usually) foreseeably negligible. Thus, the necessity and proportionality conditions internal to liability will be radically more difficult to meet and radically more difficult to know that they've been met. As a result, justification for total war does not obtain.

4.4.5 A Supposed Paradox

As shown above, Lazar further claims in pressing the Dilemma that a paradox develops out of the epistemic uncertainties involved in wartime discrimination. Recall from above:

(1) It is impossible to discriminate between liable and nonliable combatants, because of the lack of information endemic to warfare.
(2) Many combatants are not liable to be killed, because they are not sufficiently responsible for the threats that they pose.
(3) Anybody who chooses to kill [combatants], knowing both 1 and 2, chooses to kill indiscriminately.
(4) Anybody who chooses to kill [combatants] indiscriminately is maximally morally responsible for the threats that he poses, and so liable to be killed.
(5) It is therefore easy to discriminate between liable and nonliable combatants.[63]

As shown above in defeating the contingent pacifist horn of the Dilemma, Lazar's mistake here is in conflating the difficult with the impossible. By claiming that it is impossible to discriminate liability, he sets off on a path that easily results in the absurdity he intends for his *reductio*. But he needs the claim that it is impossible to discriminate for his argument to work. Consider: if he instead claims that it is *difficult* but not impossible to discriminate, the argument falls apart. For, in that case, he'd be making a rather big

---

[63] Lazar, "The Responsibility Dilemma," 197.

leap from the reality that discrimination in war is highly difficult to calling *anyone* who chooses to kill in war as necessarily acting indiscriminately. Recall the story above of Becky killing the charging man. Even if it turns out Becky's decision to kill was not fact-relative permissible, it was anything *but* indiscriminate. Indiscriminate killing would mean she makes literally no distinction between killing this charging enemy and killing a bystander who was herding goats. As we've seen, Lazar will argue that because Becky cannot be utterly certain (given all the possible epistemic constraints suffered in the chaos of war) that she is in the fact-relative right, then she cannot be certain of the moral responsibility, and hence liability, of the charging enemy. And if she is killing someone for whom she is not certain of their fact-relative liability to be killed, then she is killing indiscriminately, or so Lazar will claim. But surely this is a non-sequitur. Killing in war when one has reasonable evidence that the enemy is morally responsible and thereby liable may be, perhaps, a morally risky action—for the person could be mistaken—but it is not (whatever else it may be) a random act of violence.

Even if a soldier kills someone while not being *certain* of his or her fact-relative permissibility to do so, in the vast majority of cases the just soldier is not killing *indiscriminately* (assuming they are acting on evidence-relative permissibility) and, thus, are not themselves now maximally morally responsible for the threats he or she imposes and therefore (on the Evidence-Relative View) cannot be liable themselves to be killed. So, the defense I've outlined has a simple response: Lazar's mistake here, in this supposed paradox, is in conflating the difficult with the impossible. If it is difficult but not impossible to discriminate, the paradox falls apart. For, in that case, (1) is false because it is not impossible to ascertain liability for some combatants and thus to engage in discrimination, at least in some contexts. Because (1) is false, (3) is false. Because (3) is false, (4) does not apply to just soldiers; and (5) does not follow. Hence, there is no paradox. Instead, we know this: it is very difficult to fight justly. But it's not impossible; the just war tightrope can be walked.

As the revisionists have shown, the rejection of the MEC is a needed corrective to just war theory. And, despite fears to the contrary, the tightrope of just war can still be traversed without its aid. Yet to do so we must sharpen our understanding of what justice demands of us in war. I have tried to do some of that here. But for the revisionist approach to killing in war to be plausible, we should attempt to actually apply it. I'll argue that doing so will develop a new set of categories for enemy status in war. That is what I will do in chapter 5. First, however, to conclude this chapter, I will turn to one further attempt at re-establishing the MEC against the revisionist challenge.

4.5. Other Possible Grounds for the MEC

Given the ascendency of the revisionist view of just war theory, several writers have attempted to offer new defenses of the MEC. Rather than grounding the MEC on a simple conception of mutual threat, as is claimed by Walzer, Nagel, and other traditionalists, some search for more creative reasons to claim that unjust soldiers can permissibly kill nonliable people (including, of course, just soldiers). Yitzhak Benbaji, for example, has offered a robust defense of the full spectrum of the just war convention, including the MEC, against the revisionist challenges via a highly constrained view of the right to self-defense.[64] Another example is that of Michael Skerker, who recently defends a kind of traditionalist account.[65] Here, however, I will focus on one traditionalist response more restrained in scope than Benbaji's. Patrick Emerton and Toby Handfield have offered a defense of the MEC that focuses solely on the approach, without aiming to defend many of the implied positions that it is usually taken to generate.[66] Their strategy is intriguing. Rather than eschew the traditional reliance on mutual threat, they embrace it. That is, they hope to retain the thesis by appealing to a notion of mutual threat between combatants that grounds their mutual liability to one another. This much, of course, is nothing new in the just war canon. Emerton and Handfield's grounding of the MEC via mutual endangerment follows in this Walzerian tradition, but they offer a novel account for *how* mutual threat occurs. In particular, they claim that even *non-culpable* defensive harm can work at the individual self-defense level as grounds for mutual threat resulting in the desired symmetry. If that is correct, then the use of mutual threat to ground the MEC can stand even in the face of the revisionist pointing to a moral responsibility distinction between soldiers on opposing sides of a just cause. If their move works, then, it would be quite a challenge to the revisionists for it would radically deflate the force of the revisionist's primary argument.

---

[64] Yitzhak Benbaji, "A Defense of the Traditional War Convention," *Ethics* 118 (2008): 464–95.

[65] Michael Skerker, *The Moral Status of Combatants: A New Theory of Just War* (London: Routledge, 2020).

[66] Patrick Emerton and Toby Handfield, "Order and Affray: Defensive Privileges in War," *Philosophy & Public Affairs* 37, no. 4 (2009): 382–414.

4.5.1 Affray as Grounds for the MEC

Emerton and Handfield call this notion the principle of "affray" and derive it from the following thought experiment:

Barroom Brawl
A fight breaks out in a barroom. A number of patrons of the bar are actively perpetrating violence against one another. Another person, Smith, find himself in the midst of this fighting.[67]

Emerton and Handfield argue that, completely regardless of the culpability of those around him, Smith acquires defensive privileges simply due to the imminent danger the non-culpable defensive violence from the other patrons could hold towards him. Further, because Smith *has* such defensive privilege himself, they argue that the others in the brawl similarly gain defensive privilege against Smith since he could thereby be a likely threat, himself, in the exercising of that right. Of course, in turn, Smith would then have defensive privilege against *their* defensive harm, Emerton and Handfield argue. Once this step occurs, we see that everyone involved in the brawl will quickly have defensive privilege extended to them against the threat of harm posed by everyone else. When a state like that described in *Barroom Brawl* obtains between parties, Emerton and Handfield call this a circumstance of *affray* defined as follows:

An individual A finds himself in *affray* with B if and only if:

a. A is endangered by his physical proximity to violence perpetrated by B;
b. B's threat to A is not licensed by A's culpability;
c. B is not culpable for the danger posed to A; and
d. A is reasonably perceived to be a threat by B.[68]

In other words, "being stuck in a fight endangers A, which gives him the right to defend himself. But, if he manifests the possibility that he will exercise that right, he becomes a danger to everyone else, which gives them the right to use force against A also."[69] Thus, when two parties A and B find themselves

---

[67] Emerton and Handfield, "Affray," *Philosophy & Public Affairs*, 385.
[68] Ibid., 386.
[69] Ibid., 389.

in a state of *affray* Emerton and Handfield contend that each of A and B acquire symmetrical defensive privileges to harm one another. From here, they simply contend that soldiers in a state war are similarly caught in a state of *affray* with regard to one another and therefore have symmetrical defensive privileges and the MEC is rescued.

One may be tempted to immediately ask of the brawl scenario: but surely Smith could back away out of the brawl, right? It is not as if his only plausible option to defend himself against being injured by his "physical proximity to violence" being perpetrated near him is to add to that physical violence himself, is it? Let us unpack affray a bit. In the brawl, A sees punches flying, and worries that one may land on him. And this punch against him would land wrongly, since he is nonculpable; yet that the punch itself is flying by B is not wrongful because B is, supposedly, throwing it in defense to begin with (not necessarily against A). Here Emerton and Handfield say that A can throw a punch himself in order to block that punch that may wrongfully land on him. But why cannot A just back up, or flee to a back room in the bar, or retreat outside, or even just duck and hide under the table? Emerton and Handfield explicitly block these options as available within *affray*. But, quite surprisingly, they do not block them by pure putative restrictions on the thought experiment (e.g., "imagine that there is no physical space for Smith to escape to"). Rather, they *admit* them as possible ways one could remove oneself from being a perceived threat within affray:

> It may be possible, by one's behavior, to ensure that one is not reasonably perceived to be a threat. Smith might cower under a table, in which case it seems absurd to suppose that he is in affray with the brawlers. And no doubt there will be other, contextually variable, means by which to exit an affray by such signaling of nonviolent intent.[70]

But, they argue, these possible ways of removing oneself from affray may not be morally required of Smith due to necessity and proportionality considerations. Some of these are understandable and plausible (if we grant affray to begin with as a source for defensive privileges). So, for example, they argued that the necessity constraint would not require Smith to retreat from the affray (and not attack others), including by "cowering under the table" in cases

---

[70] Ibid., 387.

if Smith has reason to think that he personally will be exposed to a greater risk of harm by retreating than by engaging in the conflict, he almost certainly is not obliged to retreat. And even in cases where Smith is *more* likely to suffer harm by engaging in the conflict, he may be warranted in doing so, for a variety of reasons. Perhaps, by engaging, he is better able to assist those more vulnerable than himself.[71]

If we grant the mere instantiation of affray as grounding defensive privilege, then these reasons seem plausible as potentially good ones for not being morally required to retreat. However, the authors also include some rather far-reaching reasons for not requiring retreat. They worry, for example, that morally requiring Smith to duck under a nearby table, if that is the only way to not appear as a threat to others resulting in *affray*, should not be required due even to mere concerns of how this might make him *appear* to others. "Perhaps he would be warranted [to not retreat or not "cower" under a table] even by less important concerns, such as a fear of appearing cowardly or undignified if he retreats."[72] I find this to be an implausibly low (rather *incredibly* low) threshold for necessity. One should not be required to avoid harming a nonculpable person merely out of fear of possibly appearing timid in front of one's friends?[73] We may understandably worry that such thinking could justify gang violence out of a desire to look tough, or other clearly impermissible things.

But let us set aside such concerns. Rather, I wish to grant, for the sake of argument, Emerton and Handfield these points, or at least bracket them for now, and see if affray can stand on its own. Not surprisingly, I think this notion of *affray* as used by Emerton and Handfield fails to ground mutual liability between soldiers and the MEC. I argue that it fails for several reasons, even setting aside the issues raised above. First, I find that their conclusions regarding liability and self-defense in *Barroom Brawl* are mistaken to begin with on the individual self-defense level, of course. This is because the mere threat of non-culpable defensive harm is an inadequate basis for liability attribution. I could argue for this conclusion several different ways, as shown in chapter 1. But rather than rehash the rejection of the Nonresponsible Account, I will instead offer a new

---

[71] Ibid., 388. They also suggest that the protection of property, even property of relatively little value, can be a basis to not be morally required to retreat.
[72] Ibid.
[73] It might be worth reminding the reader here that people routinely die in fistfights and bar brawls like the affray Emerton and Handfield describe. A nonculpable person should die because someone is worried about looking weak? Yes, incredulously, it does seem the authors are actually making this claim.

basis for the rejection of affray here, even after granting Emerton and Handfield several points. I'll explore how the moral asymmetry used to ground liability must be *properly relevant* to the particular defensive act in question. This is important for the claim Emerton and Handfield are making, with regard to *affray*, and mutual threat is subtly distinct from a simple Nonresponsible Account, like that of Thomson. And, of course, if affray fails to ground mutual liability in *Barroom Brawl*, then it and any other approach along such lines will similarly fail to ground the MEC in war.

4.5.2 Relevant Harm

As we saw in chapter 1, Thomson famously argued that mere causal responsibility for a threat can make one liable to defensive harm.[74] Other scholars, such as Michael Otsuka, have argued instead that one must be appropriately morally *responsible* for—not merely the causation of—a threat of wrongful harm in order to be liable to defensive harm. See chapter 1.5 and 1.6 for a full review of this debate. The basic premise of the view is that some distinction of responsibility or fault or blameworthiness between actors must play a central role in determining liability. This means, amongst other things, that a moral asymmetry of some kind must exist between two actors in a forced-choice scenario that makes one liable to be killed over the other. In my view, the moral failing that matters for liability is the violation of evidence-relative norms. That is, the Evidence-Relative View (see chapters 2 and 3). I will not again re-litigate the case for my account of liability but work from within its vantage in some ways to show that *Barroom Brawl* does not adequately derive mutual defensive privileges. All of my arguments are ultimately thus constrained by this assumption. If one rejects the Responsible Account of permissible defensive harm, then, presumably, some (but not all) of my arguments here against Emerton and Handfield's account of *affray* will not succeed. However, as I'll show, the arguments should hold for the other views for the responsibility criterion within the Responsible Account; that is, both the Simple Culpability View and the Agency View.[75]

---

[74] Thomson, "Self-Defense."

[75] See chapter 1.6 above. On all rights-based accounts of self-defense, recall, defensive harm is constrained by the twin principles of proportionality and necessity which both must be met for an act of self-defense to be permissible. For all remaining discussions of self-defense in this paper, these criteria are assumed to have been met.

Notice that Emerton and Handfield's reliance on the risk of (non-culpable) harm that the parties in *Barroom Brawl* could potentially pose to one another, has an interesting parallel with the Agency View's reliance on (supposed) non-reciprocal risk imposition.[76] For the moment, let us grant that the notion of risk-imposition on others can be a proper basis for liability. I argue that even if we grant this (as Emerton and Handfield's account will require to even get off the ground), that it too must track the *right kind* of wrong-doing in its risk-imposition in order to properly assign liability. And, as I'll show below, mere defensive capability is precisely *not* the correct kind of relevant wrong to track in such cases. First, I argue that defensive capability—even if it imposes non-reciprocal risk—is itself is not relevant for tracking moral asymmetry and liability, *if* the defensive ability in question is used in a way which is justified. I call this the relevancy argument. Second, I'll argue that nearly all people have *some* level of defensive capability at all times and thus, in forced-choice cases, both parties have some capability to harm one another. This reaffirms that it is not mere defensive ability or threat of mutual harm itself but the permissibility (or impermissibility) to use it that matters for liability attribution. I, of course, hold that permissibility is of the evidence-relative kind for proper liability attribution, but here my aim is simply to show why mere capability of harm is not a relevant factor for understanding liability on any account. If that is correct, then *affray* fails as a relevant basis for anyone's liability; and the MEC cannot be grounded by it.

So, to begin, let's grant for the sake of argument that it could be in some way wrong to increase one's defensive capability such that this increased ability to do harm can impose unfair nonreciprocal risks on others. As we saw in chapters 1 and 2, this is not entirely implausible. If someone carries around multiple loaded weapons at all times—perhaps one goes to work every day wearing a vest full of hand grenades, several AK-47s (with the safeties off) slung over his shoulder, and a couple of live mortar rounds in his pocket, "just in case"—one may think that they are thereby imposing a nonreciprocal risk on others that could be relevant for who should bear the cost in a forced-choice scenario resulting from this capability.[77]

So, let's set aside different intuitions on where thresholds should be drawn on such matters and assume for the moment that it is to some degree

---

[76] See chapter 1.6.2 and 1.6.3 for a review of the Agency View and see chapter 1.6 and 1.7.
[77] McMahan, for example, holds precisely this view. See Hugh LaFollette, *In Defense of Gun Control* (New York: Oxford University Press, 2018). Also see Bradley Strawser, "Review Essay of In Defense of Gun Control by Hugh LaFollette," with Bart Kennedy, *Criminal Law and Philosophy* (April 2021).

or other impermissible to carry around an arsenal of loaded guns for this nonreciprocal risk imposition reason (as Dignitary did in *Dignitary & Guest*).[78] I propose that *even if* it is wrong to increase one's defensive capability in such a way because of resulting nonreciprocal risks doing so imposes on others, then this risk (and the resulting blameworthiness for it) is one based on the wrongful misuse (or perhaps malfunction, etc.) of the weapon. That is, the riskimposition (and resulting assumed problems certain increases in defensive capability bring with them) is not based on the risk of *permissible* use of the defensive capability. In other words, even if it is wrong to carry a gun in a certain context, it's not wrong to carry a gun based on the "risk" that it may be end up being used justifiably; it must be based on the risk that it could end up being used wrongly. And so, the supposed wrong of carrying a gun does not apply for liability purposes in a case where an agent uses it in a permissible manner because it is not a relevant instance of the risk that is the supposed source of the wrong. Even if it is wrong, in general, for one actor in a forced-choice case such as *Dignitary & Guest* to have taken on an increased defensive capability, that particular wrong is not relevant to liability determinations for the self-defense act, in question, in the same way that Dignitary's unrelated impermissible behavior she committed the night before would not be relevant.[79] Call this the Relevancy Argument for liability attribution of defensive harm.

To demonstrate the point of the Relevancy Argument, consider the following case:

Tom the Embezzler
One day Tom embezzles $200 from his employer. The next day, Tom is on his way back to his company to embezzle even more money. On the way there, however, Tom sees his friend Frank at the coffee shop. Frank is on his way to volunteer at the local soup kitchen. Sadly, at the coffee shop the two of them become caught in a kind of Tragic forced-choice scenario similar in form to *Dignitary & Guest*. In this case, a villain projects holographic images of guns onto both of their hands as they attempt to greet each other.[80]

---

[78] Again, see LaFollete. Note that I do not need this point to hold for my argument to work; I'm granting it to help Emerton and Handfield's notion of affray and get it off the ground.

[79] Let us imagine, for example, that the evening prior to the banquet Dignitary met Guest that Dignitary ordered the execution of a known-to-be-innocent political prisoner. That wrong-doing would not be relevant to liability determinations between Dignitary and Guest.

[80] Recall my definition of a Tragedy case from chapter 2.

Now who is liable in such a case? Tom or Frank? The Evidence-Relative View, recall, contends that we cannot properly claim that either is liable to be killed over the other, of course. It is a classic case of a Tragedy (in the technical sense) where both are blameless in regard to their adherence to their particular evidence-relative norms, resulting in symmetrical relational standing toward the impending harm they each pose to the other, and lack of liability to those harms. There is no liability here to be found, or so the Evidence-Relative View holds.

But what if one argues that Tom should be the liable party in such a scenario since he is the one embezzling funds and is, in fact, on his way to embezzle funds? Certainly, that action (the embezzling) is done against his evidence-relative norms and is something for which we'd rightly hold him culpable on any account. And, after all, one might even argue, this forced-choice scenario would not have occurred had Tom not been on his way to embezzle funds when he stopped at the coffee shop. On that basis, one could try to argue here that it is Tom rather than Frank who is properly liable on the basis of moral asymmetry between them. Tom was on his way to embezzle money, after all, while Frank was on his way to the soup kitchen.

But this is absurd. Clearly the moral asymmetry here between Tom and Frank—however real it is in *general* terms, is not an asymmetry that is properly relevant to the forced-choice matter of self-defense between them. That Tom is wrong in embezzling has nothing to do with the permissibility of his defensive act in the forced-choice case with Frank when the villain projects guns onto each of their hands; and thus, it has nothing to do with his responsibility and blameworthiness or lack thereof and resulting liability in this circumstance.

What *Tom the Embezzler* shows us is that in a forced-choice self-defense case that relies on some moral asymmetry between parties to distinguish liability, the moral asymmetry must be properly relevant to the act of self-defense itself that is in question.[81] Thus, mere defensive capability itself does not provide the right fit for liability attribution in cases where the defensive threat in question is used permissibly, even if we grant *ex hypothesi* that increasing one's defensive capability (by carrying a gun, say) can be wrong, just as embezzling is wrong but is not a properly relevant wrong in the *Tom*

---

[81] This is important in a variety of important cases where liability is hotly disputed. For example, the killing of Osama bin Laden. He was certainly a morally "bad man," but what matters for his liability to harm is whether that liability is relevant to the threat he poses. I discuss this at length in Strawser, *Killing Bin Laden: A Moral Analysis* (Palgrave Macmillan, 2014).

the *Embezzler* case. This is because what matters in these cases is not the risk of defensive harm itself, but whether or not that use of defensive harm is a permissible action for the defender at the time it is so used. If defensive action is taken under justified pretenses, then such a defender is not morally responsible for that particular action; wholly apart from whatever else they may be responsible for. So, the mere possession of defensive capability cannot be grounds for liability, even granting non-reciprocal risk imposition as a relevant factor for liability. The non-reciprocal risk imposition itself would have to be imposed wrongly in order to find any morally significant exercise of that capability that results in a moral asymmetry grounding liability. If the relevancy argument did not hold as a general principle, notice, any liability analysis would require a full investigation and litigation of each party's overall "total" moral blameworthiness, good and bad, in an endless regress.

Consider the following (admittedly rather far flung) story which helps illuminate the point that mere defensive capability cannot ground moral responsibility, much less culpability, for liability attribution.

Unintentional Ninja
A young child is kidnapped by a mysterious tribe of nomadic ninjas who live high in the mountains. The clan trains the child, against his will, in the powerful martial arts for which these ninjas are famous. Over the course of many years of this training, it turns out this young child is quite naturally adept at these skills and becomes one of the best martial artists the world has ever known; he is literally a walking lethal weapon and could kill anyone with a quick strike. At the age of 20, the child escapes from his long captivity and tries to resume a normal life. Call him Unintentional Ninja.

So, *Unintentional Ninja* has the capability of lethal defensive harm at any time, anywhere he goes. He cannot escape this capability. He has it innately within him, without carrying any weapons. If the increasing of Dignitary's defensive capability by showing up to the reception armed can form part of the legitimate basis for attributing liability to her (as McMahan's Agency View claims it can be), then, were *Unintentional Ninja* to find himself in the same position as Dignitary, his increased defensive capability via his martial arts skills would also be part of a legitimate basis for liability attribution. But, clearly, we should reject this. After all, *Unintentional Ninja* is not in any way at fault for having this peculiar defensive capability, and he is in the difficult position that he cannot divest himself of it. His defensive capability is now innately part of him. Holding him somehow responsible for this such that questions of liability could turn on it is absurd.

Perhaps one disagrees with me here and does not wish to grant the absurdity. That is, perhaps one holds that Unintentional Ninja should be liable in a Tragedy-type case because his defensive capability difference is, in fact, relevant. If someone holds this view, it would then only be fair to ask: what should be expected of Unintentional Ninja in order to avoid this supposedly relevant asymmetry everywhere he goes? Is he required to never go out in public or to do so in a strait-jacket or some kind of restraining device that would restrict his martial arts abilities? Imagine Unintentional Ninja did go out into public in such a restraining device, for the purpose of blocking his natural defensive capability asymmetry, but then found himself in a legitimate self-defense situation against a culpable aggressor. In that case, he wouldn't be able to (rightly) defend himself. By trying to avoid the supposed moral risk that he may create a forced-choice situation, he would have thereby prevented himself from the ability to act justly in such a forced-choice situation.[82]

This shows us, as above, that it is not the defensive capability itself that drives concern over risk imposition, but the potential impermissible use of that capability. If one is behaving properly with a given defensive capability, it is irrelevant for questions of their liability, just as Tom's embezzling is irrelevant to his liability or lack thereof over Frank. To put it another way: it may be wrong to carry firearms. But if that's true then the reason it is wrong must be because of the risk of the gun being used unjustly (or perhaps firing accidentally or being stolen and used for ill, etc.). It is not that guns are wrong to carry on the "risk" that they will be used justly.[83]

To be clear: there is certainly a difference between the Unintentional Ninja and, say, a man who seeks out a deadly weapon. The latter intentionally gained the defensive capability, and that fact might be relevant for other questions of moral blame, outside of liability. My point is simply this: at the moment, when Unintentional Ninja and intentionally armed gunman are both using defensive force, their mere possession of defensive capability is

---

[82] And note that this is the same point for Dignitary regarding her permissibility to defend against an apparently culpable aggressor. From the vantage of Dignitary, the case is no different from a legitimate self-defense case wherein a Guest really is trying to kill her. On a different point, also note that although it would take a bit of work to get there, one could extend this kind of argument for why a state should not be held liable to defensive (pre-emptive) attack for simply *having* a powerful military (as many often do), but should be held liable for that military's *misuse*.

[83] Again, see LaFollete.

not relevant in determining moral asymmetry for that very act in question. Rather, the permissibility of its use in that specific instance is what is relevant to our determination of an asymmetry to ground liability. What we want to know for the *Unintentional Ninja* case was whether he used his defensive capabilities in a permissible way. That he *could* so use them seems irrelevant (at least for liability attribution in a particular instance). And, in his case, we surely do not count his having defensive capabilities against him in determining asymmetry.[84] Generalizing then, defensive capability itself or the non-culpable threat of defensive harm does not function as a relevant basis for moral asymmetry in liability attribution; only the *culpable* threat of defensive harm is properly relevant for liability.

4.5.3 We're All Unintentional Ninjas

The second step in my argument against Emerton and Handfield's *affray* model to ground the MEC follows quickly from this point. And it is simply this: defensive capability is something that nearly everyone possesses to at least some degree in nearly all contexts. For example, most human beings capable of reading this right now have *some* defensive capability towards all others. This capability varies widely depending on the person, but nearly all possess some possibility of using some measure of defensive force, possibly even lethal force. Even if someone reading this has an increased defensive capability (perhaps someone is reading this while carrying a knife or a gun), everyone else reading this could do *something* in self-defense that could create a threat of defensive harm. So, a greater or lesser defensive capability will be a difference only in degree not in kind for any given scenario. That is, both parties in forced-choice type cases do have some level of defensive capability, however small or unlikely. We saw this explicitly in cases like *Conscientious Driver* because Pedestrian happened to be carrying an explosive device. I showed there that that fact diffuses McMahan's reliance on the nonreciprocal risk Driver imposes on Pedestrian since they both, in fact, impose risk on the other. But here I am going further by showing that, explosive device or none, we all (or nearly all) have some level of defensive capability at

---

[84] In the parallel case, then, on the Evidence-Relative View we should not count dignitary having defensive capabilities against her in searching for asymmetry. It may be wrong for her to carry the gun, in general—I'm remaining neutral on that point. But even if that is true, that supposed moral blame is inappropriately applied to determinations of liability.

any given time towards others. Dignitary and Guest both have some defensive capability against the other, even *before* we assume that Guest himself has a gun or grabs for a nearby gun from a security guard. This counts against the mere capability or threat of non-culpable defensive harm as being a properly relevant basis for liability attribution.

From this observation I can press the *reductio ad absurdum* used above even further by arguing that nearly all of us are Unintentional Ninjas to some degree. That is, nearly all of us leave the house and go out into the world everyday with some defensive capability that we could possibly use and thereby threaten others with non-culpable defensive harm. And this possibility is ever-present. If that is correct, then according to Emerton and Handfield's model of *affray*, we all exist in some limited state of *affray* at all times. That is, we are all in a kind of lesser-degreed *Barroom Brawl* right now.[85] And that sounds crazy, at least to my ears. If affray is ever present, the concept isn't doing much explanatory work, much less moral justificatory work.

Returning then to *Barroom Brawl*, I'm arguing that the conditions which here supposedly ground symmetrical defensive privileges do not track the right kind of relevant moral facts in order to adequately ground liability. When person A is surrounded by people for whom their threat of defensive harm is explicitly non-culpable, then that cannot serve to ground their liability to A's attack. Their threat of (i.e., the mere possibility of) their non-culpable defensive harm cannot ground their liability to A attacking them any more than Tom's embezzling can be the basis for making him liable to Frank or the (mere) presence of Dignitary's gun can itself make her liable to Guest. This is because in all these cases, the defensive capability is being used permissibly. And if that's true, then it cannot be a relevant ground for liability. Remember: Emerton and Handfield completely set aside questions of "who is in the right" in the brawl. (That is their point, recall, because they are trying to defend the classic MEC between combatants, grounded as it traditionally was without any reference to *jus ad bellum*.) Indeed, they stress that Smith does not know if the threat of defensive harm near him is permissible or not and so they explicitly grant that it is non-culpable. Yet, they contend, Smith gains a defensive privilege against them not due to proper

---

[85] Or, at least, the vast majority of us are. Very young children and people who are completely paralyzed or otherwise physically unable to move may not pose any defensive threat whatsoever, but the vast majority of us do pose *some* kind of potential for defensive harm of some kind to some degree, however limited it may be. Hence, according to the logic of affray, the vast majority of us are in a barroom brawl at all times. That should be all I need to show the absurdity of the view.

attribution of liability but simply because of mutual threat; and then, like some kind of liability treadmill, the others then similarly gain a defensive privilege against Smith because of the possible exercise of his own defensive privilege, and so on, and so on. Soon enough, everyone is liable to everyone else in *Barroom Brawl*.

How much more plausible, then, to say that defensive privilege against another is gained only when a party is properly morally responsible for a relevant wrong that is to be averted. But if one cannot adequately determine this, then they should refrain from delivering harm until they can do so. In other words, if you are caught in a barroom brawl and you don't know "who is in the right" in the fight, then your moral obligation is to get the hell out of the bar, duck into a back room, or (perhaps) try to stop the brawl if you can, or even hide under a table if you must. I will note anecdotally that I've found myself in the equivalent of a barroom brawl on two occasions in my life.[86] In both instances, it was easy to extradite myself from violence, if so desired. And excuses about wounded pride and such as blocks against this are simply weak and wildly disproportionate to the moral weight of potentially harming a nonliable person. I'll argue below that many excuses for an unjust soldier in war are actually similar, even when the pressures to fight in an unjust war are significant. If one is to punch another, or take up lethal arms against another, morality demands that you act on proper evidence of the justice of your act. As will be evident, this nicely dovetails with the Evidence-Relative View, although it is compatible with all versions of the Responsible Account. As will also be clear when one applied my account of liability to soldiers in war, the corollary will be that soldiers should similarly not fight if they do not have a high degree of confidence in the justice of the cause for which they fight.[87]

But it is a mistake to hold that the mere presence of a non-culpable threat around you somehow exculpates you of any wrongdoing if you join in the bar fight melee. Sure: bar fights are dangerous things. But you do not gain the right to harm others simply because there's a fight going on around you. Along the parallel lines, consider soldiers in war. Wars are also dangerous things. But, in the same way, a soldier does not gain the right to kill others simply because there's a war going on around him. If you find your state at war, do your best to figure out if your side's cause is just. If it is not, or you are

---

[86] On one occasion, it was clear who was liable to be harmed to thwart further unjust harm against a nonliable person. On the other occasion, it was completely and utterly unclear who was liable, who was nonliable, and who was even involved at all—it was mayhem.

[87] I will return to this shortly below, and discuss this at greater length in chapter 5.

not sure, then do not fight; and do not think that the mere presence or threat of non-culpable violence from the other side somehow exculpates you of any wrongdoing if you fight for an unjust cause in a criminal war. The mere threat (the mere possibility!) of defensive harm, the permissibility of which is unclear, does not give permission for violent defense or make others liable to harm. Rather, a threat must be a wrongful threat, the culpability of which one can reasonably ascertain, for it to properly result in liability that can give rise to a just defensive privilege.

So, since affray fails to give mutual liability to harm in *Barroom Brawl*, it also fails to ground the MEC for soldiers in war. In the next chapter, I will combine the work done in this chapter in defense of revisionist just war theory and the rejection of the MEC, as well as the defense of the Evidence-Relative View for the responsibility criterion of liability attribution given in chapters 2 and 3, with a new proposal for how targeting could actually work in war. This new proposal will show how a revisionist just war theory can still give us a plausible way to wage war without relying on the MEC to wrongly determine who should die by the fiat of war.

5
A New Proposal for Liability in War

It is forbidden to kill;
therefore all murderers are punished
unless they kill in large numbers
and to the sound of trumpets.

—Voltaire

5.1. Introduction

Embracing the revisionist account of just war theory in military practice would require significant changes to the ways in which war is waged and various *jus in bello* criteria are implemented. As we've seen, the difficulties such changes would bring to the operations of modern militaries have been the basis for a great deal of critique of the revisionist account. Lazar, for example, while accepting the revisionist rejection of the MEC, argues that without it, determining liability in war becomes impossible and we are left with a form of contingent pacifism.[1] Shue also points to the extreme epistemic difficulties of war and contends that we must therefore retain the MEC.[2] Walzer himself thinks the realities of war are such that he will not even entertain the possibility of what it could look like on the revisionist model. In speaking of Jeff McMahan, the scholar who has far and away done more to advance the revisionist cause more than any other, Walzer dismissively said, "What Jeff McMahan means to provide . . . is a careful and precise account of individual responsibility in time of war. What he actually provides, I think, is a careful and precise account of what individual responsibility in war would be like if war were a peacetime activity."[3] Walzer has made his opinion of the (im)

---

[1] Seth Lazar, "The Responsibility Dilemma for Killing in War: A Review Essay," *Philosophy & Public Affairs* 38, no. 2 (2010): 180–213.
[2] Henry Shue, "Do We Need a 'Morality of War'?," in *Just and Unjust Warriors: The Moral and Legal Status of Soldiers*, edited by David Rodin and Henry Shue (New York: Oxford University Press, 2008).
[3] "Response to McMahan's Paper," *Philosophia* 34 (2006): 43–45, at 43.

plausibility of the revisionist account even more clear in spoken comments.[4] What is needed then is an attempt to work out how the morality of war, properly understood by the revisionist model, might look if a sincere effort was made to apply it to the realities of modern warfare. That is what I aim to do in this chapter. It is important to note, before we dive in, that the work here is far from a complete account, and is intended to serve merely as a starting point to show a proof of concept, rather than a fully worked out approach.[5]

5.2. Degreed Status

Traditionally, as we've seen, a given populace in any war is divided simply and crudely between combatants and noncombatants; these are the only two categories for targeting decisions under the traditional just war theory rubrics. If one is a combatant, they can be targeted and killed at any time and any place in war. If one is not a combatant, then they are not to be intentionally harmed or infringed upon in any way; they have complete immunity. As we've seen, this approach to killing in war does not properly respect the rights of many individuals involved in war. Some who would traditionally be labeled combatants are not properly liable and should not be unrestricted targets of attack—both the just combatants as well as some of the less responsible unjust combatants. And, on the other side of the coin, a few who would traditionally be labeled noncombatants are, in fact, somewhat responsible to such an extent that they should not be utterly immune from any harm and may be liable to some degree of defensive harm. The traditional binary division of target status is far too imprecise a tool for the fine-grained realities of moral liability to harm.

As we saw in the last chapter, many scholars, such as Lazar, worry that without the MEC these categories would break down and, on one hand, assignment of liability will become rampant and total war will ensue, or

---

[4] Again, see note 27 in chapter 4 above for an example.
[5] David Rodin has made parallel first steps recently in exploring how we should change the laws of war to accord with the revisionist view of the morality of war. Here I am focusing solely on how the morality of combatant targeting should change to accord with the revisionist view, but I take my efforts here to be of a piece with Rodin's efforts on the legal side. See Rodin, "Superior Law." Also note that many of the arguments I make in this chapter are drawn from my initial proposals made in my paper "Walking the Tightrope of Just War," Analysis 71 (July 2011): 533–44, and a later book chapter, "Revisionist Just War Theory and the Real World: A Cautiously Optimistic Proposal," in *Routledge Handbook of Ethics and War: Just War in the 21st Century*, edited by Fritz Allhoff, Adam Henschke, and Nick Evans (London: Routledge, 2013).

else that careful restrictions on whom just soldiers can engage would become so great that military victory becomes impossible. But I responded that difficulty, even extreme difficulty, in fighting war justly does not equal practical impossibility. And even if doing away with the MEC makes determination of enemy liability *difficult*, it could still be done in a reasonable way that approximates just war. Thus, to apply the revisionist view of just war theory to targeting in war, I propose tying combatant status directly to the degreed nature of liability, insofar as it is possible to ascertain; to re-envision combatant-hood away from an all-or-nothing condition to one of degree. McMahan writes that "the extent to which a person is excused for posing a threat of wrongful harm affects the degree of his moral liability to defensive harm, which in turn affects the stringency of the proportionality restriction on defensive force."[6] We can take this principle and from it derive new categories for an unjust population that could be applied in war. (By "unjust population" I mean, similar to my use of unjust soldier, the full set of people on the side of a conflict that is pursuing an unjust war against a just cause.) This would mean that we need more complex categories of combatant and noncombatant status to better accommodate the realities of variable liability levels amongst an enemy population. I'll show that coupling this move with the understanding that liability (even "high" liability) need not always entail killing as the best response for many war situations can result in a workable and consistent form of just war. The proposal would require intricate rules of engagement (ROEs) for any given conflict based upon the most reasonable understanding a military force could have of its foes' various levels of liability and resulting combatant statuses. As will become clear below, such an envisioned approach will pair elegantly with the Evidence-Relative View of liability attribution.

Thus, rather than the binary combatant or noncombatant system of categorization traditionally used, a conflict-by-conflict rubric could be constructed that tracks differing levels of liability for a given set of unjust enemies. The distinctions could range from 1st, 2nd, and 3rd-degree combatants and the like (or more, as needed) and similar degrees for noncombatants. The basis for an adversary's degreed status would be tied to what I call "Reasonable Perceived Liability" (RPL) rather than other less adequate metrics traditionally used (such as "posing a threat"). RPL is best defined as: the best approximate determination of an enemy's degree of liability that could be reached by

---

[6] McMahan, *Killing in War*, 156.

a just force taking all reasonable efforts and epistemic due diligence to make that determination. Once broad levels of RPL are determined for a population set, correlating categories of degreed combatant and noncombatant statuses could then be applied accordingly. Specialized ROEs could then be created which best allow a military to achieve victory on behalf of a just cause, yet come as close as possible to matching the correct level of response to the RPL for each category.

By deriving enemy status from RPL, some who are traditionally labeled as combatants may be considered some lesser-degreed type of combatant with different ROEs—and vice-versa for noncombatants—all dependent upon their given RPL. What has come to be known as "narrow proportionality" can press us farther than even McMahan suggests to ever increasingly complex and restrictive ROEs resulting in a range of responses for different cases, depending on the RPL of a given enemy. McMahan explains how narrow proportionality restricts any defensive response to "(1) the magnitude of the wrongful harm to be prevented, (2) the effectiveness of the defensive act in averting the harm, (3) the magnitude of the harm inflicted on the wrongdoer, and (4) the degree of his responsibility for the threat that he poses."[7] My proposed RPL model takes these considerations and suggests we could attempt to work them *directly* into our conception of enemy status. *Pace* Lazar, under such ROEs, victory could still be attainable in certain contexts. But, it must be admitted, victory will not be attainable in all contexts of war under such restrictions. However, when it is impossible to fight justly and achieve victory, it is unjust to go to war. To fight otherwise, in a truly impossible context to follow morality's demands and win, then the war effort itself is in vain and adds unnecessary harm, death, and misery to war. Accepting this reality is one of the bullets that we must bite in embracing the revisionist view of just war theory.

I'll note that exactly what the bar is for "impossible" victory conditions here is, in my mind, perhaps a much higher threshold than many would likely hold. This is because the history of warfare is ripe with examples of surprise underdog victories against high odds. And the moral weight of a just cause against unjust aggression is so great, that it demands a valiant effort, if it is at all possible. Again, consider the 2022 just defense of Ukraine against Russia's unjust aggression. At the start of the war, many experts predicted that Russia would overrun Ukraine, and then Kiev would fall in a matter of days.

---

[7] See McMahan, *Killing in War*, 196–97.

Indeed, there are reports of Russian soldiers making dinner reservations in Kiev restaurants a week out from the start of the invasion, certain they would be conquering occupiers by that time and planning celebratory dinners. Alas, the Ukrainians, fighting for the just cause of national defense against unjust aggression, have exceeded all odds and, at the time this book is going to press, continue to wage a heroic resistance, however long the odds initially seemed.[8]

To be clear, an unjust enemy's status *should* track exactly with his or her liability. Consequently, one might object that if I am going to take the revisionist view seriously, then I should not generalize from distinct individual liability to categories of any kind—be it the traditional binary split or my proposed more complex divisions. I agree in principle but believe that by developing complex levels of enemy status we could adequately cover the vast majority of cases so that just soldiers following RPL-derived ROEs could justly engage an enemy with minimized moral risk. There is, after all, a limited, finite range of possible choices on how to engage any given enemy population in any given context. And that is primarily because there are only so many things a just force can actually do—from doing nothing to incapacitating to killing, and things in between. Thus, we can create discrete levels of enemy status tied to RPL, even if RPL is itself technically non-discrete. That is, for pragmatic reasons that do not outstrip respect for the enemies' rights, some generalizations of enemy status are permissible. The more complex divisions I'm proposing are a best approximation of what morality gives us which serve as a heuristic for the best we can reasonably do in efforts to correlate how one is treated in warfare to one's liability. It is also worth noting that this is imagined as what would be a significant moral improvement on the long history of just war theory, striving to make war ever closer to the moral ideal. However, it would still fall far short of perfect justice in that even in such an imagined scenario, some individual's liability conditions would be misattributed, misapplied, or misunderstood; including, perhaps, the categorizations themselves being insufficient. Still, it would represent a radical leap forward in the moral respect for rights within warfare.

RPL determination should account for factors such as epistemic limitations regarding one's cause, coercion to fight, other external pressures or

---

[8] There is an interesting question around this point whether the justice of the cause itself serves to improve one's chances militarily. Although perhaps it's a little idealistic to assume this is the case, there is some historical evidence for it. One is reminded of Napoleon's famous quip that "The moral is to the physical as three is to one."

confusions, and so on that were discussed and raised as challenges by Lazar and Shue.[9] As noted, this RPL determination would be accomplished by a just force researching the evidence available to an enemy populace and the various options for them to take in their support, or nonsupport, of an unjust cause. As I'll show below, while this may sound impractical and unrealistic on first glance, there are actually some real-world recent cases of militaries making exactly these kinds of determinations and behaving accordingly.

Further, recall that liability—even in war—need not necessarily constitute proper eligibility for *lethal* attack. Narrow proportionality can drive just war-fighters even farther than McMahan suggests to ever increasingly complex and restrictive ROEs that could result in a multitude of non-lethal responses being the best option for many cases, depending on the RPL of the enemy.[10] I argue that such ROEs could be workable, reasonable, and exactly the *kind* of developments that we should expect as the just war theory tradition improves over time—ever more restrictive, striving for ever more just behavior in combat.[11] Further, *contra* Lazar, I argue that, under such ROEs, military victory could still be achievable in certain contexts. I will demonstrate this below with a handful of examples that should make us cautiously optimistic about the possibilities of such a model.

So, the formal proposal is that we have more categories with simplified differences in engagement for different groups in war. It functions as a partial, additional response to the concerns raised by the Dilemma in chapter 4. More substantively, a classic problem in just war theory is how to classify people who support an unjust war effort in ways such as building tanks and munitions or other support roles. Walzer and, famously, Thomas Nagel both wrestled over this question and argued it was acceptable for a just force to kill such persons while they worked, but not when they were in their homes.[12] I'm not here to defend this position, but to raise it to show something important. And that is that even these most traditional of just war theorists recognized that liability in war is more complicated than what the meager

---

[9] Gerhard Øverland first discussed differences in liability amongst an enemy population in ways that track closely with my proposal that I will discuss below. See Øverland, "Killing Soldiers," *Ethics and International Affairs* 20 (2006): 455–75.

[10] See *Killing in War*, 196–97, for a discussion of this point.

[11] I view McMahan's work in developing a better (but more difficult) theory of liability as a sterling example of such improvements. I see the evidence-relative view as following this same path. As we've seen, these revisionist views lead to the rejection of the MEC, which makes just war far more difficult; but if this is what morality demands of us, then so be it.

[12] Walzer, *Just & Unjust Wars*, 146; Thomas Nagel, "War and Massacre," *Philosophy & Public Affairs* 1, no. 2 (1972): 140.

two-category system can deliver. By creating more divisions within these categories, with different ROEs for each, these and other perennial questions regarding difficult cases could be better resolved.

What are we to make of a military lawyer who spends all her efforts fighting to mitigate the war crimes that her unjust comrades commit? Should her status be simply "combatant" and thus liable to be killed by a just force? Or consider as a civilian target, analysts working in an unjust military's command center. Should they be immune from harm as "noncombatants"? What of soldiers in a military waging an unjust war, but who are far in the rear, fully removed from combat and almost certain to never be used to further the unjust cause? Should we treat them the same as soldiers on the front who are actively killing just soldiers to further the unjust cause of their war? Such cases, and countless others, suggest that more complex categories reflecting differing levels of liability are needed.

5.3. Deriving RPL

On my proposal, as noted, enemy soldiers under difficult epistemic circumstances for ascertaining the (in)justice of their cause, would fall into different combatant categories (with different appropriate ROEs) than those for whom a just force had reason to believe are voluntarily fighting for the unjust cause and who have better access to the injustice of their cause. Gerhard Øverland's work, "Killing Soldiers," discusses some of the differences between various liability levels of combatants amongst an enemy population in ways that track closely with my model.[13] He argues, for example, that in the case of the 2003 US invasion of Iraq, a just force would do right to distinguish between those Iraqi soldiers who were members of the Republican Guard (a volunteer force made up of well-paid proud partisans and hard-liners dedicated to Saddam Hussein and his regime) versus poorly trained and poorly informed Iraqi soldiers who were conscripted into military service under coercion and threat of death of themselves or their family.[14] A multi-faceted

---

[13] Gerhard Øverland, "Killing Soldiers," *Ethics & International Affairs* 20, no. 4 (2006): 455–75.. My proposed scheme here to track graduated combatant status with RPL is, I believe, in harmony with and follows in the vein of Øverland's position presented in that piece. Overland discusses more specifically how to resolve cases of innocent soldiers fighting each other. My rubric is an attempt to take this notion—that different liability levels amongst an enemy combatant population should result in different permissible responses—to an even broader scale, encompassing all of *jus in bello* practice.

[14] McMahan argues similarly for treating the Iraqi conscripts and members of the Republican Guard differently. See *Killing in War*, 194–95.

combatant rubric like I suggest could account for these significant differences in the liability of Iraqi soldiers in such a real-world scenario and their corresponding different levels of mitigating excuses. The RPL level for a member of the Republican Guard would be, presumably, quite different from that of the RPL for a conscripted Iraqi soldier. Consequently, this would equate to a different degree of combatant status with different ROEs for each group. In practical terms, this could mean that a theoretically just force engaged in combat against the Iraqi military at such a time might classify conscripted troops as 3rd-degree combatants whereas members of the Republican Guard would be 1st-degree combatants. The ROEs for 3rd-degree combatants could be, say, to only fire if directly fired upon, to avoid direct engagements, to seek and encourage the peaceful surrender of such enemy forces, or to seek nonlethal forms of engagement. Whereas, alternatively, ROEs for 1st-degree combatants could follow more traditional just war theory guidelines for unrestricted (or less restricted) targeting.

One can imagine a similar distinction made between some of the various Russian military units unjustly attacking Ukraine in 2022. We'll return to this in some detail below. But the accounts of many captured Russian soldiers have revealed that, for many units, the soldiers had poor information as to their missions, or even (in the early days) that they were part of an invading force. Such units would likely have an RPL difference compared to Russian troops and leaders well aware of their aims.

Another important aspect to determining an enemy combatant's liability that many critics of the revisionist view neglect is that (purported) just warfighters already take themselves to be engaged in a just war. Lazar for example fails to take this into account for a just force's apprehension of unjust soldiers. He mentions this (lack of certainty knowing "that their own cause is just") as a prohibitive factor working against the just war-fighter's ability to discriminate. I here intend to show that Lazar has this backward. If they are purportedly just war-fighters, that then *means* that they have epistemic confidence in the justice of their cause. For to wage war without confidence that one's cause is just would be to commit a Failure of Due Diligence similar to the premature shooting done by Caroline in *Caroline's Confusion*. That is, combatant liability determination does not occur in a vacuum—"from the outside"—but by those sides engaged in a given conflict itself.

This means that the level to which just war-fighters are convinced of the justice of their own military undertaking would affect their ascertaining of an enemies' epistemic view of their cause and resulting liability (and possible mitigating excuses). Assume that a just war-fighter has held herself to a skeptical position regarding her own side's justification for war and that she attained a high level of epistemic confidence on the justice of her cause before she decided to join in the war effort.[15] That is, she did full due epistemic diligence and concluded her cause was just. From this it follows that the just war-fighter, in satisfying the high level of epistemic satisfaction she would need to be justified to engage war, has at least a *prima facie* reason to hold that the enemies' side is evidence-relatively unjust to a similar degree; at least globally in terms of its overall *jus ad bellum*.[16] The question of the enemies' evidence-relative injustice of their cause is thus colored by the just war-fighters' own level of certainty of the evidence-relative justice of their own cause. Again, for a present-day example of this, imagine the Ukrainian soldier fighting to defend his home against invading Russian invaders. One would hold, as discussed in previous chapters, that the Ukrainian soldier would have a very high level of epistemic warrant to conclude they were acting on behalf of a just cause to literally defend their village against an invading force. That epistemic confidence in their own cause, counts in favor of greater confidence for the conclusions they can reach as to the enemy soldier's own cause and resulting liability.

This does not settle the matter, of course, for the enemies' epistemic access (it can be assumed) will almost certainly be limited, perhaps radically so, as to the real state-of-affairs for their side's justification. And such limitations would have to be factored into RPL for a given enemy. But the basic idea is sound: if a soldier holds a very high bar of healthy skepticism for themselves to be convinced that their own side is just, and then they *are* so convinced, this strongly implies that (most likely) there will be rather strong evidence making the case.[17]

---

[15] Lazar suggests that this, also, cannot be done, and he offers an attack against the very possibility of a just war-fighter ever having the kind of confidence in their cause I am here suggesting as an assumption for theorizing. "Our leaders could violate at least five of the standard just war theory criteria, without anybody outside the circles of power knowing about it. They might have secretly provoked the enemy into attacking, to give the appearance of a just cause; they might have adopted a disproportionate strategy; there may have been other options besides war, thus failing last resort; their intentions may be improper, say, the pursuit of resources; and they may know our prospects of success are slim, because of classified intelligence." Lazar, "Responsibility Dilemma," 194.

[16] Assuming, that is, that in no war are both sides fact-relatively just, in total *jus ad bellum* determinations. McMahan challenges the notion that both sides cannot have at least some just cause in "Just Cause for War." It is, of course, entirely possible (and probably historically highly common) that both sides of a war may be ultimately unjust, even if they each have some elements of a just cause.

[17] Notice that we do this in our theorizing about war. We assume "the just war-fighter" and then discuss her engagement of the enemy. But part of what it *means* to assume a war-fighter is just in the first place is that the war-fighter has proper epistemic warrant to so believe she is just and to take the moral risk of fighting in a war.

McMahan comments in *Killing in War* that it is hard to comprehend how a German soldier invading Poland at the outset of World War II could have possibly held that his cause was just. Even granting high levels of propaganda and nationalistic preference (and what Lazar calls "reasonable partiality"), it is hard to imagine one honestly believing his or her cause is in the right under such circumstances.[18] Far more likely is that an unjust soldier in such a case simply failed to fully or properly consider the justice of their cause—at least not to the extent that morality demands of us, given the massive moral stakes on the endeavor they were undertaking. Perhaps they mistakenly thought that—as traditional just war theory has long proclaimed—it was not their job to consider questions pertaining to *jus ad bellum*. This is the great hurdle the revisionist view must overcome. It argues that we must change the way soldiers approach the business of war in regard to their own participation therein. That, as noted in chapter 3 above, that it is theirs to question why precisely because it is theirs to do and die. And this is a change in our moral expectations of soldiers that we must make at the societal level.

This leaves an interesting question of excusing ignorance explored in chapters 2 and 3. How should the fact that a soldier simply takes *jus ad bellum* to not be their concern effect their liability determination? Is this an excusing ignorance or one for which they can be held liable? I am not sure how we can begin answering this tough puzzle. To begin, however, it seems clear that the relative accessibility or clarity of evidence that makes the unjust soldier's cause more or less manifestly unjust will run inversely correlative to how we should consider this kind of ignorance to be excusing. I'll explore this more below, but to see why this should be our approach, note that when a cause is manifestly unjust, we have historically seen soldiers drop the pretense that *jus ad bellum* was of no concern to the permissibility of their service—and this was long before the relatively recent rise of revisionist challenges to just war theory surfaced. This is critical. This shows that the obvious and evident injustice of one's cause *can* lead soldiers to see through the ignorance of a strict separation of *jus ad bellum* and *jus in bello*; that is, it is *possible*, in at least some cases. When the injustice of a cause is less evident, then, it is presumably far easier to maintain the separation in one's mind with regard to their service therein and, so, such ignorance would be more excusable of one's liability.

---

[18] Lazar's discusses the presumption in favor of one's own sources of authority, what he calls "reasonable partiality." See Lazar, "The Responsibility Dilemma," 197.

To help develop this point, McMahan offers an illuminating discussion of a Palestinian suicide bomber from Gaza.[19] Needless to say, the act the suicide bomber is carrying out is, to our eyes, a clearly wrong act. That is, it is fact-relative wrong, and we have clear evidence showing it to be such, and we thus take it to be, perhaps obviously, evidence-relative wrong as well. So, we should consider how it is that the suicide bomber could think it is permissible. Presuming, that is, that the suicide bomber does think it is permissible. It's possible he does not think it is permissible yet acts anyway and is relevantly like Morton from the chapter 2 *Morton* case. But let us presume, rather, that he is mistaken in his judgment of the act's permissibility and is more like Phillip from the *Phillip* case. In such a case, the bomber has belief-relative permission (he believes it is right to do, despite what the evidence provides). What are we to make of the suicide bomber in terms of his liability to harm? Does his ignorance give him epistemic excuse that could, even partially, excuse his liability? No, I do not think it does, and of course the Evidence-Relative View is not committed to such a conclusion, nor is any version of revisionist just war theory.

McMahan argues, for example, that we can reasonably demand of someone (at least) the mere act of minimal moral reflective equilibrium. That is, that one would ask oneself if he or she would consider someone on the opposing side undertaking the same action against his or her side as just were the conditions and roles exactly reversed. McMahan argues that the Palestinian suicide bomber would almost certainly *not* hold this (that an Israeli suicide bomber killing innocent people attending a Mosque, say, would not be justified, even if the Palestinians were keeping the Israelis under their thumb in the same way the bomber believes Israel is presently doing to them). I think this is a very reasonable assumption. And this demand for simple moral reflection on those who are about to kill others is part and parcel of Moral Epistemic Contextualism and a Failure of Due Diligence argued for at length above in chapter 2.

This, then, can give us further aspects to calculate in our RPL for a given enemy: failing to conduct even minimal moral reflection in one's actions can constitute a form of Failure of Due Diligence which can be a legitimate factor for determining one's liability. Thus, the just war-fighter's apprehension of the enemy soldier proceeds through steps. If the enemy has clear evidence that

---

[19] McMahan, *Killing in War*, 124–25.

demand even simple moral reflection, we should expect that of them (and all people, including ourselves). Ultimately all of these factors—expected moral reflection on the available evidence, the possibilities of epistemic limitations and coercion and reasonable partiality, and so forth—can culminate in some level or degree of liability which can then map onto some level of combatanthood, which correlates to resulting ROEs for the given enemy which are themselves relative to (and err on the side of caution for) the level of uncertainty for that RPL.

In discussing people's decision to go to war Lazar writes, "It is unreasonable to expect people to formulate beliefs warranting high credence, when the moral and nonmoral evidence do not support a determinate conclusion."[20] But the revisionist view and Moral Epistemic Contextualism agrees with Lazar that people should not formulate a belief warranting high credence in such a case, *particularly* if that belief then licenses killing people. Rather, when the decision to go to war involves such uncertainty, people should remain agnostic as to whether their side is just and then err on the side of caution by not taking on the moral risk of fighting in a potentially unjust war.[21] If, however, they *do* have high credence for believing they are justified to go to war, this will entail that there are (most likely) some fairly obvious reasons for the opposing side to question the justice of their cause (again, think of the German soldier invading Poland or the cognitive dissonance of the Palestinian suicide bomber, or, more recently, a Russian soldier invading Ukraine). And this reality will, in turn, be part of the calculus of RPL that just soldiers need to make in engaging the enemy. But, again, if the just forces conclude that there are good reasons to think the epistemic constraints are such that the unjust soldier has some level of excuse mitigating their unjust actions, this should then inform their RPL and correlative combatant status. And there are further limitations and factors that could mitigate an unjust soldier's liability that should also be calculated in determinations of their RPL, such as whether or not the enemy's state allows for conscientious objector status or uses coercion to force its citizens into military service, and so forth, for a wide variety of possible factors.

---

[20] Lazar, "Responsibility Dilemma," 194.
[21] This correlates nicely with Alexander Guerrero's "Don't Know, Don't Kill" principle found in his paper by the same name discussed at length above in chapter 2.

5.4. Objections and Real-World Cases

Some will argue that such a scheme makes fighting war impossible by being too restrictive on the just war-fighter; that it would "tie their hands" to such an extent that they could never have military success. It could be argued that my suggested development moves far beyond McMahanian narrow proportionality and morphs into some kind of "hyper-narrow proportionality." Granted, what I am calling for places incredibly high burdens on just war-fighters: calling on them to use near Herculean strength in their self-control and self-sacrifice under, literally, the most extreme circumstances of duress possible. But, I would counter, that is precisely *what it means* to be a just war-fighter, or aim to be one, at any rate. And this—the ever increasing demands placed on just war-fighters—is what we should expect as our moral reasoning, regarding war, improves and sharpens over time. Consider the dramatic and relatively quick moral improvements to how (purportedly) just war-fighters are expected to fight that have developed simply over the past half-century alone.[22] Far more is expected of present (putative) just war-fighters with regard to behavior in combat for issues such as careful discrimination, for example, than was ever expected of putatively just war-fighters a generation previous. Just war theory doctrine and practice has become increasingly more and more ingrained in many of the world's militaries. We should *expect* new developments in just war theory to elicit further developments for *jus in bello* practices; perhaps like those suggested here. These new arguments and developments presently being debated and the resulting casting off of various Walzerian vestments, will elicit further developments for *jus in bello* practices, such as those under consideration in this chapter.

But the likes of Shue and Lazar complain that such high demands can't be expected of soldiers operating in the vagaries of modern combat. I disagree. First, I'd ask of such scholars, "Just what do we take the aim of moral philosophy regarding just behavior in war to be?" It is to (hopefully) work out what morally right action in war would be, if it is even possible at all. If we think we have found what that is, but that it is unlikely that people will so behave, well, that is, frankly, another matter; one of how to *get* people to behave morally, not what moral behavior *is*. This is an important and often neglected point

---

[22] For a good discussion on the success of just war theory to shape contemporary military practice in the United States and other Western powers, see Martin Cook, *Moral Warrior*. Also see Michael Walzer, "The Triumph of Just War Theory—and the Dangers of Success," *Social Research* 69, no. 4 (2002): 925–46.

in debates about the morality of conduct in war. The job of the moral philosopher here is to work out what it *would be* to fight in war justly. Whether people can be convinced to do so or not is not properly our job. And this is not an "ought implies can" debate. Whether people *can* so behave in war, or *will* so behave in war are two different things. Lazar argues that it is literally impossible to fight war justly given the provisions of the revisionist view. In this chapter, I am hoping to show that he significantly overstates that case; that it is possible and, granting the limitations soldiers face, that something like what I propose (the multifaceted system of combatant status based on RPL with correlative restrictive ROEs) is what it could look like.

Second, I am simply more optimistic of the abilities of soldiers to behave justly and follow such restrictive ROEs. And this is for many reasons, including both the major changes across the past 50 years of modern warfare, and my own decades of working with and teaching ethics to actual war-fighters. It is critical to recall that when Walzer challenged the realpolitik orthodoxy in 1977 with *Just and Unjust Wars*, few thought that serious ethical constraint in war was likely to ever gain consensus much less become the orthodox view and result in actionable policy changes. But the fruit of just war theory's restraining influence is now evident in contemporary war-fighting by nearly all (so-called) Western nations' militaries. It has been a difficult shift in the thinking of contemporary war-fighters, but it has happened, generationally; and we should expect this evolution to continually occur with every new generation of war-fighter. Again, even the most "gung-ho" warrior serving in a Western nation's military today is far more acutely aware, and most likely even deeply concerned with, being careful to do his or her best to distinguish between innocent civilians and combatants than a soldier serving in those very same nation-states' militaries 100 years ago, and even 50 years ago. Be it for self-interested reasons (i.e., wanting to avoid punishment) or moral ones, the fact remains that the modern soldier in these militaries tends to act with far more awareness of *jus in bello* principles and corresponding restraint. Indeed, in most cases, today's soldier is far more concerned and careful to obey these distinctions than a soldier in the same military would have been even 20 years ago.

Moreover, this objection is largely discredited simply because the kinds of changes I'm proposing *may already be occurring*, and may have been for some time. It is hard to over-state the importance of this point. I find that many of the best scholars working on these issues in the ethics of war today tend to be rather shockingly ignorant on the actual workings of present-day military operations. Take NATO's counter-insurgency (technology strongly points) operations in Afghanistan, particularly in the years between 2009 and 2014 as one particularly powerful example. Regardless of one's assessment of the overall justification of the US and NATO forces' military operations in Afghanistan, notice that present COIN strategy provides an excellent example of this development. The average soldier in this theatre undertakes extreme caution in avoiding (what she considers to be) noncombatant causalities that would have been considered unimaginable restraint even a generation ago.[23] The soldiers have surprisingly high discipline in following incredibly restrictive ROEs. Why should we not expect that this trend could continue?

Take one clear example of this from warfare's recent history. In 2012 through 2013, NATO forces in the war in Afghanistan engaged the last vestiges of al-Qaeda groups quite differently than they engaged Taliban fighters. The former, al-Qaeda groups, they attacked "with prejudice" and, where possible, engaged and killed via drone airstrike. The latter, the Taliban, they engaged far more cautiously, avoided high death tolls and direct engagement when possible, and used extreme restraint to avoid noncombatant causalities. The point is that they treated distinct groups of enemy "combatants" within the very same theater and conflict as different *kinds* of combatants with different ROEs. Admittedly, this distinction at the time was done (most likely) on purely pragmatic and strategic grounds (on the hopes of not alienating certain groups for potential downstream negotiations). But such distinctions between combatants *could* be done for moral reasons—on the grounds of perceived differences in liability.

Further, developments over the past decades in military technology strive to be ever more discriminate in war, not less. This is *contra* Lazar who believes modern warfare makes indiscriminate combat *more* likely due to long-range artillery and "dumb bomb" munitions.[24] Perhaps this was true throughout most of the 20th Century, but such forms of warfare are today

---

[23] Granted, these strictures and constraints are often failed to be met. This war has countless tales of wrongful killing by both sides, tragically.

[24] See Strawser, "Moral Predators," where I address some of these issues directly. Lazar claims that modern war is predicated on indiscriminate weaponry such as long-range artillery, but this need not be the case. Indeed, perhaps Lazar has developed the case against such weapons, but not against the possibility of just war in principle. And, happily, the development of future weaponry appears to drive ever more toward precision and discrimination and away from the kinds of weapons such as long-range artillery. For a high-level overview of this broad trend, see my lecture: "The Ethics of Warfare and Changing Technology," World Affairs Council of Monterey Bay, Special Guest Lecturer, October, 2020.

becoming increasingly passé for much of modern conflict. Military weapons of the future enable more just behavior, not less, because they are both far more accurate and precise. Many of these kinds of weapons are already being employed.[25] Take, for one example, unmanned aerial vehicles (UAVs). I've argued at great length elsewhere that this technology could represent a significant moral improvement in warfare for precisely these kinds of reasons.[26] For the present discussion, note that these weapons enable forces to observe enemies for long, extended stretches of time before engaging them. This new ability would improve a just force's accurate determination of RPL. We've always witnessed tremendous developments in precision weaponry, which further improve the ability of just forces to behave within the strictures of RPL. All this new technology strongly points toward this kind of operational asymmetry necessary for this model as at least being possible and, in fact, increasingly common in future warfare.[27]

All of these examples give us reason to think that modern military forces could, indeed, further restrain their behavior along the lines of my proposed RPL model to achieve fighting ever more just war. Let me offer one further example of how restrictive ROEs, even if more difficult, can and are being implemented, and how we can see an arc to military restraint growing over time. Return once again to the case of NATO's military action in Afghanistan from 2009 through 2014. In that time, NATO forces' tactics and operational approaches toward the enemies they faced shifted many times and often in significant ways. General Stanley McChrystal was the NATO commander from 2009 to 2010 and he gained fame for, in part, implementing what was come to be known as a COIN strategy. COIN strategy, developed most influentially within the US military by General David Petraeus, is an approach aimed at winning over the host population to the cause against the insurgents. This should be the primary focus of all unified operations—military and diplomatic—and includes the aim of massively reducing or eliminating civilian casualties to that end with the hope of rendering the insurgents ineffective and noninfluential while simultaneously strengthening and securing

---

[25] Such as unmanned drones. Again, see Strawser, "Moral Predators." And see "The Ethics of Warfare and Changing Technology," World Affairs Council of Monterey Bay, Special Guest Lecturer, October, 2020.

[26] See, again, "Moral Predators," and also Strawser, ed., *Killing By Remote Control: The Ethics of an Unmanned Military* (New York: Oxford University Press, May 2012).

[27] For an in-depth discussion of the moral use of UAVs and the various ethical challenges to their use, see Bradley Strawser, ed., *Killing By Remote Control: The Ethics of an Unmanned Military* (New York: Oxford University Press, 2012).

one's own relations with the populace. COIN itself represents an extension of this arc of ever-increasing restrictive warfare, both that it is possible and strategically viable.

At the time, a scandalous article was published in *Rolling Stone* that ultimately led to General Stanley McChrystal's ultimate removal from his NATO command in Afghanistan. In that article, however, was this interesting and illuminating comment, "'Bottom line?' says a former Special Forces operator who has spent years in Iraq and Afghanistan. 'I would love to kick McChrystal in the nuts. His rules of engagement put soldiers' lives in even greater danger.'"[28] This was from one of McChrystal's men venting frustration at the highly restrictive ROEs that the COIN strategy being implemented at the time had placed on soldiers. People don't usually complain about restrictive policies if the policies are not actually restricting their behavior. That is why the complaint is a good sign: it means the policy's aim of forcing soldiers to be ever more careful in engaging only legitimate targets was working. Ultimately, military professionalism will outgrow such early child-rearing pains demonstrated by these kinds of complaints and accept and promote and proudly comply with such restrictive ROEs (as most military professionals already do).

There are other recent examples that show us that a movement in just war practice could, and likely is (in many cases), moving in this direction, even if any form of modern warfare is still a long way off from anything like the embrace of revisionist just war theory I am suggesting here.

Russia's unjust invasion and war in Ukraine in 2022 provides such a case. The war offers a nice real-world example where it seems there is often a discernable RPL difference among soldiers fighting on the same side. See again the discussion of Lt. Col. Astakhov Dmitry Mikhailovich's testimony and confession as to what he and his soldiers actually knew of the cause they were fighting at the outset of this book. Compare their moral standing to the unjust war effort to those generals and leaders close to Putin who knew precisely the reality of the aggression they were committing.

Presumably an advocate for Lazar's position would argue that even if just war-fighters were to actually be able to behave according to the highly restrictive ROEs correlated with RPL and the modified combatant statuses of adversaries, that military victory would then become "impossible." I disagree. There are many reasons to hold that military success could still be

---

[28] Michael Hastings, "The Runaway General," *Rolling Stone* (June 22, 2010).

attainable under such restrictive ROEs. I do admit, however, that for such a model to attain military success, rather significant asymmetries of war fighting capabilities (in favor of the just cause) would be critical.

This reality is depressing for cases where we have a clear just cause fighting an unjust cause, but the just cause does not have the military advantage, or, worse, are even outmatched. Again, one thinks of the unjust Russian invasion of Ukraine and their valiant defense against it as a stark example. The Russian military is significantly larger than that of the Ukrainians. At the outset of the war, many thought they would quickly overwhelm Ukraine.[29] It is an interesting case study in the power of morale and, perhaps, one could argue, that those who fight on the side of the just cause have certain advantages that cannot be made up for by raw military might. Additionally, different tactics combined with new, recent military technologies such as remotely controlled unmanned aerial vehicles can help to give a just cause an edge.[30] And, morally, such approaches can also radically help just forces fight with a high level of RPL restriction and yet, potentially, prevail.

Another objection my proposal faces is that expanding targeting categories would radically complicate battlefield decisions regarding collateral damage and related issues. Will expanding the categories for enemy status make battlefield decisions too difficult when soldiers confront military units consisting of individuals from different categories? First, note that all just war theorists and theories must answer this question, for even traditional theories distinguish combatants from noncombatants and military units often contain individuals from each of these two categories. So, this is not a new problem for just war theory. I grant that the question is likely more vexing, however, for the view I have proposed, given that the cases where this happens would explode in number and frequency.[31]

Two responses are in order. First, like traditional just war theories, I think an appeal to the doctrine of double effect is helpful here. The Doctrine of

---

[29] There were even rumors that some high-ranking Russian soldiers made dinner reservations in Kiev restaurants a couple weeks out from the start of the invasion, presuming that they would by then be enjoying celebratory meals. There are similar rumors that some Russian soldiers packed their service dress uniforms for parades and the like after a quick victory. I have been unable to substantiate these rumors, however.

[30] See Thomas Friedman, "Free Advice for Putin: Make Peace, You Fool," *New York Times* (April 13, 2022), https://www.nytimes.com/2022/04/13/opinion/putin-ukraine-war-strategy.html. See also, John Arquilla, *Bitskrieg: The New Challenge of Cyberwar* (Polity, 2021).

[31] For a striking recent example of this difficulty in just war theory, see Paul Richard Daniels, "Just War and Non-Combatants in the Private Military Industry," *Journal of Military Ethics* 14, no. 2 (2015): 146–51.

Double Effect (DDE) is an old concept in moral philosophy tracing its roots back to Thomas Aquinas.[32] It holds that for actions which will have multiple ('double') results, which are themselves a mix of moral outcomes, it is permissible to proceed with the act assuming it meets all of the following four criteria, which are supposed to be applied and met in order. (1) The intended result of the act is itself morally justified. (2) The bad effect may be foreseen, but not intended. (3) The good effect must result from the action, not from the bad effect. (4) The intended good result must outweigh or be proportionate to the unintended but foreseen bad result. Applied to war, this is a means of testing when so-called "collateral damage" (the unintended killing of nonliable people) is permissible in war. The Doctrine has undergone significant challenges and is the focus of much debate. Resolving that debate—indeed, even delving into it in a cursory manner—far exceeds the scope of this book. However, I do think some kind of workable DDE will be necessary for this revisionist approach to be workable in the real world. That is, soldiers should not intend to harm their enemies to a degree that is inconsistent with their liability. But some such harms, if truly unintended in the pursuit of a proportionate good aim, may still be justifiable.

The second response to the objection is equally important: the whole point of expanding the categories of enemy status is to respect the rights of individuals, including those engaged in unjust wars. Doing so will significantly increase the difficulties confronted on the battlefield for just soldiers, but these costs need to be paid if one is to take seriously the rights of an enemy population trapped in the horrors of war. My proposed model for targeting in war does that to a far greater extent than the inadequate traditional binary split of combatant and noncombatant two-category model. Further, I hope that this proposal at least partially mitigates the worries of those who find the revisionist account as wholly separated from the realities of war. The aim here is to show that something at least resembling just behavior in war is possible without relying on the crutches of traditional just war theory that has led to so many rights violations of nonliable people.

---

[32] For a nice overview of the doctrine, see Alison McIntyre, "Doctrine of Double Effect," in *Stanford Encyclopedia of Philosophy*, edited by Edward N. Zalta (Stanford University, 2018).

6
The Puzzle of Benevolent Aggression

There will be killing till the score is paid.
  —Homer, *The Odyssey*, Odysseus in reply to Eurymachus

War must be, while we defend our lives against a destroyer who would devour all; but I do not love the bright sword for its sharpness, nor the arrow for its swiftness, nor the warrior for his glory. I love only that which they defend.
  —J. R. R. Tolkien, *The Two Towers*, Faramir speaking to Frodo

6.1. Introduction

In this and the next chapter, my aim is to explore the notion of justified collective defense that is built upon a liberal commitment to individual autonomy. What would the justificatory basis for a properly liberal just war theory look like? My aim is not to give a full account of such a properly liberal just war theory, but to uncover what the moral structure any such account would entail that is grounded on a deep commitment to individual rights and proper valuing of individual autonomy. This is an important piece of my larger project in this book. Showing that a plausible liberal just war account *could* be built is a prerequisite for my attempt to take individual rights seriously in thinking on war as is done in the previous chapters of this book. It is also a central part—in some ways the most important part—of any kind of answer to Calvin with which we began this book. Calvin's question, recall once again, was simple, "How do soldiers killing each other solve the world's problems?" I have been slowly answering him throughout the book. Let's review.

We began by starting with the idea of killing itself and when it can be morally justified at all and, even, when you can kill someone and not violate their rights. Extending that Rights-Based Account of killing to soldiers challenged us to revise much of our traditional thinking on just war and to adopt some version or other of revisionist just war theory. I then tried to explore how a revisionist just war theory account could actually apply in the real world of killing in war by significantly reforming our understanding of combatants and noncombatants. Now I aim to explore how a thoroughly rights-respecting account can ever be rectified with mass, collective defense on a national level—whole groups of one state's soldiers killing the soldiers of another state.

But even speaking in this way of the aims of these next two chapters will surprise many for, after all, isn't standard Walzerian just war theory a thoroughly classic liberal enterprise in the first place? Well, as was just shown in chapters 4 and 5, much of classic just war theory does not actually properly respect individual rights. But further, even granting a Rights-Based Account of individual defensive harm and the revisionist approach discussed above, some have recently challenged that the basic and foundational premise of *any* just war theory—that group defense of a state against another aggressing state can be derived from an individual right to self-defense—cannot, in fact, be so derived.[1] In chapter 1, I reviewed a simple Rights-Based Account of individual self-defense. Can that justification be extended to collective self-defense? That is, can an individual right to self-defense extend to collective defense of something like the *state* and justify state-on-state war as we know it? Just war theory answers affirmatively that it can. But this step is surprisingly hard for liberalism to explain and justify in a way that is internally consistent. This is a problem for liberalism; it should be able to give a coherent account of how war can be justified, even if only in theory. By properly liberal, here and throughout I mean any political theory where individual autonomy is distinctively valued, is a central piece of any legitimate conception of a good life, and a critical key to human flourishing.[2] It is also meant in a classically Millian way, as one that respects individual liberty, as part of autonomy, and as the groundwork basis for rights that a properly liberal society must respect.[3]

---

[1] See below in section 6.5. This is most importantly and clearly done by David Rodin, *War and Self-Defense*. But countless other scholars have since interacted and engaged with this idea in the intervening years; some of which will be discussed below.

[2] This is the kind of commitment to autonomy typified by the likes of liberal political philosophers such as Joseph Raz as argued for in *The Morality of Freedom* (New York: Oxford University Press, 1986). Raz writes, "One common strand in liberal thought regards the promotion and protection of personal autonomy as the core of the liberal concern for liberty. This is also the view argued for in this book." Raz, *The Morality of Freedom*, 203. I discuss the value of autonomy to political liberalism in more depth in chapter 7.

[3] John Stuart Mill, *On Liberty*.

Moving from those claims to justifying the bloody defense of a state is a difficult justificatory burden. Just how deep of a problem it is for liberalism will only become clear as I press the difficulty to its extreme through the use of an unexpectedly challenging puzzle. I call it the puzzle of benevolent aggression and will outline it at length below. The puzzle is designed to isolate one particularly vexing and important problem for any attempt to build a rights-respecting liberal just war theory. My primary aim in this chapter, then, is to simply prove the following: any adequate liberal account of just war theory needs a plausible response to this puzzle. In the next chapter, I will demonstrate *how* a liberal theory of just war can respond to this puzzle and sketch what the structure of such a new liberal just war theory would look like. Here, my aim is merely to build the puzzle itself and demonstrate its force and importance.

6.2. A Justificatory Burden

So, in order to press the notion of a liberal just war theory, I investigate the implications of a particularly difficult puzzle regarding violent conflict between two states. The puzzle is designed to isolate the intuition that a group of people who have organized themselves into an independent political state are justified in defending themselves and their political project—with violent, lethal force if necessary—from an external force threatening to usurp their political self-governance. You might think that this should be a pretty straightforward and easy intuition to defend. And, of course, if an external force is attempting to literally kill all the members of a given state (presumably unjustly), then justified collective self-defense follows easily enough on nearly any standard account of individual self-defense, such as that given in the above chapters. Indeed, in such cases, the collective right to defense is simply *reducible* to the aggregate of the members' individual right to self-defense; such collective defense is warranted in response to the direct unjust threat against each of their lives. Similarly, if an external power invaded a group with the intention of, say, enslaving each of them, then most would think that collective defense would follow just as naturally. So long as one believes an individual is entitled to self-defense against their attempted enslavement, then so too would a group of individuals be so entitled against their group enslavement.

We can continue down this road—lessoning the harm intended by the invading force—until eventually we consider scenarios where an invading force's aggression is merely conditional and intends only political usurpation and not death, physical harm, enslavement, theft, or the like on the individual members of the invaded state. At such a point, many will question whether the aggressed-upon group is justified in defending their collective political project with lethal force; a decision that brings with it all the costs of war, both to themselves and the countless innocents caught in a war's crossfire, on both sides of the conflict. In particular, in such cases it will be especially hard to justify defensive war for a rights-respecting liberalism focused on the value of the individual autonomy rights of a state's members.

Note that, perhaps surprisingly, such cases are actually closest to most real-world instances of war. Some argue that in these cases the connection between individual self-defense and collective defense essentially breaks down. David Rodin has most famously and forcefully made this case in his attack on traditional just war theory's grounding of collective defense on an individual right to self-defense in *War and Self-Defense*.[4] Rodin contends that most instances of national defense are neither reducible to nor properly analogous with cases of individual self-defense. Since just war theory has traditionally simply *presumed* this connection and relies upon it for the most fundamental of its premises, Rodin concludes that in cases of conditional aggression, traditional just war theory is defunct and the case for collective defense has not been adequately made.

The puzzle I offer, then, is found in the tension created when aggression against an independent political community is *purely* conditional. Conditional here means that the aim of the aggression is solely political, and no blood whatsoever will be shed if the group simply surrenders to the political demands of the aggressing state. The tension resides between the competing goods of avoiding the costs of war on the one hand versus the preventing of an injustice against individuals' political rights on the other. But some may still think this isn't power enough of a puzzle to see the difficulty. Hence, I aim to press this tension to its most extreme form with an even stronger challenge than Rodin originally foresaw. If we make the aggression

---

[4] David Rodin, *War and Self-Defense* (Oxford: Clarendon Press, 2003). Rodin also argues that an effort to ground collective defense by analogy to individual self-defense (a classic position, held by the likes of Walzer, for example) similarly fails. I do not give this full treatment here (primarily because I agree with Rodin's rejection of analogous accounts), but I do explain Rodin's reasons for doing so more in section 5.

ever less harmful to the point where it would actually be *beneficial*, in fact, to the individual members of a given state, then it seems the costs of war may be too steep to overcome and, hence, collective defense unjustifiable. Yet many will hold that the members of a state still indeed have the right to collectively defend themselves against any external aggression which threatens their collective project of self-rule; even *benevolent* conditional aggression that is actually intended to aid (and will so aid, let's stipulate) the individual members of the state. And it is that defense intuition which presses the justificatory burden on liberalism. First, then, I must lay out the puzzle of benevolent aggression.

6.3. The Puzzle of Alpha's Benevolent Aggression

Consider the following story. Some state, Alpha, invades some neighboring state, Bravo. Each state is independently self-governed. Each state enjoys territorial integrity of some kind in which their given members' collective projects of self-rule is played out. Each state has a history of collective self-rule. But their similarities end there.

Alpha is a state wherein the rights of its individual members are upheld, and its people flourish. It is a maximally well-ordered state and delivers maximal justice to its citizens. This is accomplished through a variety of successful governance programs and policies and various cultural practices and approaches. It delivers excellent social services to its citizens; it executes fair and impartial civil and criminal justice; it effectively promotes the general welfare of all the members of Alpha, and so on. It has exceedingly low crime. It has exceedingly little poverty, and those very few in poverty are helped and given assistance until they are out of it. It does all this while not overly (unjustly) infringing upon the rights and liberties of any of its citizens. That is, Alpha is (somehow) practicing the perfectly just balance (whatever that turns out to be) between egalitarian concern for the welfare of each member that best enables each individual's autonomous pursuit of a good life *and* the libertarian concern to not overly infringe upon the autonomy of individual members to accomplish this freedom and flourishing for all.[5] It executes this

---

[5] How on earth Alpha accomplishes this is relatively unimportant for now, although some may here demur that such a utopia is not only pragmatically impossible in the real world, but impossible even in principle. I am sympathetic to such worries and see similar conceptual problems in the hopeful egalitarian libertarianism of the likes of Michael Otsuka (see Michael Otsuka, *Libertarianism*

just governance with efficiency and has been doing so for several generations; it is long-term sustainable. The individual autonomy of its members is highly valued, respected, and protected.

Bravo, on the other hand, is a state such that it barely meets the threshold of being what we might call a "minimally just" state.[6] I'll elaborate in more detail what minimally just entails below, but for present purposes this means, in the least, that Bravo is *not* committing widespread, systematic, intentional human rights violations on its people (such as genocide) and that its present governmental regime is, in at least some significant and real sense (however *minimally*), the result of a collective desire of its people.[7] That is, the actions of the state Bravo can legitimately be said to derive from the intentions of its members, in at least some minimal sense. The Bravonians are collectively engaged in the project of self-rule. However, even though Bravo is minimally just in this way, it is quite far from the just utopia of Alpha. Bravo routinely fails to deliver consistent justice to its people in all manner of ways which harms its members to greater and lesser extents. For example, due in large part to government mismanagement, Bravo's economy is in a long-term, sustained depression which leaves many of its members trapped in poverty which, in turn, restricts their individual autonomy. Many of its citizens do not have and cannot attain adequate health care, which similarly restricts their individual autonomy. In general, its people are not prospering. Racism, bigotry, and unjust discrimination of all kinds are widespread and persistent. There are a variety of inequalities and inefficiencies and outright corruption that run amuck through all levels of social and government functions. It takes literally years of slogging through bureaucratic red tape to even get something as simple as a driver's license. Severe incompetence reigns across all levels of government, and this incompetence directly harms nearly all

---

Without Inequality (New York: Oxford University Press, 2003). However, for the sake of the puzzle, let us imagine that—somehow—such a marriage of individual autonomy and egalitarian justice (the liberal dream) has been sustainably crafted by Alpha's governance.

[6] A minimally just state is usually defined negatively, such that it is a state wherein it would be traditionally considered unjustified for a foreign power to abrogate its sovereignty by force and intervene into its affairs under claims that such sovereignty does not exist due its extreme failures of justice. The phrase "minimally just" is usually used to refer to that threshold that a nation-state must fall under in order to be considered for justified humanitarian intervention (for such actions as, say, genocide or other radical humanitarian disasters brought about intentionally by an unjust state). The term is used widely by Brian Orend, amongst others. See Brian Orend, *The Morality of War* (Peterborough, ON: Broadview Press, 2006).

[7] This need not necessarily be via traditional democracy. In this chapter, I'll explore how engaging in collective political projects of this sort play out for individuals.

citizens. The justice system is broken and regularly fails to correctly apply fair and impartial legal judgments. And so on and so on. In short, Bravo does a rather poor job of protecting and upholding many of the individual rights of its people. Note that Bravo does not *intentionally* infringe upon the rights of its people in some systematic or direct manner; in that regard it is an autonomy "friendly" state, but it has serious imperfections. And those serious imperfections and ill-governance result in some non-negligible restriction of the individual autonomy and flourishing of nearly every member of Bravo. The governance is, indeed, the Bravonians' collective project; it is an extension of the autonomy of its individual members. It just turns out they are really, really bad at governing themselves and have been for countless generations and there is little hope nor reason to hope that they will improve at this project.

Alpha decides to militarily invade Bravo. Alpha does so under the best of intentions. Its aims are entirely altruistic. They intend to take over the governmental institutions of Bravo in order to deliver significantly better justice and better lives for the people of Bravo. The invasion is *conditional benevolent aggression*. It is *conditional* in that they do not intend nor desire to kill any members of Bravo and no blood will be shed *if* Bravo simply surrenders to their aggression. It is *benevolent* in that they are not intending to steal Bravo's resources or somehow abuse or misuse Bravo or otherwise harm them whatsoever. Rather, they simply intend to take-over Bravo's ruling political institutions for the sole purpose and intention of improving the lives of individual Bravonians. It is *aggression* in that the Alphonians are crossing over into the territorial integrity of Bravo by threat of force and demanding that the Bravonians surrender their collective self-governance to Alphonian rule. Presume that *were* Bravo to surrender, Alpha would indeed carry through on these intentions and would be highly successful in dramatically increasing the justice, welfare, and prosperity afforded to all Bravonians; each and every member of Bravo would have his or her individual autonomy measurably and significantly increased. Alpha has made this clear to Bravo: yes, they intend to usurp control of Bravo's political institutions, by force if necessary, but they genuinely do so for the good of the individual Bravonians. This is not some ruse on the part of the Alphonians. It is genuinely altruistic. And presume as well that this predicted result is easy to have epistemic access to and confidence in and that all members of Bravo know all of these relevant facts. That is, Bravonians have every reason to believe and trust this is Alpha's genuine aims.

However, the people of Bravo do not desire the take-over by this foreign power despite the good it would bring them both collectively and individually.[8] That is, through a referendum, or some other fair decision-making procedure that the Bravonians use for coordinating group action, they have decided they do not want Alpha to usurp their self-governance. Hence, they go to war.

6.4. The Puzzle's Challenge to Liberalism

Here then, is the puzzle proper. What moral justification do the Bravonians have, if any, for violently defending themselves against Alpha's aggression? Completely set aside whether or not Alpha is justified in their aggression—and the long debate over paternalism, benefiting others without their consent, and so on.[9] Alpha's moral justification, or lack thereof, is not what is under examination here. Whether or not Alpha's aggression is justified is a separate moral question and it is not the target of the puzzle. Rather, the question the puzzle is designed to isolate is this question: would Bravo's collective, violent, lethal self-defense against Alpha's aggression be a *just war*?[10] The hope is that the story of Alpha's aggression elicits an intuition that it is at least morally *permissible* for the Bravonians to take up arms in violent defense in such circumstances. Call this response to the puzzle the *Defense Intuition*. The challenge the puzzle presses for liberalism, then, is whether or

---

[8] This will be elaborated on below in chapter 7.6, but presume the Bravonians have followed the decision procedures they set up and agreed upon for the process of collective self-rule. They collectively decide that they do not want Alpha to take over their governance. (So, depending on the kind of group decision procedures they have set up, it may not be that all of the people of Bravo agree to the decision but simply most do, or a sizable enough majority of its people do, according to the rules they agreed upon for such decisions.) This process and the numbers themselves do matter, as I discuss in chapter 7, but for now, I will set aside the specifics of their decision procedures. Group intent is always a difficult and controversial matter, and I shall not attempt to give a proper accounting of it here. Clearly, however, given my rejection of a metaphysically robust view of the state and Walzerian-esque analogous accounts of state defense, I favor those accounts which are more modest in their assignment of shared intentions for a group. For an example of such an account that I find particularly attractive, see Michael Bratman, *Faces of Intention* (Cambridge: Cambridge University Press, 1999). However, a feature of my model is that Bratman's model is not required; the argument I offer in chapter 7 to resolve the puzzle can be run on any of the various mechanisms of collective action currently on offer.

[9] Though, for an interesting treatment of the issue, see Jonathan Parry, "Defensive Harm, Consent, and Intervention," *Philosophy & Public Affairs* 45, no. 4 (2017): 356–96.

[10] Note that on one reading of the scenario their defense is necessary, but necessary for what? It is necessary in that it is a last resort to prevent their take over. But does necessity obtain in a case like this, where what they are preventing would be such gains? I will argue that it is, but it is cheating to claim it is necessary at this stage.

not the Defense Intuition can be plausibly grounded in a distinctively liberal framework. To be clear up front: I strongly endorse the Defense Intuition. But it's defense will take some real work. Defending the Defense Intuition, I believe, uncovers a great deal of our answer to Calvin and understanding just war theory more generally.

The difficulties the puzzle presses here for liberalism should now become apparent. Why would it ever be justified for a people to violently defend themselves (which includes intentionally killing others) when, alternatively, if they did not do so their own lives would become demonstrably better? How can a group be justified to kill others in order to *block* the improvement of their own lives? In the next chapter, I will eventually argue that the proper basis for the Defense Intuition's justification is the very value which is held in such high regard by liberalism: individual autonomy. That is, that the violation of the Bravonians' individual autonomy as expressed through their project of self-governance is that which can serve as the grounding for a right to collective defense.[11] The tremendous tension, however, that is created by the Defense Intuition for a liberal account of just war theory should be clear. In the story of Alpha's aggression, we have a case wherein the aggression will actually *improve* the lives of the Bravonians precisely along the very same metrics that we'd wish to measure the costs incurred by Alpha's aggression—in this case, various collective self-determination rights that are derived (presumably) from their individual autonomy rights. That is, whatever good or value to the individuals it is that we may intuitively think is harmed when the Bravonians' collective self-rule is abrogated by Alpha such that the Bravonians are warranted to defend against this harm, it is that *same* good or value (or some good derived from it) that is *promoted* by Alpha's aggression—or at least seems to be, *prima facie*. It is precisely concerns about individual autonomy that generates the puzzle; so, it is unclear how liberalism's valuing of autonomy will be able to resolve the puzzle. Worse, we know that in effectively every war, nonliable people die, on both sides. How can Bravo justify those deaths in defending themselves from this conditional benevolent aggression?

---

[11] And I'll show further that if that's right, then if they are to be properly liberal most justified instances of modern war will be grounded in a similar basic moral structure. And, indeed, not only can a distinctively liberal framework justify war, but it is also particularly well suited to do so, given its commitment to individual autonomy.

6.5. Rodin's Challenge

At this point, however, a liberal political philosopher might think that a quick response to the puzzle is right at hand because of a simple reliance on an individual right to self-defense. That is, in order to ground the Defense Intuition, in this case, a liberal is going to think: we might need to appeal to the rights of individuals, such as the individual right to self-defense outlined in the proceeding chapters, and then simply apply that here on a large scale. As John Rawls once said, perhaps just war theory is perhaps best understood as individual rights theory "writ large." Even Rawls' rather limited enumeration of specific rights, for example, seems to provide the antidote to the puzzle. As James Griffin writes, describing Rawls on this point, "The role of human rights, on Rawls' conception of them, is quite restricted: it is to provide the justifying reasons for war and its conduct."[12] Rawls held that the proper "Law of Peoples" would be that which a set of "free and democratic peoples" would all agree upon from within the vantage of the original position.[13] And, perhaps conveniently for questions of war and international relations, "these principles, except for the last requiring a duty of assistance owed to "burdened peoples," are familiar and time-honored within international political theory . . . " and they include, "a right of self-defense and no right to instigate war except in self-defense."[14] So it may seem at first that liberalism has an easy answer here. The individual right of self-defense that each member of Bravo holds is the basis for the Defense Intuition for Bravo as a whole.

This assumption, however, is too quick and, unfortunately for liberalism, it is not going to work in the case of Alpha's benevolent aggression. David Rodin has done the most to challenge this traditional justification of collective defense as derivative from the right to individual self-defense. As noted above, this has been the traditional basis for any kind of just war theory for no less than 1600 years dating back to at least Saint Augustine. To see the puzzle of Alpha's aggression in its full light, then, it will be necessary to review his challenge in some detail. Rodin identifies two possible ways in which collective defense could be grounded on individual self-defense: analogously

---

[12] James Griffin, *On Human Rights*, 23.
[13] John Rawls, *Law of Peoples*, 38. *The Law of Peoples*, Cambridge, MA: Harvard University Press, 1999. For a good discussion of Rawls on this point, see, Samuel Freeman, "Original Position," in *Stanford Encyclopedia of Philosophy*, edited by Edward N. Zalta, Stanford University, 2008, http://plato.stanford.edu/entries/original-position/.
[14] Again, see Freeman, "Original Position."

or reductively. The analogous account holds that collective self-defense is relevantly analogous to an individual defending himself or herself from a lethal threat. Thus, if an individual can be justified to undertake violent self-defense, so too can a collective.[15] The reductive account, on the other hand, aims to simply build up a justification for collective defense as the aggregate of a collective's members' individual right to self-defense. Ultimately, Rodin concludes that deriving a right to collective defense via the individual right to self-defense is unfounded for the former, is not sufficiently analogous to the latter, *nor* can the former be reduced to a large-scale version of the latter. That is, he argues that the two ways in which the individual justification for self-defense could be applied to the moral justification for collective defense fail. If Rodin's challenge is correct, then any liberal political philosophy built upon a commitment to individual rights will (apparently) be unable to justify war.

The analogous approach, while the most common in the just war tradition and perhaps the most initially intuitive account, fails to ground collective defense for many reasons.[16] Rodin notes that, for example, many things that are traditionally justified under a defensive war would never be justified for individual practices of self-defense. One clear case would be the (supposedly) justified attacking of an enemy soldier under the context of war when that soldier was not presently a threat (e.g., if the soldier were asleep or walking unarmed, or if the defensive (justified) forces ambushed the enemy soldiers, or Walzer's famous "naked solider" cases, and so on). Notice this problem is not related to the liability differences between soldiers canvased in chapters 4 and 5 above. Rather, the problem here is in the ways even justified war and justified individual self-defense are significantly different in practice. In an analogous case, notice, an individual is *not* justified to undertake lethal self-defense if an unjust attacker is not a present and imminent threat to be thwarted (e.g., it would not be a justified instance of self-defense to kill someone now at the library because you think they will threaten you *later* when you see them at the grocery store). That is, as shown above, legitimate individual self-defense

---

[15] This view entails, I argue, a metaphysically robust view of the state (or collective) that I reject. Recently other writers in the field of the ethics of war have similarly rejected this view of the state. Most forcefully and vociferously is Helen Frowe. She proudly calls herself a "reductivist" rather than a just war "revisionist," meaning simply that all and any rights to justifiable defense is always reducible to the individual. Jeff McMahan has made similar claims rejecting the robust view of the state.

[16] Walzer, for example, in *Just and Unjust Wars: A Moral Argument with Historical Examples* (New York: Basic Books, 1977), famously offers an analogous account and a metaphysically robust view of the state called the "domestic analogy." But many other scholars throughout the just war tradition similarly invoke the analogous account to ground collective violence.

can only be employed against someone who is liable to defensive harm and liability has the internal constraints of imminent threat, usually typified in the necessity condition, and proportionality—only doing as little harm as is needed to thwart the threat, at which point further violence is unjustified. And, Rodin argues, it seems that collective defensive war, as defended by just war theory, does not possess these same constraints (or not to anywhere near the same extent) as individual self-defense does.[17] From this and other observations of apparent moral differences, Rodin argues that the analogous account cannot capture these significant disparities between the justificatory basis for individual self-defense versus collective defensive war.

So much for the analogous approach. But Rodin claims that the reductive account faces similar problems: it too is unable to adequately account for differences between the justificatory basis for individual self-defense and collective defense. The significance of these differences, even if the differences themselves are relatively small, is extreme, or so Rodin argues. This is because if collective defense is properly reducible to the individual self-defense rights of a given collectives' members, this should not be the case; these differences should not arise at all. Here, Rodin introduces conditional aggression as the most striking example of the dissimilarity that purportedly shows that collective defense is not reducible to an aggregate of individual defense. That is, he points out that nearly all real-world state-level violence is for some specific political end or purpose that is not, in fact, designed to destroy and kill the population of the defensive state. Aside from highly exceptional, unlikely, and rare scenarios, an enemy attacker's aim is not simply to kill the citizens of the target state.[18] Instead, a warring state usually aims to seize control of the government or obtain the resources of another country. And so, argues Rodin, the comparison to the individual case of self-defense is striking in its difference and the collective case cannot be reducible to it.

---

[17] Above, in previous chapters 2 and 3, I offered my account of liability and argued in chapter 3 that, in fact, justified collective defensive actions should fall under the same (or very similar) moral constraints that individual self-defense does and employ the same conception of liability. Thus, this objection here by Rodin misses my account. But I reject analogous accounts because I do not grant the existence of metaphysically robust "group rights" (and the archaic Westphalian conception of a state) that such accounts require. That is, my account of liability must rely on the reductive approach to grounding collective defense on individual defense, which will be examined next.

[18] Fernando Tesón offers the idea of an inter-planetary war wherein an alien species that was intent on destroying all human life on earth would indeed constitute such a rare care. See Fernando Tesón, "Self-Defense in International Law and Rights of Persons: Response to *War and Self-Defense*," *Ethics and International Affairs* 18, no. 1, 2004. 87–91.

To extend this argument, imagine an attacker who unjustly demands one dollar from some innocent person, such as in the following case.

Mugger
Mugger approaches Todd and demands, with the threat of physical violence, that Todd give him $1. Todd does not want to give Mugger the $1 and has the means to defend himself, but only with lethal force. That is, there is no way Todd can prevent Mugger from forcing him to give $1 except by killing Mugger. So, Todd kills Mugger.

Is Todd justified in killing the attacker for the demand of one dollar on self-defense grounds? Most agree he is not.[19] The reason is simple: such killing is not justified because Mugger, whatever else he liable to, is not liable to be *killed* because killing is not proportionate to the thwarting of stealing $1.[20] That is, Todd's killing violates the proportionality constraint internal to liability. If that's the case, then how can individual self-defense ground collective defense against conditional aggression? The real difficulty Rodin's challenge presents, then, is the following: how can a right to individual self-defense—which is usually justified because it is defending against the threat of death or direct physical harm or some other significant proportionate harm—be used to ground state warfare, which, if the attacked capitulates or surrenders, will result in little or no death or physical harm?

Thus, Rodin concludes, it is a mistake to draw the justificatory line from the *individual* right to self-defense to the justification of *collective* warfare—either by analogy or reductively. The aim of the puzzle of Alpha's aggression should now be clear: it is designed to strengthen Rodin's challenge to the most extreme form it could possibly take. The puzzle can be seen as an extension of Rodin's initial contention, but more focused on the

---

[19] Jeff McMahan demurs here by continuing the story that Rodin leaves incomplete. He argues that if one tries to prevent their dollar being taken, and then this defense of the dollar leads to their death, that an initial move of defense if one can foresee no other way of avoiding the *eventual* lethal attack could potentially be justified. One doubts how one could know this, however, and how one could base such a justification on such a weak epistemic principle. See Jeff McMahan, "Response to *War and Self-Defense*," *Ethics and International Affairs* 18, no. 1 (2004). My account of evidence-relative norms as the proper basis for liability offered above in chapters 2 and 3, of course, would not be compatible with McMahan's view here. Below, I will expand on this mugger story in applying it to my puzzle of Alpha's aggression with the story of the Benevolent Mugger and then, in chapter 7, with the story of the Strengthened Benevolent Mugger.

[20] Notice, this is the value of $1 in the present United States. We could modify the scenario such that the $1 represents tremendously greater value, perhaps even providing the only means to get water in a desert, and so forth, such that it may be proportionate to kill in its defense.

pure notion of collective defense without any appeal to any other harm being done to the state in question other than *only* the abrogation of their collective self-rule, yet with massive corresponding moral gains for all the members.

Following the story above regarding an attacker demanding one dollar from Todd, the puzzle of Alpha's aggression I offer is suggesting a case where someone wants to force Todd to *accept* money the attacker wants to give him. Consider the following, rather bizarre-sounding case.

Benevolent Mugger
Benevolent Mugger approaches Todd and demands, with the threat of physical violence, that Todd accepts $10 that Benevolent Mugger wishes to give Todd. Todd does not want the $10. Rather than accept the money, Todd kills Benevolent Mugger to prevent him from giving it to him.

Since Todd (for whatever reason) does not want to accept the money, if Benevolent Mugger then tries to *force* the gift on Todd, does Todd then have the right to violently defend himself against Benevolent Mugger? Such scenarios quickly again head down the road to discussions of paternalism and whether an agent can be justified in benefiting someone against their consent. But, although these are importantly related questions, this is not the conceptual target of the puzzle. We are not here investigating if it is morally permissible for Benevolent Mugger to engage in this forced paternalism but, rather, whether it is morally permissible for Todd to prevent the forced benefit with violence. And the intuition here is quite strong: it is *not* permissible for Todd to kill Benevolent Mugger. And, surely, if it was not permissible for Todd to kill Mugger, then it seems especially clear it is impermissible for him to kill Benevolent Mugger. But if that's the case, then how can collective defense for Bravo against Alpha's benevolent aggression be grounded on the individual right to self-defense of Bravo's members? If we have a strong moral intuition here that it would be wrong here for Todd to kill Benevolent Mugger, then how will we be able to justify the Defense Intuition for Bravo?

Recall that we are trying to find a basis to justify the Defense Intuition that is consistent with liberalism. In the original puzzle, by isolating the justificatory question on Bravo's *defense* (rather than on Alpha's aggression) and taking away all competing costs other than their collective self-rule, we hope to shine a bright light on the ultimate core of Rodin's challenge. Namely, can collective defense find any grounding on the defense of individual rights and values derived from them, such as the value of individual autonomy? Giving a liberal justification of the Defense Intuition for the puzzle of Alpha's aggression, will be challenging indeed for a quick reliance on the individual rights of Bravonians will not suffice, as was just demonstrated by Rodin's challenge and the case of *Benevolent Mugger*. Thus, it seems liberalism has a real problem in justifying collective defense in most contemporary real-world instances of war—which are nearly always cases of some type of conditional aggression—as a proper extension of individual self-defense defended thus far in this book.

In the next chapter, I hope to rescue the notion of collective defense grounded on a defense of individual rights from Rodin's challenge at its most fundamental level. That is, if I can show how a new liberal theory of just war could work, I will concurrently be giving a significant (although only partial) response to Rodin's challenge here. Rodin's challenge is particularly helpful in this regard. By focusing on the question of defense against clear cases of aggression, rather than taking a defense justification as simply assumed (as classic just war theory does), Rodin's challenge gives us a helpful way of understanding how the moral justification of collective defense should be structured, and how it cannot be structured. Hence, the puzzle of Alpha's aggression aims to continue in this vein: isolate the question of collective defense to its most bare form by stripping away questions regarding the unjust actions of the aggressor state as much as possible by turning the aggressor state into a (purported) benefactor. If the Defense Intuition can be salvaged *here* in the story of Alpha's aggression, then certainly collective defense could be justified in cases where the aggression is more clearly unjust and does not benefit the members of the aggressed-upon state in any substantive way, but rather harms them.[21] That is, if we can show that the Defense Intuition can hold for Bravo, then surely it can hold in cases of nonbenevolent, even if still conditional, aggression—like that experienced in 2022 by Ukraine from the unjust Russian aggression.

---

[21] Further, there are, of course, actual real-world cases where it seems the central question may come down to what value should be placed on the usurpation of collective self-rule, setting aside other worries. That is, the puzzle of Alphonian aggression is not totally theoretical; there are some real-world cases notably similar. I will briefly look at a couple of real-world cases that the puzzle may press on, in my concluding remarks in chapter 7.

6.6. Liberal Resolution?

So how *could* the puzzle be resolved in such a way that maintains the Defense Intuition for a distinctively liberal view? Since I reject analogous accounts of state defense to self-defense, I will have to contend that any proper justification for the violent defense of a group must be grounded on the thwarting of potential harm done to those individuals that comprise the group. And if that justification is to be properly liberal in the way I intend here, the normative value used to ground the Defense Intuition will be the distinctive role that the value of individual autonomy plays for liberalism. As already noted, in the story of Alpha's aggression, the people being defended (the Bravonians) will have their individual autonomy actually improved were they to surrender rather than fight. To justify the Defense Intuition, then, we must show what the cost is to the individual Bravonians that outweighs this future good.

But this, by itself, will not be enough to explain why the Defense Intuition holds the weight it does for a liberal theory. This is because a simple harms versus benefit calculus for the individual Bravonians could easily result in cases such that the cost in loss of autonomy for the individual manifested in Bravonians' collective project of self-rule being thwarted could be outweighed by the gains to that very same individual in other increases to their individual autonomy brought about by the new governance of Alpha. Indeed, the story of Alpha's aggression is set up so as to suggest precisely this problem: the individual Bravonians' lives would be much better (in a wide variety of ways including expansions of individual freedoms, choices, and pursuit of projects) were they to surrender to Alpha and become Alphonians (or Alpha's subjects, at any rate).[22] Thus, to resolve the puzzle, I will have to show not only *what* harm is done to the Bravonians by Alpha's unwanted aggression that justifies collective defense, but also why this harm is somehow special or unique in the weight it carries in comparison to the potential future gains for the Bravonians were they to surrender.

To preview my line of defense, let's presume that the normative weight of some particular activities (such as the collective project of political self-rule) properly derives from the benefits such projects pay to individual autonomy

[22] I'll explore in chapter 7 the possible objection against the Defense Intuition that argues that by becoming Alphonians, the Bravonians could gain all of the benefits of the aggression and none of the costs. That is, by Alpha assimilating the Bravonians into their collective enterprise, the Bravonians could still engage in a collective project. I call this the "assimilation objection." Understanding why it fails is crucial for understanding the proper role autonomy is playing in the theory and the way in which its value obtains for an individual. See chapter 7.6.

(as I will argue in chapter 7). Even if that's true, then Alpha's take-over would have the odd result of both increasing and injuring the individual autonomy of the Bravonians at the same time, albeit in different ways. There may be cases where the increase in individual autonomy to the members of Bravo would be so tremendous that any injury done to their individual autonomy by the destruction of their (present) collective governance project would be radically outweighed by future gains. But I will aim to show why that threshold *could* be very high, if the Bravonians valued their collective self-rule the right way. And that for it to be impermissible for Bravo to forcefully defend itself, this positive gap between individual autonomy gained via surrender and individual autonomy lost via surrender would have to be quite large. It could probably only be attained if the Bravonians, in fact, did not properly value their self-rule to such an extent that they weren't even effectively involved with the project. But in that case, Bravo is in danger of slipping from being a minimally just state to being a broken state.[23] So, to maintain my claim that the collective project of self-rule is so important to the Bravonians (or *could* be so important, at any rate), I will argue that the value of the individual autonomy in question is *amplified* once it is instantiated in the choice to pursue a group project. That is, I will argue in chapter 7 that we should give preference to certain properly arranged collective projects because of the way in which they can function as necessary components of a full exercising of individual autonomy. This will be why Bravo's choice for the continuation of their collective self-rule could have enough normative weight to make its defense permissible, and thereby ground the Defense Intuition in a distinctively liberal way.[24] This derives in part due to the peculiar way in which the value of autonomy itself functions and it is also due in part to the way group projects function for the individual's autonomy.

[23] As discussed, in section 7 with the case of Charlie.
[24] I demonstrate this effort in chapter 7 by constructing the value of "collective rights" out of individual autonomy. But I'll mention here that the primary way in which collective autonomy rights will carry special weight is that the individual autonomy of all members of the collective involved in the decision-making process of a given collective project are at stake. That is, even those members of a collective who disagree with any particular decision (in the minority of an agreed-upon decision-making procedure, say) still have some stake in the collective action going forth. This is because even *their* individual autonomy (those minority voices within the collective) would be violated if an external force were to thwart the collective's attempt to carry out a particular plan because part of the minority voices' autonomy is that they are part of the decisions of this collective. Thus, the individual autonomy of *all* participant members of a given collective practicing self-rule will count towards the aggregate good of that collective autonomy. But it is more than even this for I will also show below that the collective action itself can be a necessary part (a vital option) of an individual's range of choices to sufficiently ground autonomy—a necessary piece that cannot be wholly replaced, if the individual is invested in the collective project in certain ways.

6.7. The Case of Unjust Charlie

I will lay out both of those aspects of the value of collective self-rule to the Bravonians' individual autonomy next in chapter 7 (particularly in sections 2 and 3). This will give us the means by which liberalism can resolve the puzzle of Alpha's benevolent aggression while maintaining the Defense Intuition, at least in some instances. But before I conclude chapter 6's set up of this puzzle, I must first again stress that whatever this value that I hope to identify is such that it can be defended violently, that it is also *surmountable*. It could be the case that the benefit versus harm gap is so tremendous for individual Bravonians that they *cannot* legitimately justify defense of the group project such that they would be morally obligated to surrender. That is, the Defense Intuition to benevolent conditional aggression will not always be justifiable. Imagine that the individual autonomy of most Bravonians is so severely restricted presently *and* an Alpha take-over would so radically increase their individual autonomy such that the damage done to their individual autonomy in thwarting their collective governance project is simply paltry by comparison. In chapter 7, I hope to show that the damage done to individual autonomy in thwarting the collective governance project is, in most cases, actually quite large. Again, it will be hard to conceive of a real-world possibility of this sort where Bravo could also still be considered minimally just. That is, again, it may be that for the gap to be large enough to rule out the moral force behind the Defense Intuition that the individual rights of Bravonians would have to be presently so abused that Bravo fails to meet the criteria of a minimally just state. If that's the case, then it will be difficult to build a justification for the state's defense, since it itself is not a just institution worthy of defense from which no (or very few) individuals draw benefits to their own autonomy. This is assuming, of course, the Bravonians are still in some sense engaged in its governance as a collective project in such a case. If the Bravonians are not even involved in the project of self-governance at all and are instead merely abused citizens of a dictatorial regime, then the "collective project" of Bravo's self-rule is not doing any positive work for the autonomy of individual Bravonians and could not thereby ground the Defense Intuition.

And that makes sense. We certainly want to allow for cases where it is *im*permissible for the members of a given state to defend it against external forces engaged upon it for the good of its own people. Consider a third state, Charlie. Charlie is a state that is not even minimally just. In fact, Charlie falls far below whatever the threshold for "minimally just" should be. This is due to such characteristics as the following. The ruling government of Charlie is not in any way a reflection of the desires of its people. Charlonians have virtually no political freedoms; the vast majority of its members have their individual autonomy severely constrained, and they have no participation, voice, or representation of any kind in the government. Indeed, the authoritarian ruling regime of Charlie is actively killing significant numbers of various sub-groups within its borders. Sometimes this killing is systematic; at other times it is indiscriminate. Any and all resistance to the government of Charlie by most Charlonians is met with violent repression. The ruling government keeps the people in line through force, intimidation, and abuse. Every month, for example, the government of Charlie randomly abducts a small portion of its population and severely tortures them for a few weeks in order to demonstrate its power, and then releases them. Charlie is not in any way an "autonomy friendly" state. Charlie actively, systematically, and intentionally restricts the individual autonomy of the vast majority of its members. And so on.

Now, were Alpha to invade Charlie and do so under intentions identical to its invasion of Bravo—for the purpose of delivering greater justice to the people of Charlie—it would seem, indeed, to be impermissible for the Charlonians to engage in collective defense of Charlie against Alpha. Rather, they would be under a moral obligation to surrender. To defend the regime of Charlie would be to defend an unjust state that confers no positive good on the individual citizens of Charlie—or on only very few of them: those in charge. Charlie is not worth defending; indeed, it would be actively wrong to defend it.

In this case, Alpha's take-over of Charlie would result in very little loss to the individual autonomy of Charlonians, perhaps none at all. There would, of course, be some significant loss of autonomy for the few members of the ruling oligarchy but, presumably, restricting their ability to pursue projects of actively harming and oppressing others is an overall normative gain on a par with restricting the liberty of criminals by putting them in prison so that they cannot harm others. The vast majority of individual Charlonians' autonomy is not presently finding any expression in an enterprise of collective self-rule. And, thus, over-throwing the current regime does no harm to them individually and blocks no benefits to their individual autonomy as expressed through a collective political project of self-governance, because no such collective project is currently underway. In such a case, Alpha's aggression against (and subsequent rule of) Charlie is all gain to the individual autonomy of Charlie's members.

This helps better illuminate what is meant for a state to be minimally just. A minimally just state is (at least) one where the intentions of the state are in some sense a reflection of the individual intentions of its members.[25] Further, the state governance itself is some kind of collective project that gains its value (in significant part) for the role it plays as an extension of the individual autonomy of those engaged in the collective project. The intentions of the state need not be a perfect reflection of the individuals' intentions, nor do all members of the state in question need to be involved in the collective project of self-governance for it to gain this kind of value. It is merely required that the state's intentions reflect the members' intentions to enough of a degree such that it imparts substantial value to (enough of) the members' individual autonomy.[26] If it does not, it is not minimally just in this sense and, at any rate, a defense of it cannot be built upon a commitment to the value of individual autonomy. It is that value—individual autonomy—and how it can be the basis for the Defense Intuition for Bravo to which I turn, in chapter 7.

To conclude this chapter, consider again the 2022 unjust Russian invasion of Ukraine. Note that Russian state media and propaganda and Vladimir Putin, himself, effectively were claiming that Russia was nobly undertaking a military operation something along the lines of an Alpha invaded a Charlie.[27] Somehow claiming, incredulously, that they were freeing the poor, oppressed

---

[25] To just what extent this is even possible has long been contentious and debatable. For recent discussion, see Jason Brennan, *Against Democracy* (Princeton University Press, 2016).

[26] What those thresholds are, exactly, is not crucial for present purposes. Also note that it need not even necessarily be a form of democracy to meet this minimally just threshold, although it becomes difficult to imagine how a state could not be at least some form of democracy to meet the criteria of being a group project that serves as an extension of the individual autonomy of its members. I'll look at the importance of group decision-making procedures below in discussion of the legitimacy of Bravo's decision to fight, in chapter 7. Victor Tadros makes a good case that some form or democracy or other will be necessary if we are to presume that the government represents the "will of the people" in any reasonable sense. Tadros writes, "It is non-obvious how *any* set of non-democratic institutions can be seen as representing such ambitions in any reasonably large jurisdiction. In any reasonably large country, there will be disagreement as to the proper shape of political institutions. Any set of political institutions in a country will be imposed on some by others. Suppose that it is important that political institutions represent the will of the people. Only democratic institutions will secure this value, because only democratic institutions can claim to represent the will of the people. There is no proper concept of the will of the people independently of democratic institutions through which it is formed." Victor Tadros, "Law: What is it Good for?" presented at the 2011 annual Ethics, Law, and Armed Conflict Workshop on War, Oxford, Oxford University, 11. Tadros's emphasis.

[27] See the discussion, above, of how Putin claims both to his own people and to international leaders that he is attempting to "de-nazi-fy" Ukraine.

Ukrainians from Nazis.[28] Yet, in reality, the Ukrainian people's valiant defense against Russia is an amazing real-world instantiation of the plausibility of the Defense Intuition. That they have the moral permission, perhaps even the duty, to defend their independent political project against its existential threat at the hands of the conquering Russians. Notice that their justification for defense is far greater than a Bravo defense against Alpha scenario, recall, because in our puzzle Alpha genuinely intends to and actually would improve the lives of the Bravonians. The Russians, despite Putin's claims, have no such altruistic intentions for Ukraine. (And, of course, I think despite their struggles, Ukraine rises well above the minimally just threshold line that Bravo clings to.) Hence, again, we see that if we can find strong ground for the Defense Intuition for Bravo, then *surely* justification for defense of a state against unbenevolent aggression easily follows, such as in the case of Ukraine's defense against Russia. I intend to show how the Defense Intuition for Bravo can be grounded in the next chapter, and how that grounding could then extend to give us a picture of a neo-liberal just war theory that could apply in most state level defense cases in the real world. In other words, to answer Calvin, how soldiers killing one another can "solve the world's problems."

---

[28] Putin made such claims in private conversations with French President Emmanuel Macron, which Macron openly criticized and debunked. See "France's Macron: Russia's Putin alone chose war in Ukraine," *Reuters* March 2, 2022.

7
Towards a New Liberal Theory of Just War

> When a people are used as mere human instruments for firing cannon or thrusting bayonets, in the service and for the selfish purposes of a master, such war degrades a people. A war to protect other human beings against tyrannical injustice; a war to give victory to their own ideas of right and good, and which is their own war, carried on for an honest purpose by their free choice,—is often the means of their regeneration.... As long as justice and injustice have not terminated their ever-renewing fight for ascendancy in the affairs of mankind, human beings must be willing, when need is, to do battle for the one against the other.
>
> —John Stuart Mill, "The Contest in America," *Fraser's Magazine* (February 1862); later published in Dissertations and Discussions (1868), vol.1, p. 26

7.1. Introduction

Speaking broadly, the picture I offer in this chapter shows that a properly liberal theory of just war could be built out of the value derived from the individual and not through a reliance on the value supposedly derived from the state itself. By properly liberal, I here mean a political theory where individual autonomy is distinctively valued, is a central piece of any legitimate conception of a good life, and a critical key to human flourishing.[1] I will rely

---

[1] This is the kind of commitment to autonomy typified by the likes of liberal political philosophers such as Joseph Raz as argued for in *The Morality of Freedom* (New York: Oxford University Press, 1986). Raz writes, "One common strand in liberal thought regards the promotion and protection of personal autonomy as the core of the liberal concern for liberty. This is also the view argued for in this book." Raz, *The Morality of Freedom*, 203. I discuss the value of autonomy to political liberalism in more depth below in section 2. I should note up-front that some may find my employment of a Razian-type liberalism focused as it is on this particular reading of autonomy to be a strange pairing in my attempt to ground a "right" to defense for Bravo, as well as for it to be compatible with my use of rights talk throughout this book. The reason some will find it strange is because Raz is famous for, amongst other things, being a particularly ardent critic of a certain kind of rights-based liberalism. See Joseph Raz, "On the Nature of Rights," *Mind* 93 (1984): 194–214, as well as the relevant portions

heavily on the work on Joseph Raz and his liberal political philosophy, but the story I tell is not only coherent with classically liberal views espoused by the likes of John Stuart Mill, but in many ways is a direct outgrowth of such political philosophy. Indeed, I am here trying to give shape to what Mill himself pointed at, as quoted at the opening of this chapter. In discussing types of just wars, Mill specifically points to a war fought to defend individuals' own autonomy and freedom to write the stories of their own lives:

> ... a [just] war to give *victory to their own ideas of right and good*, and which is their own war, carried on for an honest purpose by their free choice,—is often the means of their regeneration.[2]

In chapter 1, I reviewed a simple rights-based account of self-defense. Can that justification be extended to collective self-defense? That is, can an individual right to self-defense extend to collective defense of the state and justify war? In this chapter, I show not only that it can, but that it can do so precisely through the distinctive value liberalism places on individual autonomy. If this is true, then not only can liberalism justify defense of the state, but it is, in fact, particularly well-suited to do so. Hence, this chapter is an exploration of what a properly liberal just war theory would look like; it is an attempt to understand what the moral blueprints of such a theory would be.

More narrowly, I will do the above and sketch what a new liberal theory of just war could look like through offering a response to the puzzle of Alpha's benevolent aggression that was laid out in chapter 6. Here I will show specifically how liberalism can respond to the puzzle. In chapter 6, I presented the puzzle and argued that any adequate liberal just war theory must be capable of handling the puzzle and, in particular, of accounting for the Defense Intuition. The Defense Intuition, recall, is that a group of people can permissibly defend against a purely conditional benevolent aggression, at least in

---

of *The Morality of Freedom*. And see chapter 1.2.4 for a partial discussion of this. One feature of Raz's view is that he downplays rights-based talk. So, it may seem that my employment of rights is inconsistent with my employment of Raz's view of liberalism and the value of autonomy. This would be a mistaken understanding of my project and of Raz's view of rights. Raz's critique of rights-based talk is of a particular kind of rights-based understanding of liberalism; Raz is not against all understandings or uses of rights, period. My project is consistent with a Razian view of rights and does not employ an understanding of liberalism of the kind Raz's critique targets. A full explication of this is beyond the scope of this book. To fully understand Raz's view here, one most read Raz.

[2] John Stuart Mill, "The Contest in America," *Fraser's Magazine* (February 1862); later published in Dissertations and Discussions (1868), vol.1, p. 26. Emphasis mine.

some cases, like that typified in the puzzle of Alpha's benevolent aggression. Through "Rodin's Challenge," I showed how a simple reliance on an individual right to self-defense cannot handle difficult cases of inter-state conditional aggression such as that presented in the more extreme version of the puzzle of Alpha's benevolent conditional aggression. Yet, many will have the intuition that the people of Bravo can permissibly defend their state if they do not wish to be usurped by Alpha. In this chapter, I will show why this intuitive response to the puzzle (the Defense Intuition) is valid and unearth what I take to be the correct basis for it. The basis for the intuition, I argue, is the distinctive and fundamental (but not absolute) value that liberalism assigns to individual autonomy. In some cases, autonomy's full expression can require group involvement and action such that the groups themselves become necessary to the maintenance of the individual autonomy of their members. I contend that states can function in this manner such that defense of a state can be a proper defense of the individual autonomy of its members. The hope is that if a proper justification can be given for collective defense in such a case as benevolent conditional aggression—where the minimal harm to the individual member is isolated—then an account for collective defense in cases against less benevolent (and malevolent) aggressors will easily follow. And, as such, we would have the necessary seeds for a new liberal just war theory that could plausibly apply in the real world.

The challenge of the puzzle is whether or not the Defense Intuition can be plausibly grounded in a distinctively liberal framework. To make the case for the Defense Intuition, then, I must show just what the cost of Alpha's aggression is and why it can outweigh (to at least grant the permissibility of defense) the value of the benefits of Alpha's aggression; even though the kinds of goods in tension derive from the same source.[3] I argue that the good that is harmed is the individual Bravonians' right to engage in certain collective projects which constitute proper extensions of their individual autonomy; in this case, collective self-rule of their own legitimate political project. As I'll explain below, their political project is the result of various collective projects each independently grounded in the value they serve as extensions of the members' individual autonomy. I follow a particular account of group projects holding that the

---

[3] By "outweigh" here, let me be clear that I do not mean to suggest some rough consequentialist calculus for justification of the Defense Intuition. Indeed, the nature of the value of autonomy is such that it does not admit to such Utilitarian cost/benefit analysis—that is part of the whole point of taking such rights seriously. I'll explain this in detail in my discussion of the peculiar value of autonomy in section 2.

collective self-rule of a given group can be (in at least some cases and granting certain commitments made by the individuals in that group) necessary to further the individual autonomy of its members. Thus, the value of their collective self-rule—and the reason defense of it can be justified on a liberal framework—can rest in the work it does for the good of individual autonomy.[4]

But, as we saw at the end of chapter 6, the vexing trouble is that it is the members' individual autonomy itself that would actually be improved—perhaps significantly so—if they were to simply surrender to Alpha's aggression. And taking up arms, of course, will incur the significant and extreme costs of war upon many of the individual Bravonians (and others). Worse still, the ravages of war tend to disproportionately harm the poorest and most oppressed of a given society. And these are the same individuals who would stand to benefit the most from the benevolent rule of the Alphonians. Thus, I must show why the individual Bravonians exercise of collective rule is peculiarly important—or *can be* properly valued as peculiarly important to individual Bravonians—and why this peculiar importance gives their collective project the value needed to justify violent defense born out of the value of individual autonomy.

The answer, I'll argue, is that part of *what it means* to properly value individual autonomy is to recognize that it is up to the individual (or group of individuals) to decide what trade-offs to that autonomy itself are permissible and which are not; at least to some degree.[5] Thus, it is up to the individual Bravonians to decide whether their individual expressions of autonomy through their collective project of self-rule is more important to them than other benefits to different aspects of their individual autonomy (such as those that could be delivered by Alpha's aggression). And not only is that decision properly up to them, but that decision itself—what trade-offs one wishes to

---

[4] See my discussion below in section 3 of Steven Wall, "Collective Rights and Individual Autonomy," *Ethics* 117 (2007): 234–64.

[5] Importantly, the valuing of trade-offs to one's autonomy is only up to the individual to a certain extent, within certain constraints or limited scope of what can count as a good project to be pursued. Which is to say that my arguments here do not take a position on perfectionism or anti-perfectionism models of state authority. By granting that there are some limits to the goods an individual can choose for trade-offs, my view is here compatible with at least a moderate form of liberal perfectionism. To say that an individual should be the arbiter of trade-offs to their own autonomy need not imply that *all* options are on the table or that governments must be completely neutral in regard to what can count as a legitimate trade-off for one's autonomy nor neutral regarding different people's conception of the good. There will be thresholds wherein at a certain point it is morally unjustifiable for the individual to grant certain trade-offs to their own autonomy. I explore this tangentially below in the case of state Charlie. For a discussion of anti-perfectionism, see Joseph Raz, *Morality of Freedom*, section II, 110–57. For a defense of liberal perfectionism, see Steven Wall, *Liberalism, Perfectionism, and Restraint* (Cambridge: Cambridge University Press, 1998).

accept for one's own autonomy—is *itself* part of the value of individual autonomy in the first place.[6]

If that is right, then we have found the liberal basis for the Defense Intuition and can build a properly liberal just war theory. The basis for it is this peculiar way in which the value of individual autonomy works: the individual (within limits) is the one who should decide what the trade-offs to his or her autonomy are best to value for that autonomy. Thus, it should be up to the Bravonians to decide if the value that their collective project of self-rule delivers to their individual autonomy is worth giving up for the benefits their individual autonomy could gain through Alphonian rule. And if the Bravonians decide that their collective project of self-rule is more important to their individual autonomy than the benefits gained from Alphonian rule, then they have a right to defend that collective project, as an extension and part of their right to defend their own individual autonomy. This will be the basic map that gets us toward a new liberal theory of just war. Consider this my opening displayed argument. From here, I will explain each of the pieces of the map in more detail and defend each turn.

7.2. The Special Value of Autonomy for Liberalism

At this point, I have said that liberalism's commitment to individual autonomy is where we can find the grounds for the Defense Intuition, but I have not yet said just what the value of autonomy is and why autonomy itself is so important to liberalism. I will try, briefly, to do that—all with an aim for why it plays the role it does in my sketch of a new liberal theory of just war. More specifically related to the puzzle, the point here is to try to show why a liberal commitment to the value of individual autonomy can yield the moral justification for the Defense Intuition for Bravo against Alpha's invasion.

At its core, liberalism is a theory about liberty as a political value. Liberty, indeed, is viewed by many as the foundational value of liberalism, by

---

[6] Again, I think this decision itself does have some self-imposed limits internal to the value of autonomy. It's not a completely open-ended decision. Can someone legitimately decide that the best way to exercise and properly value their autonomy is to sell themselves into permanent abusive slavery, for example? I don't think so. Or, rather, I think someone making such a decision is not properly valuing their autonomy, even if they make such a choice autonomously. Thus, the value of autonomy will not be able to defend the choice. But this is a very complicated (and long) discussion about the nature of autonomy. I will address this limited scope aspect of this peculiar value of autonomy I am focusing on for the Alpha-Bravo case in section 2.

definition.[7] Gerald Gaus calls the simplest conception of liberty—limiting anyone's liberty stands in need of justification—the "fundamental liberal principle."[8] This understanding of liberalism—that a presumption of noninterference in others' freedom of action is the foundational political principle—traces its roots to, of course and at least, Mill and his harm principle.[9] Within the liberal political tradition, however, there are various splits over just how this liberty is to be protected and respected. Some hold simply a negative view of liberty; that we need merely be committed to blocking the direct coercion of one person by another; that all liberty entails politically is freedom from the direct obstruction of action by others.[10] But others hold a more positive view of liberty demanding much more of our politics. The thought is that mere non-coercion of particular actions does not make someone in any meaningful sense free if an individual's actions are not properly their *own*.[11] This view argues that liberty as a political value must be understood not merely as non-coercion but, rather, as an individual *directing* his or her own life. That is, the real value of liberty is properly understood as the value of autonomy.[12] Call those who hold this view *liberal autonomists*.[13] The individual enjoying autonomy is the ruler, possessor, steward, and director of their own life, and it is *their* life. It is up to them, as individuals, to chart their life's course as they decide.[14]

Joseph Raz, the most important and influential liberal autonomist among recent and contemporary political philosophers, explains individual autonomy this way:

---

[7] British philosopher Maurice Cranston said well that, "By definition, a liberal is a man who believes in liberty." Maurice Cranston, "Liberalism," in *The Encyclopedia of Philosophy*, 458–61, edited by Paul Edwards (New York: Macmillan and the Free Press, 1967). Gerald Gaus quotes this line from Cranston in his article, "Liberalism," *Stanford Encyclopedia of Philosophy*, originally published 1996, updated in 2022., which is where I first came across it.

[8] Gerald Gaus, "The Place of Autonomy within Liberalism," in *Autonomy and the Challenges to Liberalism: New Essays*, 272–306, edited by John Christman (Cambridge: Cambridge University Press, 2009). Also see, Gerald Gaus, *Justificatory Liberalism: An Essay on Epistemology and Political Theory* (New York: Oxford University Press, 1996).

[9] John Stuart Mill, *On Liberty* (1869; repr. New York: Simpson & Brown, 2011).

[10] See Isaiah Berlin, "Two Concepts of Liberty," in *Four Essays on Liberty* (Oxford: Oxford University Press, 1969).

[11] Note that I am not here discussing the debate over the existence or nature of metaphysical freedom. That monumental debate, although relevant to many of the discussions here, falls far outside of the scope of this book, thankfully.

[12] The etymology of the word autonomy itself, of course, is a combination of "self" and "rule" (or, rather, law).

[13] The term is from Gerald Gaus.

[14] The language of "charting one's own course" is commonly employed by Steven Wall and it is likely I picked it up from him somewhere.

An autonomous person is part author of his own life. His life is, in part, of his own making. The autonomous person's life is marked not only by what it is. A person is autonomous *only if he has a variety of acceptable options available to him to choose from*, and his life became as it is through his choice of some of those options. A person who has never had any significant choice, or was not aware of it, or never exercised choice in significant matters but simply drifted through life is not an autonomous person.[15]

Raz's point that I emphasize of having a variety of acceptable options to choose from is critical for the work we'll do below regarding so-called "joint options" for a group of individuals, but it is also relevant here in tracing liberalism's valuing of liberty *as* autonomy. The reasoning, the liberal autonomist contends, is that freedom from coercion itself has no real value for an individual if they cannot purposefully build some kind of meaningful life of their own choosing within the space of that freedom. A man trapped for his entire existence in an underground cave, gripped by some addiction or obsession, spending every waking moment simply trying to survive or feed his compulsion, and never made aware of other options for his life, is not being coerced by anyone and is "free" in the minimal, negative sense. But such a person is certainly not free in the sense of enjoying any valuable exercise of autonomy.[16] And, in such a case, the liberal autonomist argues, what value is that liberty? Valuing liberty means valuing individual autonomy.

So, this strand of liberalism—liberal autonomists—is that which is committed to individual autonomy as the proper focus for liberty, as the value to be supremely protected and promoted, as a critical component of a good life, and as the proper basis for political ordering. It is this understanding of liberalism that I intend when I aim to design a properly liberal just war theory. This strand of liberalism focused on the value of autonomy has

[15] Raz, *The Morality of Freedom*, 204. Emphasis mine. Gaus gives Raz this "most important contemporary liberal autonomist" title. I certainly think it fits, given the influence of *The Morality of Freedom* and the importance with which Raz's arguments have been received. Indeed, the current importance of autonomy as a central (if not the central) commitment of liberalism and the dominance of the liberal autonomist view is due in no small part to Raz's work, influence, and responses to his work.

[16] Thanks to John Sherman for pointing out that I have here, unintentionally, more or less described the character "Gollum" from the J. R. R. Tolkien series *The Lord of the Rings*. (J. R. R. Tolkien, *The Lord of the Rings* (New York: Houghton Mifflin Harcourt, 1974).) I'd suggest those poor souls trapped in Plato's cave in *The Republic*, translated by G. M. A. Grube (New York: Hackett Publishing Co., 1992) as another picture for the non-autonomous life. Remove their chains and it seems they are still trapped and non-autonomous because their view of reality is so radically limited to mere shadows and shapes on a cave wall; they do not know that they can live a better life. Thus, even if they are not kept enslaved by anyone, they are unable to live a properly free, autonomous life.

become dominant in the last half century, encompassing liberal thinkers such as Raz, Rawls, and Scanlon but has origins (of different sorts) in both Mill and Immanuel Kant.[17] The notion is also well put by Jefferson in the United States' Declaration of Independence famous line that chief among individual's rights is, "Life, Liberty, and the pursuit of Happiness."[18]

That said, I must also note in passing that this view of liberalism is not without contention. The debate is over the use and value of autonomy. Different liberal writers will invoke autonomy, but will do so in different ways to ground and understand the good life. Some also argue for a right to autonomy as opposed to it being constitutive of a good life. Further, there are many different conceptions of autonomy itself. So up-front I admit that within this tradition are different understandings of autonomy. The view of autonomy I'm relying on looks like this "author of one's own life" version, described above by Raz, and often in similar ways by Wall. The most important aspect of this appealing view of autonomy is the need for real options for an individual to have such that they can pursue various projects as "author" of his or her life. This is not a book on autonomy, however, and I cannot here give a full accounting of it. It is rather a book about permissible defense. I hold therein that autonomy can be the value upon which certain instances of permissible defense can be based, particularly instances of collective defense. Thus, I will briefly show some of the ways autonomy holds this special value in modern liberalism as well as some reasons why so many liberal writers find this particular view of autonomy so appealing.

On some liberal views, the value of autonomy is not limited only to the "personal autonomy" necessary for an individual's ability to pursue a self-directed good life discussed thus far. Rather, autonomy is seen as foundational to even our very understanding of the good.[19] This later view is clear

---

[17] I will not here address the large debate between "personal autonomy" and the Kantian notion of "moral autonomy." Instead, I focus on how the value of autonomy is grounded in ways which will be relevant to my application of it to the case of Alpha's benevolent aggression.

[18] See "Declaration of Independence," *National Archives*, https://www.archives.gov/founding-docs/declaration-transcript. For a fascinating discussion on exactly who deserves proper authorship for the document itself, see Robert McDonald, "Thomas Jefferson's Changing Reputation as Author of the Declaration of Independence: The First Fifty Years," *Journal of the Early Republic* 19, no. 2 (Summer 1999): 169–95.

[19] Again, I will not here do justice to this debate between conceptions of personal autonomy as opposed to conceptions of moral autonomy (also sometimes referred to as "Kantian autonomy"). This is an important debate which has been recently given new life. I think the kind of personal autonomy-based liberalism I am using to ground a new liberal just war theory could work in conjunction with the moral autonomy espoused by Kant. As argued for by Gaus, I think the connections between both conceptions of autonomy may be stronger than many have previously thought. Gaus writes, in explaining the issue I'm trying to bracket here: "It is often maintained that the ideal of personal autonomy is independent of moral or 'Kantian autonomy;' the commitment to one is said not to

in Kant. He writes, for example, "Autonomy is ... the ground of the dignity of human nature and of every rational nature."[20] For Kant, the ability to act freely on the basis of our rational nature forms the very origin for our moral requirements to one another.[21] As he writes, "The ground of the possibility of categorical imperatives is this: that they refer to no other property of choice (by which some purpose can be ascribed to it) than simply to its freedom."[22] On Rawls' view, a proper Kantian interpretation of justice will depend on Kant's notion of autonomy.[23] Rawls believed that Kant held that "a person is acting autonomously when the principles of his action are chosen by him as the most adequate possible expression of his nature as a free and equal rational being."[24] As such, I think Rawls can plausibly be seen to develop a kind of bridge from this Kantian notion of autonomy to the weight put on personal autonomy seen in this strand of contemporary liberalism I am here presenting. He does this by following Kant's point above and arguing that the principles that would be arrived at in the original position would be done so autonomously, since the veil of ignorance deprives the person of the knowledge they would need to make "heteronomous" principles.[25] Thus, since free

entail a commitment to the other. Kantian autonomy is understood as... a presupposition of the very possibility of moral responsibility, while personal autonomy is typically understood as a character ideal, focusing on the value of critical self-reflection on one's desires, values and plans, or the value of choosing one's way of life for oneself, or perhaps the value of self-control." Gerald Gaus, "The Place of Autonomy within Liberalism," 272. Gaus effectively argues that the two conceptions of autonomy are more closely related than many liberal scholars think. Further, Gaus shows that a plausible case can be made that the justification of liberalism as grounded on the notion of personal autonomy may *require* moral autonomy to ground it. That is, he maintains that the two notions are independent; but that liberal personal autonomy may indeed derive from the Kantian notion of moral autonomy. In the same volume, Jeremy Waldron makes a similar argument in contending for the overlap between the two conceptions of autonomy in his essay, "Moral Autonomy and Personal Autonomy," in *Autonomy and the Challenges to Liberalism: New Essays*, 307-29, edited by John Christman (Cambridge: Cambridge University Press, 2005). Robert Taylor takes this argument even further and argues directly for a version of Kantian *personal* autonomy as opposed to merely overlap and connection as Waldron and Gaus do. See, Robert Taylor, "Kantian Personal Autonomy," *Political Theory* 33, no. 5 (2005): 602-28. For an example of a dissenting view, see Onora O'Neill, who thinks that Kant's view of moral autonomy is radically at odds with and separate from contemporary political philosophy's emphasis on personal autonomy. Onora O'Neill, *Constructions of Reason: Explorations of Kant's Practical Philosophy* (Cambridge: Cambridge University Press, 1989).

[20] Immanuel Kant, *Grounding for the Metaphysics of Morals*, 43/436 (1785; repr. New York: Hackett Publishing Co., 1993).
[21] My discussion here of Kant's view on the centrality of autonomy follows Mark Timmons' discussion of the same point in *Moral Theory* (New York: Rowman & Littlefield Publishers, Inc, 2002), 157.
[22] Immanuel Kant, *The Metaphysics of Morals*, 15/222 (1797; repr. Cambridge: Cambridge University Press, 1996).
[23] John Rawls, *A Theory of Justice* (Cambridge: Cambridge University Press, 1971), 251.
[24] Rawls, *A Theory of Justice*, 252.
[25] The point I'm trying to make here is both controversial (see note 18 above) and an admittedly radically over-simplified view of Rawls' account of autonomy. (I do not have room here to explain Rawls' full view on the distinctions he makes over political views that are and are not autonomous.

and rational people acting autonomously come to know the correct moral principles to order a just society, this Kantian sense of moral autonomy can, itself, be seen as a kind of prerequisite for the very notion of Rawls' liberal theory of justice which is so committed to personal autonomy.

Although it is perhaps not as clear in other liberal scholars, a similar line of thinking for how the moral principles for the just ordering of a society are to be arrived at through the ideal of personal autonomy can be found in much of contemporary liberalism. And even where this Kantian conception of moral autonomy is rejected as wholly distinct from the value of personal autonomy to political liberalism (for those such as O'Neill who reject the kinds of arguments given by Gaus, Waldron, and Taylor referenced in note 17), the value of *personal* autonomy in grounding the good life is still widely maintained as a key piece of many, if not most, contemporary liberal theories. As Gaus and Shane Courtland write, "That the good life is necessarily a freely chosen one in which a person develops his unique capacities as part of a plan of life is probably the dominant liberal ethic of the past century."[26]

I hope to show, then, that for liberalism this treasured autonomy is of such central importance that it can be worth defending and preventing its violation can be a justifiable cause for violence—even on a large scale and for groups. Steven Wall writes, "Autonomy is not just one intrinsic value among many; it is one of special importance. For most people it is . . . a central component of a fully good life."[27] If that is true—if we grant this view of autonomy and this version of liberalism—then it seems one would have the right to defend one's ability to pursue an intrinsically valuable component that is, itself, necessary to living a good life.

Rawls writes, for example, "A political view is autonomous if it represents, or displays, the order of political values as based on principle of practical reason in union with the appropriate political conceptions of society and person. This . . . is doctrinal autonomy" (John Rawls, *Political Liberalism* (New York: Columbia University Press, 1995), 99). But he also holds a deeper meaning of "constitutive autonomy" which says that the "order of moral and political values must be made, or itself constituted, by the principles and conceptions of practical reason" (John Rawls, *Political Liberalism*, 99). Rawls concludes that this later position is Kant's view. That sounds correct insofar as on both Kant and Rawls view, abstracting from constraints and autonomous reasoning will derive proper political and moral principles. On this discussion over Rawls' view of constitutive autonomy, I am in part following Percy B. Lehning discussion of the same in his *John Rawls: An Introduction* (Cambridge: Cambridge University Press, 2006). Lehning references Rawls: *Political Liberalism*: xliv–xlv, 98; and John Rawls, *The Law of Peoples*, 146 (Cambridge, MA: Harvard University Press, 1999), to make this case.

[26] Gerald Gaus and Shane Courtland, "Liberalism," in *Stanford Encyclopedia of Philosophy*, edited by Edward N. Zalta (Stanford University 2022).
[27] Steven Wall, *Liberalism, Perfectionism, and Restraint*, 130.

But what does it mean for a person to pursue such an autonomous life? Again, Wall: "[Autonomy] is the ideal of people charting their own course through life, fashioning their character by self-consciously choosing projects and taking up commitments from a wide range of eligible alternatives, and making something out of their lives according to their own understanding of what is valuable and worth doing."[28] If this ideal is to ever be attained, or even sought after, then people must be free to make and follow through on those projects and commitments which they choose. Blocking one's ability to do so would constitute blocking their attempt at a good life. But, as is commonly pointed out, this understanding of autonomy as a character ideal is a very difficult thing for an individual to achieve.[29] This is usually seen as a criticism, but I think, if true, it can be seen as making autonomy all the more valuable. That autonomy is something difficult to achieve makes the infringement of people successfully enjoying some autonomously pursued projects (such as the group project of self-rule, say) *all the more* harmful because there is a very real risk that they will not be able to attain it again in the future.[30]

If this valuing of individual autonomy is correct, then protecting it from unjust infringement will be of supremely high importance for such a version of liberalism. As Raz writes, the "protection of personal autonomy" can be understood "as the core of the liberal concern for liberty."[31] And if the relative harm of any given action is proportional to the good that is damaged, thwarted, blocked, decreased, or injured by that action, then the harm of unjustly infringing an individual's autonomy will be great on such a liberal view. In fact, although it may be an oversimplification, I think this understanding of autonomy offers the most plausible and straightforward view of what the ultimate disvalue to someone being killed consists in.[32] Namely, killing someone is the ultimate and permanent blocking of one's autonomy.[33]

---

[28] Ibid., 128.

[29] See Thomas E. Hill, Jr., *Autonomy and Self-Respect* (Cambridge: Cambridge University Press, 1991), for a good discussion on the importance of autonomy as for the liberal conception of the good life as well as it being particularly difficult to achieve. Hill writes, "To say that autonomy ... is an ideal is not necessarily to condemn those who lack it; for it is far from the only moral ideal, and it is very hard to achieve," p. 51.

[30] I'll review the special role that group projects can hold for individual's autonomy, in section 3.

[31] Raz, *The Morality of Freedom*, 207.

[32] See Seth Lazar for an illuminating essay on the nature of disvalue, particularly in regard to being killed, in "The Nature and Disvalue of Injury," *Res Publica*, 15, no. 3 (2009): 289–304. Also see Purves, "Accounting for the harm of death," *Pacific Philosophical Quarterly* 97, no. 1 (2016): 89–112.

[33] This point has been made countless ways and times before, of course. I raise it here to directly tie together the simple rights-based self-defense account offered in chapter 1 with a direct defense of autonomy that I need to lay out a road-map for a liberal just war theory that can withstand Rodin's challenge. For other examples of this kind of explanation of the disvalue of death (although not exactly couched in terms of the loss of autonomy, per se), see, most notably, Jeff McMahan, *The Ethics of*

So, in the most basic case of self-defense against unjust lethal harm such as in the *Defender & Attacker* case (discussed in chapter 1) we can see, even there, grounding for the right to self-defense upon the value of autonomy to the individual. One is not usually defending *only* their autonomy when they defend their life, of course.[34] But in a very real sense, they are defending their ability to continue to make their own choices. This is why I think it is so intuitively plausible to move from the claim that if one is entitled to defend themselves against being unjustly killed with violent force, then they have a similar justification (only slightly less strong, or perhaps of the same weight) to defend themselves against being unjustly enslaved with violent force. (Recall the case of *Ancient Slave* from chapter 2 and Telemaque's permissible lethal defense against Hittite Lord.) The reason the justification may be slightly less, some might argue, is because, in the enslavement case, the removal of their autonomy is not final and could be reversed. But in *both* cases, the defense of the self can be viewed as a defense of one's right to personal autonomy.

Recall as well that this progression from defense against unjust killing to defense against unjust enslavement was also discussed in chapter 6 regarding the grounding of just war on reductive or analogous accounts of individual self-defense. Rodin challenges that collective defense cannot be ground on individual self-defense because collective defense neither reduces to nor is relevantly analogous to individual self-defense, primarily because most wars are purely conditional. I noted that it seems Rodin's view is committed, however, to accepting just war as purely reductive on individual self-defense in that rare case where an invading force was explicitly aiming to wipe out the entire population (e.g., Fernando Tesón's invading alien case).[35] And it seems

Killing: Problems at the Margins of Life (New York: Oxford University Press, 2002). McMahan offers an account of the harm of killing as couched in the loss of future experiences and life as they are relationally tied to one's forward-looking commitment to them presently. This is over-simplifying, but in some ways, this can be understood as taking the harm of killing to rest in the loss of one's future exercise of autonomy.

[34] To see this, simply imagine a case where one is forced to choose between the loss of their life and the loss of their autonomy—death or benevolent slavery. Most will choose benevolent slavery, but as I mention below, I think the reason is at least in part due to the impermanence of slavery (perhaps they can escape some day and regain their autonomy) as opposed to the permanence of death. If one were forced to choose between death and a permanent loss of autonomy, the decision becomes more difficult. Even here, however, I think most would choose the permanent loss of autonomy. This simply shows that not *all* good and valuable things in life are ultimately tied to autonomy. One could still enjoy various pleasures and many other goods that need not derive from autonomy under permanent benevolent slavery. Still, the fact *that* death and permanent loss of autonomy are viewed so similarly reinforces the larger point I am making: that death includes at least the permanent loss of autonomy, and that is plausibly the largest harm death delivers to the individual.

[35] See note 15 in chapter 6 where this is discussed at length.

he'd be similarly committed to the possibility of a reductive account if an invading force was aiming to enslave an entire population—something not entirely outside of the human history of events, unfortunately.[36]

The force of Rodin's challenge for liberalism comes from abstracting from death or enslavement to lesser, conditional harms. And the puzzle of Alpha's aggression is intended to take this move all the way. But, notice, if the proper harm of death or enslavement is built on the infringement of individual autonomy, then, *if* I can show that the harm done to the Bravonians in Alpha's benevolent aggression stems from the same source, it seems plausible that a reductive account of collective defense could also follow, just as naturally as it does in the group death or enslavement case. Showing that the Alphonian invasion directly harms the individual Bravonians' autonomy through abrogation of their group project of self-governance is precisely what I've said is needed to ground the Defense Intuition and map the moral structure of a new liberal just war theory.[37] I think this can be shown through a particular view of autonomy which claims that some "joint options" for groups of people can become necessary to an individual's expression of autonomy within that group. Thus, before going further with how some aspects peculiar to the value of autonomy could potentially support the legitimacy of Bravo's defense against Alphonian aggression, I will first show how this notion of joint options works.

7.3. The Value of Group Projects to Individual Autonomy

Occasionally, we exercise our individual autonomy in a project which involves other people jointly exercising their autonomy through the same project with shared goals. In some cases, these kinds of group projects can take on particular importance to the autonomy of the members of a group because of the way they function as distinctively important options for those individuals.[38] This will be critical for my attempt to show what would have to be true of a state such that it can legitimately defend itself from an Alpha-type aggression in a way that is compatible with liberal theory. That is, I will need

---

[36] See A. H. M. Jones, "Slavery in the Ancient World," *The Economic History Review* 9, no. 2 (1956).

[37] Or, that is, Alpha's invasion *could so* harm the Bravonians' individual autonomy, given certain contexts and commitments of the individual Bravonians.

[38] This view is championed most prominently by Steven Wall in "Collective Rights and Individual Autonomy."

this understanding of certain group activities to give a liberal account of the Defense Intuition. To argue that Alpha is seriously harming the autonomy of individual Bravonians simply by abrogating their collective self-rule, I must demonstrate that the group project of collective self-rule (and group projects in general) could potentially serve such vital roles to individuals' autonomy.[39]

Some groups may have an interest in engaging in certain joint activities. Wall calls the option to engage in various joint activities *joint options*, used here as a technical term of art.[40] An example of such a joint option could be the collective self-governance of a people, such as the Bravonians' desire to engage in self-rule of Bravo.[41] Occasionally some joint options can play an essential part in the autonomy of the individuals that make up the group pursuing them. As Wall argues, these "joint options play (or can play) in the constitution of an adequate range of options for individuals."[42]

Let me explain this view more fully by first returning once again to Raz. In quoting Raz earlier, I emphasized his claim that a person is autonomous "only if he has a variety of acceptable options available to him to choose from."[43] Raz goes on to write, "If having an autonomous life is an ultimate value, then having a sufficient range of acceptable options is of intrinsic value, for it is constitutive of an autonomous life that it is lived in circumstances where acceptable alternatives are present."[44] This notion that autonomy requires an adequate range of options for an individual is the starting point for the view I am describing here: that certain group activities can become critical for the autonomy of individuals in those groups.

But what makes a particular range of alternative options adequate? There are some options which must be included in any range if it is to be adequate for individual autonomy. These Wall labels *necessary options*.[45] For example, the option to pursue romantic relationships with a person of one's own

---

[39] See Raz, *The Morality of Freedom*, 207–9 for a good discussion of collective rights being born, at least in part, out of a concern for aligning individual interests within the collective. "A collective right exists when the following three conditions are met. First, it exists because an aspect of the interest of human beings justifies holding some person(s) to be subject to a duty. Second, the interests in question are the *interests of individuals as members of a group* in a public good and the right is a right to that public good *because it serves their interest as members of that group*. Thirdly, the interest of no single member of that group in that public good is sufficient by itself to justify holding another person to be subject to a duty," 208.
[40] Wall, "Collective Rights and Individual Autonomy," 245.
[41] Wall argues that to pursue some joint options (such as self-rule) a group requires its own independent authority as well as territory to carry out their authority.
[42] Wall, "Collective Rights and Individual Autonomy," 253–54.
[43] Raz, *The Morality of Freedom*, 204.
[44] Ibid., 205.
[45] Wall, "Collective Rights and Individual Autonomy," 254.

choosing could be such an option. It is an option that *must* be included in any range of options available to an individual in "authoring one's own life" if that range is to be adequate for the individual to exercise his or her autonomy. Wall suggests the option of being able to freely express opinions about religious beliefs as another possible example of a necessary option. Thus, inclusion of *all* necessary options will be required for any range to be adequate for individual autonomy but will not be sufficient.[46] The reason for this is that an adequate range of alternatives must also include a reasonable number of diverse non-necessary options that would be worthwhile for a person to pursue.[47] But different sets of non-necessary worthwhile options will satisfy this requirement for an adequate range of options. Wall calls these *threshold options*. "Threshold options are options that, when added to the necessary options, make an option set one that provides an adequate range of options."[48] Of course, a set of alternatives for an individual that is adequate for autonomy will usually also contain other options aside from threshold and necessary options. These options Wall calls *supplementary options*.[49] Supplementary options are those options whose presence in a range does not make a range adequate, nor does their removal from a range make it inadequate—they are supplemental choices a person may have, but that are not required for an individual to have in order to fully exercise their autonomy.

Let me stop briefly to remind why this discussion is so critical for the puzzle of Alpha's benevolent aggression. If this view of various necessary, threshold, and supplementary options for the expression of autonomy is correct in all this so far, it shows what the problem will be for a liberal justification of the Defense Intuition for Bravo. Why should we presume that for individual Bravonians the joint option of collective self-governance is a necessary or threshold option and not merely a supplemental option? That is, why can't we say that the Bravonians will still have a sufficient range of acceptable options for pursuit such that their individual autonomy would not be thwarted by the removal of this one particular joint option were they to surrender? Why must *this* particular joint option of collective self-rule be

---

[46] Ibid., 254.
[47] Ibid., 254. Further, Wall adds that in addition to having a variety of worthwhile non-necessary options, an adequate range of options must "include options that enable a person to develop and exercise important human capacities," 254. Wall points us to Raz, *The Morality of Freedom*, 375, for a discussion of the importance of the option to develop various human capacities.
[48] Wall, "Collective Rights," 254.
[49] Ibid., 254–55.

considered a necessary or threshold part of that set of options available to the citizens of Bravo?

The answer I can give is purely a contingent one. But that's to be expected for not all instances of inter-state conflict will deliver justification for collective defense. That is, my answer will not obtain for all instances of Bravo-like cases where members of a group are engaged in some group project. I need not argue that joint options such as collective self-rule are necessary options, but that they could be threshold options to certain individuals in certain groups under certain conditions. Wall thinks that there are two ways this could happen, in general. The first is that a given range of options for a particular group's members is "so impoverished that the subtraction of one joint option would reduce the range below the adequacy level."[50] In such a context, a particular joint option in question, so long as it was worthwhile (and collective self-governance could be that), would be a threshold option to those members. And we could imagine something like this for the Bravonians, in fact. "We may not have much, but we're Bravonians, dammit, and no one can take that from us, at least." And so forth.

But, while plausible, this is *not* quite what we'd want for justification of the Defense Intuition of Bravo's self-rule. This is because it only gives us a very paltry reason that the joint option of their self-rule only *happens* to be a threshold option due to their otherwise impoverished opportunities for autonomous choice.[51] And all it really demands is that a given group needs *more* options; not that they need one particular joint option (such as collective self-rule) over any other. And this particularly devilish puzzle, recall, Alpha would be providing and opening up new options to Bravo.

But there is another way that a non-necessary joint option can be a threshold option. It involves the ways in which different options matter or don't matter to a given individual. An adequate range of alternatives requires not only worthwhile options, but worthwhile options that a given individual cares about or takes to be important to them in some meaningful way. As Wall explains:

> An option open to me could be worthwhile, but still it could leave me cold. I might realize that, given my talents and temperament, I cannot pursue the

---

[50] Ibid., 255.
[51] Another reason I should reject this way of the joint option of self-rule being a threshold option to Bravonians is that it would further open up my account to the assimilation objection I address below in section 7.6.

option successfully. Alternatively, I might have false beliefs about the value of the option, or perhaps I understand its value but am just not moved to pursue it. For this reason, an adequate range of options for a person must include options that are both worthwhile and can be seen by him to be worth pursuing.[52]

Further, certain options, *once chosen* or embarked upon or committed to by an individual, can "take on a special importance" for a person.[53] This is key. A particular worthwhile option can be so important to a person that it becomes to them, in their understanding of the option itself, an essential option to any attempt at pursuing an autonomously good life. Wall labels such options, *vital options*.

Take the example (given by Wall) of a highly trained flute player who loves, cherishes, and is committed to her pursuit of playing the flute more than any other activity she does. For such a person, the option to pursue a career in music wherein she can fulfill her desire to pursue her flute playing talent could become, in her eyes, not only a worthwhile option, but one "she *must* have if she is to lead an autonomous life."[54] Allow me to suggest another example of a possible vital option for an individual. Imagine a woman named Sarah.

Sarah

Sarah has longed her entire life to be a mother of children. She longs to be a caring, supportive, excellent parent to the children she is able to have and raise. She spends most of her life preparing for her longed-for role as mother. After taking tests to ensure that she is biologically able to having children, she finds and marries a good partner who similarly wishes to raise children, she reads countless books on parenting, she gets a degree in child development, she volunteers at local schools and daycare centers to better develop her parenting skills, and she eats a diet and follows an exercise regime specifically designed to create a healthy prenatal environment for her future children.

For Sarah, the option to have children of her own to raise could become, in her eyes, not only a worthwhile option, but one she must have if she is to lead

---

[52] Ibid., 255.
[53] Ibid.
[54] Ibid., 256, emphasis mine.

an autonomous life. For her, the option to have children has become a "vital option." For Sarah, having children is in many ways the entire point of her existence.

To carry the example even further, imagine that for some reason, the state she lives in forcibly sterilizes a portion of their population to promote some social good. (Granting that this action would almost certainly be unjust, of course.) If Sarah is picked (perhaps through a lottery system, let us assume) to be sterilized, I think the infringement upon her autonomy would be so great that she could make a distinctively liberal case for violent defense of her vital option of parenthood, as I propose here. That is, Sarah would be justified to use lethal force to stop such a transgression of her autonomy. (Of course, there are probably plenty of other ways to make the case for a violent defense against such an illiberal state action—such an act would likely justify violent defense even for those for whom parenting is not a vital option. This simply means the case is over-determined, in Sarah's case.)

I will note autobiographically that, for myself, the activity of parenting my children has, indeed, become precisely this kind of vital option that is necessary for any conception of the good life. I cannot imagine what a good life would even mean or consistent in were I suddenly no longer able to be a father to two humans named Toby and Norah. And a great deal of my self-identity, understanding, worth, and in any sense purpose in life is tied up in my being a father to these two. I think parenthood is something that often becomes a vital option for many; usually only after embarking on it.

Vital options will often therefore be deeply embedded in a person's very identity and how they view and understand themselves. Pursuit of a vital option for someone is part of who they believe they are. Vital options explain how an option that some might regard as merely supplemental could be a threshold option for other people. The person is committed to a particular worthwhile supplemental option in such a way that their relation towards the option itself reorients the required set of options needed for them to have a sufficient range for an autonomous life. Namely, it reorients it by changing the supplemental option into an essential threshold option, for that individual.

I should note here, importantly, that the large importance Wall attributes to the whole notion of an option requirement (or, better, a *range* of options requirement) for autonomy is something that many other liberal thinkers do *not* attribute to autonomy. Such writers are more concerned with simply blocking coercion and the like from getting in the way of autonomy. But the idea that you need a sufficient range of options, and the idea of vital options in particular, makes sense with the conception of autonomy as a central element of a good life, as opposed to a right. That is the view of liberalism I am using to sketch how a consistently liberal response to the puzzle of Alpha's aggression could be delivered. But even with this way of valuing autonomy there are other ways we could understand their importance (and how and why they could be permissibly defended). On a Razian view, for example, one condition of autonomy is independence. So, simply being subjected to the will of others would thwart one's autonomy, even if the range of options available to them was not too small. That is, one could have an adequate range like Wall demands, including all vital options accessible, yet not be properly *independent* in one's choice of those projects so as to result in in the good of autonomy.[55]

Wall places a great deal of weight on having an adequate range of options. What Wall does not put a lot of weight on is the independence option that Raz focuses on. In my view, *both* need to be emphasized and both are required. Wall gives us these distinctions of necessary, threshold, supplemental, and, ultimately, vital options. But by themselves even they need to be explained in terms of not just their value to autonomy, but *why* they hold the particular value they do for a given individual (or group of individuals). For example, Wall speaks about the notion of a vital option, as just discussed, but it seems like vitality itself is something that comes in degrees. Vital is one end of the spectrum, whereby that particular option is crucially important to one's autonomy. But there are other important options that we may say are important in special ways, and not simply supplementary to autonomy, but yet not quite what Wall calls vital options. What I see Wall doing through the vitality point dovetails with my emphasis on the *subjective* importance of an option to an individual. Some restrictions on one's options (such as the restriction Alpha's aggression might constitute) will damage some aspects of autonomy while improving other aspects of autonomy. But, as an addendum to Wall's notion of various options and, in line with my point on their degreed nature, I claim that in weighing a given range of options it is actually part of the very idea of autonomy itself that we should defer to the subjective weight placed on those options by the people whose range would be curtailed by a given action. It is that very idea that then comes into play in these conditional conflict cases. If

---

[55] An interesting case to think through in this regard is to imagine a given minority cultural group with their own distinct language. What if the language simply withers away, but not via any kind of coercion? It seems no one restricted their options, nor was their independence condition in any way violated. Yet the loss of this language could very well represent the loss of a vital option to some of those people.

you accept my view that autonomy is not just a matter of specifying a range of options that matter to people *independently* of how the individual people view those options, then you are half-way to my argument for a liberal account of the Defense Intuition. The idea is that it's up to the individual to determine how they want to lead the life they want to lead, *including* the weight given to various options and aspects of their autonomy.

Could this same argument I'm here setting up for Bravo's defense be defended through the independence condition, rather than the vital option argument? Well, again, I think we need both aspects to understand the (potential) harm here delivered. That is, the taking away of an option is a *way of* violating independence. A take-over (like Alpha's aggression) that usurps a kind of control (like self-rule) either is a kind of vetoing of certain options (vital or necessary, or perhaps threshold, depending on how they are properly related to one's self-rule), or else it violates the independence condition. I contend that however we chose to understand this, that the damage itself is quite significant for a given set of people, or at least it can be if they are properly related to it. The issue under examination here, after all, is whether one can defend the loss of a given option with lethal force. If that's the case, then it must have a central weight in the good life of the people who value it.

That one's personal autonomy can be worthy of defense, even lethal defense, is nicely captured in this passage by David Rodin.

> What of the defense of liberty? Life and liberty are often listed together as basic human goods of central importance, and it is sometimes claimed that it is justifiable to kill in defense of liberty. These assertions derive their plausibility from the observation that liberty is a necessary condition for the shaping of any meaningful life. Liberty is both a component of, and a precondition for, many of the substantive goods that we value; in part we value life because of the liberty that it enables us to exercise. For this reason, it is conceivable that it may sometimes be proportionate to defend one's liberty with lethal force, for to deprive a person of liberty in certain contexts is *to deprive them of a meaningful life.*[56]

Rodin here speaks of liberty, but the point remains the same: restrictions on certain options for an individual (which can be understood as violating independence) can harm her individual autonomy to the extent that the

---

[56] David Rodin, *War & Self-Defense*, 47. Emphasis mine.

restriction deprives her of (what she takes to be) a meaningful life. Such a deprivation, if true, would be an unjust harm worthy of defense.

From this understanding of vital options, then, the next step in constructing the liberal account of the Defense Intuition is obvious. What will matter for Bravo's collective defense of their state is simply that vital options can be joint options. And that is not hard to conceive. Imagine that the population of Bravo takes great pride in and cares deeply about their civic involvement, in voting and electing one another to office, in running the various governmental bureaucracies (even though they run them very poorly), and in making decisions for their state through their agreed-upon collective decision-making procedures. They care deeply about simply being independent Bravonians—perhaps in part for historic reasons and perhaps, even, in relation to past conditions and standings with other states, like Alpha. In short, they cherish their ongoing joint option of pursuing collective self-rule. Imagine that they care for it and are committed to it so deeply, in fact, that they view the joint option they all participate in as an essential part of their exercise of individual autonomy. Bravo's continued independence from Alpha is for the individual Bravonians a vital option. If that is right, then the defense of this joint option—this vital option—finds its ultimate value in the work it does for individual Bravonians' autonomy. The liberal justification for the Defense Intuition is then this: it is morally permissible for the Bravonians to take up arms in violent defense against Alpha's aggression because Alpha's aggression is a serious infringement upon each of their individual autonomy. (Or it could be, if they are properly related to the joint project of self-rule as just discussed.) And, as argued for above, a serious infringement upon individual autonomy is *precisely* the thing that can justify violent defense. Just as defense against unjust attack or unjust enslavement are similarly defenses against a serious infringement of individual autonomy, so too is Bravo's defense of their vital option of autonomous collective self-rule.

If this standing by individual Bravonians sounds implausible, I suggest it because of the sterility of the thought experiment. Turn instead to the 2022 war between Russia and Ukraine. First, notice that on any account of just war theory, traditionalist or revisionist, the 2022 Russian invasion, and resulting Ukrainian defense, is a clear-cut case of an unjust cause (Russian) and just defense (Ukraine) as can be imagined. As Janina Dill put well,

> Traditionalists think of the war as Ukraine exercising a collective right to defend the nation; revisionists as Ukrainians defending their rights to life

and self-determination. Either way, Ukraine has the textbook case of a just cause for war, which Russia lacks.[57]

Since the outbreak of the war, many have been inspired to see the Ukrainians fight for the very existence of their collective project called Ukraine. Their heroism inspires so many, I suggest, because it is demonstrating everything I have been speaking of here. There is the now famous instance of the handful of 13 Ukrainian soldiers, trapped on small Snake Island, right at the outset of the war. When ordered to surrender by a massive Russian warship, these men decided to tell the Russians to "Go Fuck Yourself," rather than surrender to this unjust invasion.[58] Or of the older Ukrainian "babushka" (old woman) who went right up to Russian soldiers invading her village and began putting sunflower seeds in their pocket. (The sunflower is the national flower of Ukraine.) Telling them, "Put sunflower seeds in your pocket so they grow when you die."[59] Or the now endless number of stories of Ukrainian families making the gut-wrenching decision to send the children away, and all men (and many women) of fighting age staying behind to join the defense forces.[60] This has set up powerful moments at train stations, as fathers' hug their young children being sent away to safety, as they then go to the front. Indeed, it was heard of those men interviewed as they sent their families off, "[It is] Our country, we have to protect it."[61] Many others who cannot fight have chosen to stay behind to help the defense forces in other ways, like cooking or helping with supplies.[62]

And we could easily review dozens of other examples in just the first few months of this intense and awful war. All of these endless examples give strong credence to the idea that for the Ukrainians maintaining their independent self-rule separate from Russia is to them a vital option, central to

---

[57] https://www.publicethics.org/post/the-moral-muddle-of-blaming-the-west-for-russia-s-aggression

[58] https://www.theguardian.com/world/2022/feb/25/ukraine-soldiers-told-russians-to-go-fuck-yourself-before-black-sea-island-death. It was first assumed these soldiers died in the ensuring bombardment. Thankfully, later reports revealed that they survived and escaped and, at the time of this writing, are continuing to fight in defense of Ukraine.

[59] https://www.independent.co.uk/news/world/europe/ukraine-russia-soldier-woman-confrontation-b2022993.html

[60] Alfred Hackensberger, "Ukrainian families are being ripped apart as men stay behind to fight the Russian invasion," *Business Insider*, March 3, 2022.

[61] https://www.aljazeera.com/news/2022/3/6/our-country-we-have-to-protect-it-ukrainians-who-stay-behind

[62] https://www.aljazeera.com/news/2022/3/6/our-country-we-have-to-protect-it-ukrainians-who-stay-behind

who they are and their understanding of a good life. One concludes they *must* be so oriented to their collective project in this way when we consider precisely that they are willing to risk defending it and as they step away from their own children to do so, knowing they may never see them again. (Recall again how, for many, parenthood itself is often a vital option.) I contend that as the world has watched Ukrainians shout "Slava Ukraini!" in the face of desperate odds of survival against a brutal and unjust aggression, we are witnessing precisely the kind of case where a liberal just war theory such as I am sketching could easily justify national self-defense. Of course, Ukraine's case is far afield from Bravo's in that Russia is not the altruistic Alpha in this story, despite what Russian state media may claim. Rather, just the opposite. In this way, Ukraine's collective defense justification is over-determined (similar to how Sarah's defense against sterilization likely is). However, both cases show us an example of how someone's own orientation and valuing of certain vital projects gives rise to permissible defense of their own autonomy.

7.4. Autonomy Is to Be Respected, Not Maximized

It is not simply the value of autonomy's ability to be extended from the individual to the value of group projects that makes it hold a peculiar weight in grounding the Defense Intuition in the case of Alpha's aggression. Nor is it simply my emphasis on how different aspects of one's autonomy can take on different value depending on how an individual is subjectively related to those aspects. It is also the *kind* of value that autonomy is that will allow the Defense Intuition to hold even considering the competing goods that could be delivered via Alpha's take-over (including the likely increases to individual Bravonians exercise of autonomy that would be brought by Alphonian rule). Critically, autonomy is not the kind of value that can be maximized. That is, autonomy is a value that is not commensurate with direct one-to-one weighting or comparing in an effort to attain the "most" quantity of autonomy for any given individual or set of individuals. Thinking of autonomy in this way at all is deeply wrong-headed. Autonomy, rather, is a value that is to be *respected*. This fact about autonomy helps to mitigate the initially seeming deep tension over Alpha's invasion improving some aspects of individual Bravonians' autonomy, even if we grant that it significantly harms it in other ways (by destroying their collective self-governance group project). It helps mitigate this concern because simply choosing whichever option (surrender or defense) would *maximize* the individual Bravonians' autonomy is not at all how autonomy should be protected or promoted.

Several writers have made this point using the metaphor of friendship.[63] The argument runs like this: autonomy is more like friendship than some value to be maximized such as, say, certain forms of pleasure. It would not make sense to try to maximize your "friendship quotient" by sacrificing some friendships in order to make more friendships. To think of maximizing friendship in this way misunderstands what value friendship holds. Dan Zupan makes the point well. Friendship seems to be,

> like autonomy, a value to be respected rather than ... produced. We do not show respect for friendship by betraying one friend in order to make two new friends. If friendship were like pleasure, a value to be maximized, it might make sense to talk about promoting it by betraying a friend to gain even more friends. But this does not seem to be the correct attitude about friendship. One cannot produce more friendship in this manner because the tradeoffs are incompatible with the idea of friendship.[64]

And, the argument continues, the same is true of autonomy. Zupan concludes: "We do not show reverence for autonomy if we murder one autonomous being to save two, any more than we would show respect for friendship by betraying one friend in order to gain two."[65] Scanlon argues that we are not failing to properly value autonomy if we refuse to violate the principles of autonomy with respect to a few people in order to promote the autonomy of a larger number of people.[66] In fact, to do otherwise would be to fail to understand how autonomy is to be valued in the first place: it is to be respected, not maximized.[67]

---

[63] See T. M. Scanlon, *What We Owe to Each Other* (Cambridge: Belknap Press, 1998), 160–8. And Dan Zupan, *War, Morality, and Autonomy: An Investigation in Just War Theory*, 28–31 (Burlington, VT: Ashgate Publishing, 2004).

[64] Zupan, *War, Morality, and Autonomy*, 28.

[65] Ibid., 28.

[66] Scanlon, *What We Owe to Each Other*, 165. Scanlon writes, "When we consider the things that are generally held to be intrinsically valuable, however, it becomes apparent that in most cases taking them to be valuable is not simply, or even primarily, a matter of thinking that certain states of the universe are better than others and are therefore to be promoted." Scanlon, 88. Zupan writes, along the same lines, "We do not decide that the world would be a better place if there were more friendships, then set about achieving that goal by making friends. To proceed in this way would certainly be to misunderstand the nature of friendship." 28.

[67] Christine Korsgaard also makes similar points regarding the value of autonomy, but focused on Kantian autonomy, in *Creating the Kingdom of Ends* (Cambridge: Cambridge University Press, 1996).

We can even piece together a similar line of reasoning in Rawls. Rawls held that it is one of the desiderata of *any* well-ordered society that it affirms the autonomy of individual persons.[68] Given this, if the autonomy of individual people were to be directly infringed upon in an effort to create a well-ordered society, it's plausible to think that Rawls would take this to be making a similar kind of mistake in how autonomy ought to be valued. That is, infringing upon individual autonomy in order to try to create a greater quantity of autonomy seems to be a fundamental error.[69] The bottom-line, argue Scanlon, Korsgaard, Zupan, and others is that the value of autonomy, however it is cashed out, does not lie in the fact that the world would be better were autonomy to be maximized.[70]

An interesting real-world case that Zupan discusses is Finland's decision to fight the Russians in World War II. The Finns were offered peace settlement terms that were ultimately much worse than what the Russians offered them initially. As such, we can imagine that some might argue that their individual autonomy would have been better maximized had the Finns surrendered initially even if that meant injury to their autonomy as expressed through collective self-rule.[71] The Finns response however, Zupan concludes, "shows us that to value autonomy is not the same as to maximize autonomy and does not equate to the mere preservation of life."[72]

Wall also discusses the non-maximizing nature of autonomy.[73] He points out that one problem with attempts to maximize autonomy for people in a political community is that autonomy is measured in different ways and

---

[68] Rawls, *A Theory of Justice*, 456. "... a well ordered society affirms the autonomy of persons..." See also 476.

[69] But it is possible that this is not always true in all cases. See, below, on my discussion of Mikhail Valdman's argument for the surrender of one's autonomy to people who would make better choices in directing one's life. If Valdman's argument works, one could potentially argue from somewhat similar grounds that there are conceivably times to abrogate one's autonomy in order to restore or improve their long-term autonomy. A possible case could be someone "trapped" of their own will in a cult. Perhaps this person's friends could justifiably conclude that they need to violate their friend's autonomy presently by removing him from the cult in order to restore his long-term autonomy. The problem I have with this argument is that if the person in question has become trapped in a kind of "brain-washing" by joining the cult, then they are not there as an exercise of their autonomy in the first place. In such a case, his friends would not be violating his autonomy to help him escape the brain-washing cult. This is similar, I think, to cases of severe addictions and the process of what are known as "interventions." If someone has lost their ability to freely exercise their autonomy by becoming trapped in something that robs them of it, then it does not seem to be a violation of their autonomy to try to rescue them from it. Of course, at this point, we begin to enter into the territory of the metaphysical debate over free will which exceeds the bounds intended for this book.

[70] This is drawn from Zupan.

[71] See Zupan, 29.

[72] Zupan, p. 30. Walzer also discusses the case in *Just and Unjust Wars*, 71.

[73] Wall, *Liberalism, Perfectionism, and Restraint*, 183–4.

can be improved or harmed along different dimensions. Thus, "efforts to increase development [of autonomy] along one dimension might well decrease development along another."[74] And this is precisely what I argue could be occurring in Alpha's aggression of Bravo. Even if the new prosperity, stability, improved efficiencies in governance, etc., that all came with Alpha's take-over did significantly add to the exercise of autonomy of individual Bravonians, this cannot simply be seen as a direct trade-off in comparison to the loss of autonomy they'd experience in the destruction of their joint project of self-governance. The gain in some dimensions of their individual autonomy would not directly correlate or compensate the loss in another dimension of their individual autonomy.

The reason it could not directly correlate, I argued above, is that a key piece of understanding the value of individual autonomy is the *choosing* of projects to pursue itself. If individual Bravonians have chosen their group project of self-rule, and did not choose the new governance of Alpha, then *even if* the governance of Alpha would help them better pursue projects they would have wished to pursue otherwise, those pursuits could still be seen as not fully stemming from the Bravonians' autonomy. It is not merely the ability to pursue the projects one wishes to pursue, after all, but that in some important sense one's pursuits of those projects must themselves be *one's own* if they are to be autonomous.

Let me explain. Imagine a case (taken from Wall) of a woman about to donate $50 to her favorite charity. But then a gunman appears and demands that she give $50 to the same charity she was about to give to or else he will kill her.[75] Is the charity donor acting autonomously after the gunman coerces her to give the money? She is still pursuing her own autonomously chosen project that she was going to do had the gunman not appeared, after all. Yet, most here concede that, even though she is still pursuing her project, its pursuit is no longer "hers" in the right sense for it to be a proper extension of autonomous action.[76]

---

[74] Ibid., 184.
[75] Ibid., 134.
[76] Wall argues that the reason such kinds of coercion ultimately harms one's autonomy has to do, in part, with the contingent psychological states of people in most Western societies which leads them to feel disrespected and undermine their resolve to pursue their own future projects, thereby harming their autonomy. I think it's plausible to assume that something similar could happen were the Bravonians to surrender to Alpha's aggression and that they Bravonians could foresee this damage to their autonomy.

I imagine that the same could be true for the Bravonians. Imagine, for example, that one of the goods the Alphonians were intent on bringing to Bravo was quality, universal health care. And, as it happens, imagine that the Bravonians were working on better developing their own quality, universal health care system. Even if it is the case that the Alphonian invasion could actually aid the Bravonians in bringing about or pursuing this project that they were going to pursue anyway, it seems—similarly to the woman being forced to give $50 to charity she was planning on giving—that the Bravonians autonomous choice of this group project is in some real way damaged by the *forced* imposition of the project by Alpha. This holds true even if Alpha were able to do it better than the Bravonians could.

We see here again the conjoining of both the vital options emphasis of Wall and the independence condition of Raz. If some particular aspects of my autonomy may be of more value because of my attitude towards them, then it flows from that view that different restrictions to my autonomy may be damaging to differing degrees. So, we cannot do a simple one-to-one trade-off in weighing whether Alpha's benevolent invasion will "improve" or "maximize" the autonomy of Bravonians. What will matter is how they weigh the various aspects of their autonomy. If one particular joint option is going to be trumped which is, for them, *vital* and it is centrally important to them that *they* chose it (the independence condition), then it will be no solace to explain to them these *other* options, which they have not chosen, which may be opened to them.

There's another important point here brought out by how autonomy cannot be forced on another but can be forcibly taken away. This is again related to the emphasis I place on *both* the independence condition itself and the vitality condition for certain options. I said above that Alpha's aggression (and subsequent rule) could aid in the development of autonomy for individual citizens of Bravo. This is true. But note that it will only be an *indirect* aid to their autonomy, in most cases. The harm done to the Bravonians' autonomy by Alpha's aggression, on the other hand, will be direct. The destruction of their collective project of self-rule will directly block one exercise of individual Bravonians' autonomy. Whereas the greater enabling of autonomy that would come with the improved lives, social functioning, and over all well-being of Alphonian rule, will only result in the *opportunity* for the Bravonians to then respond and exercise their autonomy in the improved autonomy-enabling environs. One could argue that this difference—the direct nature of the harm to the autonomy wrought by the invasion versus the indirect nature of the benefit to individuals' autonomy bestowed by it—further favors a moral judgment in favor of the Defense Intuition. That is, other things being equal, we usually think we have a greater moral obligation to prevent a direct, known harm rather than to promote an indirect, predicted benefit. Remembering to set aside the question of whether Alpha's aggression is itself justified or not, this still seems to add weight to Bravo's choice to defend. By defending their vital option, they would be preventing a known, direct harm to each of their individual autonomy (or the individual autonomy of those Bravonians engaged in the group project in the right way, at any rate). Whereas, not defending against Alpha's invasion would be allowing for a possible, indirect, uncertain, and only predicted benefit to obtain. In most cases of moral analysis, this counts strongly in favor of blocking the direct harm.

A further point here is relevant. The ways in which group-level functions impart value to the individuals participating in them is distinctly different than the ways individual actions can impart the same value. One of the reasons for this is that the decision-making process for group projects necessarily involves more than one autonomous choice. As Wall has shown, the "group decision" has the value or weight it does because of how it functions as an extension of the individual decisions of the group's members each making their own autonomous choices in compliance with the decision-making procedures they agreed upon for the group. This means, at least, that a thwarted group project decision is not thwarting just one act of autonomous decision making, but the combined value of the multitude of members' individual decisions to participate in the group decision-making process. I'll try to show why this is so important for the case of Alpha's invasion next in section 7.5.

7.5. The Value of Group Agency

Recall the *Benevolent Mugger* case from chapter 6. It helps to illuminate the above points on how autonomous choice and autonomous value, at the group level, functions differently than it does at the individual level. Indeed, this difference impacts the way autonomy should (or can be) valued by individuals engaged in a group project. The case was designed as an extension from the original *mugger* case demanding $1, which is supposed to offer an analogy in line with Rodin's challenge. The claim was that one would not be justified on self-defense grounds to kill a mugger demanding $1 due primarily to proportionality concerns. Similarly, Rodin claims, a collective would not be justified in defending a state against purely conditional, weak aggression. I strengthened the case to that of the *Benevolent Mugger*. And, recall, our intuitions against the permissibility of Todd's lethal defense against Benevolent Mugger are very strong. But given what was just said regarding the value joint options can play for individuals' autonomy, we should stop here. For upon reflection, we see that this case is not an accurate portrayal of Alpha's aggression after all. It is not the case that Alpha is *simply* trying to hoist some good things onto the people of Bravo. They are not, for example, simply demanding that Bravo implement their great system of health care, say, or that Bravo accept Alpha's analysis of how Bravo could improve their civil justice system, perhaps, or trying to merely give Bravo large sums of money to better help poor Bravonians. No, Alpha is demanding that they usurp power in order to enforce such goods. And that is actually quite different from the *Benevolent Mugger* case.

The common intuitive response when people are asked the question of whether Todd is justified to defend himself with lethal force against Benevolent Mugger is that he is not. But when pressed as to why this is, it is often explained that "Todd could simply drop the $10 in the trash as soon as Benevolent Mugger leaves" or something similar. The idea is that Benevolent Mugger's infringement upon Todd is actually quite minor and very temporary at best. At the worst, he is forcing a very brief holding of currency which Todd need not ever even use. Whatever infringement this is upon Todd's autonomy, it is quite negligible. The harm does not rise to the level of infringement needed to justify violent self-defense, our moral intuitions appear to demand.

But now return to the case of Alpha & Bravo. Since Alpha is actually threatening to take over Bravo's ruling institutions in order to deliver these goods to the Bravonians, the better comparison would be something like the following. Consider the following case.

Strengthened Benevolent Mugger
Strengthened Benevolent Mugger approaches Todd and demands, with the threat of lethal violence, that Todd allows Strengthened Benevolent Mugger to direct his life. It turns out that Strengthened Benevolent Mugger would be really good at this, and Todd's life would significantly improve if so directed and Todd knows this to be true. Be that as it may, Todd doesn't

want Strengthened Benevolent Mugger to direct his life. Todd wants to direct his own life. The only way for Todd to prevent Strengthened Benevolent Mugger from directing his life is to use lethal defensive force to stop him. So, Todd kills Strengthened Benevolent Mugger in defense of his own autonomy.

This is a much better analogy for Alpha's benevolent aggression. And, even if intuitions would be mixed over whether or not Todd can permissibly defend himself with violent force against Strengthened Benevolent Mugger—to my mind it is quite clear that he can—but all will agree the answers are radically more permissive than they are for the original *Benevolent Mugger* case. The reason for this is the deep value we place on individual autonomy. In *Benevolent Mugger*, the benefits-*sans*-consent that would be imposed on Todd are easily dodged, evaded, or are simply negligible in terms of Todd's ability to control and direct his life for his purposes. But in *Strengthened Benevolent Mugger*, it is precisely Todd's ability to direct his life for his own purposes that is harmed. And, at any rate, whatever intuitions are mined from *Strengthened Benevolent Mugger*, the types of solutions such as "Todd can simply drop the $10 after the mugger leaves" are no longer options for such a case. And this better fits Bravo's predicament in the puzzle of Alpha's aggression.

Hence, the problem is that Alpha's altruistic aggression forces Bravo into a surrender of judgment over their own actions, but they do not agree to this surrender. It is an unwilling surrender of judgment.[77] And, thus, the Defense Intuition contends, it is morally permissible for Bravo to defend against this forced surrender of their judgment.

How to understand group agency is complex and contentious.[78] For my argument to work, I need the agency of the group connected to the agency of the members in some important way. But I need not defend any particular account among the competing ones between individual agency and group agency. I am suspicious of the metaphysical status of groups as stand-alone agents and, as shown above and discussed in chapter 6 at length, I think a properly liberal theory cannot rely on defense of the state for *its* own good

---

[77] Raz explores this notion as it relates to the idea of authority for a state in *The Morality of Freedom*, 38–39.
[78] Among countless excellent scholarship on the topic, see Christian List and Philip Pettit, *Group Agency: The Possibility, Design, and Status of Corporate Agents* (Oxford: Oxford University Press, 2011).

to justify the Defense Intuition. But I can say, then, simply this: *whatever* the metaphysical status of group agents turns out to be, the important claim that I defend is that on a liberal account it must be the case that any appeal to a group's agency must be grounded in what it does for the individual agency that comprises that group agency (in whatever way it does), for it to succeed as an appeal for the defense of a collective project.[79]

Also, worth mentioning here that there are those who contend one's life is not necessarily harmed in any way if they surrender their autonomy to others to make good life choices for them. Mikhail Valdman made this case explicitly.[80] Valdman argues that one's life is not harmed in any way whatsoever if they are not the directors of it and they outsource their decision making to others, so long as those who make the decisions for the person make actual good decisions that are commensurate with the individual's deepest commitments. He claims that what matters for a good life is that it goes well according to the value we care most about. Whether or not we are the ones making the decisions that lead our life to go well according to our values does not matter, so long as our life does indeed go well according to those values. If he's right, then it is not the case that personal autonomy is a central component of a good life whatsoever, as has been argued for in this book. Instead, rather, the value we assign to personal autonomy is simply misplaced; it is not living a self-directed life that is valuable but leading a life that is in alignment with one's deepest values.[81]

This is an important debate. And clearly my view of the centrality of personal autonomy to any conception of a good life places my account squarely contra Valdman's thesis. But even if I am wrong in that, notice that Valdman's argument does not defeat the claims I am making for the Defense Intuition with regard to Bravo or for the permissibility of Todd's defense against

---

[79] Group intent is always a difficult and controversial matter, and I shall not attempt to give a proper accounting of it here. Clearly, however, given my rejection of a metaphysically robust view of the state and Walzerian-esque analogous accounts of state defense, I favor those accounts which are more modest in their assignment of shared intentions for a group. Again, the best example I know of this is the account offered by Michael Bratman, *Faces of Intention* (Cambridge: Cambridge University Press, 1999).

[80] Mikhail Valdman makes this case in his paper, "Outsourcing Self-Government," *Ethics* 120, no. 4 (2010).

[81] An excellent exchange over Valdman's argument for outsourcing personal autonomy was hosted by the blog "PEA Soup," and can be found at: http://peasoup.typepad.com/peasoup/2010/08/ethics-discussions-at-pea-soup-mikhail-mike-valdmans-outsourcing-selfgovernment-with-commentary-by-s.html. Steve Wall there writes a helpful précis of Valdman's paper and offers some substantive comments after which a wide-ranging discussion is engaged by the likes of Wall, David Shoemaker, David Sobel, Douglas Portmore, and Valdman himself, amongst others who work on these and related issues.

Strengthened Benevolent Mugger. The reason is that in these cases the submission and surrender of autonomy is involuntary. All we need is for Bravo to not wish to submit to others to make their decisions for them in order to avoid Valdman's argument. I can allow for the permissibility of Bravo *wanting* to surrender or of Todd not defending himself against Strengthened Benevolent Mugger as being consistent with a self-imposed (perhaps autonomously imposed?) restriction of one's own autonomy. What Valdman's argument will not impugn is that individual whose commitments are precisely such that they highly value making their decisions themselves as part of their very conception of the good life and they do not want to give up this aspect of it. In other words, since Bravo and Todd do not consent to having others usurp their autonomy, Valdman's argument doesn't even get off the ground, nor do any damage to the case for the Defense Intuition.

This brings up an important point for the permissibility of Bravo's defense and for the project of working toward a new liberal theory of just war more broadly: the people of Bravo (or any nation attempting to justify its collective defense on a similar liberal structure I am suggesting here) must already have the proper commitment towards Bravo and their collective governance for this liberal justification to succeed. The upshot is that the kind of liberal theory of just war I am sketching would not work for a group of people that did not properly value the group project of collective self-rule they are engaged in. This means that a given people must value their own collective project—their own governance, their own state, they have to care about it—and value it in the proper way such that it becomes to them a vital option, if they are to rely on a justification for its defense that is based on the value of their own individual autonomy. Such an upshot holds particularly profound implications for a liberal view of nationalism. Some might thereby immediately protest the entire project, in fact, thinking that liberalism and nationalism are inherently incompatible. But as Yael Tamir, Seth Lazar, and others have argued, this need not necessarily be the case.[82] Liberalism and some form of nationalism may be compatible. I leave this upshot unexamined here, but I view the result—that the people of a given collective must be properly invested in that collective for it to be worthy of defense as an extension of the value of their individual autonomy—as a feature, not a bug,

---

[82] See Yael Tamir, *Liberal Nationalism* (Princeton: Princeton University Press, 1993). For an interesting argument for some limited duties to a state based on associative duties that members of a state incur towards one another, see Seth Lazar in "A Liberal Defence of (Some) Duties to Compatriots," *Journal of Applied Philosophy* 27, no. 3 (2010), 246–57.

of the kind of liberal justification of just war I am proposing. It hardly seems right that a group of people could kill others in defense of a collective that they do not care about. Again, this gives greater credence to my just war theory here built on the defense of autonomy. It is worth again thinking of the Ukrainians defending their country against Russian in 2022, and their clear deep commitments to it, to some other group defending a country about which they simply do not care. One would appear justified; the other is dubious, at best.

I should stress just how modest a claim I am here making for a liberal response to the puzzle. I'm trying to explain the conditions for how liberalism *could* give an account of the Defense Intuition for Bravo. To determine whatever this actually justifies in the real-world we'd have to see if these conditions are met. And, as just explained, this kind of defense won't apply to those states that don't properly value their collective civic project. And, again, this is not a problem for the structure for a new liberal theory of just war that I am sketching here. That is, it's no objection to my account to say that if a sufficient number of people do not care about the value of their own self-rule, then a state cannot be justly defended from conditional, benevolent aggression. Rather, we should *expect* this: that liberalism would find that a given group of people's weak preference for their state can, at times, not be enough to justify bloody defense of it, is an overall normative gain. After all, otherwise it could be hard to explain why the defense of Charlie is impermissible, as was discussed in chapter 6.

7.6. The Assimilation Objection and Group Decision Thresholds

There is a rather important objection one could give to my argument for grounding the Defense Intuition in the harm Alpha's aggression does to the individual autonomy of Bravonians. I call it the Assimilation Objection and it runs as follows. The Bravonians do not have a right to violent defense against Alpha's aggression because, even if the aggression harms the individual autonomy of Bravonians via thwarting their group project of collective governance, the harm is only temporary. For once, the Bravonians are properly assimilated into Alpha's polity, they could then resume a group project of collective governance that could equally well provide the needed value to their individual autonomy. In other words, this objection contends that the joint option of their collective self-governance is not a vital option, in fact, because it is fungible; participating in the polity of a new Alpha–Bravo combined state could deliver the same goods to their individual autonomy. A related worry is that we are justifying violent defense on the basis of the Bravonians' *mere* subjective preference—and this may seem to be too weak of a basis to justify war. I will try to respond to both worries together.

There are several responses here that I think adequately can handle the Assimilation Objection, most of which has already been discussed above. As argued for in section 7.2, the idea is that making one's decision properly their own imbues it with a certain value that is a necessary component for a good life on this liberal view. And, similarly, Wall's discussion of how particular commitments for an individual need to be worthwhile *in their eyes*, helps show the importance of Bravo's preference for their own rule and why it could be reasonable for them to not accept the new polity of an Alpha-Bravo state. I'll return to this point in a moment, but one other mitigation of the worry can be found in a distinction here between that of an autonomous life in the above sense as a kind of *achievement* and that of a kind of capacity for living autonomously. The worry is that by thwarting certain group projects of individuals, the harm may not only be thwarting that particular achievement of an autonomous act but that the harm may be thwarting their capacity for autonomy itself. This could be a concern for Bravo simply surrendering to and assimilating with Alpha. The people of Bravo may have their capacity for autonomous action harmed such that they would not be able to fully participate in the polity of the new Alpha-Bravo state since they may never take it to be properly their own.

But what of the worry over mere preference being the grounds for such value that it is worth killing over? Well, although I will not give it proper attention here, a full defense of the peculiarly special value of individual autonomy suggests that mere subjective preference does indeed matter. And this need not be, note, an entirely anti-perfectionist view. That is, granting that personal preference does have an impact on our evaluation of valuable goods to an individual, this does not mean that we must be entirely neutral on the relative worthiness of possible pursuits chosen by individuals. And even on liberal perfectionist models, within a range of valuably good choices for pursuing a good life, there can still be some important weight given to the fact a particular worthy option, amongst other worthy options, was the one a given individual chose. Imagine two equally good pursuits an individual, Mary, could take to develop a good life, X or Y. Mary chooses Y. Saying that from that point forward Y is imbued with more value to Mary, and thereby her choice of Y should be particularly respected, does not seem implausible even if her choice for Y over X ultimately comes down to nothing more than "mere preference."

This is admittedly a strange seeming power that mere subjective preference apparently holds. Wall foresees the persistence of this worry in his discussion of vital options.[83] The concern is that the subjective element of vital options—that one must have access to a sufficient range of worthwhile options and to options that one *sees* as worthwhile—leaves the account too weak and too wide-open to justify the value vital options are supposed to impart. As Wall writes, "The subjective condition ... looks too undiscriminating."[84] And this particularly seems true if we are to rest so much importance on this option as essential to the Bravonians' possibility of pursuing an autonomously good life. Why should their mere subjective preference here carry as much weight as it does? What if a group of people came to orient themselves and their commitments in the right way such that, for them, the ability to pursue the joint option of ritual sacrifice of others was to become a vital option? Or what if a person was so invested and committed to watching lead paint dry that the option to them became vital—that they could not conceive of their life as autonomous without pursuing this option? If a governing authority blocked the group from sacrificing innocent people or outlawed lead paint, would this be an unjust infringement on that group or that individual's autonomy?

Some important responses are in order. First, remember, vital options must be worthwhile pursuits to begin with. This qualifier itself will help to negate much of the subjective worry as well as, of course, the paint drying case and the ritual sacrifice case. Wall also adds a reasonableness condition for vital options.[85] The thought would be that pursuing a joint option of ritual sacrifice is simply not a reasonable option to have access to, given our present society. (Wall discusses this for someone who desperately wishes to live the lifestyle of a Viking. That may have been a reasonably accessible option at one time for a certain people group; but it is no longer.)[86] It is also important to note that a vital option must be nonfungible—that is, that another equally meaningful option cannot be easily substituted for it.[87] In the

---

[83] Wall, "Collective Rights and Individual Autonomy," 256.
[84] Ibid., 256.
[85] Ibid., 257.
[86] Ibid.
[87] Ibid.

lead-paint-drying-watcher case, presumably, one could watch paint *without* lead in it dry and fulfill the same basic goal. But perhaps not—perhaps the way in which only lead paint dries has a special importance to this individual. That's not a problem for the vital options account because an individual's *belief* that a certain option is for them a vital option is defeasible. That is, people can be *mistaken* about what they think are vital options for them to have an adequate range of options.

And, at any rate, the Bravonians' desire to autonomously govern themselves seems reasonable to have access to in this imaginary society—they've already been doing it for several generations. It also seems nonfungible in the proper way that vital options should be. If what is supremely important to them is ruling themselves, then this cannot possibly be replaced by another's rule. And this will be true even if, as argued for in the Assimilation Objection, the Bravonians become participants in that new ruling polity. It might be some form of self-rule they would then participate in, but it would not be *theirs*. And the most important condition on vital options—that an option is worthwhile to pursue—certainly seems met if the notions of self-determination, democracy, and the majority of contemporary political philosophy is to have any validity. That is, whatever else it may be, the desire to participate in a joint option to autonomously govern one's own polity certainly seems worthwhile.

Note as well, we can counter most of the weight of the Assimilation Objection by combining Wall's defense of these aspects of vital options with Raz's independence condition for autonomy, as I do for my account, above. Combined, it makes it clear that it is still for the Bravonians to decide how they wish to execute their self-rule. Note this leaves ample room for a scenario where the Bravonians would so choose to shift their collective project to a shared one with the Alphonians. But in the puzzle, this is not the case and not their wish. Hence, the Defense Intuition stands, even in light of the Assimilation Objection.

This further shows why we would rightly reject a Defense Intuition for the state Charlie, considered above in chapter 6. If a group of individuals were committed to the joint option of maintaining Charlie's sovereignty such that they viewed it as a vital option for themselves, they would simply be mistaken. The reason is because the maintenance and continuation of Charlie, in it not even being "minimally just" in the ways reviewed above, is not a worthwhile pursuit. Now, perhaps if Charlie could be radically reformed, the despots removed from power, and the autonomous governance of it returned to the people of Charlie, then such a pursuit could properly be a vital option worth defending. But, as it stands, a defense of Charlie would be a defense of a genocidal, evil regime—a project most clearly not morally worthwhile. And, therefore, it is not a viable candidate as a vital option. Such musing raises interesting historical cases that could potentially fit the bill. Imagine those committed Baathists defending Saddam Hussein's rule of Iraq. Setting aside entirely the just or unjustness of the United States invasion in 2003, it seems a group deeply committed to killing to maintain Hussein's Iraq "project" would be mistaken—such a thing is not properly worthy of defense. (Whether or not that justifies invading it and bringing the horrors of war upon it, is another matter.)

One further area I have not adequately addressed is the process by which the Bravonians come to their decision to resist Alpha's aggression. Depending on how that process works out, and where the thresholds fall within that decision, this could become grounds for a very difficult objection to the kind of account I am proposing. For example, it seems that the numbers do indeed matter for how our conclusions run on the Defense Intuition, in terms of just what percentage of Bravonians want to surrender to Alpha opposed to those who wish to fight and how their decision procedures work. To keep it initially simple, I assumed that all Bravonians wish to fight. But what if it were a roughly democratic system with some kind of agreed-upon group decision-making procedures in place and that, after (say) a referendum of some kind, 95% of the Bravonians wanted to fight. Immediately, we worry about the rights of those 5%. If we press this and move it to 10% in the minority who wish to surrender, or 15%, or 45% and so forth the concern grows.[88] The concern, explicitly, is that those who wish to surrender to Alpha probably wish to do so precisely for the reason of advancing their own exercise of autonomy. And let us complicate things by suggesting (plausibly) that those who wish to surrender are not committed to the polity of Bravo in the ways necessary for its self-governance to be a vital option to them. For them, the decision to fight Alpha is all loss, since the collective self-rule of Bravo is entirely a supplemental option for their exercise of autonomy. Whereas surrender to Alpha promises to garner them a world that better enables other options they wish to autonomously pursue.

---

[88] Many thanks to Michael Hart for helpful discussion on this point and for offering the resolution I suggest. Thanks as well to Steve Wall for a helpful discussion of the importance (and difficulty) of thresholds for such group decisions.

It gets more complicated when we recognize that some will hold that the minority voters who wish to surrender are actually acting, some would argue, more rationally in this case. Of course, given what I've said above about the peculiar value that autonomy holds and, thereby, the particular importance certain group projects can take on if they enable certain aspects of individual autonomy that are particularly valued, this *need* not be true. It may not be a matter of the majority acting irrationally, but of them simply placing higher value on that value conferred by the group project as it affects their own individual autonomy. In that case, what is a liberal just war theory to say? It still seems that the minority voters have a legitimate claim. By not surrendering, their future prospects of autonomous exercise are hindered, given their detachment from the project of Bravo. Of course, much of this here is being driven by the fact that Alpha is acting altruistically and will deliver these goods. In real world cases, of course, the aggressor will usually not be benevolent and likely will impose malevolent harms. We can imagine that a minority of Ukrainians who do not wish to resist the 2022 Russian aggression as, perhaps, an example of the above group of Bravonians. But, again, in this instance the parallel does not hold because Russia is far from the altruistically intended Alpha.

Note that in my view the right solution for those Ukrainians who wish to live under Russian rule is to allow them to freely leave the territorial boundaries of Ukraine and go live in Russia. The right response to their minority view is *not* to allow those regions of Ukraine, where this sentiment is larger, to be ceded to Russia, such as the annexation of Crimea and attempted usurping of the Donbass region. The reason is because of the way in which taking over these areas still constitutes the same harm to the Ukrainians' overall project and warrants defense of it. I heard it put well to those who hold that Ukraine should simply allow Russia to have those and other regions, we can ask, "Which part of your country would you be willing to give up to Putin against your country's will?" Or, if we return to Todd and Strengthened Benevolent Mugger, perhaps we ask, "Which part of your life would you be willing to allow the mugger to direct?" The answer in both cases is, of course, none.

Returning to the puzzle, imagine it is 60% of Bravonians who are in favor of fighting—and assume they wish to fight for the right, liberal reasons laid out above: the protection of their individual autonomy as expressed through the group project of self-governance. And imagine the 40% who wish to surrender hold that view for distinctively liberal reasons. That is, they do not value the present self-governance of Bravo as an extension of their autonomy (its preservation and continued self-governance is not for them a vital option, but only a supplementary one). Rather, they wish to expand their capacities and options for an autonomously led good life by surrendering to the benign governance of Alpha; and perhaps even they wish to participate in the more functional political process of Alpha's polity.

Now it may appear that my account has a real problem. But recall, on my account, the fact that a liberal justification for the Defense Intuition does not always obtain is a feature, not a bug of the theory. That is, unless people properly value the joint project of their state in the right way, then violent defense of it does not obtain on autonomy value grounds. The question then becomes this: what is the required threshold of people within a group such that the liberal demand for defense is met? This is a difficult question. It is made more difficult by the fact that, within any society, the pay-outs various joint options deliver to different individuals' autonomy will be different depending on those individuals' subjective preference (or not) of said options.

This is a serious challenge to the kind of account I'm proposing, and I do not have a full solution to it here. And I also note that *any* theory of just war will usually have similar threshold problems. But here's one possible resolution, or at least mitigation, that a liberal theory could offer in such a case that could still preserve the Defense Intuition for Bravo at large. What if Bravo decided that those in the minority who wished to surrender to Alpha's aggression and subsequent rule should be allowed to leave Bravo and move to Alpha (or somewhere else), as suggest above in the real-world case of Ukraine? And, since simply the right to move between states is often not enough to realistically give people much of a choice, the minority voters could even be monetarily subsidized and compensated for their move, as is necessary for each individual, so as to make moving to Alpha a real, autonomy-preserving, option. Such an act by Bravo to its fellow citizens would seem to then still grant them the permissibility (for those who choose to remain) to violently defend against Alpha.

This is one possible resolution, but what if there were no such option? What if, for whatever reason, Alpha did not want to allow the refugees? (This would be strange, of course, given Alpha's intentions in all of this.) In such a case, we'd have a more difficult problem. But the difficulty of how to justly mediate such seemingly irresolvable conflicts between differing sub-groups within a given polity is nothing new for liberalism. And, perhaps then, it should not be surprising that many of the perennially vexing challenges that face liberalism at large, will also befall any attempt at a distinctively liberal just war theory.

7.7. Summary Comments on Liberal Just War

I have not here given anything close to a complete account of a new liberal theory for just war. What I have done is the following. I have tried to sketch how a distinctively liberal justification for the Defense Intuition could plausibly work. By distinctively liberal, I have meant those accounts of liberalism that take individual autonomy as an especially important and valuable component of any conception of a good life. Thus, my aim has been to chart out *how* a new liberal theory of just war could be built upon the value of individual autonomy without reliance on a value assigned to the state itself. To do this, I've argued that the value of collective self-rule for a group can rest in terms of its contribution to the individual autonomy of its members. If the members of a group value their collective self-rule in the right ways, it can be taken by them as a vital option, needed for an adequate range of options, for the full exercising of their individual autonomy. Thus, because of the high importance liberalism places on individual autonomy, violent defense against its infringement can be warranted. In this case, individual Bravonians can permissibly defend Bravo against Alpha's invasion because (and if) they hold their collective self-rule to be a vital option to their individual autonomy. I've argued that liberalism, then, with its commitment to the value of individual autonomy, is not only able to support such a moral theory of just war, but it is particularly well suited to do so. This serves as a partial response to Rodin's challenge that collective national defense cannot be grounded on individual self-defense. *Contra* Rodin, I have shown that a reductive approach can work, if the individual members of a certain group take their group project of self-governance to be particularly valuable to their own autonomy.

Recall that one upshot of resolving the puzzle of Alpha's aggression is that if a distinctly liberal case can be made for defense here in this case (where all the harm perpetrated by war against the aggressed-upon state have been stripped away and only the violation of their collective self-rule remains), then, presumably, it will be much easier to make a liberal case for defensive war against unjust aggression in real-world cases, where the aggressor state is not nearly so altruistic in its intentions as Alpha. Speaking of real-world cases, I'll note briefly that I did not intend the puzzle of Alpha's aggression to be symbolic of nor a thinly veiled analogy for the United States 2003 invasion and subsequent war in Iraq or other recent contemporary wars, such as the humanitarian interventions in Kosovo, or perhaps NATO's 2011 involvement in Libya. Compare these cases to the recent Russia–Ukraine war, and things are much clearer. There is no confusing Russia with Alpha, for there is surely no benevolent aggression here. However, the Ukrainians do seem to represent the kind of people who are properly committed to their self-governance and independence project such that their defense is justified, and even noble. But, in working on this case over the past several years, many have taken the puzzle to be possibly reflective of the United States war in Iraq in particular, so I should explain why this case fails as a relevant real-world example of the moral structure I am trying to chart here.

To begin with, the intentions of the United States in its invasion of Iraq were hardly as altruistic as Alpha's, even on the most charitable interpretation possible. Second, it's highly dubious whether Iraq itself would have met the threshold for "minimally just" that Bravo does, as discussed above in considering those Iraqis committed to defending Iraq. Iraq under Saddam Hussein seems closer in form to Charlie. Iraq's ruling government certainly did not represent the will or intentions of the people of Iraq, so it can hardly be claimed that they were engaged in a project of autonomous collective self-rule that served as a vital option to the exercise of individual Iraqi's autonomy. So, I think the kind of liberal case for just war, I have sketched here, will be of no help to either side in the war in Iraq. It seems to me that both sides of this conflict did not have proper justification to wage war.

On the defending side, the kind of liberal just war theory offered here would provide no help in justifying the Iraqis' fighting in defense of Iraq for the reasons just given: defense of Iraq would not be defending a worthwhile exercise of an individual Iraqi's autonomy through the joint option of self-rule (for that was not occurring). And the United States did not have just cause for the invasion and failed to meet the traditional *jus ad bellum* demands of classic just war theory. This is primarily because the claimed *casus belli* did not even exist (weapons of mass destruction), and, even if they had existed, the mere existence of a weapon possessed by one's strategic enemy does not give one proper, much less sufficient, moral justification for preemptively attacking them. That is, I find the arguments for pre-emptive war to be highly implausible in this case.

The parallel to an individual case of self-defense would be that an enemy of yours has a particularly powerful gun (or you think he does), and you are worried he may try to use it on you. On a Rights-Based Account of individual self-defense cases (as reviewed in chapter 1), the enemy is not liable to defensive harm from you until that harm is shown to be necessary to block his unjust threat of harm. But merely possessing a powerful weapon with the possible but unknown intent to use it does not meet this necessity threshold.[89] And even if intent *was* known, even then, one would have to be blocking an actual threat that was clearly imminent—if not already underway—not merely a predicted one.[90] Note that because of the harm done in war to individual autonomy on both sides of any conflict, the required threshold for just cause would be incredibly high under a new liberal theory of just war. (In this chapter, however, I have not engaged in whether or not, for example, Alpha's invasion was justified or not. That's an entirely different question wholly unaddressed in my work here.)

It is an open question whether the reasons of autonomy exhaust the value of collective self-rule.[91] My hunch is that it does not and that there are other important goods that collective self-rule delivers to those who participate in it. And perhaps those goods are important enough that they can justify violent defense of them. But, even if that is true, I think the high value conferred to individual autonomy by collective self-rule *can be* such that a liberal case for its defense can be built solely on autonomy grounds, as I've attempted to show here. If other values found in collective self-rule can also be grounds for legitimate defense, then that simply means there will be many cases—perhaps including the case of Alpha's invasion—where the Defense Intuition is over-determined.

---

[89] I go into much more detail on liability works in such cases where intent is unknown in the previous chapters, particularly chapter 1.

[90] Consider the real-world case of Israel and Egypt's "Six Day War" in 1967. In that case, Egyptian tanks, fully loaded and armed, were headed in full formation towards the Israeli border at top speed. The Egyptians moved all seven of their army divisions to the Sinai and were marching towards the border. In all, Egypt moved 100,000 of its 160,000 troops directly towards Israel. This all occurred following a long and simmering diplomatic crisis between the two states in which talks had broken down. As the tanks and troops were headed for Israel in what appeared to be a combat operation against them, the Israelis attacked. Technically, when they attacked, the Egyptians had not yet crossed into Israeli territory. But if ever there were a case of an imminent threat that justified a pre-emptive military strike, this was it. My point in describing it is to compare that case to the incredibly paltry "imminent threat" that was assigned by the United States to Iraq. In the Iraq case, the "imminent threat" was worry that Iraq may have a particular weapon which they may want to use on us or our allies. That hardly constitutes imminence. Thus, I remain neutral on whether a war of defensive pre-emption can *ever* be justified—if it can, perhaps the Israeli initial attack in the Six Day War could plausibly claim such a justification. But the United States invasion of Iraq cannot plausibly make such a claim. See Walzer, *Just & Unjust Wars*, 80, for a discussion of the Six Day War and pre-emptive strikes.

[91] Wall notes that he is explicitly not arguing that autonomy exhausts its value in "Collective Rights and Individual Autonomy," 245, n. 34.

8
Conclusion
Answering Calvin

"Soldiers—don't give yourselves to brutes, men who despise you and enslave you—who regiment your lives, tell you what to do, what to think and what to feel, who drill you, diet you, treat you as cattle, as cannon fodder. Don't give yourselves to these unnatural men, machine men, with machine minds and machine hearts. You are not machines. You are not cattle. You are men. You have the love of humanity in your hearts. You don't hate—only the unloved hate. Only the unloved and the unnatural. Soldiers—don't fight for slavery, fight for liberty."

—from Charlie Chaplin's speech in "The Great Dictator" (1940)

What then of Calvin's question with which this book began? Calvin, recall, asks his father, "How do soldiers killing each other solve the world's problems?" The long argument made in this book gives us a tentative answer to Calvin. Indeed, walking through the parts of my answer to Calvin here effectively reviews, step-by-step, what I have tried to do in this book. As such, it is a fitting, if overly simplified, way to conclude. I have previewed this answer to Calvin throughout the book with the various quotes placed at the beginning of every chapter. In my explanation here, I hope they will have some further resonance.

Our first response to Calvin is that soldiers killing each other usually does not solve the world's problems. Full stop. Indeed, the forlorn truth is that rather than solving our problems, soldiers killing each other more often than not simply leads to more and greater problems. Aristotle told us that "we make war that we may have peace."[1] This venerable bedrock of just war theory is a noble notion, perhaps. But in reality, it is far more often the case that, as Martin Luther King,

---

[1] Aristotle, *Nicomachean Ethics*, Book X.7

Jr. reminds us, "wars are poor chisels for carving peaceful tomorrows."[2] Indeed, given the strictures on morally permissible killing more generally, nearly all intentional killing is most often unjustified and wrong. In that regard, when soldiers kill one another, this is usually no different. However, there are times and contexts when it can be permissible for one to intentionally kill another human. These are times when someone is morally responsible for attempting to do something seriously wrong and unjust to others, and we can only stop them by killing them. That is, when it is necessary to kill as the only means to stop the wrong; not born out of any desire to kill. As Saint Augustine counseled General Boniface in antiquity, it should be "necessity, therefore, and not your will, [which] slays the enemy who fights against you."[3] And, importantly, the thing they are doing is wrong *enough* that it is proportionate to kill them in order to stop them. In these kinds of cases, we are not wronging the person we kill—we are not violating his or her rights—for we are not killing them unjustly.

But what does it mean to say someone is morally responsible for the wrongful thing we are attempting to stop? In this book, I've argued that the person needs to have good evidence available to them such that they could know what they are doing is wrong. Otherwise, they are just as morally nonresponsible for the impending wrong as we are, and it would be wrong for us to hold them morally responsible for it just because they were at the wrong place at the wrong time. In other words, they need to know—or at least, critically, *be able* to know—that what they are doing is wrong. But, of course, if someone does have available evidence to them, and fails to attend to it properly and thereby comes to the wrong belief, that false belief does not get them off the hook. As Dan Gelber asked regarding the infamous Travyon Martin case in 2012, "At what point is someone precluded from availing themselves of the justification of self-defense because of their own poor judgment?"[4] My evidence-relative account of liability attribution attempts to answer the nuances of this question and the many others that come with epistemic issues surrounding justified violence.

So, given that there can be cases like the above—where one is justified to kill another to avert a grave wrong—we next explain to Calvin that there are also times when whole groups of people work together to do something seriously wrong and unjust to others, and these people can be morally responsible for that

---

[2] From Martin Luther King, Jr.'s speech, "The Casualties of the War in Vietnam," February 25, 1967, The Nation Institute, Los Angeles.
[3] From Augustine's letter 189 to Saint Boniface (418).
[4] Dan Gelber, "Florida Defense Law Change Encourages Recklessness," *Sun Sentinel* (July 17, 2013), https://www.sun-sentinel.com/opinion/fl-xpm-2013-07-17-fl-dgcol-zimmerman-trayvon-oped0717-20130717-story.html.

impending injustice. In those cases, it can similarly be morally justified to kill these people, if we must, in order to stop the injustice, and if the injustice itself is bad enough to warrant killing. However, even then—when whole groups are killing another—we must strive to only harm those when it is absolutely necessary to stop the injustice, and only those who really are morally responsible for it, if we possibly can so distinguish them. Trying to do this will significantly change many of the ways we have traditionally thought of as waging war. Not all soldiers are fair game; and not all civilians may have complete immunity.

The kinds of things that can be wrong enough to fight and kill whole groups of people over will vary, but they will, admittedly, likely be different than the kinds of wrongs we hope to avert in usual self-defense cases. Indeed, this poses a problem for us in extending the justification from individual self-defense cases to large groups in an overly simplistic, direct way. And that is because the majority of wars are conditional in nature—if one side simply surrenders, there will be no bloodshed. But, on inspection, it turns out there will actually be such cases where the right of self-defense does so extend—and not simply to cases of war carried out for genocidal purposes. For example, if one group of people wants to stop another group from living how they want to live—to take over their control of their lives and the projects they want to pursue—this could be enough of a wrong to justify defending against it with force; even deadly force on a large scale, at least in some cases.

In such a case, soldiers defending their group's freedom to live as they wish against the wishes of another group, could very well be "solving the world's problems"—or, more accurately, preventing a tremendous moral "problem" from occurring. I should also make clear to Calvin that even in these rare cases, it is not the soldiers killing one another *itself* that "solves the world's problems," of course. That is, in any given war, at most one side is justified in killing the other. And even then, the killing itself is a regretful necessity; not something ever good in of itself. What *is* good is the preventing of the great wrong that would otherwise come about if they were not killed. We don't find any moral good in the acts of war themselves, but rather the good intrinsic in what war aims to protect. All violence which is morally permissible must be instrumentally pointed toward some good in this way, and that good is always the only good to be sought after in war. This is captured beautifully by J. R. R. Tolkien when, in the *Lord of the Rings*, the great and noble warrior Faramir speaks mournfully to Frodo about his efforts to defend Gondor from the forces of Sauron. Faramir recounts, "War must be, while we defend our lives against a destroyer who would devour all; but I do not love the bright sword for its sharpness, nor the arrow for its swiftness, nor the warrior for his glory. I love only that which they defend."[5]

But in many other cases—if not the strong majority of cases—two soldiers killing one another is simply a Tragedy. As explained in this book, by labeling it a Tragedy I mean that there often are cases where soldiers are killing one another and, indeed, it does not "solve any of the world's problems," and—perhaps worst of all—the soldiers on both sides do not even know that they are wrong to wage war. In these cases, like so many others in everyday life, people killing each other only brings about horrible amounts of pain, destruction, and suffering into this world. Too often wars are simply not worth fighting, and should not be fought, for neither side has a grievance grave enough for which it is necessary to kill whole scores of our fellow human beings. Given that the vast majority of wars are like this it is easy to become cynical about the very notion of wars ever being justifiable, much less something that "solves the world's problems." And yet, so often, history does not even question the moral permissibility of soldiers killing one another. Far too many of us simply think, uncritically, that killing in war is somehow fundamentally different than everyday murder. Voltaire rightly mocks such thinking when he writes, "It is forbidden to kill; therefore all murderers are punished unless they kill in large numbers and to the sound of trumpets."[6] Voltaire's cynicism is more than understandable. It should infuriate all who think carefully upon it but, as I've argued for in this book, the moral truth is that every unjustified and unnecessary killing of a human being is a grave and tragic wrong; be it a person walking down Main Street or a soldier on the battlefield of war.

This heartbreaking reality of war is poignantly captured in a song by the band Dispatch called "The General." The story in the song recounts a commanding general who, on the eve before a great battle, sees the enemy's soldiers in a dream. He then realizes that they are all—his own soldiers and the enemy's—tragic figures, killing one another unnecessarily, and he sends his troops home. "He said: I have seen the others, and I have discovered that this fight is not worth fighting. I have seen their mothers and I will no other to follow me where I'm going."[7] This is usually what war gives us. And this is usually what killing in any context brings us, be it in war between soldiers, or between two people on Main Street. Despite this, however, it is true that there

---

[5] J. R. R. Tolkien, *The Lord of the Rings: The Two Towers* (Mariner Books, 1955).
[6] Francois Voltaire, *Philosophical Dictionary*. Translated by Theodore Besterman, 34. (New York: Penguin Books, 2004, originally published 1764).
[7] From the song "The General" by Dispatch.

still *can* also be cases, both on Main Street and on the battlefield, where killing does solve the world's problems. There can be cases where killing preserves a great good against a great evil. War is so rarely like this that we may have trouble envisioning this with our moral imagination. But I have attempted to show how a war fought for the right reasons could do precisely this.

I admit that my liberal account of just war given in this book may sound bizarre to some, particularly given my grounding it so centrally on the notion of defending individual autonomy and freedom. But I find that its liberal roots actually run quite deep. To understand the ultimate taking of liberty— the taking of life—we must understand liberty itself. Consider this classic passage from John Stuart Mill, for example, discussed above.

> When a people are used as mere human instruments for firing cannon or thrusting bayonets, in the service and for the selfish purposes of a master, such war degrades a people. A war to protect other human beings against tyrannical injustice; *a war to give victory to their own ideas of right and good, and which is their own war, carried on for an honest purpose by their free choice,—is often the means of their regeneration.* . . . . As long as justice and injustice have not terminated their ever-renewing fight for ascendancy in the affairs of mankind, human beings must be willing, when need is, to do battle for the one against the other.[8]

As should be clear, Mill's argument here dovetails beautifully with the autonomy-based liberal just war theory I offered above in chapters 6 and 7. Interestingly, it is a different passage from Mill here that is most often cited in discussions on war. Immediately preceding the quoted passage above, Mill gives his famous line that "War is an ugly thing, but not the ugliest of things."[9] And surely Mill is right that there are, perhaps, even more heinous evils in the world, and such a line of thinking follows naturally from his Utilitarianism. But that alone does not get us the moral understanding of war that I believe we need. It is not enough to simply say that war is terrible but that there are worse things that can justify it. Rather, as I've tried to offer in this book, we need a positive, rights respecting account of permissible violence—violence that does not violate the rights of another as a

---

[8] John Stuart Mill, "The Contest in America," *Fraser's Magazine* (February 1862); later published in *Dissertations and Discussions* (1868), vol.1, p. 26.

[9] I was instructed to memorize the "not the ugliest of things" Mill quote in basic training at the US Air Force Academy in the summer of 1997. I often wonder if we are having our soldiers memorize the wrong Mill quote.

CONCLUSION 271

lesser-evil option, but rather does right in protecting the normative values we hold most dear. And that, or so I have argued, is precisely what a properly liberal just war theory delivers: "*a war to give victory to their own ideas of right and good, and which is their own war, carried on for an honest purpose by their free choice.*" One sees here in Mill that "a war to protect other human beings against tyrannical injustice" could also end up being very close, indeed, to the same thing as a war to "give victory to their own ideas of right and good." That is, both kinds of wars he mentions are to protect human beings against tyrannical injustice—whether that injustice is wrought against themselves and their own autonomy or against the liberty of others.

So, what do we say to Calvin and to those soldiers for whom he beseeches some kind of rational explanation for their killing? One could do worse than to recount the words delivered by Charlie Chaplin at the conclusion of his satirical masterpiece film, "The Great Dictator." The film was released in 1940 and ruthlessly mocks Hitler and Nazi fascism. In its final scene, the hero of the film, who happens to be an identical twin of the Hitler-parody dictator, is mistaken for the leader and pressured to make a speech to the huge crowds assembled. He takes the stage and speaks out to all people. To soldiers in particular, he makes an enduring appeal.[10] Chaplin does not call for a naïve pacifism nor a cynical resignation of the horrors of war, though either response would perhaps be understandable. Nor does he fall victim to that common mistake that soldiers' lives, and the killing they carry out in war, are somehow less worthy of our moral concern and critical engagement than any other killing. Rather just the opposite: Chaplin appeals directly to the humanity of soldiers on all sides of any war and begs of them to fight. But not to fight uncritically for those who would treat them as mere cannon fodder, but rather to unite and fight for what is right and good; indeed, to *fight* for the liberty of all people and of themselves. My hope is that this book carries along in that same tradition of Chaplin here. I am not a pacifist. War is absolute horror, it is true. And yet war can, in times of utter necessity, be justified. As many have expressed in countless ways, war is *always* a failure of some kind and a failing of us all.[11] And Chaplin, perhaps the greatest comedian who ever lived, not only understood these realities of war, but he gave them the weight and seriousness they deserve. And in the conclusion to that film, he does not give into gimmicks or anything other than impassioned argumentation. (If you have not actually watched and listened to Chaplin give

---

[10] And, in the end, I wrote this book for soldiers.
[11] Pope Francis, in September 2013, said to gatherers, "War always marks the failure of peace, it is always a defeat for humanity." See "Pope Francis: War is Always a Defeat for Humanity," *Diocese*

this speech at the end of "The Great Dictator," you must. His earnest sincerity is hard to capture in print. Watching it and remembering the time in which it was filmed and released makes it all the more compelling and gripping.) So, I hope I can follow in his same spirit here. Indeed, the themes of this book are peppered throughout that final speech from "The Great Dictator" and it is as fitting a conclusion as any I can think to offer for this book. I quote it here in full and hope that in it perhaps Calvin can find some answers. One can almost hear Chaplin speaking not only to Calvin's question inside each of us when it comes to war, but directly to those soldiers who bear the heavy burden of carrying it out. Men like Timothy Kudo and Lt. Col. Astakhov Dmitry Mikhailovich. I hope they, and the world, can hear him. His words are as true today as they were in 1940.

> I'm sorry, but I don't want to be an emperor. That's not my business. I don't want to rule or conquer anyone. I should like to help everyone—if possible—Jew, Gentile—black man—white. We all want to help one another. Human beings are like that. We want to live by each other's happiness—not by each other's misery. We don't want to hate and despise one another. In this world there is room for everyone. And the good earth is rich and can provide for everyone. The way of life can be free and beautiful, but we have lost the way.
>
> Greed has poisoned men's souls, has barricaded the world with hate, has goose-stepped us into misery and bloodshed. We have developed speed, but we have shut ourselves in. Machinery that gives abundance has left us in want. Our knowledge has made us cynical. Our cleverness, hard and unkind. We think too much and feel too little. More than machinery we need humanity. More than cleverness we need kindness and gentleness. Without these qualities, life will be violent and all will be lost....
>
> The aeroplane and the radio have brought us closer together. The very nature of these inventions cries out for the goodness in men—cries out for universal brotherhood—for the unity of us all. Even now my voice is reaching millions throughout the world—millions of despairing men, women, and little children—victims of a system that makes men torture and imprison innocent people.

of Corpus Christi (September 9, 2013), https://diocesecc.org/news/pope-francis-war-is-always-a-defeat-for-humanity. His lines have similarity to those of Martin Firrell, a noted artist and peace activist. Firrell has used the phrase "War is Failure" as the centerpiece of much public art.

To those who can hear me, I say—do not despair. The misery that is now upon us is but the passing of greed—the bitterness of men who fear the way of human progress. The hate of men will pass, and dictators die, and the power they took from the people will return to the people. And so long as men die, liberty will never perish. .....

Soldiers! Don't give yourselves to brutes—men who despise you—enslave you—who regiment your lives—tell you what to do—what to think and what to feel! Who drill you—diet you—treat you like cattle, use you as cannon fodder. Don't give yourselves to these unnatural men—machine men with machine minds and machine hearts! You are not machines! You are not cattle! You are men! You have the love of humanity in your hearts! You don't hate! Only the unloved hate—the unloved and the unnatural!

Soldiers! Don't fight for slavery! *Fight for liberty!*

In the 17th Chapter of Saint Luke it is written: "the Kingdom of God is within man"—not one man nor a group of men, but in all men! In you! You, the people have the power—the power to create machines. The power to create happiness! You, the people, have the power to make this life free and beautiful, to make this life a wonderful adventure.

Then—in the name of democracy—let us use that power—let us all unite. Let us fight for a new world—a decent world that will give men a chance to work—that will give youth a future and old age a security. By the promise of these things, brutes have risen to power. But they lie! They do not fulfil that promise. They never will!

Dictators free themselves but they enslave the people! Now let us fight to fulfil that promise! Let us fight to free the world—to do away with national barriers—to do away with greed, with hate and intolerance. Let us fight for a world of reason, a world where science and progress will lead to all men's happiness. Soldiers! In the name of democracy, let us all unite![12]

---

[12] Charlie Chaplin, *The Great Dictator*, 1940.

APPENDIX

List of Cases in Order of Appearance

A.1 Bystander on Bridge

Victim is being chased by Hitman who is trying to kill her unjustly. Victim comes to a narrow bridge, which is the only means of escape from Hitman. The bridge is blocked by Bystander who is sitting on the bridge. The only way for Victim to escape Hitman would be to knock Bystander off the bridge, thereby killing him.

A.1.1 Mafia Boss on Bridge

Victim is in the same unfortunate scenario as *Bystander on Bridge*, except that instead of Bystander blocking the way she comes across Mafia Boss sitting on the bridge. Victim knows that Mafia Boss hired Hitman to kill her unjustly.

A.2 Defender and Attacker

Defender is sitting on a park bench reading Tolstoy. She is in no way threatening harm, nor contributing to a threat of harm, nor responsible for a threat of harm, toward anyone. Attacker hates people who read Tolstoy. He charges Defender with the intent to kill her with a large sword he is swinging toward her head. Defender happens to find a small hand-gun sitting nearby, however, and she quickly shoots Attacker before his sword swings down upon her.

A.2.1 Prisoner Decision

You and I have been captured by evil terrorists who tell us that they will kill only one of us and let the other go, but they tell me that I have to decide which one of us they kill.

A.3 Falling Man

Through no moral fault of hers, Trapped finds herself at the bottom of a deep hole. Through no moral fault of his, Falling Man is thrown down the hole. Falling Man will crush and thereby kill Trapped, but she will break his fall and he will live. Trapped however, has a trusty ray-gun and could disintegrate Falling Man's body before he crushes her.

A.4 Bystander Sheila

A villain throws a javelin at Tom. Tom can save his life only by grabbing nearby woman, Sheila, and using her as a human shield, placing her body between himself and incoming javelin.

A.5 Prisoner Unintentional Decision

You and I have been captured by evil terrorists who have decided that that they will kill only one of us and let the other go. They will decide which one of us to kill by carefully watching me. If I scratch my head with my right hand, they will kill you. If I scratch my head with my left hand, they will kill me. They have not informed of any of this information—I am in the dark. But they inform you of all of this. But you are gagged and have no way of informing me.

A.6 Dignitary and Guest

Guest extends his hand to shake the hand of foreign Dignitary at a reception. Unbeknown to Guest, a third party projects a stunningly realistic holographic image of a pistol onto Guest's hand. Dignitary, who is accustomed to threats on her life, sees the hologram, forms the justified belief that Guest is about to assassinate her, and coolly draws a pistol in order to shoot Guest down in self-defense.

A.7 Conscientious Driver

A person, Driver, keeps his car well maintained and always drives cautiously and alertly. On one occasion, however, freak circumstances cause the car to go out of control. It has veered in the direction of Pedestrian whom it will kill unless she blows it up by using one of the explosive devices with which pedestrians in philosophical examples are typically equipped.

A.8 Unwitting Cell Bomber

A villain has secretly tampered with Todd's cell phone in such a way that if Todd presses the "send" button, he will detonate a bomb to which Meredith has been tied by this same villain. The villain has trussed Meredith up so that she cannot escape or alert Todd to her plight. But the villain has given Meredith a weapon with which she can kill Todd.

A.9 Coerced Killer

A mafia ring has captured a man, Sam, and his family. They have threatened to kill his family if he does not do their bidding. They give him a gun and command him to go kill an innocent woman, Sarah. Sam finds Sarah and raises his gun to kill her. Sarah is unaware of the coercion Sam is under. She just sees a random stranger trying to kill her.

A.10 Unknown Unloaded Gun

A Gunman, fully intending to kill Mark, points his gun at Mark and slowly begins to squeeze the trigger. Mark is innocent and nonliable to be killed. Gunman and Mark both reasonably believe that the gun is loaded but in fact it is not. Mark has just enough time to defend himself and kill Gunman with his own concealed gun before Gunman pulls the trigger.

A.11 Bill

Bill has evidence that if he backs his car out of the driveway, he will run over the neighbor's child. But, even though Bill has accessible evidence for this (say he can clearly see the child in the rear-view mirror, or he can recall that the child was behind the car right before he got in), Bill somehow comes to believe that his backing up the car will cause no such harm to anyone and, thus, he believes it is thereby morally permissible. Bill thus proceeds to back up his car and kills the neighbor's child.

A.12 Ethan

Ethan does not have any clear evidence that if he backs his car out of the driveway, he will run over the neighbor's child. He cannot see anyone in the mirrors, which he checks diligently, and there was no one behind him when he got in the car. The child discretely snuck up behind the car after Ethan got in, out of the purview of his sensory perception. Consequently, Ethan believes that backing up his car will not harm anyone and he believes that it would thereby be morally permissible. Unfortunately, the neighbor's child was behind the car and when Ethan backs up his car, he kills the child.

A.13 Morton

Morton is in an identical situation to Bill. Morton, however, correctly believes due to the evidence accessible to him that his backing up the car will run over the neighbor's child, and he believes that it would thereby be a morally impermissible act. Morton decides to back up the car anyway and he kills the child, just as he believed he would and had evidence that he would.

A.14 Hunter & Photographer

Paul is a nature photographer and Mike is a deer-hunter. Both are independently in separate wildernesses but are in identical evidentiary circumstances: they each see something coming through the bushes toward them. They can't quite tell what it is yet based on the evidence available—it could be a deer, or it could be a human being. If it's a deer, Paul wants to take a picture of it, but he doesn't want to take a picture of a human hiker (he doesn't want to waste the film, say, on pictures of humans). To get the shot he wants (the deer emerging from the bushes) he'll have to decide now on whether to start snapping pictures. Similarly, in Mike's identical evidentiary circumstances, if it's a deer, he wants to shoot it, but he doesn't want to shoot a human (of course). Just like Paul, Mike's best chance to bag the deer is to shoot right before it emerges from the bushes and sees him and flees.

A.15 Dogsitter

Dogsitter is taking care of a dog. Dogsitter falsely believes that dogs cannot feel pain, because he has read Descartes and believes that non-human animals are no more than automata, intricate machines, and that machines cannot feel pain. Assume that Dogsitter has evidence available to him that dogs are not automata and that they can feel pain—there are issues of *Scientific American* sitting on his coffee table that attest to this in exhaustive detail, he knows a friend who is an expert in animal psychology, he has himself witnessed many dogs exhibiting behavior that suggests they are in pain, and so on. He has even considered whether the views of a 17th century philosopher should be relied upon in this case, and has considered consulting some of the other evidence available to him with an eye to reconsidering his belief. Still, he hasn't done this, and hasn't pursued any of the evidence available to him, and he maintains his false belief. While taking care of the dogs he routinely has to roll a heavy wheelbarrow through the garage and into the yard. If he goes one route, the wheelbarrow will roll over the dog's tail while it sleeps in its bed. He could go another route, but it is slightly further, so he decides to go the route that will result in the heavy wheelbarrow rolling over the dog's tail, since it won't cause any permanent functional harm, and he believes that dogs do not feel pain. He goes this route, and the dog routinely appears to be in great pain due to the heavy wheelbarrow rolling over its tail. Still, Dogsitter tells himself, the dog is not actually feeling pain, and so he takes himself to have no moral reason to go a different route he next time. If he believed that the dog was feeling pain, he would take himself to have a moral reason to go a different route, and would do so. But he doesn't believe this, and so he doesn't go a different route.

A.16 Caroline's Confusion

Caroline is sitting in her home reading Steinbeck. Brian enters the house through the front door. He was told by Caroline's husband, Ralph, to stop by the house and pick-up Ralph's guitar, which he forgot and needs for their band practice that evening. Ralph thought that his wife Caroline was still out of town on a trip, but she has arrived home early. Ralph told Brian that no one was home, and that Brian should use the key under the front mat to unlock the door, go inside, and grab the guitar which was in the living room. Brian does so. Upon seeing a strange man enter the living room, Caroline is frightened that it may be an attacker—and she believes as much. So, she grabs her nearby revolver and shoots Brian.

A.17 Phillip

Phillip is in an identical situation to Morton. That is, Phillip correctly believes due to the evidence accessible to him that his backing up the car will run over the neighbor's child. However, unlike Morton, Phillip does not conclude that this is morally impermissible. Rather, Phillip comes to the moral conclusion that backing up cars over neighbors' children is morally permissible.

A.17.1 Ancient Slaveholder

Hittite Lord is an ancient man who lived long ago in a culture very different from ours today. The prevailing cultural norms of his time held that there was nothing morally impermissible in slave holding. The legitimacy of chattel slavery was simply taken for granted. Hittite Lord owns slaves, buys and sells human beings, requires forced labor from them, breaks up families to do so, and all corollary activities that go along with slaveholding.

A.18 Ancient Slave

Telemaque is one of Hittite Lord's slaves. He has been forced to do hard labor all of his life by Hittite Lord, he has been kept in enslavement by brutal physical force, he was forcibly removed from his parents and siblings at an early age, and he has been otherwise abused and had his rights violated in ways commensurate with being a slave. Telemaque decides to defend himself from this enslavement. One morning, when Hittite Lord orders Telemaque to work, Telemaque refuses and tries to escape his captivity. Hittite Lord blocks him and does not allow him to escape. It has become clear over many years that the only way for Telemaque to escape is that he will have to kill Hittite Lord while trying to escape. Telemaque does so, and escapes to freedom.

A.19 The Resident

Twin, the identical twin of a notorious mass murderer, is driving in the middle of a stormy night in a remote area when his car breaks down. Twin is nonculpably unaware that his twin brother, the murderer, has within the past few hours escaped from prison in just this area, and that the residents have been warned of the escape. The murderer's notoriety derives from his invariable *modus operandi*: he violently breaks into people's homes and kills them instantly. As the twin, whose car has broken down, approaches a house to request to use the telephone, the resident of the house (Resident) takes aim to shoot him, preemptively, believing him to be the murderer.

A.20 Crow Shooting

Brandon Lee, the son of Bruce Lee, was a professional actor and was filming the film *The Crow* in 1993, in North Carolina. On one day of shooting, they were filming a scene where

Lee's character enters a room and discovers his fiancée being beaten and raped by a gang of criminals. One of the actors playing the role of one of these criminals, Actor, was scripted to shoot a gun at Lee as he entered the scene. The prop used for the gun was supposed to be loaded with a kind of "dummy cartridge," similar to "blanks," that would appear to be real bullets, but would actually not be harmful. In addition to this prop, there were other prop effects staged in the room such that it would appear as if the gun was really firing at Lee (e.g., things like small explosions going off to create the appearance of bullets landing). The filming was behind schedule and the actors were not well briefed on the details of the chorography of the scene. Unfortunately, through an unintentional mix-up with the prop technicians, Actor's gun was loaded with real bullets. The mistake went unnoticed by all until filming of the scene began. Actor fired the real bullets at Lee. The bullets struck Lee and, eventually, killed him.

A.20.1 Conspiracy Crow

For a couple of weeks leading up to the incident described in *Crow Shooting*, several cast members of *The Crow* have been spreading rumors that one of the actors has it out for Lee and wants to kill him. Further, the rumors speculate that one of the actors may try to kill Lee during filming. The rumors are being spread by a malicious Prop Tech who really does have it out for Lee. The rumors have reached Lee's ears and he has good reason, say, to take them seriously and is therefore concerned about his safety and worried that an actor may try to kill him during filming. The Prop Tech is the one in charge of the guns used in filming and he intentionally gives Actor the gun loaded with real bullets with the hope that Actor will unwittingly kill Lee. From here the case proceeds as it does in *Crow Shooting*.

A.21 Just Soldier Becky

Becky is a soldier fighting for a just cause. While in theater, Becky sees a person wildly charging at her unit as they are sitting peacefully under the shade of a tree while conversing with some members of the local populace. The charging enemy is shooting wildly (indiscriminately, even) at Becky, her fellow soldiers, and the civilians all around her. Becky, holding her rifle, quickly assesses the charging man's liability as bullets whiz by her and into those around her and she decides to shoot the charging enemy.

A.22 Lt. Beaudoin

On April 6, 1945, American soldier 1st Lt. Raymond Beaudoin was leading his platoon over flat, open terrain near Hamelin, Germany—just a few miles from the still active Nazi concentration camp of Bergen-Belsen. Nazi soldiers ambushed Beaudoin's unit with machine guns and automatic weapons, laying down devastating fire which pinned his unit to the ground. Beaudoin instructed his men to dig in and take up defensive positions against the enemy fire. Despite these attempted defensive measures, the platoon was losing men quickly. Things became more dire when the enemy brought up strong reinforcements to the rear of Beaudoin's unit and was preparing to attack from that direction. Three of Beaudoin's troops, sent back to obtain ammunition and reinforcements, were killed by Nazi sniper fire. To defend himself and his troops from the unjust enemy combatants' attack, Beaudoin decided to attack the most damaging enemy sniper nest 90 yards to the right flank, and thereby divert attention from the runner who would attempt to pierce the enemy's line and secure help. Crawling over exposed ground, he relentlessly advanced, undeterred by eight rounds of bazooka fire directed toward him or by rifle fire which ripped his uniform. Ten yards from the enemy position, he stood up and charged. Upon reaching the enemy position, he shot and killed two occupants of the nest; a third, who tried to bayonet him, he overpowered and killed with the butt of his carbine.

A.23 Barroom Brawl

A fight breaks out in a barroom. A number of patrons of the bar are actively perpetrating violence against one another. Another person, Smith, find himself in the midst of this fighting.

A.23.1 Tom the Embezzler

One day Tom embezzles $200 from his employer. The next day, Tom is on his way back to his company to embezzle even more money. On the way there, however, Tom sees his friend Frank at the coffee shop. Frank is on his way to volunteer at the local soup kitchen. Sadly, at the coffee shop, the two of them become caught in a kind of Tragic forced-choice scenario similar in form to Dignitary & Guest. (Perhaps a villain projects holographic images of guns onto both of their hands as they greet each other.)

A.24 Unintentional Ninja

A young child is kidnapped by a mysterious tribe of nomadic ninjas who live high in the mountains. The clan trains the child, against his will, in the powerful martial arts for which these ninjas are famous. Over the course of many years of this training it turns out this young child is quite naturally adept at these skills and becomes one of the best martial artists the world has ever known; he is literally a walking lethal weapon and could kill anyone with a quick strike. At the age of 20, the child escapes from his long captivity and tries to resume a normal life. Call him Unintentional Ninja.

A.25 Mugger

Mugger approaches Todd and demands, with the threat of physical violence, that Todd give him $1. Todd does not want to give Mugger the $1 and has the means to defend himself, but only with lethal force. That is, there is no way Todd can prevent Mugger from forcing him to give $1 except by killing Mugger. So, Todd kills Mugger.

A.25.1 Benevolent Mugger

Benevolent Mugger approaches Todd and demands, with the threat of physical violence, that Todd accepts $10 that Benevolent Mugger wishes to give Todd. Todd does not want the $10. Rather than accept the money, Todd kills Benevolent Mugger to prevent him from giving it to him.

A.26 Sarah

Sarah has longed her entire life to be a mother of children. She longs to be a caring, supportive, excellent parent to as many children as she can reasonably have and raise. She spends most of her life preparing for her longed-for role as mother. After taking tests to ensure that she is biologically able to have children, she finds and marries a good partner who similarly wishes to raise children, she reads countless books on parenting, she gets a degree in child development, she volunteers at local schools and daycare centers to better develop her parenting skills, and she eats a diet and follows an exercise regime specifically designed to create a healthy prenatal environment for her future children.

A.26.1 Strengthened Benevolent Mugger

Strengthened Benevolent Mugger approaches Todd and demands, with the threat of lethal violence, that Todd allows Strengthened Benevolent Mugger to direct his life. Strengthened Benevolent Mugger would be really good at this, and Todd's life would significantly improve if so directed and Todd knows this to be true. Be that as it may, Todd doesn't want Strengthened Benevolent Mugger to direct his life. Todd wants to direct his own life. The only way for Todd to prevent Strengthened Benevolent Mugger from directing his life is to use lethal defensive force. So, Todd kills Strengthened Benevolent Mugger.

Bibliography

Alexander, Edward Porter. *Military Memoirs of a Confederate*. New York: De Capo Press, 1993. First published New York: Charles Scribner's Sons, 1907.
Allhoff, Fritz. *Terrorism, Ticking Time-Bombs, and Torture*. Chicago: University of Chicago Press, 2012.
Anscombe, G. E. M. "War and Murder." In *Collected Philosophical Papers*. Vol. 3: *Ethics, Religion, and Politics*, 51–61. Minneapolis: University of Minnesota Press, 1981.
Aquinas, Thomas. *Thomas Aquinas: Selected Writings*. Edited by Ralph McInnery. New York: Penguin Classics, 1999.
Aristotle. *Nicomachean Ethics*. Translated by David Ross. New York: Oxford University Press, 1998.
Arquilla, John. *Bitskrieg: The New Challenge of Cyberwar*. Polity, 2021.
Atkins, E. M. and R. J. Dodaro, eds., *Augustine: Political Writings*. Cambridge: Cambridge University Press, 2001.
Bainton, Ronald. *Christian Attitudes Toward War and Peace: A Historical Survey and Critical Re-evaluation*. Nashville: Abingdon Press, 1960.
Baiss, Bridget. *The Crow: The Story Behind the Film*. New York: AbeBooks, 2000.
Bazargan-Forward, Saba. "Defensive Liability Without Culpability." In *The Ethics of Self Defense*, edited by Christian Coons and Michael Weber, 59–85. Oxford University Press, 2016.
Beach, Waldo and H. Richard Niebuhr. *Christian Ethics: Sources of the Living Tradition*. 2nd ed. New York: John Wiley & Sons, 1973.
Benatar, David. *Better to Never Have Been: The Harm of Coming into Existence*. Oxford: Oxford University Press, 2006.
Benbaji, Yitzhak. "A Defense of the Traditional War Convention." *Ethics* 118 (2008): 464–95.
Berlin, Isaiah. "Two Concepts of Liberty." In *Four Essays on Liberty*. Oxford: Oxford University Press, 1969.
Bourke, Joanna. *An Intimate History of Killing*. London: Granta, 1999.
Bratman, Michael. *Faces of Intention*. Cambridge: Cambridge University Press, 1999.
Brayton, Abbott A. and Stephana Landwear. *The Politics of War and Peace: A Survey of Thought*. Washington D.C.: University Press of America, 1981.
Brennan, Jason. *Against Democracy*. Princeton, NJ: Princeton University Press, 2016.
Broome, John. "Fairness." *Proceedings of the Aristotelian Society* 91 (1991): 87–101.
Burri, Susanne. "The Fair Distribution of Bad Luck." Unpublished manuscript.
Burri, Susanne. "The Toss-up Between a Profiting, Innocent Threat and His Victim." *The Journal of Political Philosophy* 23, no. 2 (2015): 146–65.
Burri, Susanne. "Morally Permissible Risk Imposition and Liability to Defensive Harm." *Law and Philosophy* (2020): 381–408.
Cantor, Joanne. "'I'll Never Have a Clown in My House'—Why Movie Horror Lives On." *Poetics Today* 25 (2004): 283–304.

Carr, Craig and Michael Seidler, eds. *The Political Writings of Samuel Pufendorf*. New York: Oxford University Press, 1994.
Chignell, Andrew. "The Ethics of Belief." In *The Stanford Encyclopedia of Philosophy*, edited by Edward N. Zalta. Stanford University (March 5, 2018), accessed May 1, 2011. http://plato.stanford.edu/entries/ethics-belief/#BelCon
Chomsky, Noam. "American Decline: Causes and Consequences." *Al Akhbar* (August 24, 2011), accessed November 1, 2020. https://chomsky.info/20110824/
Christie, Lars. "Causation and Liability to Defensive Harm." *Journal of Applied Philosophy* 37, no. 3 (2020): 378–92.
Clark, Nell. "Here's how propaganda is clouding Russians' understanding of the war in Ukraine." *NPR* (March 15, 2022)., accessed June 6, 2022. https://www.npr.org/2022/03/15/1086705796/russian-propaganda-war-in-ukraine
Clifford, William K. "The Ethics of Belief." *Contemporary Review* 34 (1877): 1–10.
Coady, Tony. *Morality and Political Violence*. Cambridge: Cambridge University Press, 2008.
Coady, Tony. "Terrorism and Innocence." *Journal of Ethics* 8 (2004): 37–58.
Coady, Tony. "The Status of Combatants." In *Just and Unjust Warriors: The Moral and Legal Status of Soldiers*, edited by David Rodin and Henry Shue, 153–75. New York: Oxford University Press, 2008.
Cohen, G. A. *Rescuing Justice and Equality*. Cambridge, MA: Harvard University Press, 2008.
Cook, Martin. *The Moral Warrior*. Albany, NY: SUNY Press, 2004.
Cranston, Maurice. "Liberalism." In *The Encyclopedia of Philosophy*, edited by Paul Edwards, 458–61. New York: Macmillan and the Free Press, 1967.
Daniels, Paul Richard. "Just War and Non-Combatants in the Private Military Industry," *Journal of Military Ethics* 14, no. 2 (2015): 146–51.
Davidson, Donald. "The Development of the Just-War Tradition." In *Nuclear Weapons and the American Churches: Ethical Positions On Modern Warfare*. Boulder, CO: Westview Press, 1983.
Davis, Nancy. "Abortion and Self-Defense." *Philosophy & Public Affairs* 13 (1984): 175–207.
See "Declaration of Independence," *National Archives*, https://www.archives.gov/founding-docs/declaration-transcript
Delaney, Neil Francis. "Two Cheers for 'Closeness': Terror, Targeting, and Double Effect." *Philosophical Studies* 137 (2006): 335–67.
DeRose, Keith. "Assertion, Knowledge and Context." *The Philosophical Review* 11, no. 2 (2002): 167–203.
DeRose, Keith. "Contextualism and Knowledge Attributions." *Philosophy and Phenomenological Research* 52 (1992): 913–29.
DeRose, Keith. *The Case for Contextualism: Knowledge, Skepticism, and Context*. Vol. 1. Oxford: Clarendon Press, 2009.
Dill, Janina. "The Moral Muddle of Blaming the West for Russia's Aggression." *Public Ethics* (April 6, 2022), accessed April 7, 2022. https://www.publicethics.org/post/the-moral-muddle-of-blaming-the-west-for-russia-s-aggression
Dipert, Randall. "The Ethics of Cyberwarfare." *Journal of Military Ethics* 9, no. 4 (2010): 384–410.
Draper, Kaila. "Defense." *Philosophical Studies* 145, no. 1 (2009): 69–88.
Draper, Kaila. *War and Individual Rights: The Foundations of Just War Theory*. Oxford: Oxford University Press, 2015.

Dunn, Kathleen. "Interview with Jeff McMahan." *Wisconsin Public Radio* (May 9, 2011). http://wpr.org/wcast/download-mp3-request.cfm?mp3file=dun110509e.mp3&iNoteID=97290

Dworkin, Ronald. "Rights as Trumps." In *Theories of Rights*, edited by Jeremy Waldron, 154–55. New York: Oxford University Press, 1984.

Dworkin, Ronald. *Taking Rights Seriously*. Bristol: Duckworth, 1977.

Egerton, Douglas R. *He Shall Go Out Free: The Lives of Denmark Vesey*. 2nd ed. Lanham: Rowman and Littlefield, 2004.

Emerton, Patrick and Toby Handfield. "Order and Affray: Defensive Privileges in Warfare." *Philosophy & Public Affairs* 37, no. 4 (2009): 382–414.

Fabre, Cécile. "Harming, Rescuing and the Necessity Constraint on Defensive Force," *Criminal Law and Philosophy* 16, no. 3 (2002): 525–38.

Feldman, Fred and Brad Skow. "Desert." In *The Stanford Encyclopedia of Philosophy*, Winter 2020 Edition, edited by Edward N. Zalta Stanford University (September 22, 2020), accessed October 10, 2022. https://plato.stanford.edu/archives/win2020/entries/desert/

Ferzan, Kimberly Kessler. "Justifying Self-Defense." *Law and Philosophy* 24 (2005): 711–49.

Finnemore, Martha. *The Purpose of Intervention*. London: Cornell University Press, 2003.

Fletcher, George. *Rethinking Criminal Law*. Originally published Boston: Little, Brown, 1978; Reprinted New York: Oxford University Press, 2000.

Fletcher, George. "Proportionality and the Psychotic Aggressor: A Vignette in Comparative Criminal Theory." *Israel Law Review* 8 (1973): 367–90.

Fletcher, George. *Rethinking Criminal Law*. Boston: Little, Brown, 1978.

"France's Macron: Russia's Putin alone chose war in Ukraine." *Reuters*, March 2, 2022.

Freeman, Samuel. "Original Position." *Stanford Encyclopedia of Philosophy*. April 3, 2019, accessed May 10, 2011. http://plato.stanford.edu/entries/original-position/

Friedman, Thomas. "Free Advice for Putin: Make Peace, You Fool." *New York Times* (April 13, 2022).

"From Where to Eternity." *Sopranos*. Season 2, Episode 9. Transcript accessed October 2, 2011. http://www.tvfanatic.com/quotes/shows/the-sopranos/page-2.html#ixzz1oef8Yxwv

Frowe, Helen. "Threats, Bystanders and Obstructers." *Proceedings of the Aristotelian Society* 108, no. 3 (2008): 365–72.

Frowe, Helen. "A Practical Account of Self-Defence." *Law and Philosophy* 29, no. 3 (2010): 245–72.

Frowe, Helen. *Defensive Killing*. Oxford: Oxford University Press, 2014.

Frowe, Helen. "Equating Innocent Threats and Bystanders." *Journal of Applied Philosophy* 25, no. 4 (2008): 277–90.

Frowe, Helen. "Risk Imposition and Liability to Defensive Harm." *Criminal Law and Philosophy* 16, no. 3 (2022): 511–24.

Gardner, John and Francois Tanguay-Renaud. "Desert and Avoidability in Self-Defense." *Ethics* 122, no. 1 (2011): 111–34.

Gardner, Molly. "What is Harming?" In *Principles and Persons: The Legacy of Derek Parfit*, edited by Jeff McMahan, Tim Campbell, James Goodrich, and Ketan Ramakrishnan, 381–96. New York: Oxford University Press, 2021.

Gaus, Gerald. *Justificatory Liberalism: An Essay on Epistemology and Political Theory*. New York: Oxford University Press, 1996.

Gaus, Gerald, and Shane Courtland. "Liberalism." In *The Stanford Encyclopedia of Philosophy*, edited by Edward N. Zalta. Stanford University (February 22, 2022), accessed October 1, 2011. http://plato.stanford.edu/Entries/liberalism/

Gaus, Gerald. "The Place of Autonomy within Liberalism." In *Autonomy and the Challenges to Liberalism: New Essays*, edited by John Christman, 272–306. Cambridge: Cambridge University Press, 2009.

Gelber, Dan. "Florida Defense Law Change Encourages Recklessness." *Sun Sentinel*, July 17, 2013. https://www.sun-sentinel.com/opinion/fl-xpm-2013-07-17-fl-dgcol-zimmerman-trayvon-oped0717-20130717-story.html

Gewirth, Alan. *Human Rights: Essays on Justification and Applications*. Chicago: University of Chicago Press, 1982.

Ginet, Carl. "Deciding to Believe." In *Knowledge, Truth, and Duty: Essays on Epistemic Justification, Responsibility, and Virtue*, edited by Matthias Steup, 63–76. New York: Oxford University Press, 2001.

Gordon-Solomon, Kerah. "What Makes a Person Liable to Defensive Harm?" *Philosophy and Phenomenological Research* 97, no. 3 (2018): 543–67.

Gosselin, Abigail. "Global Poverty and Responsibility: Identifying the Duty-Bearers of Human Rights." *Human Rights Review* 8 (2006): 35–52.

Griffin, James. *On Human Rights*. New York: Oxford University Press, 2008.

Gross, Michael. "Assassination and Targeted Killing: Law Enforcement, Execution, or Self-Defense?" *Journal of Applied Philosophy* 23, no. 3 (2006): 323–35.

Grossman, David. *On Killing*. London: Back Bay Books, 1995.

Guerrero, Alexander. "Don't Know, Don't Kill." *Philosophical Studies* 136, no. 1 (2007): 59–97.

Hackensberger, Alfred. "Ukrainian families are being ripped apart as men stay behind to fight the Russian invasion." *Business Insider*, March 3, 2022.

Hanna, Jason. "The Moral Status of Nonresponsible Threats." *Journal of Applied Philosophy* 29, no. 1 (2011): 1–14.

Hastings, Michael. "The Runaway General." *Rolling Stone* (June 22, 2010).

Hauerwas, Stanley. "Pacifism: Some Philosophical Considerations." In *The Morality of War: Classical and Contemporary Readings*, edited by Larry May, Eric Rovie, and Steve Viner, 80–97. Upper Saddle River, NJ: Prentice Hall, 2005.

Haque, Adil. *Law and Morality*. New York: Oxford University Press, 2017.

Herr, Michael. *Dispatches*. London: Picador, 2004.

Hill, Benjamin and Henrik Lagerlund, eds. *The Philosophy of Francisco Suarez*. New York: Oxford University Press, 2012.

Hill, Thomas E., Jr. *Autonomy and Self-Respect*. Cambridge: Cambridge University Press, 1991.

Himma, Ken. "Artificial Agency, Consciousness, and the Criteria for Moral Agency: What Properties Must an Artificial Agent Have to be a Moral Agent?" *Ethics Information and Technology* 11, no. 1 (2009): 19–29.

Hohfeld, Wesley Newcomb. *Fundamental Legal Conceptions as Applied in Judicial Reasoning*. New Haven: Yale University Press, 1946.

Hurka, Thomas. "Proportionality in the Morality of War." *Philosophy & Public Affairs* 33, no. 1 (2005): 34–66.

Jones, A.H.M. "Slavery in the Ancient World." *The Economic History Review* 9, no. 2 (1956).

Kaldor, Mary. *New and Old Wars: Organized Violence in a Global Era*. Palo Alto, CA: Stanford University Press, 1999.

Kamm, Francis. M. *Creation and Abortion: A Study in Moral and Legal Philosophy.* Oxford: Oxford University Press, 1992.
Kamm, Francis. M. *Intricate Ethics: Rights, Responsibilities, and Permissible Harm.* New York: Oxford University Press, 2006.
Kant, Immanuel. *Grounding for the Metaphysics of Morals.* Translated by James W. Ellington. New York: Hackett Publishing Co., 1993; first published 1785.
Kant, Immanuel. *The Metaphysics of Morals.* Edited by Mary Gregor. Cambridge: Cambridge University Press, 1996; first published 1797.
Kaufman, Whitley. "Rethinking the Ban on Assassination." In *Rethinking the Just War Tradition*, edited by M. W. Brough, John W. Lango, and Harry van der Linden. Albany, NY: SUNY Press, 2007: 99–114.
Kaufman, Whitley. "Self-Defense, Innocent Aggressors, and the Duty of Martyrdom." *Pacific Philosophical Quarterly* 91, no. 1 (2010): 78–96.
Kershnar, Stephan. "An Axiomatic Theory of Just War: Forfeiture Theory." In *Who Should Die? The Ethics of Killing in War*, edited by Bradley Strawser, Michael Robillard, and Ryan Jenkins. New York: Oxford University Press, 2018.
Kershnar, Stephen. "Assassination and the Immunity Theory." *Philosophia* 33, no. 4 (2005): 129–47.
Kershnar, Stephen. "The Moral Argument for a Policy of Assassination." *Reason Papers* 27 (2005): 45–67.
Khurshudyan, Isabelle and Sammy Westfall. "Ukraine puts captured Russians on stage. It's a powerful propaganda tool, but is it a violation of POW rights?" *Washington Post* (March 9, 2022).
Korsgaard, Christine. *Creating the Kingdom of Ends.* Cambridge: Cambridge University Press, 1996.
Kudo, Timothy. "On War and Redemption." *New York Times* (November 8, 2011), accessed December 20, 2011. http://opinionator.blogs.nytimes.com/2011/11/08/on-war-and-redemption/
Kymlicka, Will. *Contemporary Political Philosophy: An Introduction.* New York: Oxford University Press, 2001.
LaFollete, Hugh. *In Defense of Gun Control.* New York: Oxford University Press, 2018.
Lazar, Seth. "A Liberal Defence of (Some) Duties to Compatriots." *Journal of Applied Philosophy* 27, no. 3 (2010): 246–57.
Lazar, Seth. "Responsibility, Risk, and Killing in Self-Defense." *Ethics* 119, no. 4 (2009): 699–728.
Lazar, Seth. "Risky Killing and the Ethics of War." *Ethics* 126, no. 1 (2015): 91–117.
Lazar, Seth. "The Nature & Disvalue of Injury." *Res Publica* 15, no. 3 (2009): 289–304.
Lazar, Seth. "The Responsibility Dilemma for *Killing in War*: A Review Essay." *Philosophy & Public Affairs* 38, no. 2 (2010): 180–213.
Lazar, Seth. "War and Associative Duties." D.Phil. diss, University of Oxford, 2009.
Lee, David. *Up Close and Personal: The Reality of Close-quarter Fighting in World War II.* London: Greenhill, 2006.
Lehning, Percy B. *John Rawls: An Introduction.* Cambridge: Cambridge University Press, 2006.
Lichtenberg, Judith. "How to Judge Soldiers Whose Cause Is Unjust." In *Just and Unjust Warriors: The Moral and Legal Status of Soldiers*, edited by David Rodin and Henry Shue, 112–31. New York: Oxford University Press, 2008.

List, Christian and Philip Pettit. *Group Agency: The Possibility, Design, and Status of Corporate Agents*. Oxford: Oxford University Press, 2011.
Lloyd, Sharon. "Democratic Responsibility and Moral Liability: A Hobbesian Account." Unpublished manuscript.
Lockhart, T. *Moral Uncertainty and Its Consequences*. Oxford: Oxford University Press, 2000.
Lucas, George. "Advice and Dissent: 'The Uniform Perspective.'" *Journal of Military Ethics* 8 (2009): 141–61.
Mason, Elinor. "Between Strict Liability and Blameworthy Quality of Will: Taking Responsibility." In *Oxford Studies in Agency and Responsibility* (2019): 241–64.
Marshall, S. L. A. *Men Against Fire: The Problem of Battle Command*. Gloucester: Peter Smith, 1978.
May, Larry. *War Crimes and Just War*. Cambridge: Cambridge University Press, 2007.
McDonald, Robert. "Thomas Jefferson's Changing Reputation as Author of the Declaration of Independence: The First Fifty Years." *Journal of the Early Republic* 19, no. 2 (Summer 1999): 169–95.
McIntyre, Alison. "Doctrine of Double Effect." In *The Stanford Encyclopedia of Philosophy*, edited by Edward N. Zalta. Stanford University (December 24, 2018). https://plato.stanford.edu/entries/double-effect/
McMahan, Jeff. "Duty, Obedience, Desert, and Proportionality in War: A Response." *Ethics* 122, no. 1 (2011): 135–67.
McMahan, Jeff. "Innocence, Self-Defense and Killing in War." *Journal of Political Philosophy* 2 (1994): 193–221.
McMahan, Jeff. "Just Cause for War." *Ethics and International Affairs* 19 (2005): 1–21.
McMahan, Jeff. *Killing in War*. Oxford: Clarendon Press, 2009.
McMahan, Jeff. "Necessity, and Noncombatant Immunity." *Review of International Studies* 40, no. 1 (2014): 53–76.
McMahan, Jeff. "On the Moral Equality of Combatants." *Journal of Political Philosophy* 14 (2006): 377–93.
McMahan, Jeff. "Response to *War and Self-Defense*." *Ethics and International Affairs* 18, no. 1 (2004): 75–80.
McMahan, Jeff. "Self-defense and Culpability." *Law and Philosophy* 24 (2005): 751–74.
McMahan, Jeff. "The Basis of Moral Liability to Defensive Killing." *Philosophical Issues* 15 (2005): 386–404.
McMahan, Jeff. *The Ethics of Killing: Problems at the Margins of Life*. New York: Oxford University Press, 2002.
McMahan, Jeff. "The Ethics of Killing in War." *Ethics* 114 (2004): 693–732.
McMahan, Jeff. "The Morality of War and the Law of War." In *Just and Unjust Warriors*, edited by David Rodin and Henry Shue, 9–43. New York: Oxford University Press, 2008.
Merari, Ariel. *Driven to Death: Psychological and Social Aspects of Suicide Terrorism*. Oxford: Oxford University Press, 2010.
Metaxas, Eric. *Amazing Grace: William Wilberforce and the Heroic Campaign to End Slavery*. New York: HarperOne, 2007.
Meyer, Robinson. "Another Victim on this Election: The Verb 'To Trump,'" *The Atlantic* (October 25, 2016). https://www.theatlantic.com/technology/archive/2016/10/ave-atque-trumpe/505259
Mill, John Stuart. *On Liberty*. New York: Simon & Brown, 2012. First published 1869.
Mill, John Stuart. "The Contest in America." *Fraser's Magazine*, February, 1862.

Moody-Adams, Marilyn. "Culture, Responsibility, and Affected Ignorance." *Ethics* 104, no. 2 (1994): 291–309.

Morkevicius, Valerie. "Hindu Perspectives on Just War." In *The Prism of Just War: Asian and Western Perspectives on the Legitimate Use of Military Force*, edited by Howard Hensel, 169–94. London: Ashgate Press, 2010.

Morkevicius, Valerie. "Shi'i Perspectives on Just War." In *The Prism of Just War: Asian and Western Perspectives on the Legitimate Use of Military Force*, edited by Howard Hensel, 145–69. London: Ashgate Press, 2010.

Mulet, A. and J. Benedito, J. Bon, C. Rossello. "Ultrasonic Velocity in Cheddar Cheese as Affected by Temperature." *Journal of Food Science* 64 (2006):1038–41.

Münkler, H. *Die Neuen Kriege*. Reinbek at Hamburg: Rowohlt, 2003.

Nagel, Thomas. "War and Massacre." *Philosophy & Public Affairs* 1, no. 2 (1972): 123–44.

Narveson, Jan. "Is Pacifism Consistent?" *Ethics* 78, no. 2 (1968): 148–50.

Narveson, Jan. "Pacifism: A Philosophical Analysis." *Ethics* 75, no. 4 (1965): 259–71.

National Priorities Project. "Cost of War," accessed September 1, 2010. http://www.nationalpriorities.org/costofwar_home

Natfali, Tim. "The Worst President in History," *The Atlantic* (January 19, 2021), https://www.theatlantic.com/ideas/archive/2021/01/trump-worst-president-history/617730

Neff, Stephen C., ed. *Hugo Grotius on the Law of War and Peace: Student Edition*. Cambridge: Cambridge University Press, 2012; first published 1625.

Nelkin, Dana Kay. "Liability, Culpability, and Luck." *Philosophical Studies* (2021): 3523–41.

Nicol, Mark. *Condor Blues*. Edinburgh: Mainstream, 2007.

Nozick, Robert. *Anarchy, State, & Utopia*. Oxford: Basil Blackwell, 1974.

O'Neill, Onora. *Constructions of Reason: Explorations of Kant's Practical Philosophy*. Cambridge: Cambridge University Press, 1989.

Orend, Brian. *The Morality of War*. Peterborough, ON: Broadview Press, 2006.

Orend, Brian. *War and International Justice: A Kantian Perspective*. Waterloo: Wilfrid Laurier University Press, 2000.

Osiel, Mark. *The End of Reciprocity*. Cambridge: Cambridge University Press, 2009.

Otsuka, Michael. "Killing the Innocent in Self-Defense." *Philosophy & Public Affairs* 23 (1994): 74–94.

Otsuka, Michael. *Libertarianism Without Inequality*. New York: Oxford University Press, 2003.

Otsuka, Michael. "Licensed to Kill." *Analysis* 71, no. 3 (2011): 523–32.

Øverland, Gerhard. "Killing Civilians." *European Journal of Philosophy* 13 (2005): 345–63.

Øverland, Gerhard. "Killing Soldiers." *Ethics and International Affairs* 20, no. 4 (2006): 455–75.

Pagden, Anthony and Jeremy Lawrance, eds. *Vitoria: Political Writings*. Cambridge: Cambridge University Press, 1992.

Parfit, Derek. *On What Matters*. Vol. 1. New York: Oxford University Press, 2011.

Parfit, Derek. *Reasons and Persons*. Oxford: Clarendon Press, 1984.

Parry, Jonathan. "Defensive Harm, Consent, and Intervention." *Philosophy & Public Affairs* 45, no. 4 (2017): 356–96.

"PEA Soup." Internet blog. http://peasoup.typepad.com/peasoup/2010/08/ethics-discussions-at-pea-soup-mikhail-mike-valdmans-outsourcing-selfgovernment-with-commentary-by-s.html

Plato. *The Republic*. Translated by G. M. A. Grube. New York: Hackett Publishing Co., 1992.

Pleasance, Chris. "Show us mercy.. we thought we were liberating Ukraine from the Nazis." *The Daily Mail* (March 7, 2022). https://www.dailymail.co.uk/news/article-10585541/Ukraine-war-Russian-POW-begs-mercy-invading-forces.html

"Pope Francis: War is Always a Defeat for Humanity." *Diocese of Corpus Christi* (September 9, 2013). https://diocesecc.org/news/pope-francis-war-is-always-a-defeat-for-humanity

Purves, Duncan. "Accounting for the harm of death." *Pacific Philosophical Quarterly* 97, no. 1 (2016): 89–112.

Purves, Duncan. "Harming as making worse off." *Philosophical Studies* 176 (2019): 2629–56.

Quong, Jonathan. "Killing in Self-Defense." *Ethics* 119 (2009): 507–37.

Quong, Jonathan. "Liability to Defensive Harm." *Philosophy & Public Affairs* 40 (2012): 45–77.

Quinn, Warren. "Actions, Intentions, and Consequences: The Doctrine of Doing and Allowing." *The Philosophical Review* 98, no. 3 (1989): 287–312.

Rawls, John. *A Theory of Justice*. Cambridge: Cambridge University Press, 1971.

Rawls, John. *Political Liberalism*. New York: Columbia University Press, 1995.

Rawls, John. *The Law of Peoples*. Cambridge, MA: Harvard University Press, 1999.

Raz, Joseph. "On the Nature of Rights." *Mind* 93 (1984): 194–214.

Raz, Joseph. *The Morality of Freedom*. New York: Oxford University Press, 1986.

Renzo, Massimo. "Political Authority and Unjust Wars." *Philosophy and Phenomenological Research* 99, no. 2 (2019): 336–57.

Renzo, Massimo. "Manipulation and Liability to Defensive Harm." *Philosophical Studies* 178 (2021): 3483–501.

Rigstad, Mark. "Putting the War Back in Just War Theory: A Critique of Examples." *Ethical Perspectives* 24, no. 1 (2017): 123–44.

Rodin, David. "Superior Law." Presented at the annual Ethics, Law, and Armed Conflict Workshop on War. Oxford: Oxford University, 2011.

Rodin, David. "The Moral Inequality of Soldiers: Why *Jus in Bello* Asymmetry Is Half Right." In *Just and Unjust Warriors: The Moral and Legal Status of Soldiers*, edited by Henry Shue and David Rodin, 44–68. New York: Oxford University Press, 2008.

Rodin, David. *War and Self-Defense*. Oxford: Oxford University Press, 2002.

Rosen, Galen. "Culpability and Ignorance." *Proceedings of the Aristotelian Society* 103, no. 1 (2003): 61–84.

Ross, William D. *Foundations of Ethics*. Oxford: Clarendon Press, 1939.

Rowe, Thomas. "Can a Risk of Harm Itself Be a Harm?" *Analysis* 81, no. 4 (2022): 694–701.

Russell, Frederick. *The Just-War in The Middle Ages*. New York: Cambridge University Press, 1975.

Ryan, Cheyney C. "Self-Defense, Pacifism, and the Possibility of Killing." *Ethics* 93 (1983): 508–24.

Ryan, Cheyney C. *The Chickenhawk Syndrome: War, Sacrifice, and Personal Responsibility*. London: Rowman and Littlefield, 2009.

Rysiew, Patrick. "Epistemic Contextualism." In *The Stanford Encyclopedia of Philosophy*, edited by Edward N. Zalta. Stanford University (December 15, 2020), accessed May 1, 2011. http://plato.stanford.edu/entries/contextualism-epistemology/index.html.

Sagan, Scott and Benjamin Valentino. "Just War and Unjust Soldiers: American Public Opinion on the Moral Equality of Combatants." *Ethics and International Affairs* 33, no. 4 (2019): 411–44.

Sandel, Michael. *Justice: What's the Right Thing to Do?* New York: Farrar, Straus and Giroux, 2010.
Scanlon, T. M. "The Responsibility of Soldiers and the Ethics of Killing in War." *Philosophical Quarterly* 57 (2007): 558–72.
Scanlon, T. M. "Thomson on Self-Defense." In *Fact and Value. Essays on Ethics and Metaphysics for Judith Jarvis Thomson*, edited by Alex Byrne, Robert Stalnaker, and Ralph Wedgwood, 119–213. Cambridge, MA: Bradford Books, the MIT Press, 2001.
Scanlon, T. M. *What We Owe to Each Other*. Cambridge: Belknap Press, 1998.
Shakespeare, William. *King Henry V (The New Cambridge Shakespeare)*, edited by Andrew Gurr. Cambridge: Cambridge University Press, 2005.
Shamash, Hamutal. "How Much is Too Much? An Examination of the Principle of Jus in Bello Proportionality." *Israel Defense Forces Law Review* 2 (2005): 103–48.
Sher, George. "What Makes a Lottery Fair?" *Nous* 14, no. 2 (1980): 203–16.
Shue, Henry. "Do We Need a 'Morality of War'?" In *Just and Unjust Warriors: The Moral and Legal Status of Soldiers*, edited by David Rodin and Henry Shue, 87–111. New York: Oxford University Press, 2008.
Skerker, Michael. *The Moral Status of Combatants: A New Theory of Just War*. London: Routledge, 2020.
Slote, Michael. "Is Virtue Possible?" *Analysis* 42 (1982): 70–76.
Smith, Holly. "Culpable Ignorance." *The Philosophical Review* 92, no. 4 (1983): 543–71.
Steinbuch, Yaron. "Captured Russian Officer apologizes to Ukraine for 'genocide,' begs for mercy." New York Post. (March 7, 2022). https://nypost.com/2022/03/07/captured-russian-officer-apologizes-to-ukraine-for-genocide/
Steinhoff, Uwe. "Debate: Jeff McMahan on the Moral Inequality of Combatants." *Journal of Political Philosophy* 16 (2008): 220–26.
Steinhoff, Uwe. "Killing Them Safely: Extreme Asymmetry and Its Discontents." In *Killing By Remote Control: The Ethics of an Unmanned Military*, edited by Bradley Jay Strawser. New York: Oxford University Press, 2013: 179–210.
Steinhoff, Uwe. "Torture: The Case for Dirty Harry and Against Alan Dershowitz." *Journal of Applied Philosophy* 23, no. 3 (2006): 337–53.
Steinhoff, Uwe. "The Liability of Justified Attackers." *Ethical Theory and Moral Practice* 19, no. 4 (2016): 1016–30.
Steinhoff, Uwe. "The Indispensable Mental Element of Justification and the Failure of Purely Objectivist (Mostly "Revisionist") Just War Theories." *Zeitschrift Für Ethik Und Moralphilosophie* 3, no. 1 (2020): 51–67.
Steup, Matthias, ed. *Knowledge, Truth, and Duty: Essays on Epistemic Justification, Responsibility, and Virtue*. New York: Oxford University Press, 2001.
Strawser, Bradley, with Adam Henschke and Fritz Allhoff, editors. *Binary Bullets: The Ethics of Cyberwar*. New York: Oxford University Press, 2016.
Strawser, Bradley. *Killing bin Laden: A Moral Analysis* New York: Palgrave Macmillan, 2014.
Strawser, Bradley. "Moral Predators: The Duty to Employ Uninhabited Aerial Vehicles." *Journal of Military Ethics* 9, no. 4 (December 2010): 342–68.
Strawser, Bradley. "Response to Rodin," Paper presented at Oxford's Institute for Ethics, Law, and Armed Conflict Annual Workshop, Oxford, UK, August 2011.
Strawser, Bradley. "Review Essay of In Defense of Gun Control by Hugh LaFollette." With Bart Kennedy, *Criminal Law and Philosophy* 15 (April 2021): 311–16.
Strawser, Bradley. "Revisionist Just War Theory and the Real World: A Cautiously Optimistic Proposal." In *Routledge Handbook of Ethics and War: Just War in the 21st*

Century, edited by Fritz Allhoff, Adam Henschke, and Nick Evans, 76–90. New York: Routledge Press, 2013.

Strawser, Bradley. "Walking the Tightrope of Just War." *Analysis* 71 (2011): 533–44.

Strawson, Peter. *Freedom and Resentment*. In *Free Will*, edited by G. Watson, 72–93. Oxford: Oxford University Press, 1982.

Tadros, Victor. "Law: What is it Good for?" Presented at the annual Ethics, Law, and Armed Conflict Workshop on War. Oxford: Oxford University, 2011.

Tamir, Yael. *Liberal Nationalism*. Princeton: Princeton University Press, 1993.

Taylor, Robert. "Kantian Personal Autonomy." *Political Theory* 33, no. 5 (2005): 602–28.

Tennyson, Alfred. "Charge of the Light Brigade." In *Tennyson: Selected Poems*, edited by Christopher Ricks, 215–16. New York: Penguin Classics, 1995.

Tesón, Fernando. "Self-Defense in International Law and Rights of Persons: Response to War and Self-Defense." *Ethics and International Affairs* 18, no. 1 (2004): 87–91.

Thomson, Judith Jarvis. "Self-Defense." *Philosophy & Public Affairs* 20, no. 4 (1991): 283–310.

Thomson, Judith Jarvis. "Self-Defense and Rights." In *The Lindley Lecture*. Lawrence, KS: Lawrence University of Kansas Publications, 1976.

Thomson, Judith Jarvis. *The Realm of Rights*. Cambridge, MA: Harvard University Press, 1990.

Tiechman, Jenny. *Pacifism and the Just War*. Oxford: Basil Blackwell, 1984.

Timmons, Mark. *Moral Theory*. New York: Rowman & I Littlefield Publishers, Inc, 2002.

Tolkien, J. R. R. *The Lord of the Rings: The Two Towers*. Boston: Mariner Books, 1955.

Uniacke, Susan. *Permissible Killing: The Self-Defence Justification of Homicide*. Cambridge: Cambridge University Press, 1994.

US War Department. *The War of the Rebellion: A Compilation of the Official Records of the Union and Confederate Armies*. Washington D.C.: Government Printing Office, 1899.

Valdman, Mikhail. "Outsourcing Self-Government." *Ethics* 120, no. 4 (2010): 761–90.

Vitoria, Francisco de. "On the Law of War." In *Political Writings*, edited by Anthony Pagden and Jeremy Lawrence. Cambridge: Cambridge University Press, 1991: 303–22.

Voltaire, Francois. *Philosophical Dictionary*. Translated by Theodore Besterman. New York: Penguin Books, 2004; originally published 1764.

Waldron, Jeremy. "Moral Autonomy and Personal Autonomy." In *Autonomy and the Challenges to Liberalism: New Essays*, edited by John Christman, 307–29. Cambridge: Cambridge University Press, 2005.

Walen, Alec. *The Mechanics of Claims and Permissible Killing in War*. New York: Oxford University Press, 2019.

Wall, Steven. "Collective Rights and Individual Autonomy." *Ethics* 117 (2007): 234–64.

Wall, Steven. "Neutrality and Responsibility." *The Journal of Philosophy* 98, no. 8 (2001): 389–410.

Wall, Steven. "Perfectionism in Politics: A Defense." In *Contemporary Debates in Political Philosophy*, edited by John Christman and Thomas Christiano. Oxford: Blackwell Publishing, 2009: 99–118.

Wall, Steven. *Perfectionism, Liberalism, and Restraint*. Cambridge: Cambridge University Press, 1998.

Wall, Steven. "Rawls and the Status of Political Liberty." *Pacific Philosophical Quarterly* 87, no. 2 (2006): 245–70.

Wallace, David Foster. "Consider the Lobster." In *Consider the Lobster: And Other Essays*. New York: Little, Brown, and Company, 2005.

Wallach, Wendell and Colin Allen. *Moral Machines: Teaching Robots Right from Wrong*. New York: Oxford University Press, 2009.

Walsh, Declan. "Osama bin Laden 'Revenge' Attack Kills Scores in Pakistan." *The Guardian* (May 13, 2011).

Walzer, Michael. *Just & Unjust Wars: A Moral Argument with Historical Examples*. New York: Basic Books, 1977.

Walzer, Michael. *Arguing About War*. New Haven: Yale University Press, 2004.

Walzer, Michael. "Response to McMahan's Paper." *Philosophia* 34 (2006): 43–45.

Walzer, Michael. "The Triumph of Just War Theory—and the Dangers of Success." *Social Research* 69, no. 4 (2002): 925–46.

Wang, Marian and Braden Goyette. "Bin Laden Reading Guide: How to Cut Through the Coverage." *ProPublica*, accessed August 5, 2011. http://www.propublica.org/blog/item/bin-laden-reading-guide-how-to-cut-through-the-coverage

"What We Know About the Fatal Shooting on Alec Baldwin's New Mexico Movie Set," *New York Times* (April 2022).

Weintraub, Robert. "How Donald ruined the Word Trump," *Slate* (February 14, 2017), https://slate.com/culture/2017/02/how-donald-ruined-the-word-trump.html

Welkos, Robert W. "Bruce Lee's Son, Brandon, Killed in Movie Accident." *The Los Angeles Times* (April 1, 1993), accessed November 15, 2018. https://www.latimes.com/archives/la-xpm-1993-04-01-mn-17681-story.html

Wertheimer, Roger. "Reconnoitering Combatant Moral Equality." *Journal of Military Ethics* 6 (2007): 60–74.

"White House Press Briefing by Senior Administration Officials on the Killing of Osama bin Laden." *Office of the White House Press Secretary* (May 2, 2011), accessed May 30, 2015. http://www.whitehouse.gov/the-press-office/2011/05/02/press-briefing-senior-administration-officials-killing-osama-bin-laden

World War II History Reference Library. "Raymond O. Beaudoin," accessed August 1, 2010. http://www.worldwariihistory.info/Medal-of-Honor/Germany.html

Yoder, John Howard. *The Original Revolution*. Scottdale, PA: Herald Press. 1971.

Yoder, John Howard. *The Politics of Jesus*. Grand Rapids, MI: William B. Eerdmans Publishing Co., 1972.

Yoder, John Howard. *When War is Unjust*. Minneapolis: Augsburg Publishing, 1984.

Zimmerman, Michael. "Is Moral Obligation Objective or Subjective?" *Utilitas* 18, no. 4 (2006): 329–61.

Zimmerman, Michael. *Living with Uncertainty: The Moral Significance of Ignorance*. Cambridge: Cambridge University Press, 2010.

Zimmerman, Michael. "Moral Responsibility and Ignorance," *Ethics* 107, no. 3 (1997): 410–26.

Zohar, Noam J. "Collective War and Individualistic Ethics: Against the Conscription of 'Self-Defense.'" *Political Theory* 21 (1993): 606–22.

Zupan, Dan. "The Logic of Community, Ignorance, and the Presumption of Moral Equality: A Soldier's Story." *Journal of Military Ethics* 6 (2007): 41–49.

Zupan, Dan. *War, Morality, and Autonomy: An Investigation in Just War Theory*. Burlington, VT: Ashgate Publishing, 2004.

Index

For the benefit of digital users, indexed terms that span two pages (e.g., 52–53) may, on occasion, appear on only one of those pages.

ability, 73, 156, 161–62, 175, 179, 191, 198–99, 221–22, 231–34, 246–47, 249, 253, 258
accident, 47, 133n.20, 179
accounting, 69–70, 210n.8, 225–26, 231, 234n.32
addiction, 230, 248n.69
Afghanistan, 3, 197–200
Africa, 140n.5
agency, 17–18, 42–43, 46, 57–58, 74, 82–83, 158, 251–56
  the Agency View, 56–57, 58–60, 61–64, 65–68, 69–70, 72–75, 85–86, 87, 109, 112, 115–16, 119–25, 131, 133–34, 162, 166–67, 174–75
  See also group agency
aggression, 160, 236, 244, 246–47, 248–49, 250–52, 256–57, 260, 262, 263–64
  benevolent, 13, 27n.32, 203–23, 231n.17, 236, 238–39, 241–42, 253, 256, 263–64
  conditional, 214, 215, 216–17, 220
  international, 137–38, 143, 200, 261
  unjust, 5, 6–7, 21–22, 187–88, 245–46, 263–64
  unprovoked, 164n.58
airstrikes, 198
aljazeera, 245n.61, 245n.62
allies, 164n.58
Alphonians, 227, 228, 236, 246–47, 250–51
  puzzle of aggression (*see* benevolent aggression)
altruism, 209, 222–23, 245–46, 253, 261, 263–64
American, 61, 138n.4, 141, 142n.15, 164. *See also* USA

analytic philosophy, 3, 4–5, 66–67, 71–72, 101n.51, 105n.61, 129, 136
antebellum, 148–49
Aquinas, Thomas, 141–42, 201–2
Aristotle, 137, 141n.10, 266–67
St. Augustine, 17, 137–38, 140, 141–42, 143, 212–13, 266–67
autonomy
  and individuals, 12–13, 25, 154–55, 203–5, 210–11, 216–17, 218–19, 220–23, 246–51, 270–71
  and political liberalism, 203–23, 224–65

battlefield, 201, 202, 269–70
the Belief-Relative view, 75, 86n.26, 95
  and duties, 89–90
  and liability attribution, 89, 94–95
  and permissibility & impermissibility, 75–76, 76n.5, 79n.15, 81–82, 84, 93, 94–95, 96–97, 106n.63
  and responsibility, 10
benevolent aggression *See* aggression
blame, 6–7, 180n.84
blameworthiness, 17–18, 38n.59, 42–43, 57–59, 82–84, 87, 88, 103, 125, 174, 175–76, 177–78
Bravonians, 203–23, 226–28, 236–37, 238–39, 244, 246–56, 263
Burri, Susanne ix, 10–11n.1, 41n.66, 44n.71, 63n.112, 65n.113, 66n.116, 84n.24, 116n.3, 117n.5, 118
Bystanders, 28–31, 34, 35–36, 44–45, 46–48, 49–55, 56, 65–66, 82–83, 88, 123–24, 159, 168–69

Calvin & Hobbes, 7
capabilities, 175–76, 177–83, 200–1

296 INDEX

CAPACITIES, 158, 233, 238n.47, 257, 261–62
casualties, 199–200, 267n.2
causation, 9–10, 19n.6, 24n.24, 35–37, 105n.61, 115, 157, 174, 197–98
certainty (and uncertainty) 4, 39, 77n.6, 77n.7, 77n.10, 92n.39, 158–59, 160–62, 167–68, 191–92, 195
Charlonians, 220–23
Christianity, 18n.2, 140, 141–42, 141n.10, 141–42n.12
citizens, 6, 156n.52, 195, 207–9, 214, 220, 221, 238–39, 250–51, 262
civilians, 139, 153n.46, 153n.48, 155–56, 157, 163, 165–68, 190, 197, 199–200, 267–68
claimant, 22
Coady, Tony, 18–19
Coerced Killer, 68, 87, 125
coercion, 68, 87, 88, 125, 188–89, 190–91, 194–95, 228–29, 230, 241–42, 249n.76
COIN, 197–98
collateral damage, 141–42n.12, 201–2
collective action, 210n.8, 219n.24
combatants, xi, 137–39, 143, 146, 147, 154, 160–61, 164, 165–70, 185–90, 197, 198, 201, 203–4
  liability of, 157–63, 169, 185–91, 198
  moral status xi, 2–3, 10, 11–12, 19n.6, 56–57, 138–39, 143, 144, 170, 181–82 (*see also* MEC)
commensurate, 106, 246–47, 254
conditional aggression, 206–7, 214, 215, 216–17, 220, 225–26
conquest, 104, 140, 187–88, 222–23, 272
consent, 5n.5, 150–51, 210–11, 216, 253, 254–55
consequentialism, 19–22, 226n.3
conspiracy, 134–35
contextualism, 89–99, 103–4, 107, 111, 121–25, 134–35, 194, 195
criminals, 132–33, 221–22, 279–80
culpability
  and blameworthiness, 82–83, 97–98, 104, 125
  and liability to harm, 17–18, 26, 42–43, 59, 67–69, 123n.13, 171, 178, 182–83

and responsibility, 17–18, 35n.52, 36n.53, 42–43, 58, 72–73, 74, 77n.6, 85, 100n.50, 102n.53, 103n.56
  Simple Culpability View, 56–59, 62–63, 69–70, 72, 74–75, 78, 85–86, 87, 88–89, 109, 114, 115–16, 125, 174
culture, 101–2
cyberwar, 155n.50, 201n.30

death, 3–4, 25n.27, 45, 50–51, 112–14, 117, 129n.17, 131, 132, 133n.20, 159, 187, 190–91, 198, 206, 211, 215, 234–35nn.32–34, 236, 245n.58
deception, 81, 159–60
Declaration of Independence, 230–31
defensive killing, 1, 12–13, 18n.5, 19n.6, 25, 29, 29n.37, 153–54
democracy, 208n.7, 222n.25, 222n.26, 259, 273
deontology. *See* Kant
DeRose, Keith, 90n.31
dictators, 6–7, 220, 266, 271–72, 273
dignity, 149, 231–33
dilemmas, 49–50, 126, 139, 184n.1
  and the Evidence-Relative View, 162–69
  The Responsibility Dilemma for Revisionists, 140n.5, 155–58, 160–61, 189–90, 192n.15, 193n.18, 195n.20
distribution, 47n.80, 66, 117–19, 125, 131
disvalue, 25n.25, 33, 234–35
Doctrine of Double Effect (DDE) 141–42n.12, 184
Dostoevsky, 83–84n.23
doxastic, 83n.20, 98–99
Draper, Kaila ix, 18–19, 21–22, 42n.67, 43
drones, 155n.50, 199n.25
duties, 5, 48n.81, 72–73, 88–93, 96–97, 98–99, 103–4, 122–23, 124, 255n.82
Dworkin, Ronald, 229n.11

economy, 208–9
Egypt, 265n.90
election, 21n.11
eliminative, 50–52, 199–200
embezzling, 176, 177–78, 179, 181–82, 281
Emerton, Patrick, 11–12, 27n.32, 170, 171–72, 173–75, 180–82
Empire, 140, 141

enslavement, 106, 205, 206, 234–36, 244, 279
epistemic
  contextualism, 12–13, 83n.22, 89–99, 111, 122–23, 124, 194, 195
  duties, 5, 72–73, 88–89, 91, 92–93, 96–97, 98–99, 103–4, 122–23
  justification, 5, 59, 83n.20, 96–97
  uncertainty, 3, 6–7, 158–59, 161–62, 168
epistemology, 98–99, 229n.8
equality, 2–3, 10, 11–12, 19n.6, 118, 137–39
  See also moral equality of combatants
ethical theory, 166n.61
Europe, 141–42, 164n.58
the Evidence-Relative View
  and intricate symmetries, 110–36, 180n.84
  and liability attribution, 10, 72–73, 74–75, 78, 85–89, 108–9, 162–65, 174, 177, 185–86, 189n.11, 194
evil, 3–4, 5, 19–22, 23–24, 33, 34, 34n.48, 53, 55, 62–63, 71, 83–84n.23, 94–95, 101–2, 110–11, 112–13, 116–17, 118–19, 131, 135–36, 141–42, 160–61, 259–60, 269–71, 275, 276
execution, 176n.79

Fabre, Cecile ix, 18–19
the Fact-Relative View, 10
  and norms, 75–76, 112–13, 119–20
  and obligations, 76
  and liability, 10, 130, 168–69
  and permissibility & impermissibility, 10–11, 79, 81–84, 86, 87, 93, 94–95, 96–97, 98–99, 108–9, 111, 113, 114, 115–17, 119, 120, 125–26, 130–31, 132, 133–34, 135–36, 162, 163, 165, 168–69, 192n.16
  and wrongdoing, 75–76, 113–14, 115–16, 119–20, 126, 130–31, 194
fair distribution, 47n.80, 66, 117, 118–19, 118n.8, 125, 131
fairness, 118, 118n.6, 118n.7, 118n.8
fascism, 271–72
Fletcher, George, 23n.20, 42–43n.68
flourishing, 204, 207–9, 224–25

foreseeability, 62–64, 98–99, 120–21, 122–23
frameworks, 4, 13, 18–19, 74–76, 93, 94, 119–20, 210–11, 211n.11, 226–27
Frowe, Helen ix, 18–19, 26n.28, 29n.37, 42–43nn.67–68, 50nn.85–86, 51–55, 63n.112, 167n.62, 213n.15

Gaus, Gerald, 228–29, 229nn.7–13, 230n.15, 231–32n.19, 233
Gaza, 194
Geneva conventions, 141–42
genocide, 164n.58, 208–9
God, 68, 77, 79, 112, 130, 140, 141–42, 273
greed, 273
group agency, 251–56
group projects, 13, 218–19, 222n.26, 234, 236–47, 249, 250–52, 255–57, 261–62, 263
Guerrero, Alexander, 90–91, 90n.30, 90n.32, 91n.37, 92, 93, 94n.42, 95, 99n.49, 100n.50, 102n.53, 103–5, 108, 195n.21
Gunman, 68–69, 179–80, 249, 277

Handfield, Toby, 170, 171–72, 173–75, 180–82
happiness, 104, 230–31, 272, 273
hastings, 200n.28
hell, 150–51
Hinduism, 18n.2
Hobbes, Thomas, 45, 156n.52
holograms, 59, 113, 121, 130–31, 276
humanitarian intervention, 208n.6, 263–64
Hussein, Saddam, 190–91, 259–60, 264

ideal, 188, 231–32n.19, 233, 234, 234n.29
ignorance, moral, 93n.40, 99–109
immunity, 27n.34, 137–38, 143, 154n.49, 167, 185, 267–68
impermissibility, 10–11n.1, 93, 99, 103–4, 175
incompatibility, 139, 145–46, 155–56, 247, 255–56
Independence, 241–44, 250–51, 259, 263–64
  Declaration of, 230–31, 231nn.17–18

INDEX

individuals, 1, 2, 24–25, 113, 135–36, 146–47n.31, 147, 185, 201, 202, 205, 206–7, 208n.7, 211, 212, 218, 220, 222, 224–25, 226–29, 230, 236–39, 242–43, 246–47, 250–52, 257–58, 259–60, 262
injustice, 3–4, 6, 190–92, 193, 206–7, 224, 267–68, 270–71
innocence, 3–4, 7, 19n.6, 95n.43, 159
intelligence, 3–4, 192n.15
intention, 9, 32–33, 50n.87, 53, 70, 112–13, 122–23, 125, 132–33, 134–35, 136, 143, 152, 158–59, 178–83, 185, 192n.15, 208–9, 210n.8, 211, 220–21, 222–23, 230n.16, 254n.79, 262–64, 266–67, 276
  See also Unintentional Ninja
intervention, 23n.20, 110–11, 112, 117n.4, 118–19, 125–26, 130–32, 208n.6, 210n.9, 248n.69, 263–64
intuition, 27n.32, 33, 40, 65–66, 70, 125, 205, 206–7, 210–11, 212, 216–19, 218n.22, 220, 222–23, 226–27, 228, 236, 238–39, 244, 246–47, 254–55, 256–57, 259–60, 262, 263, 265
invasion, 5n.5, 6–7, 26n.28, 112, 135–36, 160, 164n.58, 187–88, 190–91, 200, 201, 201n.29, 209, 221, 222–23, 228, 236, 244, 245, 246–47, 250, 251, 259–60, 263–65
involuntarism, 83n.20, 254–55
Iraq, 3, 160, 190–91, 200, 259–60, 263–64
Israel, 23n.20, 146n.28, 194, 232n.20

Jesus, 18n.2, 140
jus ad bellum, 6n.6, 137–39, 141, 141–42n.12, 143, 144, 153, 181–82, 191–92, 192n.16, 193, 264
jus in bello, 6n.6, 56–57n.97, 137–39, 141, 143, 144, 153, 184–85, 190n.13, 193, 196, 197
just combatant, 154, 158, 160–61, 185
justice, 3–4, 6, 18n.5, 34, 47, 86n.26, 118–19, 135–36, 141–42n.12, 143–44, 153–54, 162–63, 169–70, 182, 188, 188n.8, 190–95, 206–10, 221, 224, 231–33, 251–52, 267–68, 270–71
justified

aggression, 96–97, 159, 166n.61, 194, 203–23, 250–51, 267
belief, 59, 91, 92–93, 129, 276
killing, 12–13, 19–20, 44, 70, 115–16, 148, 152, 235–36, 266–69
and *morally*, 12–13, 34, 148, 159, 201–2, 203–4
rights-infringement, 31n.44
self-defense, 34, 35, 40, 135–36, 175, 177–78, 203–23, 226–27, 241, 251–52, 255–56, 263–64
and waging war, 137–39, 143, 164n.58, 191–92, 195, 203–23, 264–65, 265n.90, 271–72
just war theory, 1–3, 3n.3, 10–13, 19n.6, 40n.61, 73, 88–89, 110–11, 135n.21, 137–83, 184–202, 203–23, 225–26, 228, 231–32n.19, 234–35n.33, 236, 245–46, 261, 262–63, 264, 270–71

Kamm, Frances, 18–19, 19n.6, 42–43n.68
Kant, Immanuel, 230–33, 231–32nn.19–22, 232–33n.25
Kantianism, 231–33, 231n.17, 231–32n.19, 247n.67
Kaufman, Whitley
Kershnar, Stephen, 31n.43
Korsgaard, Christine, 247n.67, 248

language, 27, 27n.35, 37, 45n.73, 55n.95, 56n.96, 75–76, 229n.14, 242n.55
law, 95n.44, 141–42, 141–42nn.12–13, 146n.29, 146n.30, 148n.35, 149n.37, 149n.38, 151–52n.43, 152n.45, 154n.49, 185n.5, 212, 212n.13, 214.18, 222n.26, 229n.12, 232–33n.25, 267n.4
Lawrence, Jeremy, 95n.44
Lawrence, KS, 1n.2, 33n.45
Lazar, Seth ix, 11–12, 11n.2, 25n.25, 27n.34, 40n.61, 40n.63, 56–57n.97, 58, 58n.101, 66, 66n.114, 67n.117, 95n.45, 113n.1, 117, 117n.5, 121n.10, 153n.47, 156, 156n.52, 157, 158–60, 158n.53, 161–62, 161n.55, 163, 165–66, 165n.60, 168–69, 168n.63, 184n.1, 185–86, 187, 188–89, 191, 192n.15, 193, 193n.18, 195, 195n.20, 196–97,

198–99, 198n.24, 200–1, 234n.32, 255–56, 255n.82
Lazar's paradox, 111, 119
leadership, 145n.27
legitimacy, 102, 149, 222n.26, 236, 279
lethal
  attack, 166, 189, 215n.19
  force, 133, 180–81, 205, 206, 215, 241, 243, 252, 281
  harm, 29, 118, 125, 234–35
  self-defense, 180–81, 210–11, 213–14, 234–35, 243, 251–53, 282
  threats, 32–33, 182, 212–13, 252–53, 282
  and *Unintentional Ninja*, 178–79, 281
liability, 4, 10–11n.1, 12, 18–19, 22, 24, 24nn.22–24, 28, 29, 33, 34, 36, 37, 39, 40, 44–45, 49, 59n.103, 59n.104, 66, 67, 75–76, 87, 92–93, 94, 97–98, 105, 110, 114–15, 116, 118, 131, 131n.19, 132, 135–36, 146, 146–47n.31, 147, 153–54, 154n.49, 158, 160, 164, 165, 166n.61, 168, 177–78, 177n.81, 184–85, 188, 189, 189n.9, 190n.13, 191, 193, 194, 198, 201–2, 213–14, 214n.17, 215, 265n.89, 280
  and blameworthiness, 38n.59, 57, 59n.102, 82, 175–76, 176n.79, 177, 179, 180n.84
  and culpability, 17–18, 40–41, 42–43, 57, 69, 139, 78, 82–83, 115–16, 125, 170, 173–74, 175, 178, 179–80, 181–83
  and responsibility, 9–11, 17–18, 26, 26nn.29–31, 29, 30n.38, 38, 40–41, 42, 46, 51–52, 54, 56–57, 56–57n.97, 60, 61, 62, 63, 65, 70, 71, 76, 85, 89, 93, 98–99, 101, 108, 113, 115, 119, 122–23, 136, 139, 155–56, 157, 162, 163, 174, 178–79, 182, 183, 185, 267
liberalism, 12, 154–55, 204, 204n.2, 206–7, 210, 216–17, 218, 220, 224–25n.1, 225, 228, 230, 230n.15, 231–32n.19, 233, 234–35, 236, 241–42, 255, 262
libertarianism, 44n.70
  And autonomy, 207–8, 207–8n.5
  and benevolent aggression
  and just war theory

liberty, 25, 28, 204, 204nn.2–3, 221–22, 224–25n.1, 228–29, 229n.7, 229n.9, 229n.10, 230, 234–35, 243, 266, 270, 273
License, 92, 99, 102, 103–4, 105–6, 108, 171, 195, 208–9
logic, 3, 12–13, 18n.5, 22–23, 30–31, 76–78, 150–51, 181n.85
Lord, 102, 105, 107, 108–9, 140, 230n.16, 234–35, 268–69, 279
luck, 47n.80, 117n.5, 123, 123n.13

machine guns, 164, 280–81
malevolent, 225–26, 261
malicious, 21–22, 133–34, 280
maximizing, 247, 248–49
McChrystal, Stanley, 199–200
McMahan, Jeff ix, 1, 9–10, 18–19, 18n.5, 20n.7, 22, 25n.26, 26, 26nn.29–31, 27n.34, 38–39n.60, 41n.65, 42–43nn.67–69, 43, 44n.70, 45n.73, 55n.95, 56n.96, 56–57n.97, 57, 57n.99, 58n.100, 59, 60n.105, 61, 62, 62n.109, 62n.110, 63, 65, 66–67, 68, 69n.118, 69n.119, 74n.2, 75–76, 86, 86–87n.27, 95, 95nn.43–45, 98n.48, 105n.61, 109, 117n.5, 119, 121, 121n.10, 123n.11, 123n.12, 123n.14, 126, 127n.16, 143n.19, 145n.27, 148n.36, 150n.40, 153n.47, 154, 154n.49, 156, 156n.52, 158, 158n.53, 162, 162n.57, 165–66, 166n.61, 175n.77, 178–79, 180–81, 184–86, 184n.3, 186n.6, 187, 187n.7, 189, 189n.11, 190n.14, 192n.16, 193, 194, 194n.19, 196, 213n.15, 215n.19, 234–35n.33
mercy, 6n.6, 140
metaphysics, 65n.113, 116n.3, 232nn.20–21
military, 1, 140, 141n.10, 143, 156n.52, 179n.82, 184–85, 189, 190, 196, 198–99, 199nn.26–27, 200–1, 201n.31
  and US, 142n.15, 155n.50, 167, 190–91, 196n.22, 197–98, 265n.90
  and UK, 197, 199
  and Russia, 6–7, 191–92, 195, 201, 222–23

military
  commanders, 1
  force, 141n.10, 167, 185–86, 199–200
  service, 140, 190–91, 195
  units, 191, 201
  victory, 185–86, 189, 200–1
mistakes, 3, 11–12, 54, 58, 72–73, 75, 76–77, 84n.24, 86n.26, 96–97, 108, 113, 121, 122–23, 132–34, 158–60, 161–62, 168, 173–74, 182–83, 193, 194, 215–16, 248, 258–60, 271–72, 279–80
mitigation, 88, 125, 257, 262
moral equality of combatants thesis (MEC) 2–3, 10, 11–12, 19n.6, 56–57n.97, 138–39, 138n.4
moral ignorance thesis, 100, 100n.50, 103, 103–4n.57, 104, 104n.59, 105–6, 105n.61
morality, 2, 11–12, 18n.2, 19n.6, 20–21n.10, 26n.31, 33, 62–63, 76–77, 77n.6, 78, 96–97, 102, 103–4, 118–19, 126, 126n.15, 136, 137–38, 139–40, 145–46, 145n.25, 146–47n.31, 147n.32, 148, 149, 151, 151–52n.43, 152n.45, 154, 154n.49, 155–56, 182, 184–85, 184n.2, 187, 188, 189n.11, 193, 196–97, 204n.2, 208n.6, 224–25n.1, 227n.5, 230n.15, 234n.31, 237n.39, 237n.43, 238n.47, 247n.63, 247n.64, 253n.77
Morkevicius, Valerie, 141n.10
murder, 82n.19, 126–27, 150, 164n.58, 184, 247, 269, 279

Nagel, Thomas, 145n.25, 170, 189–90
Napoleon, 188n.8
Narveson, Jan, 18n.2
nationalism, 255–56
nation-state, 12–13, 143n.18, 160, 197, 208n.6
NATO, 197–200, 263–64
Nazis, 6, 83–84, 83–84n.23, 164, 222–23, 271–72, 280–81
necessity, 17, 19n.6, 69, 117, 140, 141, 143, 166, 167–68, 173, 174n.75, 264–65, 266–67, 268–69, 271–72
  and proportionality, 26–28, 38–40, 172, 213–14

neo-liberal. *See* liberalism
Nicomachean, 137, 141n.10, 266n.1
ninjas (unintentional) 178–83, 281
noncombatant, 3, 27n.34, 137–38, 141–42n.12, 143, 153n.46, 155–56, 157, 165–68, 185–87, 190, 197–98, 201, 202, 203–4
noninterference, 228–29
nonlethal, 131, 190–91
nonliability, 28–31, 62, 65, 68–69, 87, 96–97, 111, 114–16, 117, 119, 127–28, 130–31, 133–34, 162–63, 164–65, 166–67, 168, 170, 182, 201–2, 211
the Nonresponsible View, 17–18, 40–62, 64–66, 67–68, 69–70, 71, 74, 82–83, 106–7, 113, 115, 116, 127–28, 166–67, 173–74, 267
norms, 10, 72, 75–76, 79, 85, 86n.26, 87, 88, 93, 94–95, 96–97, 101–2, 112–16, 119–20, 121–22, 125–29, 130–31, 132, 133–35, 165, 174, 177, 215n.19
Nozick, Robert, 41
nuclear weapons, 141n.10

obligation, 30n.38, 76–77, 77nn.6–10, 78, 81–82n.18, 82, 92n.38, 138n.3, 182, 221, 250–51
The Odyssey, 203
oligarchy, 221–22
Orend, Brian, 208n.6
Orthodoxy, 1, 142n.17, 145n.27, 154n.49, 197
Otsuka, Michael, 18–19, 19n.6, 42n.67, 43, 44, 44n.70, 46, 46nn.76–77, 47–48, 47nn.79–80, 49n.84, 58–59, 59n.103, 74n.2, 174, 207–8n.5
Oxford (over 98 appearances)

pacifism, 18n.2, 35n.51, 137–38, 137n.1, 156, 157, 158–62, 165–66, 167–68, 184–85, 271–72
Pagden, Anthony, 95n.44, 142n.14
Palestine, 194, 195
Parfit, Derek, ix, 75, 77–78, 77nn.6–11, 79
paternalism, 210–11, 216
peace, 75–76, 137, 140, 141, 141–42nn.10–12, 142n.13, 143, 201–2, 248, 266–67, 272

peacemakers, 140
peacetime, 148n.36, 184–85
perfectionism, 227n.5, 233n.27, 248n.73
permissible defensive harm, 13, 17–70, 26n.28, 72, 85, 106–7, 126, 127, 139, 174
persons, 20, 25n.26, 50–51, 148, 149, 189–90, 214n.18, 247n.67, 248
phenomenological, 19n.6, 90n.31, 138n.3, 144–45
philosophers, 18–19, 25n.27, 40–41, 65, 84n.24, 116, 116n.3, 124–25, 204n.2, 224–25n.1, 229
Plato, 38n.59, 90n.31, 212n.13, 230n.16
police, 128
policy, 197, 200
politics, 18n.2, 141–42n.12, 144–45, 157, 176n.79, 221–23, 226–27, 228–29, 230–31, 248–49
  freedom, 220–21
  institutions, 146n.30, 205, 206–7, 208n.7, 209, 218–19, 221–22, 222n.26, 261–62
  philosophy, 1, 18n.2, 19n.6, 41n.66, 44n.70, 95nn.43–44, 140n.5, 204, 212–13, 224–25, 229, 229n.8, 231–32n.19, 233, 259
  realism, 137–38
  violence, 206, 214
Pope, 271–72n.11
poverty, 22n.15, 207–9
POW, 5, 6–7
power, 6, 23–24, 81, 141–42, 141n.11, 150, 192n.15, 196–97, 201, 205, 206–7, 208n.6, 210, 220–21, 245, 251–52, 258, 259–60, 273
predators, 155n.50, 198n.24, 199nn.25–26
President, 21n.11, 223n.28
Princeton, 222n.25, 255n.82
prisoners (prisoner decision only shows up)
propaganda, 5n.5, 7n.7, 193, 222–23
proportionality, 13, 23n.20, 26–28, 26n.31, 30–31, 38, 138–39, 143, 165–66, 167–68, 172, 175, 185–86, 187, 189, 196, 213–14, 215, 251–52
psychology, 93–94, 278
public good, 237n.39

Purves, Duncan, 25n.26, 25n.27, 234n.32

Quinn, Warren, 50n.87
Quong, Jonathan, 10–11n.1, 19n.6, 28n.36, 42n.67, 42–43n.68, 50n.85

racism, 208–9
radical, 2, 77n.11, 141, 188, 208n.6
rational, 1, 83–84n.23, 105n.61, 231–33, 261, 271–72
Rawls, John, 212, 230–33, 248
Raz, Joseph, 204n.2, 224–25, 230n.15, 234–35, 237, 242–43, 253n.77
Realism, 137–38
Realpolitik, 137–38, 146, 197
Reasonable Perceived Liability (RPL), 12, 186–87, 188–89, 190–95, 196–97, 199–201
reasonableness, 258–59
reasoning, 3, 4–5, 8, 22n.13, 44, 46, 52–53, 101–2, 149, 196, 230, 232–33n.25
reductio ad absurdum, 105–6, 107, 149, 168–69, 181
reductive, 212–13, 214, 215–16, 235–36, 263
religion, 140
Renzo, Massimo, ix, 59n.104, 138n.3
Plato's Republic, 230n.16
Republican, 190–91
Repugnant Conclusion, 42n.67
responsibility and culpability. *See* culpability; responsibility
restraint, 197–98, 199–200, 227n.5, 233n.27, 248n.73
retreat, 27n.32, 30–31, 172, 173–74
revisionist just war theory, 11–12, 73, 88–89, 110–11, 135n.21, 137–83, 184–202, 203–4, 213n.15, 244–45
rigor, 3, 4–5
risk imposition, 58, 63n.112, 66–67, 110–11, 119–22, 175, 177–78, 179
Rodin, David ix, 9–10, 12–13, 18–19, 21–23, 25n.25, 26n.28, 30–31, 35, 36–37, 37n.57, 42n.67, 43, 44n.70, 45, 45n.74, 56–57n.97, 74n.2, 75n.4, 132, 146n.29, 148–49, 151–52, 154n.49, 184n.2, 204n.1, 206, 212–17, 225–26, 235–36, 243–44, 251–52, 263

ROEs, 185–87, 188, 189–91, 194–95, 196–98, 199–201
Roman, 140, 141
Rosen, Gideon, 77n.6, 78n.13, 93, 101n.51
Russia, 6, 187–88, 200, 222–23, 223n.28, 244–46, 245nn.57–59, 261, 263–64
  and invasion of Ukraine (*see* Ukraine)
Ryan, Cheyney, 35n.51, 55, 56n.96

sacrifice, 196, 258–59
Scanlon, T.M., 65n.113, 116, 116n.3, 230–31, 247, 247n.63, 247n.66, 248
science, 137–38, 140, 273
security, 121n.10, 140n.7, 180–81, 273
Shakespeare, William, 144n.21
Shue, Henry, 19n.6, 56–57n.97, 145–46, 145n.26, 146–47nn.28–31, 147–48, 147nn.32–33, 151–52, 151–52n.43, 152n.45, 154, 155–56, 184–85, 184n.2, 188–89, 196–97
slaveholders, 102, 103, 104, 104n.59, 148–49, 151–52, 279
slavery, 102, 102nn.52–54, 103, 149, 151–52, 228n.6, 235n.34, 236n.36, 266, 273, 279
slaves, 102, 103–4, 105–6, 106n.62, 107, 234–35, 279
Smith. *See* thought experiments
Sniper, 29–30, 130–31, 132, 164, 280–81
society, 29n.37, 77n.6, 118n.6, 204, 227, 231–33, 232–33n.25, 248, 248n.68, 258–59, 262
soldiers, 3–7, 9, 12–13, 34n.49, 70, 84, 111–12, 119, 129n.17, 135–36, 137–39, 143–48, 150–51, 152–70, 171–72, 173–74, 182–83, 185–86, 187–88, 189n.9, 190–93, 194, 196–98, 200, 201–2, 203–5, 213–14, 222–23, 245, 266–73
  and moral equality (*see* moral equality of combatants [MEC])
  and non-combatants (*see* non-combatants)
Sopranos, 150–52, 150n.39
sovereignty, 208n.6, 259–60
Stanford, 38n.59, 90n.31, 202n.32, 212n.13, 229n.7, 233n.26

Steinhoff, Uwe, ix, 135n.21, 138n.3, 166n.61
Strawser, Bradley, 12n.4, 26n.28, 31n.43, 154n.49, 155n.50, 175n.77, 198–99nn.24–27
subjective, 10–11n.1, 123n.12, 242–43, 256–59, 262
subjectivist, 95, 95n.45
suicide, 194, 195
surrender, 150–51, 163, 190–91, 206–7, 209, 215, 218–19, 220, 221, 227, 238–39, 245, 246–47, 248, 248n.69, 249n.76, 253, 254–55, 257, 260, 261–62, 268
survival, 49n.83, 245–46
symmetry, 65–66, 86, 113–16, 117, 118–19, 134–35, 136, 151n.41, 152–53

Tadros, Victor, ix, 18–19, 38–39n.60, 42n.67, 222n.26
Taliban, 198
targets, 139, 144, 150–51, 152–53, 156, 156n.52, 165–66, 167, 185, 200, 224–25n.1
Taylor, Robert, 231–32n.19
Tennyson, Alfred, 137, 143n.20
terrorism, 19n.6, 20n.9
theology, 18n.2, 140, 142
Thomism. *See* Aquinas, Thomas
Thomson, Judith Jarvis, 1, 1n.2, 9–10, 18–19, 18n.3, 65n.113, 116n.3
thought experiment, 4–5, 7, 49–50, 64, 66–67, 68, 112, 122–23, 124–25, 129–30, 135–36, 145n.27, 171, 172
Tolkein, JRR, 203, 230n.16, 268–69, 269n.5
torture, 20n.9, 150, 220–21, 272
treaty, 143n.18

UAVs
Ukraine, 5, 5n.5, 6–7, 6n.6, 7n.7, 26n.28, 112, 135–36, 160, 187–88, 191, 195, 200, 201, 201n.30, 217, 222–23, 222n.27, 223n.28, 244–46, 245n.58, 245n.59, 261, 262, 263–64
understanding (65 appearances)
Uniake, Susan, 18, 18n.4, 41n.66
Unintentional, 53, 132–33, 141–42n.12, 276, 279–80

Unintentional Ninja, 15, 178–83, 281
United States, 141n.11, 148–49, 150,
    196n.22, 215n.20, 230–31, 259–60,
    263–64, 265n.90
    and invasion of Iraq (*see* Iraq)
    and Vietnam War (*see* Vietnam)
    US War Department, 142n.15
unjust aggression, 5, 6–7, 21–22, 187–88,
    245–46, 263–64
unjust attacker, 96–97, 213–14
unprovoked, 160, 164n.58
Utilitarianism, 21–22, 270–71
Utopia, 41n.66, 207–8n.5, 208–9

vegetarianism, 105n.61
victims, 144–45, 272
Vietnam war, 267n.2
villains, 82n.19
violating, 29, 33, 36–37, 42–43, 46, 47,
    113–15, 115n.2, 124, 133–34, 243–44,
    248n.69, 266–67
violence, 12–13, 18, 18n.2, 19n.6, 30–31,
    156n.52, 168–69, 171, 172, 173–74,
    182–83, 213–14, 213n.15, 215, 216, 233,
    252–53, 267, 268–69, 270–71, 281, 282
virtue, 83n.20, 102n.53, 114
voluntarism, 83nn.20–22

Walen, Alec CP.P8
Wall, Steven, 224–65, 229n.14,
    236–37nn.38–41

Wallace, David Foster, 105n.61
Walzer, Michael, 1, 1n.1, 2–3, 137–38,
    138nn.2–4, 142, 142–37nn.16–1,
    144–46, 144n.23, 145nn.25–27,
    146.28, 148, 148n.36, 151–
    52n.43, 154, 170, 184–85, 189–
    90, 189n.12, 196, 196n.22, 197,
    206–7, 213–14, 213n.16, 248n.72,
    254n.79, 265n.90
warfighters CP.P10, 191, 196
warrants, 88, 261
warriors, 19n.6, 56–57n.97, 145n.26,
    146n.28, 154n.49, 184n.2
Washington, 5n.5, 141–42n.12, 142n.15
weaponry, 198–99, 198n.24
welfare, 207–8, 209
Westphalia, Treaty of, 143n.18, 214n.17
World War II, 141–42, 164, 193, 248
worthiness, 17–18, 58–59, 59n.102,
    164n.58, 257–58
wrongdoing, 21–22, 126, 138–39, 182–83

Yale, 22nn.14–17
Yoder, John Howard, 18n.2, 140n.6

Zeitschrift, 113n.1, 138n.3
Zimmerman, Michael, 77–78, 77nn.6–11,
    78n.13, 79, 80n.16, 93n.40, 100–
    1nn.50–51, 104
Zupan, Dan, 247, 247nn.63–64, 247n.66,
    248, 248n.70, 248nn.71–72